Fundamentals of Permanent Establishments

This considerably updated and expanded second edition acknowledges the original contribution to Chapters 1-6 made by the first edition, *Permanent Establishments – A Planning Primer* © 1993 (Kluwer Law & Taxation Publishers, Deventer, Boston) by Robert L Williams, Member of the Washington and District of Columbia Bars, then an International Tax Partner with Ernst & Young, St. Helier, Channel Islands, UK and by Professor John C Huston, Member of the Washington and New York State Bars, then Professor of Law, University of Washington, Seattle, Washington, USA.

Fundamentals of Permanent Establishments

Robert L Williams

Wolters Kluwer
Law & Business

Published by:
Kluwer Law International
P.O. Box 85889
2508 CN The Hague
The Netherlands
E-mail: sales@kluwerlaw.com
Website: http://www.kluwerlaw.com

Sold and distributed in North, Central and South America by:
Aspen Publishers, Inc.
7201 McKinney Circle
Frederick, MD 21704
USA
E-mail: customer.service@aspenpublishers.com

Sold and distributed in all other countries by:
Extenza-Turpin Distribution Services
Stratton Business Park
Pegasus Drive
Biggleswade
Bedfordshire SG18 8TQ
United Kingdom
E-mail: kluwerlaw@turpin-distribution.com

Printed on acid-free paper.

ISBN 978-90-411-4948-0

Printed and Bound by CPI Group (UK) Ltd, Croydon, CR0 4YY

Table of Contents

Abbreviations

Agency PE	Article 5(5) of OECD MC; cf. Articles 5(5) and 6 of UN MC
BEPS	base erosion and profit shifting
CAS PE	Article 5(3) of OECD MC
CTS	*Consolidated Treaty Series* (Parry, ed., 1979)
LHUSTC	Legislative History of United States Tax Conventions (1962)
Ltr. Rul.	Letter Ruling, U.S. Internal Revenue Service
MC	Model Convention
NRE	nonresident enterprise
OECD	Organization for Economic Co-operation and Development
PE	permanent establishment
'PE-Free' Zone	Articles 4, 6 and 7 of OECD MC; cf. Article 4, 7 and 8 of UN MC
POB	a fixed place of business
POB PE	Articles 5(1,2) of OECD MC
Rev. Rul.	Revenue Ruling, U.S. Internal Revenue Service
Services PE	Article 5(3)(b) of UN MC
UN	United Nations

Foreword

Taxpayers engaged in cross-border business activity face – among other commercial and tax complexities – increasing permanent establishment ('PE') tax risk with respect to their foreign operations. Not only are governments constantly revising their international and domestic tax rules, but also tax authorities are significantly increasing their enforcement efforts and deploying new examination techniques (including the emerging use of data analytics, joint audits, etc.). At the same time, business is evolving and globalizing. The interaction of rapidly changing rules, increased enforcement, and evolving business operations creates a challenging environment for tax directors of global businesses who must understand and manage their company's PE risks.

This book is intended to be a primer for those new to the PE concept as well as a go-to reference book for international tax practitioners. It covers the fundamentals of the international rules relating to PEs and also aims to provide the reader with an appreciation of the historical development of the various PE concepts and their evolution to the present. This new edition includes three key updates that reflect the continually changing circumstances in which global business and trade are carried out today.

One new chapter addresses the application of PE concepts in the context of the digital economy, a part of the economy that has grown and evolved since the last edition was published. A second new chapter focuses on the PE issues associated with the global trend of centralized operating models, which have been or are being implemented by many multinationals to capture business synergies and efficiencies in order to maintain and enhance their competitiveness. The third new chapter addresses the issue of Service PEs, a concept that was added to the UN Model Convention in 1980 and was included as an optional provision in the OECD commentary in 2008. This chapter also addresses the PE aspects of secondments.

In taking the reader through the issues, Lee Williams explores the theoretical aspects of the rules themselves and the commentary on those rules and also looks at the application of the concepts as illustrated in international case law and tax rulings which underscore the complexity in applying the rules to real life circumstances. I think that Lee can be confident that there will be many grateful readers who find this book has brought them a broader perspective and understanding of the PE concept and the central role it plays in international tax law.

EY is pleased that Lee reached out to his alumni organisation for support in producing this new edition. We have assisted in updating the discussion of the rules, regulations and case law from multiple jurisdictions and we have served as a sparring partner for Lee on various fine points and nuances. We trust that our efforts have benefitted Lee and the content of this book as much as the focused review of this important element of international tax law has benefitted us. Special thanks for the tremendous contributions of Tigran Mkrtchyan, Ai-Leen Tan, Sebastiaan Kuijper, Helen Childers, and the EY International Tax Knowledge team in Kerala, India.

Alex Postma
International Tax Services Leader, EY

Chapter 1
Historical Development of the Concept

In its 1977 report,[1] the Committee on Fiscal Affairs of the Organization for Economic Co-operation and Development observed that at the beginning of that year, 179 bilateral conventions for the avoidance of double taxation with respect to taxes on income and on capital had been concluded amongst the members of that organization.[2] The 2010 OECD MC lists 904 treaties among its then 32 OECD member countries. Because the right to enter into double taxation conventions is by no means confined to the members of the OECD but includes the 193 countries of the UN,[3] and in view of the acceleration of the rate at which tax and commercial treaties are being entered into all over the globe, there are now over 3,500 tax treaties.

What seems to astonish newcomers to the area is the degree to which the language of each of these tax treaties conforms to that of all of the others. These treaties are uniform 'laws' in the same sense as are the Uniform Acts adopted by the legislatures of American states. This intricate network of bilateral conventions functions like a Uniform Code of International Taxation.

At the center of virtually all tax treaties currently in force is the concept 'permanent establishment.' The term must be understood to describe that degree of economic penetration which, according to the agreement of treaty partners, justifies a nation in treating a foreign person for income tax purposes in the same manner as domestic persons are treated. When a treaty governs the tax relations between the foreign person's country of residence and the country which is his[4] host, 'permanent establishment' supplants the taxing nexus of the domestic tax law of the host country. When he acquires a 'per-

---

1. Model Double Taxation Convention on Income and on Capital, Report of the OECD Committee on Fiscal Affairs (1977).
2. *Id.* at 8.
3. The 3 countries which are not UN members are Kosovo, the Vatican and Taiwan (the latter with 25 treaties).
4. The English language badly needs a pronoun that is understood by all to mean 'he, she, or it.' The need is met in some treaties by the older custom of using the masculine singular pronoun. *See* e.g., the former 1971 United States–Japan treaty 9(5) ('where such broker or agent is acting in the ordinary course of his business.' While treaties use the word "person" to refer to an individual, a company or any other body of persons, some use the pronoun "he" even though in the particular PE context, the foreign person referenced may well be a company.

manent establishment,' the nation of his residence yields taxing jurisdiction to the nation in which he has acquired a permanent establishment – by granting him either tax exemption or tax credits with respect to income earned in the host country. Moreover, the foreign person must file tax returns in the local language and comply with local tax laws.

Prior to reaching the crucial point of economic penetration, the foreign person enjoys exemption as to his business income and is subject to reduced rates of taxation of his income from investments. Precisely when the foreign person arrives at the crucial point becomes a question of enormous financial significance. The acquisition of 'permanent establishment' is the language in which treaties describe the event. This singular concept – permanent establishment – appears to have operated effectively for thirteen decades while only in the last two decades attracting significant attention from legal commentators.[5] The concept has a history that is somewhat out of the ordinary.

1.1 ORIGINS IN DOMESTIC LAW

While what is regarded as the first contemporary double taxation convention was entered into just before the turn of the twentieth century,[6] its most important single concept is not original with it. The permanent establishment idea adopted in that convention appears to have been a product of the legal laboratories of German States, which expended considerable effort in the latter part of the nineteenth century towards avoiding double taxation.

---

5. The 1976 prototype of this book was Williams, 'Permanent Establishments in the United States,' 29 *Tax Lawyer* 277 (1976), reprinted as updated in *Income Tax Treaties* 189 (Bischel ed. 1978) and with Professor John Huston as co-author, published as *Permanent Establishments – A Planning Primer* (1993 © Kluwer Law International), the first edition of this book. Following significant early contributions by Vogel and Skaar, some impressive texts have since been written in the area, including Reimer (Germany), Mehta (India), Tittle (USA), and Rawal (India) as well as articles by practitioners and law professors, e.g. Nitikman (Canada), Pijl (Netherlands), Russo (Italy) and Jones (UK). Reimer, a disciple of Vogel, has co-authored a 12 country book on the concept, also published by Kluwer. Mehta has summarized and reproduced some 70 recent Indian, European and North American cases and rulings in a useful reference volume for those seeking to delve into case law. Tittle has an excellent analysis of the US model tax treaty and its expression in the US–Canada Treaty. Rawal's treatise covers Indian law and the Indian concept of Service PEs and he is writing a forthcoming book on the subject of Service PEs. The obligation owed by this second edition to the research and thought leadership of these authors is acknowledged and will become further apparent as the reader progresses through this primer.
6. *See* Carroll, 'The Historical Development of Income Tax Treaties,' in *Income Tax Treaties* 51, 52 (Bischel ed. 1978) (An impressive body of international tax law has been developed since 21 June 1899, when Austria–Hungary and Prussia signed the first convention for the avoidance of double taxation of income and property listed in the collection of treaties published by the League of Nations and the United Nations').

Its initial appearance fifty years earlier in the Prussian Industrial Code had found the permanent establishment concept performing tasks not involving taxation.[7] The concept had assumed fiscal guise by 1869,[8] and by 1891 it had found definition in Prussian tax statutes.[9] Thus, when the time for forging a double-taxation convention had arrived, the basic tools were at hand.

1.2 FIRST TREATY APPEARANCE

The first contemporary tax treaty was the 1899 convention entered into by Austria–Hungary and Prussia.[10] It is written in German and, although brief, contains the principal elements found in contemporary tax treaties. It uses this language to define its pivotal concept:

> 'The term "business establishment" includes branch establishments, factories, depots, offices, places where purchases and sales are effected and other business facilities by which the owner, partner, manager, or other permanent representative carries on his normal business activities.'[11]

1.3 FIRST PERIOD – PRE LEAGUE OF NATIONS

This 1899 treaty became the model for the relative handful of tax treaties entered into before World War I. Virtually the same language continued to appear in most tax treaties entered into prior to 1927.

The English-speaking researcher is likely to derive from the materials of the time the impression there was considerable disagreement concerning the nature of the core concept. Translating the German–Czechoslovak treaty

---

7. *See* Skaar, at 72 (1991). Skaar's Chapter 7, entitled, 'The History of the concept of PE,' is an excellent narrative description of the origins and early years of the permanent establishment concept.
8. *Id.* at 73.
9. *Id.* at 74 (describing parallel development in German domestic tax statutes).
10. Austria/Hungary–Prussia, 21 June 1899, 187 *Consolidated Treaty Series* (Parry ed. 1979) [hereinafter cited 'CTS.'] *But cf.* Carroll, 'The Historical Development of Income Tax Treaties,' in *Income Tax Treaties* 51 (Bischel ed. 1978), who states that this was 'the first convention ... listed in the collection of tax treaties published by the League of Nations and the United Nations.' Pijl, Part I at 15 refers to an earlier 1869 Prussia–Saxony income tax treaty which only referred to the term *stehendes Gewerbe* (standing business, as opposed to itinerant business) without referring to agencies.
11. Translation by Professor Peter Rohn, Director of the University of Washington Treaty Research Centre.

of 1921,[12] the League of Nations Secretariat employed the term 'business establishment.' Translating the Austrian–Czechoslovak treaty of 1922,[13] the Secretariat rendered the term 'industrial establishment.' The identical term in the Italian–German tax treaty of 1925[14] becomes 'establishment.' Translations into French during the same period evidence comparable variations.[15]

Reference to the originals reveals little variation in German texts. The core term – *Betriebstätte* – was employed in the 1899 progenitor and in virtually all German-language tax treaties from that day to this.[16] That a standard English translation of that term was not settled for the first 30 years of its existence must not obscure the fact that this core concept emerged, seemingly fully-developed, so long ago.

A jarring counter indication appeared in 1905 in the Austrian–Hungarian treaty with Württemberg.[17] There the term *Gewerbebetrieb* is defined in terms almost identical to those employed to define *Betriebsstätte* in the 1905 Austrian–Hungarian treaty with Bavaria,[18] and in the 1908 Austrian–Hungarian treaty with Baden.[19] Just why *Betriebsstätte* was abandoned in this single instance has never been explained.

The basic concept (hereafter to be called 'permanent establishment') does not want for definitions. It was defined in the 1899 treaty; it is defined more elaborately in the years after the war. These definitions are the best evidence of the content of the permanent establishment concept in the early years of the twentieth century, before the League of Nations intervened. They also supply some of the reasons for the League's intervention.

One observes that, from the very outset, treaty-makers believed that domestic agents of certain kinds and qualities constituted the permanent establishments of foreign persons. The 1899 Convention between Austria–Hungary and Prussia placed agents within the permanent establishment concept. The language earlier quoted lists particularly partners, managers, and permanent representatives. The terms are rarely absent in German-language treaties signed in the first three decades of the twentieth century. The few French texts of the era are parallel.

---

12. Germany–Czechoslovakia, 31 December 1921, 17 LNTS No. 447.
13. Austria–Czechoslovakia, 18 February 1922, 14 LNTS No. 371.
14. Italy–Germany, 31 October 1925, 53 LNTS No. 1261.
15. Various translations produced '*établissements d'exploitation*,' '*établissements servant a l'exercice d'une industrie*' and '*établissements stables*.' *See generally*, Carroll, 'U.S. Tax Treaties with the European Community Member Countries: Corporate Aspects,' *Tax Management Portfolio* T.M. 41-3rd. (1974).
16. More recent tax conventions spell the term '*Betriebsstätte*.'
17. Austria/Hungary–Württemberg, 4 February 1905, 198 CTS 111.
18. Austria/Hungary–Bavaria, 6 October – 11 November 1903, 194 CTS 144.
19. Austria/Hungary–Baden, 7 November 1908, 208 CTS 15.

These provisions rather strongly favored imposition of taxation on the foreign person by a generous definition of permanent establishment. The German–Czechoslovak treaty of 1921 included a special provision allotting the imposition of special taxes on 'hawking and other itinerant trades' irrespective of the presence or absence of permanent establishment.[20] The hawking provision appears again in the Austrian treaty with Hungary of 1924.[21] Rather than exempting the commercial traveler, these early provisions assured that he and his employer would both be taxed.

The treaties started lengthening after the experience of a quarter of a century. The objects of permanent establishment provisions began to diverge. The Poland–Czechoslovak treaty of 1925 states, for example:

> 'If there is no place of establishment as defined above, a lucrative undertaking shall be deemed to be established in the place in which it is in fact carried on.'[22]

In the very next paragraph it provides:

> 'For the purposes of this Convention the term "working establishment" shall not include the following: journeys made by the head of the undertaking to obtain orders, delivery of orders, delivery of goods on commission to an established dealer, delivery to customers of goods transported from one country to the other or of goods lying in warehouses belonging to a transport undertaking or to a forwarding agent, providing that such transactions are not carried out by offices or employees of the undertaking.'[23]

Two years later the Austrian–Swiss treaty of 1927 provided:

> 'Where an independent agent merely negotiates business for the firm he represents, without maintaining on its behalf any warehouse, and without being authorized to conclude on its behalf any transactions, this shall not be regarded as constituting the maintenance of a business establishment (*Betriebsstätte*).'[24]

---

20. Germany–Czechoslovakia, 23 April 1925, 44 LNTS No. 1091.
21. Austria–Hungary, 8 November 1924, 44 LNTS No. 1096, Art. 3(5).
22. Poland–Czechoslovakia, 23 April 1925, Art. 2, 44 LNTS No. 2091.
23. *Ibid.*
24. Austria–Switzerland, 1927, 85 LNTS No. 1935, Art. 5(2).

The English translation of the treaty between Poland and Danzig of 1929 bears repeating:

> 'The fact that an undertaking maintains business connections with the other territory through a really independent representative (broker, commission agent, etc.) shall not, however, be taken to mean that the undertaking maintains a business establishment (*Betriebsstätte*) in such territory.'[25]

The quoted passages support the inferences that by 1927 most of the elements of the contemporary agency-permanent-establishment construct were in existence. The business partner and the (simple, unqualified) agent were there from the start. In the quoted passages one can detect the emergence of the agent engaged in preliminary or auxiliary activity, the agent of independent status, the purchasing agent. Between the simple definitions of the earlier treaties and the more elaborate formulae of the later, quite substantial variations in the breadth of the permanent establishment concept had been created. In two treaties, the subsidiary is recognized.

1.4 SECOND PERIOD – LEAGUE OF NATIONS 1928 MODEL TREATY

While the post-war development of tax treaties proceeded along the original German lines, a new phase in that development was marked with the 1919 Meeting of the International Chamber of Commerce and the 1920 Brussels Financial Conference.[26] Both of these gatherings appealed to the new League of Nations to assume a leadership role in the elimination of double taxation. The League responded in late 1921 by asking a committee of four prominent economists to conduct a study of double taxation. The economists responded with an extensive report in April of 1923.[27]

The Council of the League of Nations referred the report to a panel of technical experts who were senior tax administrators of a number of European

25. Danzig–Poland, 29 May 1929, Art. III; League of Nations, 'Double Taxation and Fiscal Evasion,' Supplement No. I to the Collection of International Agreements and Internal Legal Provisions for the Prevention of Double Taxation and Fiscal Evasion, League of Nations Doc. No.C345.M.102.1928.II,at 10.
26. *See* Carroll, A-4. As to the importance of both of these meetings in the history of double taxation conventions, *see* Ehrenzweig & Koch, *Income Tax Treaties 1* (1949).
27. The committee consisted of Professor Bruins of the Commercial University of Rotterdam; Professor Senator Einaudi of Turin University; Professor E.R.A. Seligman of Columbia University; and Sir Josiah Stamp of the University of London.

nations – the tax administrators of the former Central Powers being notably absent. Represented on the original panel were Belgium, Czechoslovakia, France, Italy, the Netherlands, Switzerland, and the United Kingdom.[28] An enlarged committee[29] met in London in April of 1927. One of the products of this committee was a series of model bilateral tax treaties.

The committee undertook preliminary studies in 1927. The first of these studies, entitled 'Draft Bilateral Convention for the Prevention of Double Taxation,' contained a sharply revised definition of the core concept in the area:

> 'The real centres of management, affiliated companies, branches, factories, agencies, warehouses, offices, depots, shall be regarded as permanent establishments. The fact that an undertaking has business dealings with a foreign country through a *bona fide* agent of independent status (broker, commission agent, etc.), shall not be held to mean that the undertaking in question has a permanent establishment in that country.'[30]

The differences between the 1899 treaty and the draft convention were significant and profound. The three terms of prior conventions – partners, managers, agents – were reduced to a single word: agencies.

> '[A]gencies ... shall be regarded as permanent establishments.'

Not all agencies qualified: '[A] *bona fide* agent of *independent status*' had been placed beyond the permanent establishment definition.

The Commentary on the Draft evidences earmarks of careful deliberation. In its first appearance, the new term 'permanent establishments' is italicized. Business establishment, industrial establishment, and establishment – all three of its predecessors are to be supplanted by it. The strongly geographic flavor of the core concept at this time is unmistakable: providing 'a list of the establishments which are considered as permanent,'[31] the Committee submits the following:

---

28. League of Nations Document E.F.S.73.F.F.19 (4 *Legislative History of United States Tax Conventions* [hereinafter *LHUSTC*] 4003). Economic and Fiscal Commission, 'Report on Double Taxation' (1923).
29. The enlarged committee included representatives of Argentina, Germany, Japan, Poland, the United States, and Venezuela. League of Nations Doc. No. C.216.M.851.927.11, 'Double Taxation and Tax Evasion' 6; 4 *LHUSTC* 4120 (1927).
30. Article 5 (second paragraph), *id.* at 11; 4 *LHUSTC* at 4125.
31. League of Nations Document C.216.M.85.1927.11, at 15; 4 *LHUSTC* at 4129. Mitchell Carroll repeats this language at 2 *International Lawyer* 692, 701. Pouring content of this importance

> 'real centres of management, affiliated companies, branches, factories, agencies, warehouses, offices, depots, no matter whether such establishments are used by the traders themselves, by their partners, attorneys or their other permanent representative.'[32]

The Committee notably advanced the concept of the independent agent. The language of prior treaties certainly does not provide much support for the concept.[33] Nor is there much in the Committee's prior published reports that seems to compel adoption of the rule. The rule in the 1927 Draft Convention and the following explanation in the Commentary state:

> 'Nevertheless, the fact that an undertaking has business dealings with a foreign country through a *bona fide* agent of *independent status* (broker, commission agent, etc.) shall not be held to mean that the undertaking in question has a permanent establishment in that country. The words "*bona fide* agent of *independent status*" are intended to apply absolute independence, both from the legal and economic point of view. The agent's remuneration must not be below what would be regarded as a normal remuneration. The Committee has not expressed an opinion on the point whether purchasing offices or sales offices are to be considered as places of business, this being a question of fact.'[34]

One notes the impact of the final sentence: the commentator announces that the purchasing office – a fixture in tax treaties since 1899 – had its status under review. (The sentence probably should be interpreted as meaning 'we could not reach agreement.')

The 'General Meeting of Government Experts on Double Taxation and Tax Evasion' convened in Geneva on 22 October 1928 for the purpose of reviewing the draft treaties. Some interesting changes occurred. First of all, the term 'affiliated companies' disappeared from the permanent establishment definition in both the treaty text[35] and the Commentary.[36] Between 'branches' and 'factories' a new term 'mining and oil fields' was added. The same term was moved out of the second paragraph of the Commentary and into the third. The word 'workshop' followed 'factories'

---

into a term so recently coined as the English rendering of *Betriebsstätte* places some strain on credulity.

32. *Ibid*. Note the appearance of the term 'attorneys.'
33. Other than its contemporaneous appearance in the 1927 Austrian–Swiss Treaty.
34. *Ibid, n. 32*.
35. Draft Convention No. la, Article 5, *id*. at 8.
36. Commentary, Article 5, *id*. at 12.

The Commentary contains not a word to explain the deletion of 'affiliated companies.' Yet the time of their constituting automatic permanent establishments was about to come to an end. In the midst of trivia, the independent-entity concept seems to have begun life.

1.5 THIRD PERIOD – THE 1943 MEXICO DRAFT AND THE OECD 1963 DRAFT AND 1977 MODEL

By the time that the Technical Experts exited in 1928 and the League of Nations Fiscal Committee moved to center stage, the elements of 'permanent establishment' were in place. The years between the wars were times of development and refinement of concept. By the middle of World War II, there was a surprising degree of agreement on the critical language. In its 'Mexico Draft' of 1943, the League of Nations Fiscal Committee defined the term as follows:

> '1. The term "permanent establishment" includes head offices, branches, mines and oil-wells, plantations, factories, workshops, warehouses, offices, agencies, installations, professional premises and other fixed places of business having a productive character.
> 2. A building site (*chantier de construction*) constitutes a "permanent establishment" when it is destined to be used for a year at least or has been in existence for a year.
> 3. The fact that an enterprise established in one of the contacting States has business dealings in another contracting State through an agent of genuinely independent status (broker, commission agent, etc.) shall not be held to mean that the enterprise has a permanent establishment in the latter State.
> 4. When an enterprise of one of the contracting States regularly has business relations in the other State through an agent established there who is authorized to act on its behalf, it shall be deemed to have a permanent establishment in that State.
> A permanent establishment shall, for instance, be deemed to exist when the agent:
> A. Is a duly accredited agent (*fondé de pouvoir*) and habitually enters into contracts for the enterprise for which he works; or
> B. Is bound by an employment contract and habitually transacts business on behalf of the enterprise in return for remuneration from the enterprise; or
> C. Is habitually in possession, for the purpose of sale, of a depot or stock of goods belonging to the enterprise.

5. As evidence of an employment contract under the terms of B above may be taken, moreover, the fact that the administrative expenses of the agent, in particular the rent of the premises, are paid by the enterprise.
6. The fact that a broker places his services at the disposal of an enterprise in order to bring it into touch with customers does not in itself imply the existence of a permanent establishment for the enterprise, even if his work for the enterprise is, to a certain extent, continuous or is carried on at regular periods, and even if the goods sold have been temporarily placed in a warehouse. Similarly, the fact that a commission agent (*commissionaire*) acts in his own name for one or more enterprises and receives a normal rate of commission does not constitute a permanent establishment for any such enterprise, even if the goods sold have been temporarily placed in a warehouse.
7. A permanent establishment shall not be deemed to exist in the case of commercial travelers not coming under any of the preceding categories.
8. The fact that a parent company, the fiscal domicile of which is one of the contracting States, has a subsidiary in the other State does not mean that the parent company has a permanent establishment in that State, regardless of the fiscal obligations of the subsidiary toward the State in which it is situated.'[37]

The sort of difficulties that the Fiscal Committee had been thrashing out is evident – sorting out the tax attributes of agency relationships under various legal systems had obviously required considerable effort.

The appearance in 1963 of the OECD Draft Income Tax Convention heralded the beginning of a new era in international taxation. The Draft was widely accepted as a pattern on which bilateral tax conventions might thereafter be shaped. Countries such as the United States joined the swelling ranks of those nations which were adopting the OECD Draft language.[38] And, more importantly, the basic nexus provisions of the domestic tax law of some nations were made to conform to the language of the Draft.[39]

There were, of course, variations. The United States continued to insist on treaty language concerning source of income, for example.[40] And there

37. League of Nations Fiscal Committee, Report on the Work of the Tenth Session of the Committee, League of Nations Doc. No. C.37.M.37.1946.II.A., 25 April 1946 (4 LHUSTC 4299).
38. The first full-scale effort was in the treaty with France. *See* Lazerow, *OECD Draft Influence on United States Income Tax Treaties* (1976).
39. Japan is a prime example. *See* Huston, Miyatake & Way, *Japanese International Taxation* § 2.01 (1983-1987).
40. *See, e.g.*, the former 1971 United States–Japan treaty, article 6.

was plenty of negotiating over just what should and should not constitute the 'business income' that would be subject to this treatment, rather than some other.[41] But in the main, the problems now surrounding tax treaties center on the interpretation of terms almost universally adopted, rather than with language peculiar to this or that convention.

The language of the Draft was only slightly modified in the OECD Model of 1977. However, the extensive rewriting of the Commentary makes the Model a document of unique value to researchers.

1.6 FOURTH PERIOD – THE 1980 UN MODEL, SERVICES PEs AND E-COMMERCE

The concerns of third-world countries were brought into focus in 1980 by the publication of the 1980 United Nations Model Double Taxation Convention Between Developed and Developing Countries.[42] Significant modifications in the basic permanent establishment definition and a broadening of the primary right to tax in the country of source were major thrusts of the document.[43]

In response to the policies of its source country members, who greatly outnumbered the OECD residence country membership, the 1980 UN Model:

1. created a new "asset and agency-free" *Services PE* category in the midst of the construction assembly project type of PE, itself already an exception to the fixed place of business PE;
2. reduced the minimum time threshold for construction PEs from 12 months (OECD) to 6 months; the same 6-month time threshold applied for the new Services PE provision;
3. deleted the "PE free"[44] exception for "delivery" warehouses, stocks and agents from OECD Articles 5(4) and 5(5);
4. added a new Article 5(6) insurance company PE for non resident enterprise (NRE)[45] insurers who collect premium or insure risks through non independent source country agents – another "asset and agency-free" type PE.

---

41. *See* de Ravel d'Esclapon, 'International Tax Treaties and Industrial and Commercial Profits,' in *Income Tax Treaties* 75 (Bischel ed. 1978), reprinted from *U.S. Taxation of International Operations* (1981).
42. UN Doc. ST/ESA/102, UN Sales No. E.80.XVI.3 (1980).
43. *See* Vogel (1997, 3rd edition), at 281, para. 5a ('The definition adopted in UN MC extends the State of source's power to impose tax and in some fields does away completely with the permanent establishment test').
44. Tittle appears to have coined this apt term.
45. A number of abbreviations are used in this book, which will be identified only when first used. For a complete list of terms used, see the Glossary following the Table of Contents.

The current form of the UN Model is the 2011 MC. Aside from the above changes from the OECD Model and the retention of Article 14 Fixed Base taxation of individuals, the current Commentary of the UN Model closely follows the Commentary of the OECD Model.

In 1992, the OECD Fiscal Committee announced a plan for periodic updating of the 1977 Model. The first of these 'Updates' appeared in that year. The definition of permanent establishments has not changed although the OECD Model has been updated several times, most recently in 2010.[46] What has changed significantly are provisions in the OECD's Commentary to article 5, as well as intervening reports of the OECD Committee on Fiscal Affairs which have found their way into the Article 5 Commentary on such issues as software, e-commerce, container leasing and transfer pricing.

In its 2008 Commentary Update,[47] the OECD introduced its own concept of alternative 6-month Service PE provisions, which was not incorporated into the OECD Model, but has been adopted by some OECD countries, e.g., the 2007 Fifth Protocol to the US–Canada Treaty. These provisions add to the traditional asset or agency type PEs in favor of a 6-month "boots on the ground" type of Services PE.[48]

Some far reaching changes were proposed in an OECD 12 October 2011 *Discussion Draft* revising the article 5 Commentary with respect to 25 enumerated issues. These proposed changes covered a range of topics relating to PE issues identified in the 2009 IFA meetings as well as evolving case law on such issues as business restructuring, commissionaires, toll manufacturing, secondments, attributed PE issues relating to an NRE's use of independent contractors, one shot and recurrent time period place of business (POB) PEs, PE POB attribution through use of customer offices and related issues.

Following objections and comments from business and trade groups on these proposed changes, the OECD Working Party issued a revised Discussion Draft on 19 October 2012 which retreated from some of the more far

46. In 2000, the OECD deleted article 14 dealing with the taxation of professionals and other self-employed persons with a source country "fixed base" lasting 6 months. Article 14 has also been deleted from the 2006 US Model. The OECD deemed that a fixed base was the same as a permanent establishment and such persons should be taxable or not under article 5. Article 14 remains in the UN Model with the UN Commentary providing an option to remove it, but with a number of concomitant conforming changes which suggest article 14 might have an independent role, particularly in view of the Services PE provision in the UN Model and the alternative Services PE provisions in the OECD Commentary. For just one example, under the OECD model with a Services PE provision inserted, the fixed POB protection of article 14 is gone for a principal, who cannot be his own deemed agent PE but could be taxed under the Services PE provision which does not require a POB.
47. The 2008 Update of the OECD Model Commentary on Art. 5 results primarily from the previously published report, entitled "The Tax Treaty Treatment of Services: Proposed Commentary Changes". The report was released as a public discussion draft on 8 December 2006.
48. *See* the discussion at Chapter 2.1D. *See also* Chapter 7.

reaching changes, but also left unanswered questions concerning the erosion of traditional bricks and mortar PE and dependent agency concepts.

At the Request of the G20, the OECD published in July 2013 *An Action Plan on Base Erosion and Profit Shifting* (BEPS), which proposed 15 Actions to be reviewed and discussed in a scheduled manner. Two of these Action Plans – dealing with Treaty Abuse and BEPS in the Digital Economy – were published on 14 and 24 March 2014 respectively.

Chapter 2
Elements of the Basic Definition: Fixed Place of Business

2.1 FIXED PLACE OF BUSINESS – THE ASSETS PE

Article 5(1) of the OECD and UN Model Conventions state that a 'permanent establishment' is defined as simply 'a fixed place of business through which the business of an enterprise is wholly or partly carried on.'[1] The OECD Model Commentary explains:

> 'This definition, therefore, contains the following conditions:
> – the existence of a "place of business", i.e., a facility such as premises or, in certain instances, machinery or equipment;
> – this place of business must be "fixed", i.e. it must be established at a distinct place with a certain degree of permanence;
> – the carrying on of the business of the enterprise through this fixed place of business. This means usually that persons who, in one way or another, are dependent on the enterprise (personnel) conduct the business of the enterprise in the State in which the fixed place is situated.'[2]

Case law and OECD Commentary[3] indicate five key tests underlying the definition of a fixed place of business PE – all of which must be met:

---

1. OECD Model 5(1).
2. OECD Model Commentary, Art. 5(1), para. 2.
3. As to the *authority* of the Commentary, *see* Tremblay 38:7 and Reimer, p 21. In general, the Commentary may have significant interpretative authority if both treaty parties are OECD members and neither has made a reservation (to the treaty) or observation (about its Commentary) and the provision or its content predates the treaty. *See*, for a critical analysis of the Vienna Convention on the Law of Treaties and the role of subsequent Commentary on previously concluded treaties, Lang and Brugger, *The Role of OECD Commentary in Tax Treaty Interpretation* 3 April 2008, at http://www.wu.ac.at/taxlaw/institute/staff/publications/langbrugger_australiantaxforum_95ff.pdf

   In practice, the Commentary, since 1992 and particularly in recent years has tended to back away from bright line tests and to make skewed or "spectrum" comments which are not

1. *Character* of the 'place' – e.g., office, premises, machinery, equipment
2. *Geographic fixation* of the place – including certain exceptions allowed by treaty or domestic law for different places which are commercially and geographically connected
3. *Permanence* – the NRE must conduct an enterprise through the place with some 'permanence,' i.e., there must be a minimum duration of such enterprise, usually 6 to 12 months beginning or ending within the fiscal year; both tax rulings and the OECD Commentary recognize some exceptions for 'one shot' or 'recurrent' multi-year trading activity. Also subsumed here are beginning and ending dates and 'interruptions'
4. *At the disposal* – The 'place' must be either owned, rented or 'at the disposal' of the NRE (if it has multiple users) – this is a control of the place test
5. *Whose business is conducted* at the place – The enterprise conducted in the source state must be that of the NRE. This factor looks at the role or not of principals, employees or agents (other than deemed agent PEs who would moot the enquiry). Included are automatic equipment PEs (such as servers, pipelines or gaming equipment operated without source country personnel), persons who may be either NRE or affiliate employees (secondment issues), independent contractors and agents, warehousing/delivery agents, commissionaires, contract and toll manufacturers, and contract joint venturers who do not share profits or losses.

A. Character of a 'Place of Business'

It is now well established that a place of business can include not only an office, premises, workshop, mines, oil wells, an aircraft hangar, farms, installations or pipelines[4] or other immovable fixed places of business, but also movable property which is not moved. The place must be associated with the conduct of

always reconcilable, inviting courts and tax authorities to make selective reference to certain provisions and ignore others (*See e.g.*, Nitikman, in his article on the *Dudney* case (discussed in Chapter 2.1.D.1) refers to the "schizophrenic" approach of the Commentary to the 'at the disposal' requirement). It also seems that the OECD has adopted a *dynamic* rather than *static* view as to the application of subsequent interpretation (in the Commentaries) to previously concluded treaties – a position on which not all, particularly developed, countries agree. *See* OECD MC 2010, Introductory Notes nos. 33 *et seq*. *See* also, OECD Model Commentary, Art. 5(1), para. 3.1 (a PE must be determined according to the way business is currently conducted – a reference to today's supply chain models in contrast to historic decentralized models).

4. *Bundesfinanzhof*, No. II R 12/92 (30 Oct. 1996), discussed in Mehta, at 8.

business and generally does not include buildings not used for business, such as homes and places of accommodation.[5]

Machinery or other movable equipment which is not moved can be a fixed POB if the NRE conducts business regularly through such stationary property with the required degree of permanence and the property is 'at the disposal' of the NRE. So qualified, vending machines as well as 'a work bench in a caravan, restaurants on permanently anchored river boats, steady oil rigs, or a transformator or generator on board of a former railway wagon qualify as places (and may also be "fixed"...).' However property must be tangible to constitute a POB. Software, securities, patents, goodwill or other intangible economic assets cannot themselves constitute a PE.[6]

In the *German Pipeline* case,[7] the Court held that the Dutch owner of an underground oil pipeline in Germany used to transport third party customers' petroleum products had a fixed place of business PE, even through the pipeline was fully automatic and operated entirely by personnel in the Netherlands.

The use of stationary equipment as a POB is an evolving area. Most of Australia's tax treaties provide that:

> '"Permanent establishment" includes, by virtue of paragraph (b) of its definition in subsection 6(1) of the ITAA 1936: ... a place where the person has, is using or installing substantial equipment or substantial machinery; ...'[8]

The provision has provoked a fair number of rulings, which generally look at the equipment's size, quantity (if multiple pieces of equipment are involved), value and importance (whether the equipment plays a core role in profit making activity. The most important criteria are substantial size and value.

In *ATO ID 2006/337*, the Australian Tax Office (ATO) ruled that the computer system of a NRE engaged in securities trading was not a substantial equipment PE. The equipment consisted on ten pieces of hardware weighing 164 kilograms and worth $200,000, including servers and routers and software used for market access and trading algorithms.[9]

5. *See* Reimer at 38 'This is why social facilities such as rest homes, or living quarter of employees do not constitute PEs under Article 5(1) OECD MC.' *Finanzgericht München* 16 EFG 55, 56 (1966).
6. Reimer at 35.
7. *Bundesfinanzhof*, No. II R 12/92 (30 Oct. 1996), discussed in Mehta, at 8.
8. ATO Interpretative Decision (ID) 2006/337. All Australian tax decisions and rulings can be viewed online at http://law.ato.gov.au/atolaw/searches.htm.
9. *See also Games Co*, Administrative Appeals Tribunal (Australia) Case U162 dated 5 August 1987 (87 ATC 942) (discussed in Mehta at 28) which involved the taxability of a loan out company of a US professional golf player who earned substantial endorsement fees by competing for 24 and 28 days in Australian golf events; the Tribunal held that 'substantial equipment'

In *TR 2002/5*, the ATO ruled construed the domestic definition of a permanent establishment to include the word 'fixed.' Thus, the use or installation of substantial equipment or machinery in Australia should meet the OECD test of geographic permanence if carried on 'habitually' at a fixed place as stated by McHugh J. in *Thiel vs FCT*.[10] *TR 2002/5* states that, while the test of time permanence does not literally require 'permanence', it is a question of fact and, in the absence of a treaty time requirement, will be assumed met by a period of six months.[11]

The use of equipment as a POB with e-commerce businesses and e-tailing was dealt with in a 2002 OECD Fiscal Committee Report which is discussed in detail in Chapter 8 (PEs in the Cloud). The taxation of e-commerce has been again addressed as one of 15 Action Plans proposed in the OECD's July 19, 2013 Report on Base Erosion and Profit Shifting (BEPS) and is the subject of a discussion draft issued March 24, 2014.

While the OECD 2013 BEPS proposals will be further discussed in the updated online version of this book, the basic popular premise that international tax law has not kept pace with the developments in international trade can be questioned. As discussed in Chapter 8 (E-Commerce) it would appear that case law and rulings have adequately addressed changes in the digital economy and that further changes are not needed and could seriously erode the role of the permanent establishment concept in promoting international trade.

There are a handful of decisions which illustrate how the OECD BEPS proposals could undermine the traditional concept of a 'fixed place of business' PE. For example, in *Amadeus Global*,[12] a Spanish based company developed a *fully automatic* airline computer reservation system (CRS) with mainframe servers in Germany and accessed in India through the Internet by unrelated travel agents. Amadeus contracted with an Indian company to solicit Indian travel agents who subscribed to the CRS system through the Indian company. Amadeus had no office, employees or dependent agents in India.

The Indian travel agents could access the CRS either through their own computers or through IBM computers with dumb terminals supplied free as an incentive by Amadeus to a minority of agents. These agents could not move

---

could not include a set of golf clubs or anything else associated with the taxpayers' activities in Australia; cf. Article 17, taxation of artists and athletes. *And see*, *Golf in Dubai LLC*, In re [2008] 174 Taxmann 480 (AAR – New Delhi), also discussed in Mehta at 32 and reproduced in Mehta, Appendix One, which held that 2 Indian golf courses rented by a UAE company for a weeks' tournaments did not constitute a fixed place of business for failure of the permanence test.

10. (1990) 171 CLR 338 at 359; 90 ATC 4717 at 4728; 21 ATR 531 at 544.
11. *See e.g.* United States–Australia 5(2)(f & g) (9 months for CAS project; 6 months for oil and gas exploration).
12. *Amadeus Global Travel Distribution SA vs DDIT* (2011, 11 Taxmann.com 153 (Delhi), discussed in Mehta at 12 and Nitikman at 237 and reproduced in Mehta, Appendix One).

the computers, which were only of use to send or receive information from the CRS system and could not process it.

Agents not supplied with such a computer could access the CRS system through their own computers configured with a 'node' supplied by SITA, an unrelated French telecom company to whom Amadeus paid a service fee. Amadeus paid its Indian solicitation agent a $0.84 fee 'per click' by an Indian travel agent using the CRS system. Amadeus' source of income was a net booking fee paid by the airlines pursuant to separate Participating Carrier Agreements. The airlines also compensated the Indian booking agents, the booking being concluded and both payments being made offshore.

ITAT considered the OECD Commentary, paragraph 4 (the 'at the disposal' requirement) and found that it stated the law in India. However, ITAT went on to find that the dumbed down IBM computers handed out free as an incentive to some travel agents, together with linked leased telephone lines, constituted a 'fixed place of business' PE of Amadeus in India over which it retained complete 'control' – despite the fact that Amadeus was not in the 'business' of providing computers or leased telephone lines. Amadeus had no control over the travel agent's offices in which such computers were located, any Indian travel agent could access the CRS system through his own computer and Amadeus received no income from any person in India, had no personnel and no activities there.

The facts in an earlier *Galileo*[13] case were similar but even more devoid of any PE connection to India. There, a US based CRS provider had a huge US Master Computer System with 18 main-frame computers connected to airlines' servers which continually exchanged flight and seat availability data on a real time basis. 6 categories of unrelated players used or were involved with the CRS system: passengers, travel agents, an unrelated Indian solicitation agent, SITA, Galileo and the airlines. Galileo also provided computers to its unrelated Indian solicitation agent, but only for the first two years as the computers then became obsolete. The computers had no significant value and were provided to only 265 out of 800 Indian travel agents.

As in *Amadeus*, ITAT held that Galileo had an Indian fixed place of business PE due to the computers because the CRS system existed 'in part' in the dumbed down computers over which Galileo maintained complete control, as well as the SITA telecom connection. The Court also held that such use was not 'preparatory or auxiliary' to Galileo's business.

---

13. *Galileo International Inc. vs DCIT, DDIT* (2008, 19 SOT 257 (Delhi), also discussed in Mehta at 18 and reproduced in Mehta, Appendix One).

Interestingly, in a third decision, *Western Union Financial Services Inc vs ADIT*,[14] the US based money transfer company dealt with a variety of independent agents in India with regard to the transmission of funds from the US to India via a Money Transfer Control Number (MTCN) provided by the US sender to the Indian recipient, who provided the MTCN to an Indian agent who inputted it into a computer system using Western Union's software. ITAT held, in accordance with the OECD Commentary, that software, like any intangible, could not be a place of business.

The *CRS* decisions do not appear to follow OECD commentary since the provision of telecom connections and purely transmissional hardware was clearly ancillary to the CRS business conducted through offshore servers and software. It is also questionable whether a third party telecommunication network could be a POB of a user[15] since it is similar to a telecommunication 'roaming' agreement, which the OECD Commentary states does not constitute a PE. Finally, the provision of disparately located non programmable computers to some but not all travel agent users can hardly be said to meet the requirements of a single 'fixed' place of business at the disposal of the CRS provider.[16]

B. Geographic Fixation of the Place of Business – a Fixed Place

1. Basic Rule

A place of business must have a specific geographical location. If not fixed to the soil, it must lie on, or under it, be a part of or be attached to it or docked within territorial waters. Thus far, a country's air space has not been the locus of a fixed place and the Commentary rules out taxation of satellites in geostationary orbit.[17]

As stated by the OECD Model Commentary:

> 'According to the definition, the place of business has to be a "fixed" one. Thus in the normal way there has to be a link between the place of business and a specific geographical point. It is immaterial how long an

14. *Western Union Financial Services Inc vs ADIT* (2007, 104 ITD 34 (Delhi), discussed in Mehta at 25 and reproduced in Mehta, Appendix One.
15. *See e.g.*, OECD Commentary, article 5(1), para. 9.1, that a telecom roaming agreement is a contract with an independent contractor and does not constitute a PE.
16. *Cf.* Roberto Greco de Souza Ferreira, The traditional Concept of Permanent Establishment and the New Economy – The Position Taken by the OECD and the Issues Faced by the Brazilian Tax System, 9 July 2003. Mr Ferreira is associated with Stroeter, Royster & Ohno Advogados, (Steel Hector & Davis LLP) http://www.mondaq.com/article.asp?articleid=21845&login=true (last viewed May 26, 2013) (Brazil would not treat server as a PE unless both used and controlled by the NRE for core business activities).
17. OECD Model Commentary, Art. 5(1), para. 5.5.

> enterprise of a Contracting State operates in the other Contracting State if it does not do so at a distinct place, but this does not mean that the equipment constituting the place of business has to be actually fixed to the soil on which it stands. It is enough that the equipment remains on a particular site ....'[18]

The OECD Model Commentary closes the excerpt with a cross-reference to a statement made in connection with construction and installation projects:

> 'The very nature of a construction or installation project may be such that the contractor's activity has to be relocated continuously or at least from time to time, as the project progresses. This would be the case for instance where roads or canals were being constructed, waterways dredged, or pipelines laid. Similarly, where parts of a substantial structure such as an offshore platform are assembled at various locations within a country and moved to another location within the country for final assembly, this is part of a single project. In such a case, the fact that the work force is not present for twelve months in one particular place is immaterial. The activities performed at each particular spot are part of a single project, and that project must be regarded as a permanent establishment if, as a whole, it lasts more than twelve months.'[19]

One is prompted to inquire whether the cross-reference is intended to imply that this variety of fixedness is applicable across the board, or whether it is meant to apply only in the case of construction projects. There is debate whether Art. 5(3) is (1) a deeming (stand-alone) provision, i.e. a CAS project PE may exist independently of Art. 5(1) conditions; or (2) a *lex specialis* case of Art. 5(1), i.e. the requirements of Art. 5(1) – apart from the permanence test which is specified in Art. 5(3) – must be met in order for a CAS project PE to be constituted.[20] The 'stand-alone' view would seem the better construction. While a fixed place of business at a construction site can constitute a PE, it can only do so under Article 5(1) and not Article 5(3).[21] Conversely, a construction

18. OECD Model Commentary, Art. 5(1), para. 5. In the second paragraph of the Commentary preceding, the Fiscal Committee stated: 'A place of business may thus be constituted by a pitch in the market place ...' – an illustration of classic ineptness if that place of business could under no circumstances constitute a permanent establishment.
19. OECD Model Commentary, Art. 5(3), para. 20.
20. For a detailed discussion of the arguments for and against these approaches, see Pijl, The relationship Between Article 5, Paragraphs 1 and 3 of the OECD Model Convention, 33 *Intertax* (International Tax Review), 4 (2005), pp. 189-193.
21. OECD Model Commentary, Art. 5(3), para 16.

site PE can exist without a fixed place of business in the Article 5(1) sense.[22] The issue is further discussed in Chapter 3.8.

Nonetheless, some loosening of fixation is found in the OECD Commentary's observation that one or more different sites can be a single fixed POB if 'geographically and commercially' connected. The examples refer to 'campus' like situations[23] and distinguish work done at different discrete locations, which should not be aggregated due to lack of geographical coherence.[24]

According to a US Court, this view apparently does not apply to bank branches. The US Court of Claims stated in its 2005 *Nat West III* opinion that 'there was no precedent for treating six branch offices as six separate permanent establishments in either the United States or the United Kingdom.' The Court aggregated 6 US branches of Nat West bank into a single US branch because that is the way Nat West and the Bank of England had accounted for them.[25]

2. *Touring and Moving Target Rulings*

Some early American rulings have stretched the concept of a fixed place of business beyond fixedness. A series of American *Race Horse* rulings held that a French owner of racing stables had a US fixed place of business when he entered more than one horse a year in American horse races.[26] Although the French owner had a racing stable in the US, the races occurred at different locations in the U.S.

While this ruling is questionable in view of both the fixed place of business and 'permanence' requirements, another controversial American ruling found a PE when a Swiss entrepreneur demonstrated his specialized logging equipment with the assistance of specially trained Swiss employees in various United States forests over a period of time expected to last two years.[27]

The ruling relied on the *ipse dixit* observation that the taxpayer's business was a type which could not be conducted from a fixed place of business. Neither this nor the *Race Horse* rulings were based on the dependent-agency concept nor involved a fixed place of business in the traditional sense. Thus

22. *See e.g., CIT vs T/HAM*, 15 Taxmann.com 102 (2011Uttarakhand) which held that a construction project which was itself less than 6 months could not become one by the continuation of a project office, which in any effect ITAT held was only used for preparatory and auxiliary activities, discussed in Mehta at 182 and reproduced in Mehta Appendix One.
23. OECD Model Commentary, Art. 5(1), paras 5.1-5.4.
24. OECD Model Commentary, Art. 5(1), para. 5.4.
25. *National Westminster Bank, PLC vs United States* 69 Fed Ct. Claims 128, 140-41 (2005) aff'd (NatWest IV), 512 F.3d 1347, 1349 (Fed. Cir. 1008), discussed in Tittle at 83.
26. Rev. Rul. 58-63 (1958-1 CB 624) as modified in Rev. Rul. 60-249 (1960-2 CB 264), discussed *infra* in Section 2.2 K.
27. Rev. Rul. 56-165, 1956-1 CB 849.

they could be viewed as aberrational. Support for this conclusion is found in a New Zealand ruling[28] which held that an Australian theatre touring company which arranged performances at different theatres in New Zealand did not have a PE because there was no single fixed place of business.

Similarly, in an *Alaskan Fishing* case[29] the Norwegian Supreme Court held that the combination of a Norwegian fishing vessel, use of a Seattle quay to equip the fishing vessel and off season storage of fish pots at Dutch Harbour Alaska did not create a fixed POB PE in Alaska.

In contrast, a *Dutch Drilling Ship*[30] case held that an employee working on board a ship engaged in oil exploration offshore India, Indonesia and Malaysia had a fixed POB where the ship was mobile within a geographic and commercially coherent area such as an 'oil exploration block'; however the lower court found that the ship was not a PE because its period of operation failed the permanence test.[31]

In *Alphawell Ltd. and Richard Pegrum vs Ministry of Finance*,[32] a UK tax resident employee of a family owned company acted as exploration advisor to Statoil over a 4 year period involving various trips to Norway and use of different offices provided by Statoil. The Norwegian Supreme Court held that the company did not have a Norwegian fixed POB since the employee worked at different places for differing periods of time.

However in a *French Canal Boat*[33] case, a UK company operated 3 canal boats on tours through French inland waterways booked and paid for through its US parent. The French Supreme Administrative Court held that the canal boats constituted a French fixed POB of the UK company.

The extension of the fixed POB PE to 'moving target' business ventures erodes the 'fixed' requirement as a number of disparate 'places' could become 'fixed' within some subjectively perceived geographical or time spectrum. The better analysis is that 'moving target' business cannot be a fixed POB PE – apart from the limited commercial and geographic connectivity test applied to construction project PEs, which is a discrete type of PE which arguably does not share the Article 5(1) requirement of geographic fixity.[34] This view appears endorsed by the OECD 2012 Revised Discussion Draft which states:

---

28. Case 5, 17 Aug. 1965, 3 NZTBR 49, discussed in Mehta at 10.
29. Case No. 15B/1984 (25 Jan 1984) discussed in Mehta at 55.
30. Case No AWB09/563 (25 May 2009, *Rechtbank Breda*) discussed in Mehta at 60.
31. Both of these diverse rulings involved factual situations where the taxpayer would benefit from a finding of a PE.
32. Case No. 56/994 (10 Jun 1994) discussed in Mehta at 61.
33. Case No. 94137 (23 Nov 1992 *Conseil d'Etat*) discussed in Mehta at 59.
34. A similar concept can however aggregate non disparate POBs which are commercially and economically connected within a source country into a 'single POB PE. *Cf. National Westminster Bank, PLC vs United States* which aggregated 6 US branches of Nat West bank into a single US branch because that is the way Nat West and the Bank of England had accounted for them.

> 'The Working Party concluded that a moving ship would typically not constitute a fixed place and a shop aboard such a ship would not, therefore, constitute a permanent establishment. It was noted, however, that a specific area to which the operation of the ship would be restricted could itself have commercial and geographic coherence and, therefore, could constitute a fixed place of business depending on the circumstances.'[35]

Thus, floatable oil rigs are not fixed POB PEs while anchored ones may be.[36] Similarly, offshore fishing is beyond the pale of a fixed POB or any other kind of PE. Equipment and machinery must remain at a fixed location. However the second sentence of the above Working Party comment above introduces a subjective element. Is this an endorsement of the result in the *French Canal Boat*[37] case above? Can a defined journey constitute a fixed POB?

In a *Turkish Yacht* case,[38] a UK operator of yachts for foreign tourists had a PE in Turkey because the yachts themselves were considered places of business through which the business of the UK company was carried on and each was fixed and followed a specific excursion route. A PE existed, although the day-to-day operation of the yachts was performed by a Turkish sub-contractor (which raises other issues, discussed later in this section). The time requirement was also found to be met, given the seasonal nature of the business activities.

C. Permanence of Business Operations – Minimum Duration, Recurrent and One Shot Ventures

A 'fixed' place of business displays other facets. One turns next to the temporal aspect of the concept. The OECD 2012 Revised Discussion Draft confirms what commentators and practitioners have generally believed to be a minimum 6-month bright line test:

> 'Since the place of business must be fixed, it also follows that a permanent establishment can be deemed to exist only if the place of business has a certain degree of permanency, i.e. if it is not of a purely temporary

35. Issue 5, paragraph 30.
36. Reimer at 47, who notes the potential source country taxability of floating rigs under articles 6 (real estate income) or 13 (real estate gains); *Gerechtshof 's-Gravenhage*, Rolno. 4287/87-M-1, Beslissingen in Belastingzaken, Nederlandse Belastingrechtsspraak 1992/51: DTC Netherlands–UK, discussed in Reimer at 44.
37. Case No. 94137 (23 Nov 1992 *Conseil d'Etat*) discussed in Mehta at 59.
38. Supreme Administrative Court, 3rd Chamber E.2009/4489, 25 October 2010, Case K.2010/3276, discussed in S. B. Law, T. Mkrtchyan, Vienna Conference on 'Treaty Case Law Around the Globe', European Taxation 12 (2011), pp. 548-555, at 549.

> nature … Whilst the practices followed by *member* countries have not been consistent in so far as time requirements are concerned, *experience has shown that permanent establishments normally have not been considered to exist in situations where a business had been carried on in a country through a place of business that was maintained for less than six months* (conversely, practice shows that there were many cases where a permanent establishment has been considered to exist where the place of business was maintained for a period longer than six months.)'[39]

1. Six Months Minimum Duration Cases

Several cases, particularly in Germanic countries, have held that a minimum 6-month duration requirement applies to a POB PE. In a *Swiss Consultant*[40] case, the Austrian Supreme Administrative Court held that a Swiss consultant who provided consultancy services to an Austrian client for about 9 months had a fixed POB PE in office space provided by the client. The then Austrian–Swiss Treaty was based on the OECD Draft Model which did not provide a minimum time frame for a fixed business PE. Nonetheless, the Court referred to later OECD Article 5 Commentary and German jurisprudence as requiring a minimum 6 months' time period for a permanent establishment.

Similarly in *PGS Geophysical AS vs Norway*,[41] the Norwegian Supreme Court held that two stand-alone oil exploration ships operating off the Ivory Coast did not constitute a fixed POB and further, failed a 6 months minimum duration test, which was not in the Treaty, but which the Court inferred from common interpretation.

And a *Dutch Drilling Ship*[42] case held that an employee working on board a ship engaged in oil exploration offshore India, Indonesia and Malaysia had a fixed POB where the ship was mobile within a geographic and commercially coherent area such as an 'oil exploration block'; however the lower court found that the ship was not a PE because its period of operation failed a 6-month permanence test.[43]

In *Rev. Rul. 67-322*,[44] the IRS held that a Danish company operating a restaurant in the Food Pavilion of the New York World's Fair for 6 months

---

39. *OECD 2012 Revised Discussion Draft, para. 6* (emphasis added).
40. *Verwaltungsgerichtshof*, Case No. 96/14/0084 (21 May 1997), discussed in Mehta at 29 and 72.
41. Case No. 2004-01003-A (8 June 2004) discussed in Mehta at 72.
42. Case No AWB09/563 (25 May 2009, *Rechtbank Breda*) discussed in Mehta at 60 and 72.
43. Both *PGS Geophysical* and *Drilling Ship* involved factual situations where the taxpayer would benefit from a finding of a PE.
44. 1967-2 CB 469.

in each year 1964 and 1965 had a fixed POB PE there due to the minimum 6 months of operation in each year.

Rev. Rul. 77-45[45] involved a Canadian company (Canco) which provided through its employees construction site supervisory and planning services for the unrelated general contractor of a US client. The US client provided office furniture and equipment *gratis* to Canco's US onsite employees. The ruling involved the 1942 US–Canadian Treaty which did not contain a CAS PE provision. While the IRS held that such activities could constitute a fixed POB PE, it held that mere 'supervisory and planning' services did not amount to construction activity. Further it found no fixed POB PE *both* because the use of the provided furniture and equipment was not separately bargained for (i.e., rented) by Canco and because such use was for less than 1 year.

See also ATO TR 2002/5,[46] an Australian tax ruling which in the absence of a specified term, would apply a 6 months' required term.

2. *One Shot Ventures (Less Than 6 Months)*

The OECD Commentary recognizes two exceptions to the general 6 months' minimum duration rule:

> A place of business may, however, constitute a permanent establishment even though it exists, in practice, only for a very short period of time because the nature of the business is such that it will only be carried on for that short period of time. It is sometimes difficult to determine whether this is the case.... One exception has been where the activities were of a recurrent nature; in such cases, each period of time during which a place is used needs to be considered in combination with the number of times during which that place is used (which may extend over a number of years). Another exception has been made where activities constituted a business that was carried on exclusively in that country; in this situation, the business may have short duration because of its nature but since it is wholly carried on in that country, its connection with that country is stronger.[47]

These exceptions test the thesis and are discussed in the OECD 2012 Revised Discussion Draft: namely (1) the one shot business venture and (2) the recurrent same place business venture. As evidence of the first, The Revised Draft

45. 1977-1 CB 413.
46. http://law.ato.gov.au/atolaw/view.htm?docid=TXR/TR20025/NAT/ATO/00001 (last viewed at May 26, 2013).
47. *OECD 2012 Revised Discussion Draft, para. 6* (emphasis added).

provides the example of a non-resident who, upon learning of a 4-month TV documentary filming project near her parents' home, converted it into a cafeteria to cater to the film crew onsite for 4 months, after which the cafeteria business was closed.[48]

Because all aspects of the business occur within the source country within this less than 6-month time frame, the Commentary posits that a fixed POB PE is created for this 4-month business. Over objections that this type of thinking could throttle onsite businesses catering to the Olympic summer and winter games, the Revised Draft creates a specific exception for such providers at four week sporting events.[49]

The objections go further however than that concession.[50] The one shot business example confuses the 'core business activity' rule negating the PE-free status of certain preparatory or auxiliary activities under Article 5(4) with the permanence rule of an Article 5(1) fixed POB PE. The exception would engulf the 'permanency' requirement of a fixed place of business.

An illustration is the *Fugro Engineers BV vs ACIT*[51] involving the provision of geotechnical services by a Dutch Company at various Indian oil drilling locations for 3 customers over periods of 13, 14 and 37 days. ITAT found both a fixed place of business and that the permanence test was met because the period required was long enough for the Dutch company to complete its project.[52] The ruling holds that a fixed POB PE, unlike the 6-month limited CAS PE, does not require any period of time to constitute a POB PE. Further ITAT held that a moving vessel present in Indian waters for 91 days was a 'fixed' place of business.

A more temporal view was expressed in a Canadian Interpretation Bulletin:[53]

> '[D]espite the use of the word "permanent", the length of time that a fixed place of business is used in Canada by a non-resident carrying on a business is not a deciding factor in determining the existence of a permanent establishment. Also, the words "fixed" and "permanent" refer to the continual carrying on of a business at a particular work site and do not mean that the place of business must exist for a lengthy

48. OECD 20112 Revised Discussion Draft, proposed para. 6.2.
49. *Id.*
50. *See e.g.*, Reimer, at 49, and Business & Industry Advisory Council comments to OECD 2011 Discussion Draft, argue for an across the board minimum 6-month bright line test.
51. (2008, Delhi), 26 SOT 78, discussed in Mehta at 77 and reproduced at Mehta, Appendix One.
52. http://www.bmradvisors.com/upload/documents/TES%2024%20Oct%20081248782732.pdf (last viewed April 7, 2014)
53. IT-173R2 (30 January 1989), summarized at 2 *International Tax Treaties Service*, Art. 13, page 8.5001 (Edwardes-Ker ed. 1986).

> period or that it must be a permanent type of building. Consequently, a temporary field office erected by a contractor from the US to carry on building or other operations would be a "fixed" place of business ...'

Most countries will tax an individual physically present within the country for 6 months as a 'resident.' A similar 6-month test should apply to corporate and joint venture NREs.[54] Certainty for taxpayers and collectors is more important here than a perceived loss of revenues from one shot ventures, which could include any number of short term consulting projects. It is worth noting that both the UN Services PE and the OECD Commentary Services PE provisions require a minimum source country presence of 6 months.

3. Recurrent Multi-Year Ventures

The second OECD 2012 Revised Draft exception applies to recurrent ventures. Here, an example is provided of an NRE which conducts oil drilling in the Arctic for 3 months of each year over a 5 year period – 3 months being a limit provided by seasonal weather conditions. The Draft considers that this venture could meet the fixed POB permanence requirement – due to the specific requirements of this business even though drilling in any year is less than 6 months.[55] The Draft adds that the specific conditions of other businesses could require even shorter annual periods of enterprise activity.

This example does find support in some rulings. In *Joseph Fowler vs MNR*[56] the Canadian Tax Court found a fixed place of business when a US resident sold goods at the Vancouver Pacific National Exhibition for at least 3 weeks a year over a 15 year period. The taxpayer also sold his goods at two California fairs. The Court's findings were influenced (1) by the (seasonal) nature of the activities and (2) the fact that the activities in Canada formed a significant part of the overall activities of the taxpayer:

> 'Conceptually the Vancouver sales were actually being conducted at, or from, a place of business having the same attributes as that of a "place of management", as a "branch" of the whole operation, or as an "office". The matters of mobility and the three-week time period are not in themselves overly material when taken into context. Indeed, it was the very nature of the business itself that mandated these aspects.'[57]

---

54. *Accord*, Reimer 2013 at 44.
55. *Id.* at para. 61.
56. *Joseph Fowler vs MNR*, (1990) D.C.T. 1834; (1990) 2 C.T.C. 2351 (Tax Court Canada).
57. *Id*, at para. 10.

The *Pollens*[58] case involved an Austrian company which seasonally produced pollens at a rented Austrian barn with a container placed in front equipped with a desk, telephone and fax machine. Each harvesting season, the Austrian company employed a Swiss agricultural engineer (for less than 6 months) who worked in the container, in the field and in the barn. The Austrian Supreme Administrative Court held that the Swiss engineer had an Austrian fixed POB.

A *German Consultant*[59] case involved a German resident who provided technical services to a French company at its premises through a room provided for his use including other projects. However he spent only 2-3 days a month at such office which led the Court to conclude the room was not at his disposal.

Nitikman points out[60] that the United States Internal Revenue Service struggled with the issue of temporal fixedness in back-to-back rulings published in 1967.[61] In the first of these, the Service ruled that the ten-week run of a French cabaret show created no permanent establishment at the resort hotel at which it played.[62] In contrast, the Danish restaurant at the New York World's Fair was ruled a permanent establishment, although it operated only six months in each of two years.[63]

Just where the US line might be today is impossible to determine. One letter ruling permitted a theatre performance to run for periods totaling perhaps ten months over two calendar years without resulting in the acquisition of a permanent establishment.[64] One suspects that the Service is applying a rule of thumb and that business operations conducted in the United States at specific sites for twelve months over the course of two years are to be regarded as permanent establishments under that rule.

It is difficult to reach definitive conclusions as the operative dates in a large number of the road-show letter rulings published are concealed.[65] On the other hand, 'the elements of permanency and identifiability which are the indicia of a permanent establishment'[66] may simply be absent in the case of touring theatrical productions mounted by foreign individuals and corporations.

---

58. Case No. 2000/15/0118 (18 Mar 2004, *Verwaltungsgerichtshof*)
59. Case No. III 84/96 (2 Dec 1998 *Finanzgericht Nürnberg*) discussed in Mehta at 117.
60. *See* Nitikman, Part 1, at 162.
61. Rev. Rul. 67-321, 1967-2 *C.B.* 470; Rev. Rul. 67-322, 1967-2 *C.B.* 469.
62. Ltr. Rul. 5903189290A.
63. Ltr. Rul. 6704066110A.
64. Ltr. Rul. 7746041 ('during August through October, 1976, January, 1977, February 1977, and August through December, 1977').
65. *See, e.g.*, Ltr. Ruls. 8217103, 8210043, 8115049, 8026067, 7946043, and 7943045. Since 1985, the IRS refused to rule on whether a permanent establishment exists, but in Rev. Proc. 2005-12 reinstated its willingness to give pre filing agreement rulings in the PE area.
66. Case 5, 3 *N.Z. Tax'n Bd. of Rev. Rept.* 49, 59 (1965).

The administrative complexities of taxing recurrent ventures suggest the exemption should be reined in.[67] The OECD 2012 Revised Draft deleted a 2011 example of a sculptor who sold his sculptures at a fair over a 3-week period for each of 15 years.[68] A number of objections were made to this example. When is the threshold year in which a PE is acquired? Once passed, is the sculptor required to file back returns for the earlier years? If back year returns are filed is there exposure to VAT without the opportunity to recover input VAT credits?

Once the recurrent period extends beyond 2 or perhaps 3 years, the associated retrospective administrative and compliance issues would seem to make the recurrent trading exception less tenable. Commentators have suggested a solution of a 6-month bright line test[69] with an exception for recurrent activities only if the same enterprise is conducted in the source country for at least 2 months of every year.[70] Such a limitation would basically cap the recurrent exception at 3 years, which is within the statute of limitations period for tax collection by most countries.[71]

4. *Beginning and Ending Dates*

Finally, related to the concept of permanence are the beginning and ending dates of a source country venture. The OECD 2012 Revised Discussion Draft states:[72]

> 'Where a place of business which was, at the outset, designed to be used for such a short period of time that it would not have constituted a permanent establishment but is in fact maintained for such a period that it can no longer be considered as a temporary one, it becomes a fixed place of business and thus – retrospectively – a permanent establishment. A place of business can also constitute a permanent establishment from its inception even though it existed, in practice, for a very short

67. Reimer at 54, who cites a Norwegian case involving 50 stays in 600 days in different offices in 2 different cities, held no PE. Reimer summarizes other cases denying a fixed POB PE as including traveling circuses, ice skating shows, dancing and music groups and horse races.
68. *Cf.* Fowler above, which involved just such facts.
69. *See e.g.* Reimer at 49.
70. *See e.g.*. Business & Industry Advisory Council (BIAC) Comments on the OECD 2011 Discussion Draft. In substance, BIAC (which represents more than 2000 businesses with respect to OECD issues) proposed that the OECD reaffirm the 12-month rule; if a 6-month rule had to be specified, it should be a minimum and the recurrenct time frame should be reasonably short e.g. source country presence in each year should be a minimum of 2 months or 6 months over 3 years.
71. *Eg.* Internal Revenue Code of the United States §6501(a).
72. Revised amended Commentary, para. 6.6.

period of time, if as a consequence of special circumstances (e.g. death of the taxpayer, investment failure), it was prematurely liquidated.'

Two principles are established here. First, it is reasonably stated that a POB intended to last for a short period of time can meet the permanence requirement if it lasts longer. However the second point is surprising – a fixed place of business intended to last a long period of time but which lasts only a short period of time due to an unexpected event, such as death of the taxpayer, nonetheless meets the permanence requirement. The latter view has been rightly questioned[73] as the existence of a POB is a facts and circumstances, not a subjective intent test.

5. *Deviations in State Practice*

Damaging the fabric of Permanent Establishments as an International Uniform Code of Source Country Taxation of NREs are some deviations in practices of individual countries. For example, a *Belgian Trade Fair*[74] lower court ruling found that a French company had a fixed place of business by its sale of wares in several Belgian trade fairs each year, each fair lasting about a week. The case was decided under an esoteric article 4(4)(h) of the Belgian–French tax treaty which included as a PE facilities at the disposal of traveling salesman for a total period of 30 days in any year.

Similarly, Australian treaties incorporate a domestic law provision classifying the use of 'substantial' equipment within Australia as a POB PE. What is 'substantial' is defined by 4 domestic law criteria which may not comport with traditional PE interpretation.

Oil exploration and exploitation provide a tempting target for countries with offshore oil reserves. Most of the Dutch treaties have a provision taxing as a PE such offshore activities performed by an enterprise for more than 30 days in the taxable year. Such clauses are also found in treaties of Norway, the UK and the United States.[75]

Some Indian treaties have intricate provisions taxing technical services income alternatively under either Article 12 or Article 5. A number of Indian Treaties also separately apply the UN MC Services PE provision to third party services (e.g., a 3- to 6-month provision) and to related party services, with

---

73. Reimer at 50.
74. Case No G1 08/0446 (15 May 2008 *Rechtbank* van *Eerste Aanleg Gent*) discussed in Mehta at 81.
75. Skaar at 425, Reimer at 69; such a provision is also in the Nordic Treaty between Iceland, Norway, Sweden, Finland and Denmark.

services rendered an affiliate under the US–India treaty being taxable even if rendered on only one day during the year (e.g. no time limit).[76]

In *2 Afs 29/2012-18*,[77] the Czech Supreme Administrative Court held that the permanence requirement was not relevant for POB PEs, because – unlike CAS PEs – no duration test was contained in Art. 5(1). Consequently, the taxpayer had a PE in the Czech Republic, even though his activities had lasted for less than 6 months.[78]

Finally, some source countries have differing rules relating to the required registration of local or representational offices or branches with potentially severe consequences for getting it wrong. Great care and appropriate advice should be sought in advance re such requirements.

D. 'At the Disposal' of the NRE (Control of the POB by the NRE)

It is now well established that a place of business may be owned, rented or otherwise 'at the disposal' of the NRE. But it must meet *one* of these 3 conditions. And all 3 relate to the 'control' of the NRE over (1) a place of business with respect to (2) the conduct of its *own* business (3) *through* that place.[79] Thus:

1. An NRE who *owns* a POB (such as a warehouse) has the legal right to control the use and occupancy of that space and thus has control over it.
2. Similarly a *tenant* of business premises has a similar legal leasehold right to control the use and occupancy of facilities or premises leased by it.
3. Finally an NRE which uses a designated part of a place of business owned, leased or used by *another* enterprise, which could include premises of a customer, supplier or other enterprise, can have a POB if such space is 'at its disposal.'

The 'at the disposal' test was not in the 1963 OECD Draft Model or the 1977 OECD MC nor is it in the present 2010 OECD MD. It was added in 1974 by paragraph 4 of the 1963/77 OECD Commentary and by 2002 had become a sine qua non fixture of the definition of the OECD MC requirement that an

76. *See generally*, Rawal (*The Taxation of Permanent Establishments: An International Perspective* (2006)), who has a whole chapter on these variations.
77. Czech Supreme Administrative Court, 29 May 2012, 2 Afs 29/2012-18; IBFD Tax Treaty Case Law Database.
78. A similar view was taken in *Fugro Engineers BV vs ACIT*, (2008) 122 TTJ 655 (Delhi).
79. *Accord*, Reimer at 56, Nitikman, *id*. at 222.

NRE's business be conducted 'through' or 'in' a source country fixed place of business.[80]

1. *The OECD 1977 Commentary is Ambiguous*[81]

The meaning of 'at the disposal' of an NRE is at the heart of a considerable amount of ambiguity in the OECD Commentary, which the 2012 Revised Draft has done little to clarify. The Commentary clearly recognizes the test in the case of ownership or rental of a fixed POB, but lacks clarity when it gets to the third case of a third person's POB 'at the disposal' of an NRE. For example:

> 'A place of business may also exist where no premises are available or required for carrying on the business of the enterprise and it simply has a certain amount of space at its disposal. It is immaterial whether the premises, facilities of installations are owned or rented by or are otherwise at the disposal of the enterprise. A place of business may thus be constituted by a pitch in a market place, or by a certain permanently used area in a customs depot (e.g., for the storage of dutiable goods).'[82]

The second sentence seemingly negates the first, while the next paragraph postulates that not only is no formal legal (even contractual) right required, but that a POB may exist which the NRE 'illegally' occupies to carry on its business.[83]

The Commentary then illustrates these 'concepts' by four examples, two of which are hardly instructive, one of which is questionable and the last refuted by case law. Example 1 (a salesman who regularly visits the office of his customer's purchasing director to take orders does not have a POB there) and Example 3 (a road transportation enterprise which makes daily deliveries at a customer's loading dock does not have a POB there) simply state the obvious.

Example 2 involves an NRE employee who is allowed to occupy the offices of a subsidiary company *for a long period of time* to ensure compliance with the subsidiary's contract with the NRE. This use is stated to constitute a POB PE of the NRE. The 'long period' language might save this example, but without it the example is questionable. A parent clearly has a 'stewardship' right to supervise its subsidiaries and compliance with an already executed

80. The 1977 MC change in terminology from 'in' to 'through' does not appear to have had any substantive significance. Nitikman, *id* at 220. The 'at the disposal' language is not in the 1996 US MC.
81. The latter term is used by Nitikman in his leading commentary on the 'At the disposal' concept, *'The Painter and the PE,'* Canadian Tax Journal (2009) vol. 57, no 2, 213-58, at 220.
82. OECD Commentary, para. 4.
83. *See* Nitikman, *Id.* at 224 re this latter claim.

contract would seem to be more in the nature of an Article 5(4) PE-free type of auxiliary activity. This example also comes close to endorsing the facts of the *Philip Morris* case,[84] which has been widely criticized for overlooking normal stewardship or ancillary affiliate functions to establish a group wide PE in derogation of the parent-subsidiary exception of Article 5(7).[85]

The fourth example finds a POB PE from a painter's spending 3 days a week painting the large office building of his main client over a two year period.[86] This painter example has been criticized by Germany[87] and several commentators.[88] Although painting may be his main business and the permanence requirement met, case law affirms that the client's office building is not 'at the disposal' of the painter. It is an 'object of his business' and not the place of his business. As stated by Nitikman:[89]

> 'As noted above, the BIAC was so upset by this example that it made several lengthy submissions to the OECD to revise or eliminate it. Germany entered an observation to this example (paragraph 45.7 of the commentary). One senior authority has clearly expressed his "doubts" concerning the correctness of the example. The painter example appears to contradict the commentary in paragraph 4, the example in 4.2, the requirement for the office to be at the employee's disposal in paragraph 4.3, the example in paragraph 4.4, and the requirement for disposal in paragraphs 4.6, 41, 41.1, 42, 42.3, and 42.5. The Canadian

84. *Ministry of Finance (Tax Office) vs Philip Morris (GmbH)*, May 25, 2002, no. 7682/ (Supreme Court of Cassation), unofficial English translation, *Ministry of Finance vs Philip Morris* (2002), 4 ITLR 90.
85. *See* Section 5.8 and fn 225 et seq.
86. OECD Commentary, para. 4.5.
87. Decision of the *Bundesfinanzhof*, IR 30/07, issued June 4, 2008, published September 10, 2008, reversing the decision in FG Cologne, January 24, 2007, 13 K 336/07 (EFG 2007, 1349). And see further authorities cited by Nitikman in his 'Painter' article at 251, notes 108 and 109.
88. The best criticism appears in Nitikman, *The Painter and the PE*, Canadian Tax Journal (2009) vol. 57, no 2, 213-58 at 250; *see also*, Reimer, who notes at 61 that the OECD simply ignored the 'at the disposal' requirement; *see* comments to the 2011 Discussion Draft by Knut Olsen who objecting to the famous 'painter' example, stated that Peter might not be allowed to operate his business for other clients at Clientco premises, or to take customers, clients and other business relatives onto the premises, or have his own employees stationed there, or use the premises outside working hours, on holidays or during weekends; or to refurbish and redecorate the premises or use his own equipment or furniture, or to set up company logo or sign or adverts around the premises, Peter would not pay rent and Client would use the premises when he is not using them. Such premises are not 'at the disposal' of Peter. *See also*, re the 'at the disposal requirement,' Richard G. Tremblay, *'Permanent Establishments in Canada,'* in Report of Proceedings of the Forty-First Tax Conference, 1989 Conference Report (Toronto: Canadian Tax Foundation, 1990),38:1-69, at 38:21-22. Vogel at 286 (1997 3rd ed.), Philip Baker *id.* at sections 5b.08-5b.09.
89. *Id* at 249.

> decisions discussed above [*Dudney, et al.*] are clearly contrary to the painter example, as is the decision in *Ericsson Radio Systems AB vs DCIT*. In my view, this example is simply out of step with the balance of the commentary on article 5. '[footnotes omitted]

The fact that a PE could be found under an applicable PE Services provision illustrates the harm this example does to the traditional concept of a place of business through which the NRE conducts *his* business at his place of business, not his customer's.

2. *Use of Client Offices or Equipment*

The clearest expression of what 'at the disposal' means in the context of the use of customer premises is the leading Canadian case of *Dudney*,[90] which involved facts similar to the 'painter' example and which held the client's premises were not a POB PE.[91] In fact, *because* of the *Dudney* ruling, the US–Canada Tax Treaty was amended in the 2006 Fifth Protocol to add an OECD PE Services provision (Article V(9)[92] because such extended use of a customer's premises did not constitute a place of business of under the Treaty without such a provision.[93]

William Dudney was a Houston resident computer expert hired as an independent contractor to train employees at Pan Canadian Petroleum in Calgary, where he spent 300 days in one year and 40 the next. He took no equipment with him to Canada, had no business cards identifying him with PanCan, had no Canadian business license and was not indicated as working at PanCan in its directory or otherwise. He invoiced his work on an hourly basis, usually on invoices send from the USA, where he was paid:

---

90. *Dudney vs Regina*, 99 DTC 147 (T.C. Canada 1998), aff'd 2000 DTC 6168 (F. Ct. App. Canada, 2000)
91. In terms of commentary, one could not quarrel with Nitikman's observation:
    'Perhaps the simplest and yet clearest definition of what it means for a place of business to be at a non-resident's disposal is suggested by Baker: "These cases confirm that the fixed place of business need not be owned or leased by the foreign enterprise provided that it is at the disposal of the enterprise in the sense of having some right to use the premises for the purposes of its business and not solely for the purposes of the project undertaken on behalf of the owner of the premises." Nitikman, at 251, quoting Baker, *Double Tax Conventions*, section 5B.09.
92. Tittle at 212.
93. Article V(9)(b) is broader than the suggested OECD Commentary Services PE provision, in that it does not require the presence of personnel in Canada for 183 days, implying that services provided by an automatic machine installed there could be taxable under the Services provision. Tittle at 215. More likely, it would seem that a fixed place of business might exist through the provision of such machinery.

> '[Dudney] was at first provided with a small room from which to work. After three months he was moved to a larger room, which he shared with a number of other consultants. Later he was moved to another room in a different building, also occupied by PanCan. For the most part, the actual training, or mentoring, of the PanCan personnel took place in the offices of the people being trained, or in a conference room. Sometimes there would be meetings or consultations in the space provided to the trainers. Their use of that space was strictly limited, however. It was available to them for the purpose of the contract only. They could not conduct any other business from there, they could use the telephone only for business related to the PanCan contract, and their access to the building was controlled by a magnetic card system, and restricted to business hours, on weekdays only.'[94]

The Canadian court held *Dudney* had no office or fixed place of business 'at his disposal' and hence no PE in Canada. The Court added:

> 'A Canadian lawyer does not acquire a fixed place of business in the office of a client in the United States merely by attending to the client's affairs there, even if the client insists on the lawyer's personal presence.'[95]

South of the border, *Dudney* was followed in a 2010 *Mexican Circuit* court decision[96] which involved consulting services provided to the Mexican government by employees of a US firm who traveled to Mexico for one week a month over a period exceeding 12 months. The US employees were allowed to use a meeting room there. The Court ruled that the US firm did not conduct its business at the premises of the government company since the use of its facilities was limited to compliance with just one single item of business derived from the services agreement with the government company.

The Court followed *Dudney* and also accepted Klaus Vogel's view that 'disposition' of a place of business did not exist if a client permitted access to its facilities for purpose of a service provider's complying with agreements of services related to planning, supervision or any other specific project.[97] Specifically, the court found instructive that the US company was not allowed to conduct its business in the way that it normally did in the US with full disposal

94. Discussed and quoted in Tittle at 213.
95. *Id.* at 215.
96. Ruling issued by 13th Administrative Tribunal of the First Circuit in the case *DA 233/2009* in connection with R.F. 159/2010-2865, discussed in EY ITS Tax Alert 20 January 2011.
97. Vogel on Double Taxation Conventions (3rd ed. Kluwer 1997) at 287, para. 26.

of the offices, did not conduct marketing activities from the government offices, provide services to other clients or receive requests from other clients or perform any other of its regular business activities from the government office.

Where premises or a part thereof are actually leased for the conduct of the lessee's business, they will likely result in a 'fixed place of business' of one or another sort. The status of an NRE's *rented* shed adjoining a *Botswanan Abattoir*, used for the processing of fresh animal hides, was found by a South African court to constitute a fixed place of business.[98]

Similarly, in a *German Toll Manufacturing*[99] case, a Swiss company rented space in a German company's warehouse and established production facilities there for the production of salad dressing by the German company pursuant to the Swiss company's formula. The Swiss company provided raw materials to the German company and arranged transportation of the raw materials and the finished salad dressings. Although the German Federal Tax Court found that the contract manufacturing in the rented facility amounted to a fixed place of business, it held there was no PE of the Swiss company because the business conducted there was that of the German and not that of the Swiss company.

In an *Abattoir*[100] case, a Polish company entered into contract slaughtering agreements of one to two years duration with German slaughterhouses. The German slaughterhouse provided work benches for the Polish employees who worked separately from the German employees, and were provided work clothes and utensils by the Polish company, but who had access to a common cafeteria and washrooms at the German slaughterhouse. The German company-provided workbenches were held a fixed POB of the Polish company in Germany.

The OECD's 2012 Revised Discussion Draft provides a similar example relating to toll manufacturing by a subsidiary in source country premises contracted by the NRE parent. The Draft adopts the CARCO example of the 2009 IFA meetings in finding that the parent did not have a fixed POB PE merely because its subsidiary manufactured products for it to its specification and materials provided[101] The OECD drafters also extended this principle to service providers.

98. *See Transvaal Associated Hide and Skin Merchants vs Collector of Income Tax, Botswana*, 19 *S. Afr. Tax Cas*. 97 (Ct. of App., Botswana 1967) (shed constitutes permanent establishment); *see also* Judgment of 24 March 1976, HR, Neth., No. 17,812, summarized at 1 *International Tax Treaties Service*, Art. 5, page 58 (Edwardes-Ker ed. 1986).

99. Case No. 3k 309/91 (11 May 1992), Court of First Instance of Baden-Wurttemberg), discussed in Mehta at 43.

100. Case no 9K6931/98 K dated 6 Nov. 2000, *Finanzgericht Münster*, discussed in Mehta at 45.

101. Revised Draft Commentary at para. 4.2.

Scanwell AB and Mats Johanson vs Mun. of Stavanger,[102] involved a Swedish family owned company whose sole employee was an engineer stationed for 178 days on an oil drilling platform on the Norwegian continental shelf. The Norwegian Court found that the Swedish company (which was managed by the engineer's wife) had a fixed POB PE in Norway consisting of a desk in living quarters on the platform furnished the engineer. About 25% of the engineer's work was performed at this desk, the remaining 75% consisting of his management of the physical operations onboard the platform.

The *Pollens*[103] case involved an Austrian company which seasonally produced pollens at a rented Austrian barn with a container placed in front equipped with a desk, telephone and fax machine. Each harvesting season, the Austrian company employed a Swiss agricultural engineer (for less than 6 months) who worked in the container, in the field and in the barn. The Austrian Supreme Administrative Court held that the Swiss engineer had an Austrian fixed POB.

In the *Hotel Chain*[104] case, a UK company entered into a hotel management contract with a German hotel owner to provide a general manager and marketing. While the German Federal Tax Court found the UK company had a fixed POB PE, it limited it to the space required for the general manager, finding that the rest of the hotel did not constitute a POB PE of the UK company.

A *US Warehouse* ruling[105] involved a UK company which contracted with a US public warehouse to store an amount of inventory sufficient to deliver from time to time to a US distributor customer as needed by its customers. The IRS ruling holds that no POB PE was created in the United States.

In *Toronto Blue Jays Baseball Club vs Minister of Finance*[106] the Court held that the provision to the Blue Jays of locker rooms, coaches' rooms and training rooms at away games (about 50% of the total) did not constitute a fixed POB PE because the Blue Jays lacked ownership, management and control over such premises.[107]

In the *German NATO*[108] case, a Dutch company contracted with a German company to provide cleaning services for NATO aircraft. The Dutch company's employees could access a locker room, telephone, showers and a changing room at the NATO airport. The German Federal Tax Court held no

---

102. Case No. 33—1989 (15 Feb 1991, Gulating Court of Appeals, Norway).
103. Case No. 2000/15/0118 (18 Mar 2004, *Verwaltungsgerichtshof*).
104. Case No IR 80-81/91 (3 Feb 1993, *Bundesfinanzhof*).
105. US Letter Ruling 77-49-009 (non-binding private ruling).
106. 18 Taxmann.com 206 (2012 CA Ontario) discussed in Mehta at 103 and reproduced in Mehta Appendix Two.
107. This was another case in which the taxpayer would have benefitted from a PE finding, which would relieve it of having to make health care contributions on players' behalf.
108. Case No. IR 30/07 (4 Jun 2008 *Bundesfinanzhof*) discussed in Mehta at 118.

PE existed because the 'at the disposal' requirement meant, in the absence of ownership or a tenancy, that the company must have a legal right such that it could not be removed from the facility without its consent.

To similar effect, see a *Butcher*[109] decision which held that a Dutch butcher who used the premises of his German customers did not have a PE. These decisions are in line with a long-standing German approach to the 'at the disposal' test, i.e. in order for a POB to be at the disposal of an NRE, that NRE must hold 'a legal position which, *ipso jure*, may not be withdrawn or terminated without his consent'. That does not, however, mean that a formal rental agreement or ownership of the POB is always required.[110]

In *Ericsson Radio Systems AB vs DCIT*[111] the ITAT held that the Swedish telephone manufacturer did not have a fixed POB at the offices of its Indian subsidiary which Ericsson's employees used during their visits to India – because they did not have a legal right to use such premises.

To the contrary is *Motorola Inc vs DCIT.*[112] The US telecommunications equipment supplier stationed some of its employees at the offices of its Indian subsidiary and paid their salaries. ITAT found that Motorola had a fixed POB at offices of its Indian subsidiary, finding that these employees worked both for Motorola and its Indian subsidiary, were given certain perquisites by the subsidiary and since both worked together at the same affiliate offices it had to be presumed that they had the right to use such offices.

In *Rolls Royce Plc vs DDIT*[113] the UK manufacturer of jet engines had an Indian subsidiary whose Indian offices expenses were paid by Rolls Royce at cost plus a 5% markup. ITAT held that the Indian office had to be within the 'control' of Rolls Royce in order to constitute a fixed POB PE. On the facts, Rolls Royce's employees were frequently in India and used the office while there. The Indian affiliate's offices were found to be a POB PE because it was available to Rolls Royce's employees.

In *Ezra Shahmoon vs MNR, 1975 DTC 275 (3 Jul 1975),* the Canadian Tax Review Board held that a US resident who conducted substantial real estate transactions in Canada through the office premises of a company of which he was president, and also maintained a Montreal apartment in which he stayed with his wife for two months annually, did not have a fixed POB in Canada. The Board held Shahmoon did not have ownership or control over the offices of the company of which he was a president.

---

109. Case no 13 K 560/88E (24 Jun 1992 *Düsseldorf Finanzgericht*) discussed in Mehta at 120.
110. *See* BFH of 14 July 2004, I R 106/03.
111. 95 ITD 269 (2005 Delhi) discussed in Mehta at 120 and reproduced in Mehta Appendix One.
112. *Id.*, delivered as a combined judgment with *Ericsson* and *Nokia Networks OY vs DCIT,* discussed in Mehta at 121.
113. *Rolls Royce vs Deputy Director of Income Tax* (ITAT Delhi, October 26, 2007) (online: http://www.itatonline.org/).

A *Heart Surgeon*[114] case involved an Italian heart surgeon who had a contractual right to use Belgian medical institute facilities for a certain project. The Belgian ruling holds however that no PE existed because the surgeon did not have a right to use the facilities for any purpose other than the certain project.

Engineering Services[115] involved a French resident who provided power plant consulting services to clients in Germany. At various times he rented in Germany a hotel room, a room in a pension, a room as a sub-tenant and an apartment. The Court held that only the apartment could be regarded as a fixed POB PE because he had no legal right to use the hotel room, pension, or sublet room for the conduct of business.

In contrast, in *Seagate Singapore,*[116] the Indian Authority for Advance Rulings (AAR) found that a Singapore manufacturer of computer hard drives had a fixed POB PE by contracting with independent Indian bonded warehouses to import and separately store Seagate's disks in bonded warehouses, delivering them on an 'as needed' basis to Seagate's OEM purchasers (such as Dell) who would then be directly invoiced by Seagate. As in the *US Warehouse* ruling, Seagate had no employees at the warehouses and none of the agents were authorized to bind Seagate to any transaction. The ruling can be criticized as it is a classic example of an independent agency relationship. Even if a POB existed in a part of the warehouse, the business conducted there was that of the independent warehouses in the ordinary course of their business and should not have constituted a PE of Seagate.

In a *Swiss Consultant*[117] case decided before *Dudney*, the Austrian Supreme Administrative Court held that a Swiss consultant who provided consultancy services to an Austrian client for about 9 months had a fixed POB PE in office space provided by the client, even though that space could also be used by the client's employees. The ruling rejected the taxpayer's claim that such office space could not be his POB because it was not 'exclusively' at his disposal.[118]

---

114. Discussed in Mehta at 106. *See* Queiroli, *Belgian Court Provides Interpretation of PE under Treaty,* Tax Notes International at 945 (16 Mar 2009).
115. Case No. 4K/2608/95 (24 Apr 1998 *Finanzgericht Rheinland-Pfalz)* discussed in Mehta at 116.
116. *Seagate Singapore International Headquarters Pvt. Ltd* (2010) 189 Taxmann 181 (AAR – New Delhi) discussed in Mehta at 34 and reproduced in Mehta at Appendix One.
117. *Verwaltungsgerichtshof,* Case No. 96/14/0084 (21 May 1997), discussed in Mehta at 29.
118. *See also, ATO Ruling 2002/5*, which contains the following example: '42. HKco is a computer service provider and a resident of Hong Kong. It successfully tenders to train the employees of Ausco, a company resident in Australia, in a new computer system. To undertake the training, HKco sends four of its employees to Australia for six months. Ausco provides HKco employees with a room in one of its offices for that six months. Because HKco has at its disposal a room in Ausco's offices for six months and carries on its business at or through that room, HKco has a place at or through which it carries on its business in Australia.'

The OECD Commentary does state that premises may be 'at the disposal' of an NRE even though they are not used 'exclusively' for the business of its enterprise. The OECD 2012 Revised Discussion Draft finds that premises are at its 'disposal':

> 'where an enterprise is allowed to use a specific location that belongs to another enterprise or that is used by a number of enterprises and performs its business activities at that location on a continuous basis over an extended period of time...'[119]

Looking at the case law, the OECD's reference seems rather directed to joint activities, such as an aircraft hangar owned by 5 airlines which is made available to an unrelated aircraft repair company which services all 5 airlines at that location – i.e., a vertically integrated customer-supplier relationship – or a group distribution center – i.e., a horizontally integrated relationship – where the use of common facilities has economic and functional justification.[120]

On balance, case law would seem to support a requirement that an NRE's use of a third party office is not at its 'disposal' unless the NRE has the right to use the premises on the same basis as it would its own leased or owned premises – for example to use the third party location as its own 'office,' to conduct its own business there for clients other than the owner of the third party premises and to have independent access to and use of such premises.

Otherwise, every entrepreneur who performs services over an extended period at the premises of a client, customer or supplier would be attributed the POB of his client, customer or supplier. If a PE were to exist in such a situation, it could not be because the NRE were attributed the POB of his client, but rather because of the application of a Services PE provision, if any. If no Services PE provision applied, no fixed POB should be attributed to the NRE from its use of its client's premises.

An illustration is *Rev. Rul. 77-45*[121] involving a Canadian company (Canco) which provided through its employees construction site supervisory and planning services to the unrelated general contractor of a US client. The US client provided office furniture and equipment *gratis* to Canco's US onsite employees. The ruling involved the 1942 US–Canadian Treaty which did not contain a construction assembly site (CAS) PE provision. While the IRS held that such activities could constitute a fixed POB PE, it held that mere 'supervisory and planning' services did not amount to construction activity. Further

119. Revised Draft at para 4.2.
120. Each of the joint owners would have sufficient operational control, though not exclusionary control over the joint facilities. Reimer at 59.
121. 1977-1 CB 413.

it found no fixed POB PE *both* because the use of the provided furniture and equipment was not separately bargained for (i.e., rented) by Canco and because such use was for less than one year.

3. *Home Office Cases*

There are a number of cases which discuss when an employee's home office is the POB of an employer company. Generally, these cases find that a home office is a POB where the employee is a principal, especially if a shell 'loan-out' services company were involved. In contrast, a home office of cross border employees or agents is generally not attributed to larger companies unless the company had no office in the source country and the employee either used his own home for company business or was compensated to do so.

In the *Universal Furniture Ind. AB vs Norway, Stavanger Byrett*,[122] a Swedish furniture company sold its furniture in Norway through a Norwegian resident salesman who made sales calls Monday through Thursday and used his home office on Friday to write up sales reports and plan the next week's activities. His Swedish employer reimbursed his home office phone, fax and equipment charges first directly and then through increased salary. Sales were received directly from Norwegian customers or through the salesman. The Norwegian court found that the salesman's home office was a Norwegian fixed POB PE of the Swedish company.

In *Air Conditioning Consultant*[123] a Dutch family owned Swiss domiciliary company provided air conditioning and cold storage technology services through its principal shareholder employee outside Switzerland and the Netherlands. However, all commercial activities were conducted by the shareholder employee at his Dutch home office, which the Court found a fixed POB PE. On the facts, it would seem the court could also have found a dependent agency PE in the Netherlands.

In *S.V. G.J.G. vs Belgium*[124] a Belgian agent of a Dutch principal received clients in his apartment where he concluded agreements. The agent's business card and the Dutch company's invoices to the clients bore the apartment's address, which was held to be a fixed POB PE of the Dutch Principal.

In *Sunbeam Corporation (Canada) Ltd vs Minister of National Revenue*[125] an Ontario based manufacturer of electrical appliances employed a commis-

122. Case No. 99-00421 A (19 Dec 1999 Stavanger County Court), discussed in Mehta at 45.
123. Case No. 101/82 MII dated 28 Mar. 1983, *Gerechtshof 's-Gravenhage* (Hague Court of Appeals, Netherlands).
124. No. 10 (18 Feb 1992) at 268-70 (*Revenue General de Fiscality* (Oct. 1992) discussed in Mehta at 89.
125. (2012) 18 Taxmann.com 213 (S. Ct. Canada) discussed in Mehta at 47 and reproduced in Mehta Appendix Two.

sion-paid salesman in other provinces including Quebec. The salesman had no inventory and no authority to bind the company. They had home offices, but were not compensated by Sunbeam for maintaining such offices or any required equipment there and their home offices were not listed in the telephone directory as offices of Sunbeam. The Canadian Supreme Court held that the salesmen's home offices did not constitute a fixed POB PE of Sunbeam in the salesman's respective provinces.

In this case, the taxpayer (Sunbeam) would have benefited from having a POB PE from salesmen's home offices in Quebec as such would have entitled it to claim a deduction in computing its own liability in Quebec. A parallel situation applies in European countries (e.g. Norway, Germany, France, Belgium, Netherlands, Luxembourg and Austria) with respect to resident taxpayers claiming a PE with respect to operations in another country, as its related profits there would then be exempt from home country taxation. There is thus a duality of perspective in which both taxpayers and tax collectors can argue for a PE in a number of European and Canadian PE cases – which ensures that the general body of precedent is neither taxpayer nor tax collector biased.

Knights of Columbus[126] was a similar Canadian case which held that the home offices of insurance field agents of the US insurance taxpayer did not constitute a fixed POB PE of the employer insurance company in Canada. The insurance company did not pay the home office expenses of the employees, who the Court said conducted their own business there, as insurance agents, and not the business of the employer insurance company.

American Income Life Insurance vs the Queen[127] involved a similar fact pattern. In holding that AIL did not have a fixed POB through the offices of its Canadian agents, the Tax Court noted that the agents conducted their own business at such premises and not AIL's business. Further the agents controlled their own office premises, were not reimbursed by AIL for any office expenses and equipment, received no instructions from AIL concerning the running of their offices and bore their own entrepreneurial risk.

The OECD 2012 Revised Discussion Draft Commentary is consistent with the above case law. Acknowledging that the source country home office of a principal individual of an enterprise can be attributed to her enterprise if she used it for such business for an extended period of time, the Draft adds:

> 'In many cases, the carrying on of business activities at the home of an individual (e.g. an employee) will be so intermittent or incidental that the home will not be considered to be a location at the disposal of the

126. *Knights of Columbus vs The Queen* (2008 TCC 307).
127. 18 Taxmann.com 204 (16 May 2008) discussed in Mehta at 95 and reproduced in Appendix Two.

enterprise (see paragraph 4.2 above). Where, however, a home office is used on a regular and continuous basis for carrying on business activities for an enterprise and it is clear from the facts and circumstances that the enterprise has required the individual to use that location to carry on the enterprise's business (e.g. by not providing an office to an employee in circumstances where the nature of the employment clearly requires an office), the home office may be considered to be at the disposal of the enterprise.'[128]

E. Whose Business is Conducted at the Place

The enterprise conducted in the source state *must be that of the NRE*. This factor determines whose business is conducted at the place by focusing on how business is conducted at the place, whether by employees or other 'dependent' agents (*other than* deemed agent PEs whose authority would moot the POB enquiry) or whether business can be conducted without any source country personnel. Included are automatic equipment PEs (such as servers, vending machines, pipelines or gaming equipment operated without source country personnel), persons who may be either NRE or affiliate employees (secondment issues), independent contractors and agents, warehousing/delivery agents, commissionaires, contract and toll manufacturers, and contract joint venturers who do not share profits or losses.

1. Automated POB PEs

It is a settled principle that certain source country equipment or machinery which may be automatically operated or operated by non-resident personnel can be a fixed POB PE.[129] The operation of such equipment and/or machinery must constitute a part of the core business of the NRE and cannot be merely preparatory or auxiliary to that business.

Thus, an oil pipeline which is used to transport an NRE's own oil will generally *not* be regarded as a POB PE as the transportation of the NRE's own oil is auxiliary to its main business of refining and selling its products. However, an oil pipeline which is used to transport third party owned oil for a fee is central to the pipeline company's business and will be a POB PE even if entirely operated by personnel outside the source country, as in the *German*

128. OECD 2012 Revised Draft at para 4.8.
129. Reimer at 41.

Pipeline case.[130] A similar Italian ruling found that a Swiss RR company had a fixed POB PE due to railroad tracks and a train terminus in Italy.[131]

Similarly automated gaming equipment, vending machines and similar core business equipment owned and serviced by an NRE can be a fixed POB PE, even if the operation of such machinery is automatic and does not require source country operation.[132] If however, such equipment is leased to an operator without active maintenance and servicing by source country personnel of the NRE, the POB will be that of the lessee and nor the lessor, as the business conducted through it is that of the lessee and not that of the lessor.

These principles have generally been applied by the OECD Commentary with respect to source country servers and other hardware used in e-commerce and e-tailing businesses with source country customers. The following five cases involving e-commerce businesses have focused on whether source country hardware is used by the NRE as an integral part of its business or rather is auxiliary to it, the control over such hardware exercised by the NRE in terms of configuration and programming of hardware as opposed to mere ownership or leasing for data storage and the importance of such hardware with respect to mainframe servers and equipment maintained or operated by the NRE elsewhere.

In a *Swiss Server*[133] case, a German company owned an Internet server kept in leased premises in Switzerland. Operation of the server did not require the services of NRE employees in Switzerland. However the server did contain programs and data relating to the NRE's Swiss clients and which was provided to such clients as a core part of its business. The court found that a Swiss PE did exist (and hence the Swiss profits attributable to such PE were exempt from German tax). In so ruling, the Court found that none of the Article 5(4) PE-free provisions applied. The server did not constitute a facility used for the purpose of 'storage, display or delivery of goods or merchandise' because software data are not 'goods or merchandise' (such being limited to items which could listed on a balance sheet). The Court also found that the server was not used for the purpose of advertising, the supply of information or similar activities of a preparatory or auxiliary character – as the provision of such information was a significant part of the core business of the NRE. Finally, the Court found that paragraphs 42.1 to 42.10 of the OECD Commentary (dealing with e-

130. *Bundesfinanzhof, No. II R 12/92 (30 Oct. 1996),* discussed in Mehta, at 8; OECD 2012 Revised Discussion Draft, revised amended Commentary at para. 10.2.
131. R. Russo & C Romano, *Italian Tax Consequences of Permanent Establishments,* Bulletin for International Taxation, 456, 457 (Aug-Sept 2010).
132. Reimer at 35: OECD OECD 2012 Revised Discussion Draft, revised amended Commentary at para. 10.2.
133. Case No. II/1224/97 (6 Sep 2001, *Finanzgericht* of Schleswig Holstein) discussed in Mehta at 50.

commerce) provided that server hardware would constitute a PE if the content provider owned the server and conducted its business through the server.

Mehta comments that the Italian tax authorities reached a similar conclusion in *Resolution 119*[134] involving a French provider of online video games to Italian subscribers. Although it had no employees in Italy, the French company owned two servers through an Italian Internet service provider. The French company configured the servers and their operation (including online delivery of game services to Italian customers) directly from France. The Italian tax authority's ruling found a PE, holding that the servers could constitute a fixed place of business PE where the (1) servers were at the disposal of the NRE, (2) were located in the same place for a significant period and (3) were used to carry out the NRE's core business.[135]

The French tax authorities appear to have taken a somewhat different view with the presumption that in the absence of source country personnel a source country server would have a preparatory or auxiliary role unless the server 'completely performed the enterprise's core business functions.'[136]

In contrast, two Indian ITAT rulings in *Amadeus Global* and *Galileo* have held that the incidental provision of dumb terminal computers to a minority of Indian users of an offshore based airline computer reservation system (CRS) constituted a fixed POB PE of the offshore CRS enterprise.[137]

2. *The Requirement that the Business of the NRE Be Conducted There*

A place of business, no matter how well furnished, must actually be used by the NRE to conduct its core business in the source country state. In *MNR vs Tara Exploration & Development Company Limited*,[138] a Canadian company which was managed and controlled in Ireland, and hence resident there, used the Toronto office address of a related company for Canadian compliance purposes, but did not conduct business there. The Canadian Supreme Court held that no fixed POB existed in Canada.

In *Danish Power Project*,[139] a Swedish company entered into a partnership with a Danish company (P1), which was owned by another Danish partner-

---

134. (28 May 2007) discussed in Mehta at 52, who cites M. Rossi, *Tax Authorities Issue Ruling on Permanent Establishment,* Tax Notes International, June 4, 2007, p. 1006.
135. Russo & Pedrazzini, *Permanent Establishments under Italian Tax Law: An Overview,* European Taxation 289, at 393 (Aug-Sept 2007).
136. Mehta at 53, citing Mboma, *France, OECD Take Different Views of Unstaffed Servers as Permanent Establishments,* Tax Notes International (3 Jun 2002) at p. 1107. The ruling is in line with the French 'complete cycle of business' concept.
137. *Amadeus* and *Galileo,* discussed at length supra under 2.1 A at footnote 12 et seq.
138. [1974] S.C.R. 1057.
139. Case LSR 641-1220-1, Danish Administrative Tax Court (24 June 1996) discussed in Mehta at 126.

ship (P2) involving electricity companies and a Danish city. P1 was formed to construct a power station and leased a site therefore from P2. P1 then contracted with P2 to plan and supervise the construction of the power plant using unrelated contractors over a 4 year period. The Danish tax authorities asserted that the Swedish company had a POB PE (through the P1 partnership) from the *commencement* of this 4 year construction period even though the Swedish company earned no income and paid only lease rentals during this period. The Court held that no PE existed as to the Swedish company as P1's core business was *operating*, not building a power station and this business could not commence until the plant was completed. The unrelated contractors could have a CAS PE, but not P1 as the property owner.

3. *The Mere Leasing of Real or ICS Property Does Not Create a PE of the Lessor*

From early rulings, case law has established the general principle that that the mere leasing or renting of source country real property does not constitute POB of the lessor as any business conducted there is that of the lessees.[140] As stationary substantial equipment can also constitute a POB, case law has extended this principle to the rental of such movable equipment at a stationary site. The reason is that such leasing or rental constitutes passive activity producing passive income which is from, but not through the source country place of business. In each case, the activity conducted at the source country place of business is that of the lessee and not that of the lessor and hence the lessor has no PE.

The OECD Model recognizes this principle and exception in the following Commentary:[141]

> 'If an enterprise of a State lets or leases facilities, ICS [industrial, commercial or scientific] equipment, buildings or intangible property to an enterprise of the other State without maintaining for such letting or leasing activity a fixed place of business in the other State, the leased facility, ICS equipment, building or intangible property, as such, will not constitute a permanent establishment of the lessor provided the contract is limited to the mere leasing of the ICS equipment, etc. This remains the case even when, for example, the lessor supplies personnel after installation to operate the equipment provided that their respon-

140. Reimer 2012 at 40: 'By contrast, the renting-out or leasing-out of property or know-how, the holding of shares, or the granting of loans (and, therefore, the receipt of rental or leasing payments, dividends, interest or royalties) do not in themselves constitute a business or enterprise.'
141. OECD Commentary, para. 8.

> sibility is limited solely to the operation or maintenance of the ICS equipment under the direction, responsibility and control of the lessee. If the personnel have wider responsibilities, for example, participation in the decisions regarding the work for which the equipment is used, or if they operate, service, inspect and maintain the equipment under the responsibility and control of the lessor, the activity of the lessor may go beyond the mere leasing of ICS equipment and may constitute an entrepreneurial activity. In such a case a permanent establishment could be deemed to exist if the criterion of permanency is met.'

The OECD view is amply supported in case law. Thus, *Elizabeth Herbert vs Comm'r*[142] held that the leasing of a single Washington D.C. men's clothing store did not constitute a trade or business even though checks were paid, tax returns made, and repairs were authorized through the office of a Washington D.C. holding company of which the taxpayer was a minority stockholder. Herbert paid only taxes, mortgage principal and insurance premiums (all expenses of ownership, rather than occupancy). No PE was found.

A similar case is *Inez De Amodio vs Commissioner*[143] in which real estate brokers were employed to lease, manage and sell two US commercial properties of a Swiss resident. The brokers were found to be independent agents even though they only acted on the taxpayer's instructions as to which properties to sell or lease. The business conducted by them was their own, not that of the Swiss landlord. Hence the Court held the Swiss resident did not have a US POB PE.[144]

In the United States, triple net leases are typically used by real estate investment trusts (REITs), to maximize cash flow and minimize any business activity. In a triple net lease, the tenant assumes the cost of repair, insurance and local taxes on the property and the landlord has no active business involvement. The income is of a passive investment character and will not itself create a PE through the leased premises.

DDIT (International Taxation) vs Dharti Dredging & Infrastructural Ltd[145] involved an Indian company which hired a dredger from a Dutch company which also provided crew. However, the crew was under the direction of the Indian lessee, which also paid their salaries, food, accommodation and insurance on the dredger. ITAT held that the dredger was only let for hire and did not

142. 30 *T. C.* 26 (1958) (former United States–United Kingdom treaty).
143. 34 *T.C.*894 (1960), *aff'd, 299* F.2d 623 (3rd Cir. 1962).
144. The taxpayer actually wanted a US PE, enabling him to deduct expenses, as the gross income was taxable anyway under article 6. Today, the Internal Revenue Code offers an election for non-residents to be treated as though *they* were engaged in a US trade or business, and thus to claim expenses. IRC §§ 882 (c) and 871(d).
145. 44 SIT 586 (2011 Hyd) discussed in Mehta at 136 and reproduced in Mehta Appendix One.

conduct any business of the Dutch lessor. Hence, there was no PE. Similarly, *Nederlandsche Overzee Baggermaatschappij BV vs DDIT* held that bareboat leasing of a dredging vessel did not constitute a POB PE of the lessor.[146]

In *Whirlpool India Holdings Ltd vs DDIT*[147] Whirlpool's US holding company seconded high level employees to its Indian subsidiary and paid their salaries through its Indian branch (due to local law restrictions on paying key personnel salaries). ITAT held that the branch did not constitute an Indian PE as no business was conducted through it, and further that the seconded employees were employed by the Indian subsidiary.

Similarly, in a *German Toll Manufacturing*[148] case, a Swiss company rented space in a German company's warehouse and established production facilities there for the production of salad dressing *by the German company* pursuant to the Swiss companies formula. The Swiss company provided raw materials to the German company and arranged transportation of the raw materials and the finished salad dressings. The German Federal Tax Court found that the *rented* contract manufacturing facility amounted to a fixed place of business, but that the German, not the Swiss, company conducted business there and thus there was no Swiss company PE.

The OECD's 2012 Revised Discussion Draft provides a similar example relating to toll manufacturing by a subsidiary in source country premises contracted by the NRE parent. The Draft basically adopts the CARCO example of the 2009 IFA meetings in finding that the parent did not have a fixed POB PE merely because its subsidiary manufactured products for it to its specification and materials provided[149] – that is, the manufacturing facilities were the place of business of the subsidiary and not of the parent.

Just as the mere leasing of offices or ships does not create a fixed POB PE of the lessor, so also the mere hiring of employees does not create a POB or Service PE of the NRE providing or seconding such employees. These employment issues are discussed in detail in Chapter 7 – *Permanent Establishments – Service PEs and Secondments*.

4. *Joint Venturers Who Are Not Partners or Dependent Agents*

The Anglo Saxon concept of general and limited partnerships attributes the authority and office of a general partner to all other partners including limited

146. (14 May 2010) (bareboat lease charter of dredger was not an Indian PE of the lessor) discussed in Mehta at 138.
147. 10 Taxmann 31 (2011 Delhi), discussed in Mehta at 184 and reproduced in Mehta Appendix One.
148. Case No. 3k 309/91 (11 May 1992), Court of First Instance of Baden-Wurttemberg), discussed in Mehta at 43.
149. Revised Draft Commentary at para. 4.2.

partners. In common law, the classic definition of a partnership is a joint venture by two or more entrepreneurs to share venture profit and losses.

Yet in large construction or assembly projects two or more unrelated NREs will not infrequently form a contractual joint venture to bid on the project but divide up the project bid on distinct and discrete construction/assembly lines (like building excavation/ construction and design/installation of specialized plant equipment) with neither venturer sharing its project revenue costs or income with the other.

Such a contractual joint venture if blanketly considered as a common law partnership (which it is not) could have unintended consequences on the joint venturers – e.g., if one project component were completed at a loss and the other at a profit, the profitable venturer's profit might be deemed taxable in part to the loss venturer and vice versa resulting in partial non taxation of the profitable venturer and partial taxation of the loss venturer.[150]

Although the situation usually will typically arise in CAS PEs, the 2012 Revised Discussion Draft Commentary deals with the situation with regard to POB PES. Its conclusion is that the economically correct formulation should be that a transparent contractual joint venture should be disregarded for purposes of profit attribution and the PEs of the two venturers considered independently of the other:

> '10.3 Different enterprises may collaborate on the same project and the question of whether their collaboration constitutes a separate enterprise (e.g. in the form of a partnership) is a question that depends on the facts and the domestic law of each State. Clearly, if two enterprises carried on by different persons each carrying on a separate enterprise decide to form a company in which these persons are shareholders, the company constitutes a legal person that will carry on what becomes another separate enterprise. It will often be the case, however, that different enterprises will simply agree to each carry on a separate part of the same project and that these enterprises will not jointly carry on business activities and share the profits thereof even though they may share the overall output from the project or the remuneration for the activities that will be carried on in the context of that project (e.g. what is considered to be a "joint venture" according to the law of some countries). In such a case, it would be difficult to consider that a separate enterprise has been set up. Although such an arrangement would be referred to as a 'joint venture' in many countries, the meaning of 'joint venture' depends on domestic law and it is therefore possible that, in some

150. US Internal Revenue Code Sec. 704(b) permits the allocation of separate income streams if the allocation has substantial economic effect (i.e., is not 'recouped' through another allocation).

> countries, the term 'joint venture' would refer to a distinct enterprise. Although such an arrangement would be referred to as a 'joint venture' in many countries, the meaning of 'joint venture' depends on domestic law and it is therefore possible that in some countries, the term 'joint venture' would refer to a distinct enterprise.'

Tax treaties rarely address expressly an NRE's participation in domestic joint ventures but there are exceptions. For example, the Sweden–Bulgaria tax treaty contains a deeming provision to the effect that '[t]he participation of a Swedish enterprise in a joint venture, set up in accordance with the Bulgarian legislation, shall be deemed to be a place of business [permanent establishment] situated in Bulgaria.'[151]

With respect to *transparent* partnership ventures, the OECD's solution to this situation is found in the OECD 2012 Discussion Draft paragraph 19.2 which states that the CAS minimum time threshold would be applied at the partnership entity level but taxation would be limited to the profits of each partner which would be taxable under the treaty of residence of that partner. The Revised Draft provides the following example (summarized):

> 'Country A company and Country B company form a Country B partnership to undertake a CAS project in Country C which will last 10 months. The A-C Treaty has the OECD 12 month period for a CAS PE, while the B-C Treaty provides for an 8 month CAS PE. Although the partnership has a CAS PE, Country C can only tax the profits of B attributable to that PE since the CAS project did not last the 12 month's required under A-C Treaty to tax the profits of A.'

5. *Attribution of Business of Subcontractors to Main Contractors*

OECD Treaty Article 5 creates at least 3 'PE-free' zones:[152]

1. An NRE with no source country POB, CAS or dependent agent has no PE there under articles 5(1, 2, 3)
2. An NRE with a source country POB and/or dependent agent whose activities are limited to warehousing, delivery, purchases, manufacture by another enterprise or other similar preparatory or auxiliary activities has no PE there under article 5(4, 5)

151. Art. 4(4) of the Sweden–Bulgaria tax treaty. This treaty uses the term 'place of business', rather than permanent establishment.
152. The term 'PE-free' appears to have been coined by Tittle, and is a useful acronym.

3. An NRE who merely trades in a source county through a general commission agent, commissionaire, or other *independent* agent acting in the course of such agent's business *and who may have authority to bind the NRE*, or through any other *independent contractor*, principal, customer or supplier who is conducting his own business, has no PE there under article 5(1, 2, 5, 6, 7).

Generally, therefore mere dealings with an independent contractor are not attributed to a NRE. If the contractor is commonly controlled, but not authorized to bind the NRE, the transfer pricing rules will establish the appropriate source country profit to be allocated to the independent contractor.

Nonetheless, a German 1963 Supreme Court case recognized that the time spent on a CAS by a sub-contractor can be aggregated with the time spent on the site by the NRE general contractor in determining whether the OECD 12-month minimum period is met for a CAS PE. This authority is limited to where only a 'part' of the CAS work is contracted out to subs, and the general remains actively involved at the site with 'boots on the ground.'[153] With limited exceptions discussed below this concept has not been extended to POB PEs.

A ruling involving the role of independent contractors is the *Norwegian Safe Service*[154] case. That case involved a Swedish supplier of catering services to offshore oil well drilling platforms. The Swedish company subcontracted this contract to an unrelated independent Norwegian catering company. The Swedish company had no employees on the rig and conducted no business there. However, Article 21(2)(a) of the Nordic Treaty (between Denmark, Iceland, Norway, Sweden and Finland) provided that the provision of services relating to offshore natural resource exploration or development for a period of 30 days constituted a PE.

Although no comparable provision or precedent exists in the OECD or the UN Models, the OECD 2012 Revised Discussion Draft states that an NRE can have a fixed POB PE by dealing in a source country entirely through independent agents:[155]

> 'An enterprise may also carry on its business through subcontractors, acting alone.... In that case, a permanent establishment will only exist for the enterprise if the other conditions of Article 5 are met. In the context of paragraph 1, that will require that these subcontractors

153. Comments of Deloitte-Netherlands to October 11, 2011 OECD Discussion Draft on Article 5 Commentary changes, Ernst & Young at 77.
154. *Offshore Accommodation Service AB vs Government of Norway*, Case 327/2001.
155. OECD 2012 Revised Discussion Draft, para. 19, criticized by United States Council for International Business in comments to the OECD October 21, 2011 Discussion Draft, EY publication at 90.

> perform the work of the enterprise at a fixed place of business that is at the disposal of the enterprise for reasons other than the mere fact that these subcontractors perform such work at that location (see paragraph 4.2 above) ... ; in the absence of employees of the enterprise, however, it will be necessary to show ... that the enterprise clearly has the effective power to use that site, e.g. because the enterprise owns or has legal possession of that site and controls access to and use of the site. Paragraph 19.1 illustrates such a situation in the case of a construction site; this could also happen in other situations. *An example would be where an enterprise that owns a small hotel and rents out the hotel's room through the internet has contracted the on-site operation of the hotel to a company that is remunerated on a cost plus basis.*' [Emphasis added]

The above principle plus the hotel example was widely criticized in 2011 comments on the Draft and its propositions are not shared by leading commentators. As stated by Reimer:

> 'A dispute has arisen on whether a PE can be constituted by the on-site planning and on-site supervision of the erection of a building. While there is no doubt that situations in which the enterprise carries on both supervisory and proper building activities qualify, the mere supervision or planning has been regarded as insufficient under Article 5(3) OECD MC by some authors (which makes the twelve-month period inapplicable so that Article 5(1) and (2) OECD MC apply). Where the taxpayer is involved in planning and/or supervision, and the contractor functions as the main contractor but has transferred the entire 'real' work to subcontractors, prominent scholars have held that the taxpayer did not meet the requirements of Article 5(3) OECD MC.'[156]

The OECD 2012 Revised Discussion Draft position of attribution of subcontractors to a non operating general contractor would appear inappropriate for the following reasons:

1. German subcontractor CAS precedent is specifically limited to meeting the CAS time period by tacking on the time spent by a subcontractor engaged for only a *part* of the project where the general is on-site and actively supervising the subcontractor while carrying out its own

156. Reimer at 75, citing Baker, P, *Double Taxation Conventions*, loose-leaf ed. Art 5 at m.no. 5B.16, referring to *Cour Administratif d'Appel de Nancy* decision of 9 May 1996, Case No. 94-914, RJF 6/97, no 604.

functions on-site.[157] Such precedent does not establish a POB through the premises used by a subcontractor[158]

2. The *Norwegian Safe Service* case is not in point. It is based on a unique offshore Nordic Treaty provision which is not in the OECD or the UN Models[159]
3. The OECD hotel example *ignores* two lines of case precedent discussed above: (1) the mere leasing or renting of source country real property through offshore personnel cannot constitute a fixed POB of the lessor; and (2) if the lessor has no employees or dependent agents at the leased premises, it conducts no business there and the premises are the POB of the lessee or operator[160]
4. Under Article 5(5) no PE can exist merely through source country services provided by an independent contractor[161]

2.2 'PRIMA FACIE' EXAMPLES OF A FIXED PLACE OF BUSINESS

A. An 'Office'

Article 5(2) of the OECD and UN model conventions states:

> '2. The term "permanent establishment" includes especially:
> a) a place of management;
> b) a branch;
> c) an office;
> d) a factory;
> e) a workshop, and

---

157. *See e.g.* comments of US Council for International Business to the OECD 2011 Discussion Draft
158. *See* comments of Deloitte Netherlands to the OECD 2011 Discussion Draft to the effect that the original 1977 Commentary when article 5(3) was inserted at the request of the Netherlands (per Pijl as a stand-alone concept, not as stairstep provision as in the UN version), intended that only where the general contractor contracted out 'parts of' a CAS project would the time of subcontractors be counted towards the 12-month requirement – the implication being that the general contractor would remain involved itself at the site and in supervision of the sub beyond mere control of access to the site and legal responsibility for the project; thus, there is no authority to extend this concept to complete subcontracting.
159. *Id.*
160. *See e.g.* comments of the Federation of Swedish Enterprises to the OECD 2011 Discussion Draft (independent subcontractor cannot create a PE unless it is a dependent agent PE of the NRE; subs carry on their own business, not that of the NRE)
161. *See* comments of Deloitte Netherlands to the OECD 2011 Discussion Draft.

f) a mine, an oil or gas well, a quarry or any other place of extraction of natural resources.'

The Commentary of both models provides that this non exhaustive list of illustrative items will in fact be permanent establishments only if all the requirements of Article 5(1) are met.[162] That means, with respect to an 'office' for example, that all of the criteria discussed in prior Section 2.1 must be met, namely:

1. *Character* of the premises as a physical 'place' e.g. an office (or a branch, factory, workshop, farm, forestry, mine, well or other place of natural resource extraction)
2. *Geographic fixation* of the place – including some spatial delimitation allowed close but different places which are commercially and geographically connected, e.g., campus offices, expanding mines or quarries
3. *Permanence* –there must be a minimum duration of such enterprise, usually 6 to 12 months
4. *At the disposal* – The 'place' must be either owned, rented or 'at the disposal' of the NRE (if it has multiple users) – this is a *control* of the place test
5. *Whose business is conducted* at the place – The enterprise conducted in the source state *must be that of the NRE* – aside from automatic equipment, this means that the *core* business of the NRE must be connected through the place by the NRE usually with its own 'boots on the ground'.

In *Whirlpool India Holdings Ltd vs DDIT*[163] Whirlpool's US holding company seconded high level employees to its Indian subsidiary and paid their salaries through its Indian *branch* (due to local law restrictions on paying key personnel salaries). ITAT held that the branch did not constitute an Indian PE as no business was conducted through it, and further that the seconded employees were employed by the Indian subsidiary. Thus, a branch is not per se a fixed POB PE. Similarly, in *CIT vs BKI/HAM*,[164] ITAT held that the operation of a project office after completion of a CAS project could not be tacked on to create a CAS PE because the office was used for preparatory or auxiliary activities.[165]

162. Para. 12, Reimer 2013 at 67.
163. 10 Taxmann 31 (2011 Delhi), discussed in Mehta at 184 and reproduced in Mehta Appendix One.
164. 15 Taxmann.com 102 (2011 *Uttarakhand*).
165. *But cf. Pipeline Construction*, Case No. A00131 (28 Aug 2008) (Adm've Court of Lucerne) which found that a branch office could exist merely by enumeration in Article 5(2).

A characteristic of the definition of permanent establishment definition found in double-taxation conventions is thus a listing of those places that *could* constitute, in the minds of the treaty partners, fixed places of business through which the business of an enterprise may be carried on provided the other requirements of article 5(1) are met.

Rarely heading the list (but almost never omitted altogether) is the term 'office.'[166] In view of the ubiquitousness of the term, the relative dearth of attention that the 'office' has received in cases and rulings is surprising. Judge Van Fossen, in a rare Tax Court opinion on the topic, compiled its essential elements:

> '[The Canadian corporation involved] had no real office in the United States; no officers, directors, or employees here; no bank account or books of account; no telephone listing; its name did not appear on any door or office; it had no employee or agent established here who had "general authority" to contract for his employer or principal, such authorized agent being one of the definitive tests of a "permanent establishment" under the treaty.'[167]

Just what does having a 'real office' require? In a well-known American opinion,[168] the Tax Court held that a noted author's 'office at his house was his fixed place of business ... and that his office therefore was a "permanent establishment".'[169] Of what did that office consist? 'Part' of the author's Connecticut farmhouse was 'converted ... to the use of an office,'[170] the court noted. He claimed depreciation deductions on 'furniture and fixtures.' There is mention of his 'typing manuscripts.'[171] He claimed a modest amount of 'salaries and wages' as business deductions.[172] The author's wife acted as his business agent.[173] The result is physical space of uncertain dimensions, peopled by the author, his wife, and one, perhaps two, others. There was a typewriter atop some sort of furniture. Matters of bank accounts, books of account, telephones and their listings are not mentioned. Whether the name was on the outer door,

---

166. *See*, e.g., Ltr. Rul. 6011165960A ('An "office" is a fixed place of business').
167. *Consolidated Premium Iron Ores Ltd. vs Commissioner,* 28 *T.C.* 127, 151, aff'd, 265 F.2d 320 (6th Cir. 1959). As to the separateness of the issue of the contracting agent, *see* Case No. F85, 6 *Tax'n Bd. of Review Cas*. (Australia) 483, 494 (1955); Judgment of 23 January 1985, *Bundesfinanzhof*, IR 292/81, *BStBl*. II 1985, p. 417, summarized at 1 *International Tax Treaties*, Art. 5, page 46 (Edwardes-Ker ed. 1986).
168. *Georges Simenon vs Commissioner,* 44 *T.C.* 820 (1965).
169. *Id.* at 850.
170. *Id.* at 846.
171. *Id.* at 849.
172. *Id.* at 827.
173. *Id.* at 826.

or was even painted on the mailbox does not appear. Yet the court seemed to have no trouble in concluding that the author had created an 'office.' One has the sense that removal of a few more of the basic elements might finally alter the characterization. But which elements and in what order and amounts is simply unclear.

The minimum physical requirements for a 'real office' may yet be stated.[174] However most of the litigated cases and rulings have focused on the use of third party owned or leased offices and whose business is conducted there. See the discussion in Section 2.1 D above on the 'at the disposal' requirement as applied to the use of customer or supplier offices, the permanence and fixedness of such use and whether such use is by the NRE in pursuit of its core profit making business[175] (e.g., the *Dudney* case, *home office* cases and similar precedent).

In *Brick Work*[176] a Danish company employed about 8-10 workers in Norway for half of each month, with a small office at its disposal at the premises of a VAT representative. The office was held a fixed POB PE. However, in *Fiebert vs MNR*,[177] a Canadian resident who spent 3-4 days a week in Toronto, maintained a US residence as well, which he claimed was a POB PE. The Court rejected the claim finding that to be an 'office' such premises had to be staffed and equipped to carry out the day to day business.

B. 'Place of Management'

Article 5(2) includes 'a place of management.' The Commentary explains that the term is included since it is not necessarily an 'office.' It need not be included in treaties between countries which do not have the concept of a 'place of management.'[178]

---

174. These physical requirements are treated independently of the business activity requirements (*see* Sections 4.05 and 4.06) and the preparatory and auxiliary activities exceptions (*see* Sections 6.01 through 6.13). Note that offices on building sites or construction or installation projects are not permanent establishments until the treaty time limit on the site or project has expired. *See* § 3.07, *infra*. As to home offices of employees of the taxpayer, *see Sunbeam Corporation (Canada) Ltd vs Minister of National Revenue*, 62 *D.T.C.* 1390 (S. Ct. Canada 1962). *See also* Tremblay, at 38:17.
175. The OECD Commentary, in para 3, has backtracked on the original requirement that a POB PE have a 'productive' character. This disclaimer is misleading as it is clear that such place must be used for the core business *of the NRE* as opposed to preparatory or auxiliary activities. Activities which are a part of such *core* business are by nature productive of profit making even if the particular POB is only a cost center which does not have its own revenue or allocation of NRE profit.
176. Case No. 91-01618 A (16 Jun 1992 Eidsivating Court of Appeal) discussed in Mehta at 196.
177. 86 DTC 1017 (25 Nov. 1985, Tax Court Canada).
178. OECD Commentary, para 13.

One may deduce that a place of management, in treaty terms, shares at least some of the characteristics of an office, perhaps even a head office, and some aspects of professional premises. Again, assuming the existence of business[179] being carried on through this place of management, by what other characteristics may one recognize it? The answer is surprisingly complex.

1. Modes of Expression

If United States tax treaties are any guide, there are at least three expressions of the place-of-management concept. The first is the OECD Draft formula: 'a place of management.'[180] This is an original formulation; the Mexico and London Drafts did not include the term. It is far and away the most popular.

Treaties with Commonwealth nations tended to use Commonwealth terminology – simply 'management'[181] – a somewhat ambiguous reference since historically Anglo-Saxon corporate *residence* has been defined as the place where a company is 'centrally managed and controlled,' e.g., where its board or directors meet and decide corporate policy, or lacking an operative board, the place where the real operations of the company are directed by those acting for it. But this is a residency test. If met, unless a treaty dual residence provision applies, the NRE is a full tax resident of the country in which it is managed and controlled and generally taxable on its worldwide income (except for European countries applying the territoriality principle).

There is a European concept of the *place of effective management* which seems surprisingly similar. *Audio Visual Consultancy*[182] was a Swiss incorporated loan-out company providing AV services through a Dutch director (the other two directors were outside Swiss professionals). The Court held the company was effectively managed in Holland by the Dutch director and hence taxable on all its income as a Dutch resident company. Since however the company was also Swiss resident under the dual residence tie-breaker clause of the Netherlands–Swiss Treaty Article 2(4), the Court found that the proper

---

179. 'As these examples are seen against the background of the general definition given in paragraph 2, it is assumed that the Contracting States interpret the terms listed, "a place of management" ... etc. in such a way that such places of business constitute permanent establishments only if they meet the requirements of paragraph 1.' OECD Model Commentary, Art. 5, para. 11. One such requirement is 'the carrying on of the business of the enterprise through this fixed place of business.' *Id.*, para. 2. *See* OECD Draft Commentary, Art. 5, paras. 7 and 8.
180. OECD Draft 5(2)(a). The term does not appear in the United States Model Conventions. The reasons for its omission are said to be 'the continued ambiguity of the term and the opportunity for developing countries to interpret it too broadly.' *See* Bischel, 'Basic Income Tax Treaty Structures,' in *Income Tax Treaties* (Bischel ed. 1978) 1, at 25.
181. *See, e.g.*, United States–Australia, United States–Ireland, United States–New Zealand, United States–Pakistan, United States–United Kingdom.
182. Case No. 21,286 (24 Nov 1982, Hoge Raad).

basis of taxation was its Dutch PE acquired by having a place of management in Holland.[183]

The third term is '*seat* of management.' Although said to be French in origin,[184] its occurrence in some treaties craves explanation and it may be just a French translation of a place of management.[185]

Although theoretically different in several respects,[186] these modes of expression have been only slightly distinguished one from the other in the cases and rulings published to date.

2. *A 'Place of Effective Management'*

Common to the three modes of expression is the term 'management.' An Australian tribunal attempted to define this term in the following language:

> 'Management ... is this – that the business of the company is being carried out by agents directing their care and attention to that particular business and who have control of it – not purely ministerial.'[187]

Decided cases indicate that the principle cuts two ways. On the one hand, it is clear that 'management' means the possession of actual decision-making power, and that a layer of powerless directors interposed between the enterprise and the decision-maker will simply be ignored.[188] On the other hand, the place where that person actually makes these decisions is crucial, irrespective

183. *See also, Air Conditioning Consultant,* Case No. 101/82 MII (28 Mar 1993, *Gerechtshof 's-Gravenhage*), another Swiss domiciliary loan-out case which found a Dutch place of management by an operative owner.
184. *See* United States–France 4(2)(a) (1967) (but not United States–France (1932) or United States–France (1939)).
185. *See,* Technical Explanation, United States–Trinidad and Tobago, Article 9, 3 *Tax Treaties* (CCH) ¶ 9750: 'The proposed Convention uses the term "a seat of management" which was the term used in our Convention with France. The technical explanation of our French Convention explains the definition of the term "a seat of management" and its difference in meaning from the term "a place of management" as follows: "It should be noted that this convention uses the term 'seat of management' where the OECD model convention and prior agreements to which the United States is a party used the term 'place of management'; both terms are translations of the French term 'un siege de direction' and it is believed the translation found in this convention is the more accurate. Prior agreements in which the term 'place of management' appears will be interpreted therefore as if the words 'seat of management' had been used."'
186. *See* Roberts & Warren IX/12F(l)(a).
187. The statement is attributed to counsel for the Commissioner of Taxation. Case No. F 85, 6 *Tax'n Bd. of Rev.* 483, 494 *(Austl. Bd. of Rev.* No. 1 1955).
188. *See* Judgment of 24 November 1982, HR, Neth., *BNB* 83/103, summarized at 1 *International Tax Treaties Service,* Art. 5, page 59.001 (Edwardes-Ker ed. 1986); Judgment of March 28, 1983, Lower Court of the Hague, Neth., *BNB* 1984/279, summarized in 1 *International Tax Treaties Service,* Art. 5, page 59.5003 (M. Edwardes-Ker ed. 1989).

of the title that he or she bears. For example, a Dutch lower court has held that a Netherlands Antilles corporation was actually managed by a clerk. The clerk had authority to bind the corporation and did so in practice.[189]

While an employee denominated a 'clerk' may in fact manage an organization, another denominated 'touring manager' may not. Although he 'attended to hotel accommodation, supervised the setting up of scenery and exercised overall direction of production' of a traveling theatrical enterprise, he had no power 'to stop a show from going on, to employ a new artist, to alter the conditions of engagement of an artist or the amount of advertising expenditure, to hire a particular theatre or to pay any sum which was not within the day-to-day expenditure of the company.'[190] The New Zealand Tax Board concluded on these facts that the touring manager's 'duties were limited in scope and consisted only of the performance of a variety of domestic tasks arising out of the day-to-day production of a show on tour.'[191]

> '[W]e are satisfied that the touring manager was no more than a representative of his employer and that, as A. said in the course of cross-examination, he "(carried) out the management policy of the company in accordance with (his) instructions." It is apparent from the evidence that those instructions may have been given almost from day to day.'[192]

The same conclusion was arrived at as regards a person representing an English company on the boards of directors of two other companies, both of which were Australian domestic corporations, with whom the English company was doing business. 'But a representative is not a "management", and there is no evidence of any managerial duties carried out by him' concluded the chairman of the Australian tax board.[193] In concurring, one board member pointed out that the amount of goods in question, the prices of those goods, and the major agreements under which the goods were produced were all arrived at outside of Australia. 'On the evidence,' he commented, 'there is no person or board in Australia who may in any manner control any of these matters … I fail to see any management of the taxpayer in Australia.'[194]

---

189. Judgment of 22 January 1982, Decision No. 2 Lower Court of The Hague, Neth., *BNB* 1984/9, summarized in 1 *International Tax Treaties Service,* Art. 4, pages 34.5006 and 34.5007 (Edwardes-Ker ed. 1986).
190. Case 5, 3 *N.Z.Tax'n Bd. of Rev.* 49, 52-53 (N.Z. 1965).
191. *Id.* at 59. Note that the applicable convention, Australia–New Zealand II(l)(m)(i) (1960), specifies 'a management,' rather than 'a place of management.'
192. *Ibid.*
193. Case No. F 85, 6 *Tax'n Bd. of Rev.* 483, 494 *(Austl. Bd. of Rev.* No. 1 1955).
194. *Id.* at 504. Separate opinion of Member Bock.

3. *Management or Technical Expertise?*

Another quality of 'management' formed the subject of an example appearing in an official exchange of correspondence in 1964, in which Assistant United States Treasury Secretary Stanley S. Surrey outlined two situations and asked for (and received) agreement on both of them. Both involve 'place of management' in the United States–Luxembourg tax convention. The first is as follows:

> 'As an example of a case in which it is feared might arise, let it be assumed that a Luxembourg manufacturing enterprise enters into a contract with a U.S. firm for the supply and installation of certain precision equipment at the U.S. firm's plant located in the United States. It is required that top-level personnel of the Luxembourg enterprise be present in the United States for the purpose of directing and supervising the installation of the equipment delivered by the enterprise. Such personnel do not exercise any authority to conclude contracts in the name of the Luxembourg enterprise. The project lasts for less than 5 months and no office or branch is maintained in the United States inasmuch as the Luxembourg firm does not generally carry on business in the United States.
>
> In such a case, it is true that important decisions with regard to the Luxembourg enterprise's business in the United States are made at the place in the United States where services contemplated in the contract are being performed. These are, however, in the nature of technical decisions relating to the completion of the task which was undertaken by the manufacturer and would not be considered by the U.S. Government to constitute decisions involving the "management" of the Luxembourg enterprise's business in the United States. Therefore, for purposes of the imposition of the U.S. tax under the treaty, no permanent establishment would exist in the United States.'[195]

While it may be difficult to articulate, the line between 'technical decisions relating to the completion of the task' and 'management' is probably fairly clear.

4. *Ownership Distinguished*

'Management' does not mean ownership. In reaching its result in the case of the Netherlands Antilles corporation managed by the clerk, the lower court of The Hague rejected the assertion that a subsidiary be deemed managed in

---

195. *International Tax Treaties Service, OECD Income* Article 5, page 84 (Edwardes-Ker ed. 1977).

the country in which its sole shareholder resided.[196] Subsequently, the highest court in the Netherlands concluded that the normal influence of a sole shareholder over the affairs of a corporation does not constitute 'management' of that corporation.[197]

Similarly, 'management' should not mean the right of a shareholder to monitor and supervise the performance of its subsidiaries ('stewardship').

5. *Requirement of Situs*

'Management' seems to need a situs. A German partnership hired Netherlands construction workers for German builders. The partners were both Dutch residents. They conducted virtually all of their business either in weekly or semi-weekly meetings conducted in the office of their German tax advisor or in an automobile while they drove around Germany. The High Court of the Netherlands held that the partnership had no place of management in Germany. Carrying on business activities in Germany and exercising effective management while so doing is not enough. A place of management is required. After having decided (for reasons that do not appear) that the tax advisor's office could not be considered a place of management, the court appears to arrive at the same conclusion regarding a motor vehicle.[198]

6. *Permanence*

The temporal aspect of the place-of-management concept has been a source of concern. In the 1964 official exchange of correspondence earlier mentioned, Assistant Secretary of the Treasury Surrey wrote:

> 'It has been suggested ... that the casual or temporary use of premises in Luxembourg, and the contemporaneous rendering of management decisions at such place, by a director or an executive official of a U.S. enterprise could constitute a "place of management" within the meaning of the treaty. Under such a rule, a hotel room in Luxembourg from which a visiting executive of a U.S. corporation chances to make a decision with respect to the conduct of the corporation's business would be a place of management.'

---

196. Judgment of 22 January 1982, Decision No. 2 Lower Court of The Hague, Neth., *BNB* 1984/9, summarized in 1 *International Tax Treaties Service,* Art. 4, pages 34.5006 and 34.5007 (Edwardes-Ker ed. 1986).
197. Judgment of 1 July 1987, HR, Neth., *BNB* 1987/306 *(Mees en Hope).*
198. Judgment of 22 January 1982, Decision No. 2 Lower Court of The Hague, Neth., *BNB* 1984/9, summarized in 1 *International Tax Treaties Service,* Art. 4, pages 34.5006 and 34.5007 (Edwardes-Ker ed. 1986).

Asserting that the result would violate the general rule that requires 'a degree of continuity and permanency and would prevent the mere casual or temporary use of facilities or premises by a person making management decisions from being held to constitute a permanent establishment,' he noted that no position taken in the treaty negotiations was contrary to his view.[199]

The agreement between the representative of the Grand Duchy and one of the most prestigious and respected of American tax law professors may well establish that 'mere casual or temporary use' of a hotel room in Luxembourg City does not constitute a permanent establishment even when it is the situs of management decisions. The parameters of 'casual or temporary use' under the United States–Luxembourg convention are subjective however and the very fact of this exchange of correspondence indicates that the question may again be asked, by other officials under other tax treaties.[200]

C. A 'Branch'

'Branch' is one of the most common (and durable[201]) terms to appear in treaty specifications of permanent establishments.[202] Yet the treaties contain no definition of the term, and relatively little concerning the nature of the branch appears elsewhere in international tax literature. One American source volunteered that '[a] "branch" is generally understood to be an office or other establishment of a corporation incorporated under the laws of a country other than the one in which the branch is located.'[203] A 1955 Australian tax decision adds detail and some color:[204]

> 'It is of some assistance to note the basic concept of "permanent establishment" is defined[205] as meaning "a branch or other fixed place of business." Both of these terms imply an identifiable *locus* of operations where in a commercial sense it could be said, "There is the taxpayer

---

199. Letter of Surrey to Schaus, dated 14 May 1965, 1 *International Tax Treaties Service,* Art. 5, page 83 (Edwardes-Ker ed. 1977). A comparable agreement had been arrived at in a 1965 Memorandum of Understanding with the Federal Republic of Germany. Memorandum of Understanding, United States–Federal Republic of Germany, 18 October 1965, 1 *International Tax Treaties Service*, Art. 5, page 90 (Edwardes-Ker ed. 1977).
200. *See* Bischel, 'Basic Income Tax Treaty Structures,' in *Income Tax Treaties* (Bischel ed. 1978) 1, at 25. *See also* Tremblay at 38:28-33.
201. 'Branch establishments' appeared as a term in the original tax treaty. *See* quote in Section 1.2, *supra*.
202. *See*, e.g., OECD Model 5(2)(b).
203. Gifford & Streng, *International Tax Planning* 1 (2d ed. 1979).
204. Case No. F 85, 6 *Tax'n Bd. of Review Cas.* 483 (Board of Review No. 1, Sydney, Australia 1955) and subject to the lesser Services PE time period.
205. Under Article III of the former United Kingdom–Australia convention.

> company's branch," or "That is where the taxpayer company carries on its business in Australia." A branch or other fixed place of business connotes, in my view, something physical and separately identifiable as the place of business of the non-resident enterprise.'[206]

The difficulty with these definitions is that they do not attempt to distinguish 'branch' from other permanent establishment descriptives – 'office' and 'place of management' in particular.[207] Indeed, they raise the question whether any difference may exist. Some indication as to what comprises a branch appears in a West German decision. There, an American bank set about to open a German branch. The rental of office space, the hiring of staff, the application for and receipt of governmental permission to engage in the banking business, and the transfer of the capital required in order to conduct the operation all occurred in 1971. The branch opened for business on 5 January 1972. A net worth tax, due from foreign enterprises having permanent establishments in Germany on 1 January 1972, was held properly exacted.[208] The activities mentioned were 'more than preparatory'; they amounted to the conduct of business.[209] The branch was a permanent establishment even before it opened its doors.

The issue is whether this place, called a 'branch,' differs in any material way from another, called an 'office.' One has the sense that there is a difference, and that the difference arises from an affirmative act of the taxpayer. Decided cases and rulings reveal that characterizing offices, factories, places of management, and dependent agents as permanent establishments tends to be an activity in which government agencies engage. Taxpayers are usually found to be resisting such characterization.

Taxpayers do not seem to resist characterization as branches. The reason may well be that branches are the creatures of taxpayers. A foreign corporation announces that, at a given place and time, it shall be present in the source jurisdiction for the purpose of doing business, operating under the same trade

206. *Id.* at 493 (*dictum*).
207. *See* Ltr. Rul. 6011165960A (taxpayer asserts that it is considering 'the opening of a "Branch" in the United States'; issue resolved in terms of an 'office'; both terms appear in the applicable treaty).
208. Judgment of 30 January 1981, BFHE, West Germany (No. III R 116/79) *BStBl* II, 15 September 1981, p. 560; summarized at 1 *International Tax Treaties Service*, Art. 5, page 42 (Edwardes-Ker ed. 1986).
209. The OECD seems to disagree: 'A permanent establishment begins to exist as soon as the enterprise commences to carry on its business through a fixed place of business. This is the case once the enterprise prepares, at the place of business, the activity for which the place of business is to serve permanently. The period of time during which the fixed place of business itself is being set up by the enterprise should not be counted, provided that this activity differs substantially from the activity for which the place of business is to serve permanently.' OECD Model Commentary, Art. 5(1), para. 11.

name that it uses in its country of residence. It is said to 'open a branch.'[210] In the process, it signals to the source-jurisdiction taxing authorities that it has opted in favor of being taxed as a permanent establishment in the source jurisdiction. Given a fixed place of business, 'a certain degree of permanence, and the conduct of business through that fixed place,'[211] a permanent establishment in the nature of a branch may be said to exist.[212] And it exists in fact because the taxpayer has planned that it exist and has executed that plan.[213]

D. A 'Store or Other Sales Outlet'

The absence of the term from the London and Mexico Drafts, as well as from the OECD Draft and OECD Model,[214] seems to have done little to stem the enthusiasm of some treaty nations for characterizing a 'store or other sales outlet' as a permanent establishment. For some reason, the term tends to appear most frequently in treaties between developed nations and third-world countries.[215] It has been considered in neither cases nor rulings. Indeed, it has received little attention anywhere.

One may obtain at least a hint as to the meaning of the phrase by examining the treaty materials of the United States. The term (or one of its variants) has appeared at various times in several older United States treaties.[216] Judging from the technical explanations accompanying these treaties, the attitude of the Americans and their treaty partners has generally been uncritical. The technical explanation accompanying the 1980 United States treaty with Jamaica is a rare exception. There, 'a store or premises used as a sales outlet' elicited this explanation:

---

210. *See*, e.g., Ltr. Rul. 6011165960A('[T]he time has now come for you to consider the opening of a "Branch" in the United States ...').
211. OECD Model Commentary, Art. 5(1), para. 2. No permanent establishment results from the conduct of only preparatory or auxiliary activities through a branch. *See* Ltr. Rul. 8442107.
212. Whether a branch exists before the formal requirements of local commercial law have been fulfilled is a concern of several domestic legal systems. *See* Vogel, at 297, para. 52.
213. Ltr. Rul. 6102066160A(concluding that the maintenance of a showroom 'constitutes a branch or fixed place of business') is probably erroneous. *See* Rev. Rul. 62-31 (concluding that comparable facts created 'a fixed place of business').
214. And the two United States Models patterned on the OECD Model.
215. *See*, e.g., Japan-Philippines 5(2)(a) (1980).
216. *See*, e.g. United States–Barbados 5(2)(f) ('a store or premises used as a sales outlet'); United States–Bermuda 3(2) ('premises used as a sales outlet'); United States–Cyprus 9(2)(f); United States–Jamaica 5(2)(f) ('a store or premises used as a sales outlet'); United States–Korea 9(2)(f); United States–Morocco 4(2)(g). *See also* United States–Aruba 5(2)(e) ('a store or premises used as a sales outlet'); United States–Israel 5(2)(g); United States–Sri Lanka 5(2)(f) ('a store or premises used as a sales outlet')

> 'The ... reference to a premises used as a "sales outlet" does not mean that premises used by an enterprise for the mere delivery of goods is a permanent establishment; additional significant activity by the enterprise at the premises, such as the negotiation of sales and delivery of goods, is necessary for the premises to constitute a "sales outlet" and a permanent establishment of the enterprise.'[217]

One notes that the storage-display-or-delivery exception in this treaty is unique. Ruled out of the use of facilities or the maintenance of a stock of goods for the excepted purposes is 'goods or merchandise held for sale by such enterprise in a store or premises used as a sales outlet.'[218] The technical explanation volunteers at this point:

> 'The term "sales outlet" is intended, however, to mean a place of business where the enterprise conducts activities which contribute significantly to the conclusion of sales, not a place where goods are merely delivered.'[219]

A second technical explanation of the same year, accompanying the United States–Bangladesh tax convention, speaks of the term 'a store or other sales outlet' in the following language:

> 'The reference to premises as a "store or other sales outlet" does not mean that premises used by an enterprise for the mere occasional delivery of goods is a permanent establishment; in such case, additional significant activity by the enterprise, such as the negotiation of sales and delivery of goods, is necessary for the premises to constitute a permanent establishment of the enterprise.'[220]

The Bangladesh convention contains an atypical provision stating that the use of facilities or the maintenance of a stock for the purpose of occasional deliveries is not to constitute a permanent establishment.[221] Technical explanations of other treaties deal with the language in question quite superficially.[222] Although one might expect the earlier discussions to be carried over into the later technical explanations, in fact they are not.

---

217. Technical Explanation, United States–Jamaica, Art. 5, 2 *Tax Treaties* (CCH) 5050.
218. United States–Jamaica 5(3)(a) and (b).
219. Technical Explanation, United States–Jamaica, Art. 5, 2 *Tax Treaties* (CCH) 5050.
220. Technical Explanation, United States–Bangladesh, Art. 5, 1 *Tax Treaties* (CCH) 950.
221. United States–Bangladesh 5(5).
222. *See*, e.g., Technical Explanation, United States–Cyprus, Art. 9; Technical Explanation, United States–Bermuda, Art. 3.

It is a paradox that the only rulings regarding sales outlets involve treaties from which the store-or-other-sales-outlet phrase is absent. The first of these rulings, a letter ruling issued in 1954,[223] interpreting the language of an unspecified treaty, involved a showroom maintained by the taxpayer's company. There, a group of salesmen solicited orders from samples for the merchandise of the company and that of another (presumably foreign) corporation. Quoting from the dependent-agency language of the treaty, the author of the ruling concluded that the commission paid the company by the other company was not subject to United States income tax.

A Revenue Ruling[224] issued in the same year, involving the United States treaty with the United Kingdom, involved almost identical facts. The ruling specifies (as the letter ruling did not) that both of the principals involved were foreign corporations. The selling corporation did not manufacture in the US; it simply sold the goods manufactured by the other corporation and collected commissions on the sales. As in the earlier ruling, neither corporation maintained a stock of goods in the United States. After citing the dependent-agency language of the United Kingdom treaty, the author of the ruling concluded that the commissions were not subject to United States income tax.

Virtually the same facts elicited the contrary conclusion in a private letter ruling issued in 1961.[225] As in the first letter ruling, the identity of the treaty is concealed. Noting that that treaty 'states, among other things, that the term "permanent establishment" ... means a branch, management, factory or other fixed place of business,' the author concluded that 'the maintenance of a showroom and a group of salesmen in ... constitutes a branch or fixed place of business by your company.'

The final step was taken the following year in a second Revenue Ruling.[226] The facts differ only slightly from those of the earlier rulings. Here an 'office,' rather than a 'showroom,' was involved. The salesmen were joined by 'general clerks,' and both were 'empowered only to run the office, to arrange for the appointment of distributing agents for the merchandise offered by the corporation, and to solicit orders generally.' The ruling specifies that not only was there no stock of goods, but that the employees did not 'have the authority to negotiate and conclude contracts on behalf of the corporation.'

The author of this ruling concluded that the 1954 Revenue Ruling had been incorrectly decided. Had the question been whether the manufacturing company had a permanent establishment in the United States, the inquiry regarding dependent agency (i.e., whether the sales company employees had

223. Ltr. Rul. 5405286160A.
224. Rev. Rul. 54-588, 1954-2 *C.B.* 657.
225. Ltr. Rul. 6102066160A.
226. Rev. Rul. 62-31, 1962-1 *C.B.* 367.

authority to bind orders for the products of the manufacturing company) would have been appropriate. But the sales company, by maintaining the showroom, 'clearly has a fixed place of business in the United States, constituting a permanent establishment within the meaning of the convention, for the carrying on of its commission business.'[227]

Finally, the activity of exhibitors at conventions, fairs, and exhibitions seems relevant. A single letter ruling[228] deals with a foreign corporation's promoting exhibitions of goods and craftsmanship of unrelated suppliers in two American cities. Each exhibition is to last two weeks. The Internal Revenue Service ruled that the renting of space in exhibition halls and charging admission to view the exhibit would not be considered doing business through a permanent establishment. The ruling closed with this caveat:

> 'However, if [the foreign corporation] engages in exhibiting and selling its [own] goods during its presence in the United States, it shall be carrying on an enterprise which is "engaged in trade or business in the United States through a permanent establishment situated therein" within the meaning of Article III(1) of the United States–... income tax convention.'

The ruling seems to echo the OECD Model Commentary:

> 'If a fixed place of business ... is deemed not to be a permanent establishment, this exception applies likewise to the disposal of movable property forming part of the business property of the place of business at the termination of the enterprise's activity in such installation ... Since, for example, the display of merchandise is excepted [under the "storage, display, or delivery" rubric], the sale of the merchandise at the termination of a trade fair or convention is covered by the exception. The exception does not, of course, apply to sales of merchandise not actually displayed at the trade fair or convention.'[229]

One is compelled to conclude from all of this that a 'store or other sales outlet' is a permanent establishment, whether or not the language appears in a particular treaty. Further, a mere sales solicitation office is sufficient, whether intended for one's own goods or services or those of an unrelated supplier.

---

227. *Id.* at 369. The ruling revokes Rev. Rul. 54-588. It was cited and followed in Rev. Rul. 65-263, 1965-2 *C.B.* 561, which involved the sale in the United States of services to be performed in Canada.
228. Ltr. Rul. 6207256130A.
229. *See also* OECD Model Commentary, Art. 5(4), para. 29.

A sales-solicitation-office permanent establishment consists first of all of a fixed place of business, described as a 'showroom' or a 'sales office.' This place of business is inhabited by persons engaged in the business (under one scenario) of soliciting orders intended to be accepted outside of the United States – either by the enterprise operating the place of business or by a client of that enterprise.

The trade-fair-or-convention clause would indicate that (under a second scenario) sales and deliveries to customers from stock on any regular basis should produce the permanent establishment characterization for the place of business, even if operated for relatively short periods of time.[230] Alternatively, a dependent-agency permanent establishment could exist under those (generally older) treaties which apply to an agent filling merchandise orders out of source country stock.

At the center of it all seems to be the act of the salesperson persuading the customer that he or she cannot live without ordering – or purchasing on the spot – the product in question. Given this activity in a fixed place over a reasonable period of time, there is a permanent establishment.

Several United States Revenue Rulings[231] hold that no permanent establishment exists in the case of a foreign supplier which enters into a consignment sales arrangement with a related or unrelated United States seller. The seller took possession of the goods upon arrival of each shipment to the United States. Title to the goods remained in the supplier (according to the contract between them) until the instant before the seller sold each item to a customer. Presumably, the result would be the same if the seller were to provide a separate area of a department store operated by it solely for the display of the goods of the foreign supplier.

E. 'Factory'

Although the term has appeared in the vast majority of tax treaties,[232] the term 'factory' seems to have all but escaped definition. In the one instance in which the term appears to have come into question, the factory in question was owned and operated by an Australian company, an entity separate and distinct from the taxpayer – an English company which held shares in it but was not its parent. The Australian company produced articles (the nature of which was deliberately concealed from the reader). It sold a portion of its production to

---

230. This is one explanation for the conclusion that the temporary Danish pavilion restaurant at the 1964-1965 New York World's Fair constituted a permanent establishment. *See* Rev. Rul. 67-322, 1967-2 *C.B.* 469.
231. Ltr. Rul. 8318080; *see also* Rev. Rul. 76-322, 1976-2 *C.B.* 487.
232. The term is probably the most popular of the listed permanent establishment examples. It occurs in almost every tax treaty.

the taxpayer company and was duly paid for articles supplied. The Australian government argued that:

> 'where, as here, there is a factory catering especially for the needs of the taxpayer company, it should be held to be "a factory" for the purposes of the definition.'[233]

The Taxation Board of Review declined to adopt the government's view on the ground that the factory simply did not belong to the English taxpayer. The OECD's official attitude toward foreign ownership would indicate that a factory need not be owned by a foreign enterprise in order to be its permanent establishment; leased premises would clearly suffice.[234] The Australian government failed in this instance because the factory was neither.

A foreign enterprise operating in a building or series of buildings and, for a 'permanent' period, producing items of tangible personal property for sale to customers as its principal line of business probably has a fixed place of business in the nature of a factory.

F. 'Workshop'

Of all of the major terms, 'workshop' seems the one most thoroughly ignored. Introduced into the model-treaty bloodline in a 1928 revision to the 1927 League of Nations Bilateral Convention,[235] it has been a fixture in model tax treaties ever since.[236] What it actually means is entirely uncertain. Its inclusion in 1928 probably carries some special weight in the United Kingdom. A dictionary definition of that era explains that in Britain, the term had, by various acts of Parliament:

> 'been declared to be any place in which collective manual labor, under an employer having right of access to or control over the place, is done by way of trade or in making, repairing, or the like, articles to be sold, and in which no machinery moved or worked by any mechanical power is used.'[237]

---

233. Case No. F 85, 6 *Tax'n Bd. of Rev.* 483, 495 (*Austl. Bd. of Rev.* No. 1 1955).
234. OECD Model Commentary, Art. 5(1), para. 4.
235. *See* 'Double Taxation and Tax Evasion,' Report presented by the General Meeting of Government Experts on Double Taxation and Tax Evasion, 1928 (C.562.M.178.1928.II), 4 *LHUSTC* 4151.
236. *See* Mexico Draft, Prot. Art. V(l), London Draft, Prot. Art. V(l), OECD Draft 5(2)(e), OECD Model 5(2)(e), UN Model 5(2)(e).
237. *Webster's New Int'l Dict.* 2350 (1933).

Contemporary dictionaries de-emphasize the more austere aspects of the older definitions: power tools are permitted, but the hand-work aspect remains foremost. It is doubtful that the treaty term embraces the newer use of 'workshop' to mean an adult education course or seminar involving professional skills or the arts.[238]

It seems to be assumed that the essential hand-work results in the production of some products and the repair of others. The concept seems to share a long border with the 'factory' idea. In particular, each seems to deal with tangible personal property. While engaged in manufacturing proper, the workshop seems a bright-line sort of concept. When the hand-work is applied to the property of others, the margins of the workshop concept grow dim. An auto-repair garage is probably a 'workshop,' but is a dry-cleaning plant? A hair-styling salon? A fast-food outlet? Is the issue whether the active participants do business while wearing business suits with white shirts or blouses? Seemingly, it becomes an 'office or other fixed place of business' if they do.

G. 'Warehouse'

Although it appeared in the London and Mexico Drafts,[239] the term 'warehouse' is missing from the OECD Draft and 1977 and later Models. The 1963 OECD Draft Commentary explains its absence in the following terms:

> 'The purpose of including the term was, of course, to cover those warehouses in which the business of letting storage space or other facilities to third persons was carried on. The insertion of the term was not intended to treat as a permanent establishment a warehouse controlled by an enterprise, but used only for the storage, etc. of its own goods. It was, however, suggested that to insert the term would cause confusion and that the term "warehouse" in paragraph 2 [that is, among the agreed-example permanent establishments] read together with *a)* and *b)* of paragraph 3 [exempting the use of facilities or the maintenance of a stock for "storage, display or delivery"] would be misleading. It was accordingly decided not to include the term "warehouse" in paragraph 2.'[240]

The authors of the Commentary seem satisfied that storage of one's own goods in a warehouse 'controlled' by an enterprise does not create a permanent establishment. The sort of warehouse that constitutes a permanent establishment

238. *Webster's Third New Int'l Dict.* 2635 (1981).
239. *See* London Draft, Prot. Art. V(l); Mexico Draft, Prot. Art. V(l).
240. OECD Draft Commentary, Art. 5(1), para. 9. Vogel, at 302, para. 62.

is that maintained by an enterprise engaged in public warehousing. In their words:

> 'A warehouse in which the business of letting facilities for storage, etc. to third parties is carried on will be a permanent establishment under the general definition of paragraph 1 [which states the general fixed-place-of-business rule] even though it is not specifically mentioned in the list of examples in paragraph 2.'[241]

1. American Warehouse Rulings

In rulings separated by more than two decades, the United States federal taxing authorities ruled that English corporations who maintained warehouses in the United States, and in fact delivered from the stock in these warehouses from time to time, had no permanent establishment in the United States. The earlier of the rulings states:

> 'The mere ownership of a warehouse in the United States by a United Kingdom enterprise does not mean that such enterprise has a permanent establishment therein.'[242]

The later ruling cites its predecessor with approval, but shifts the focus slightly. 'The above described warehousing' did not constitute engaging in trade or business in the United States through a permanent establishment, it concluded.[243] The English corporations operated entirely through 'home-office' transactions, had no employees in the United States, solicited orders only through agents of independent status who served a number of English exporters, and ordinarily shipped direct from Britain to the customer.

The absence of the term 'warehouse' from the Article 5(2) list of permanent establishment examples of either of the treaties involved[244] is significant. There seems no doubt that engaging in the commercial warehousing business creates a permanent establishment. Whether the space is owned or merely leased seems immaterial. By the same token, the use of warehouse space for storage and for at least occasional (or extraordinary) deliveries in respect of home-office transactions is permissible – at least in the absence of 'warehouse' in

241. *Ibid.*
242. Rev. Rul. 56-594, 1956-2 *C.B.* 1126, 1126. The ruling seems to involve the party involved in Ltr. Rul. 5509205580A (which differs in that it identifies the product as shoes).
243. Ltr. Rul. 7749009.
244. I.e., United States–United Kingdom 11(1)(1) (1945) and United States–United Kingdom 5(2) (1975).

the list of permanent establishment examples in the applicable tax convention. This view was espoused in a 1980 decision of the French *Conseil d'État*.[245]

2. *The UN Model Provision*

The authors of the United Nations Model Convention appear to hold a different view. In the Commentary accompanying the permanent establishment provisions of the convention is found the following statement:

> 'Developing countries often wish to broaden the scope of the term "permanent establishment" and some believe that a warehouse should be included among the specific examples. However, the deletion of "delivery" from the excluded activities described in subparagraphs (a) and (b) of paragraph 4 means that a "warehouse" used for any purpose is (subject to the conditions in paragraph 1 being fulfilled) a permanent establishment under the general principles of the Article.'[246]

That a warehouse will constitute a permanent establishment if used as a source of deliveries, under the terms of a treaty configured on the United Nations Model, seems inescapable. The deletion of 'delivery' from the usual 'storage-display-or-delivery' phrase is plainly intended to have that effect. The fact that the American taxing authorities reached a contrary result in the rulings just mentioned, without reference to storage-display-or-delivery,[247] will probably not be persuasive.

The UN Model has not proved entirely popular with treaty negotiators from developed countries.[248] Hence, the deletion of 'delivery' from the list of exempt activities has occurred to date only infrequently.[249]

---

245. Judgment of 25 July 1980, *Conseil d'Etat* (Req. No. 11.535) summarized at 1 *International Tax Treaties Service*, Art. 5, page 34.5011 (Edwardes-Ker ed. 1986). The editor suggests that the appearance of the term 'a sales outlet' in the applicable (France–Algeria) treaty had no effect on the outcome because, although deliveries were made from the warehouse in question, the sales had all been effected in home-office transactions.
246. UN Model Commentary, Art. 5, para. 4
247. While the term appears in Article 5(4)(a) and (b) of the 2001 United States–United Kingdom treaty, it is entirely absent from the 1945 treaty under which Rev. Rul. 56-594,1956-2 *C.B.* 1126 was decided.
248. *See*, e.g., Ritter, 'Requirements of Developed Countries from Double Tax Treaties with Developing Countries,' *UN Draft Model Taxation Convention* 42 (1979).
249. The 2004 United States–Bangladesh 5(4)(a) tax treaty contains such a provision. *See* Rosenbloom, 'Trends in Tax Treaties Between the United States and Developing Countries,' in *UN Draft Model Taxation Convention* 18 (1979): 'The United States believes that some provisions of the UN Model are questionable (... treatment of "delivery" as evidencing a permanent establishment) ....' *Id.* at 21. Note that the 1976 United States–Philippines convention limits the customary exception to 'storage, display, or occasional delivery.'

3. *US Treaties*

The United States treaties with Barbados, Jamaica, and the Netherlands Antilles contain a specific provision that seems to eliminate the issue. Under these treaties, the term 'permanent establishment' includes 'a warehouse, in relation to a person providing storage facilities for others.'[250] That warehouses otherwise related engage *ipso facto* in exempt activities seems assumed.

H. Other Named Places

Aside from terms involving agriculture and extraction (which are dealt with in the following pages[251]), the list of terms describing fixed places of business is virtually complete at this juncture. There will always be one or another aberrant provision. A sign of its times, perhaps, is the following term that appears in the current Belgian treaty with France:

> 'facilities in either State at the disposal of organizers or entrepreneurs of any kind of entertainments, amusements or games whatsoever as well as travelling shows, travelling salesmen, artisans or other persons carrying on one of the activities which come within the scope of this Article, where such facilities are at their disposal in that State for a total period of at least thirty days during any calendar year.'[252]

I. Agricultural and Timber Land

No reference to agricultural or timber land appears in the OECD Draft or Model Conventions. Although the term 'plantation' had appeared in the Mexico and London Drafts, its omission from the Draft and Model was not even mentioned in the OECD commentaries. Nevertheless, references to plantations, farms, and forests are not uncommon in contemporary double-taxation conventions and the 2012 OECD Revised Discussion Draft specifically acknowledges that farms can be a POB PE if the requirements of Article 5(1) are met.[253]

The crucial terms are undefined. The absence of any mention in the OECD commentaries means that local laws will govern the meaning of 'farm,' 'plan-

250. United States–Barbados 5(2)(g); United States–Jamaica 5(2)(g). The identical provision appears at Japan-India 5(2)(g).
251. Sections 2.10, 2.11, Chapter 3, and Chapter 4.
252. Belgium–France 4(4)(h).
253. *See*, e.g., Belgium–Israel 5(2)(g) ('a plantation'); Cyprus–United Kingdom 5(2)(h) ('a farm or plantation'); United States–Australia 5(2)(g) ('an agricultural, pastoral, or forestry property'). The OECD 2012 Revised Discussion Draft recognizes that farms can be a PE, Article 3.2, with collateral consequences for taxation of e.g. effectively connected investment income.

tation,' and like terms. Although one cannot doubt that the 'fixedness' requirement is easily managed, the requirement of engaging in business is another matter.

The proper treatment of the rental situation is somewhat obscured in a Canadian Income Tax Appeal Board case[254] involving Alberta wheat land owned by an American corporation headquartered in Utah. One of the problems confronting the Board was simply whether land leased pursuant to a share-cropping arrangement by the corporation constituted its permanent establishment in Canada. The corporation employed a Canadian agent who arranged the sale of the landlord's share of the crop, withheld Canadian tax, and forwarded the balance to it. It had no other connection with Canada. The 1942 tax treaty between Canada and the United States contained a rather rudimentary definition:

> 'As used in this Convention ... the term "permanent establishment" includes branches, mines and oil wells, farms, timber lands, plantations, factories, workshops, warehouses, offices, agencies and other fixed places of business of an enterprise, but does not include a subsidiary corporation.'[255]

It provided in addition that the term 'industrial and commercial profits' did not include 'income in the form of rentals.' The conclusion drawn by the Board as to the meaning of this language is at least questionable:

> 'From this definition, it would appear that the possession of a farm in one of the countries by an enterprise of the other country would be considered as a permanent establishment of that enterprise in the country in which the farm was situated. Possibly the intention of the terms of the Convention was that, if the enterprise itself conducted farming operations on such a farm situated in the territory of the other contracting state, it would be considered to be carrying on business in that state and subject to taxation on the industrial and commercial profits arising from the farm. But, if the farm was rented to some third party, and all that was received by the enterprise was income by way of rentals, then the [treaty provision excluding rentals from industrial-and-commercial profits] would apply ...'[256]

254. *D.H. Peery Estate, Inc. vs Minister of National Revenue*, 52 *D.T.C.* 202 (Income Tax Appeal Bd. 1952).
255. United States–Canada (1942), Prot. 3(f).
256. *D.H Peery Estate, Inc. vs Minister of National Revenue*, 52 *D.T.C.* 202, 206 (Income Tax Appeal Bd. 1952); *see* Tremblay at 38:13. The OECD 2012 Discussion Draft confirms this view, see proposed Article 5 Commentary, para. 3.2 (The determination of whether a farm or

The conclusion was not questioned in the 1980 case of *Halcrow vs Minister of National Revenue*[257] in which twenty-four persons, all but one of whom were Americans, purchased a Manitoba farm. Four of the persons actually operated the farm. The Board quoted the language of the *Peery Estate* case set out above, and concluded that the group 'carried on a business or operating a farm [sic]' and had a permanent establishment in Canada.

While the results in both cases are probably correct, the conclusion (if such it be) that a fixed-place-of-business permanent establishment existed in the former case appears to be contrary to the OECD model commentary. Sharecropping is a form a renting agricultural property in exchange for rent paid in kind (a share of the crop, which is sold for cash). One of the basic 'conditions' set out in the OECD Model Commentary seems to be missing:

> 'the carrying on of the business of the enterprise through this fixed place of business. This means usually that persons who, in one way or another, are dependent on the enterprise (personnel) conduct the business of the enterprise in the State in which the fixed place is situated.'[258]

Contrary to earlier practice,[259] the OECD Model includes as income from immovables, taxable in the country of source, 'income from agriculture and forestry.'[260] While the provision is likely to resolve most of the practical problems in the area, it does not directly address the issue of the existence of a permanent establishment by reason of such activities.[261] The result should be that mere ownership of a farm and receipt of farm rental income (including sharecropping proceeds) does not itself create a permanent establishment.

J. Rental Real Estate

The specific mention in contemporary treaties of farms, plantations, pastoral and timber lands has generated almost nothing by way of cases or rulings. In contrast, the major field of rental real estate is dealt with under general permanent establishment principles, and authority abounds.

---

an apartment rental building is a POB PE must be made independently of whether such income is taxable as real estate income under Article 6. PE status can affect taxability of connected interest, dividends, nonresident employees of a source country PE, and non-discriminatory taxation of a source country PE

257. 1980 *C.T.C.* 2801 (Tax Review Bd. 1980).
258. OECD Model Commentary, Art. 5, para. 2.
259. *See* Skaar, at 242.
260. OECD Model 6(1).
261. *See* OECD Model Commentary, Article 6, para. 1 ('Although income from agriculture or forestry is included in Art. 6, Contracting States are free to agree in their bilateral conventions to treat such income under Art. 7 [Business Profits]').

Real estate rental activity breaks into two divisions, depending on whether the taxpayer is the lessee of rental realty or is its owner. The lessee's questions are relatively simple and may be resolved in terms of 'fixed places of business' of one or another sort. The status of a rented shed adjoining an abattoir, used for the processing of fresh animal hides,[262] is not atypical of these questions.

The landlord's problems are more complex. After getting off to rather a bad start, the field seems to have settled into a fair amount of certainty. Unfortunate beginnings came in several forms. In the first place, the United States Tax Court produced a dictum to the effect that the concepts of permanent establishment and 'engaged in trade or business' were coextensive.[263] They clearly are not. Secondly, Canadian tax officials became entangled with the term 'enterprise' in at least two cases in which valuable opinions regarding permanent establishment might otherwise have been made.[264] Finally, the Belgian authorities instituted a bright-line rule: foreigners who owned real estate in Belgium would be deemed to have permanent establishments in Belgium.[265] The rule was quickly dispatched in the courts.[266] It was subsequently withdrawn.[267]

A new factor colors these controversies. In most instances appearing in the case law, a finding that the taxpayer has no permanent establishment in the source country translates into exemption of the taxpayer's business income from source-country taxes. Farms, plantations and the like also produce business income. The stakes in this area are different, due to widespread acceptance of the rule that neither rents nor gains realized on the disposition of

262. *See Transvaal Associated Hide and Skin Merchants vs Collector of Income Tax, Botswana*, 19 *S. Afr. Tax Cas.* 97 (Ct. of App., Botswana 1967) (shed constitutes permanent establishment); *see also* Judgment of 24 March 1976, HR, Neth., No. 17,812, summarized at 1 *International Tax Treaties Service,* Art. 5, page 58 (Edwardes-Ker ed. 1986).

263. *See Lewenhaupt vs Commissioner,* 20 *T.C* 151, 161 (1953).

264. *See Rutenberg vs Minister of National Revenue,* 1979 *C.T.C.* 459 (Fed. Ct. of App. 1979); *Abed Estate vs The Queen,* 82 *D.T.C.* 6099 (Fed. Ct. of App. 1982). The term does not appear in the current United States–Canada convention. *Cf. Shahmoon vs Minister of National Revenue,* 1975 *C.T.C.* 2361 (real estate investments and apartment for taxpayer's personal use in Montreal – no permanent establishment in Canada).

265. Ruling of the Tax Authorities, No. Ci. RH 61/260.221, summarized at 1 *International Tax Treaties Service,* Art. 5, page 23 (Edwardes-Ker ed. 1986). The authorities may have been misled by the Judgment of 7 October 1970, Lower Tax Court of Brussels, Belg., *Bulletin der Belastingen* No. 484, April 1971/15,799, summarized at 1 *International Tax Treaties Service,* Art. 5, pages 22-23 (Edwardes-Ker ed. 1977-86).

266. *See* Judgment of 30 April 1973, Lower Court of Brussels, Belg., 1973 *La Revue Fiscale, 7,* 8, 9/423, summarized at 1 *International Tax Treaties Service,* Art. 5, page 23 (Edwardes-Ker ed. 1986); Judgment of 15 December 1976, Brussels Court of Appeal, Belg., *Algemeen Fiscaal Tijdschrift,* April 1977/125, summarized at 1 *International Tax Treaties Service,* Art. 5, page 27 (Edwardes-Ker ed. 1977).

267. Circular of tax authorities, Belg., No. Ci.RH.61/293.709, summarized at 1 *International Tax Treaties Service,* Art. 5, page 28 (Edwardes-Ker ed. 1979).

real property constitute 'business profits.'[268] Rents from the leasing and gains from the alienation of realty are usually taxable in the source country. Hence, controversies concerning the presence of a permanent establishment tend to be pursued for collateral reasons.[269]

The Belgian circular in which the earlier ruling was withdrawn[270] seems representative of the rule as it presently exists. First of all, rental realty owned by a foreigner is not *ipso facto* the permanent establishment of that foreigner. Secondly, the rendering of services to the tenants of that realty will alter the result if it amounts to 'the carrying on of professional activity.' Foreign landlords are warned by Belgian counsel to write leases in which the tenant is responsible for all services which might otherwise be provided by a landlord.[271] Just how much activity will result in crossing the line is difficult to ascertain, especially as tolerance levels seem to vary from country to country.[272] However, given the fixedness that characterizes real estate investments, and given a measure of permanence, crossing that business activity line completes the traditional recipe for a permanent establishment.

K. Ships/Equipment/Containers/Race Horses

The concept of any sort of personal property constituting the fixed-place element of a permanent establishment seems to have been quite late in emerging. No mention of it appears in the early products of the League of Nations Fiscal Committee.[273] The OECD Model seems equally silent.

---

268. *See* de Ravel d'Esclapon, 'International Tax Treaties and Industrial and Commercial Profits,' in *Income Tax Treaties* 75, 91 (J. Bischel ed. 1978). The terms 'business profits' (in headlines) and 'profits' (in text) have supplanted the earlier term 'industrial or commercial profits' [sometimes 'industrial *and* commercial profits']. The concepts are probably identical.
269. In earlier American cases, for example, 'force-of-attraction' treatment was often at stake. *See* Williams, 'Permanent Establishments in the United States,' in *Income Tax Treaties* 189, 200 (J. Bischel ed. 1978).
270. Circular of tax authorities, Belg., No. Ci.RH.61/293.709, summarized at 1 *International Tax Treaties Service*, Art. 5, page 28 (Edwardes-Ker ed. 1979).
271. Editorial, 1 *International Tax Treaties Service,* Art. 5, page 28 (Edwardes-Ker ed. 1979).
272. *See* Judgment of 27 February 1984, Conseil d'Etat, Fr., Req. Nos. 37.377, 37.378, and 37.379, summarized at 1 *International Tax Treaties Service,* Art. 5, page 34.5016 (Edwardes-Ker ed. 1986) (apartment ownership plus real estate dealings – no permanent establishment); *Shahmoon vs Minister of National Revenue,* 1975 *C.T.C.* 2361 (real estate investments and apartment for taxpayer's personal use in Montreal – no permanent establishment in Canada); *De Amodio vs Commissioner,* 34 *T.C.* 894 (1960), *aff'd 299* F.2d 623 (3d Cir. 1962).
273. *See,* e.g., Draft Plurilateral Double-Taxation Convention (1931-1933), 4 *LHUSTC* 4232.

1. Substantial Equipment or Machinery Clauses

Such clauses may have originated as late as 1950. Mitchell B. Carroll, for half a century one of the major personages in the field of tax treaties, stated:

> 'The 1950 [United States] Treaty with Canada added to the 1942 definition ... the use in one State of substantial equipment or machinery at any time in any taxable year by an enterprise of the other state. The Canadian authorities wanted this addition in order to tax American construction enterprises on earnings from short jobs North of the border.'[274]

A parallel provision was tested in a 1957 Australian case.[275] There, an American pharmaceutical firm closed its branch operation in Australia and licensed an English company to manufacture and distribute its product in Australia. As a part of the governing agreement, the American firm agreed to lend to the English company the machinery necessary for the manufacture of the product. Specifically, it loaned four separate machines, denominated a mill, a tank, an extruder, and a capper. The machinery was held to constitute a permanent establishment of the American firm. Finding that the machinery represented all of the machinery employed in producing the product, the chairman of the Australian tax review board ruled:

> 'The meaning of "substantial" is relative and in the case where the machinery required is not extensive, and the whole is involved, it is "substantial".'[276]

One member of the board took an absolutist view:

> 'No doubt that the term "substantial" is somewhat relative; but it seems to me, as a matter of degree, that the loaned equipment, as described *supra* from the evidence, and occupying as it did, floor space equivalent to the average post-war suburban home, could not reasonably be regarded as other than substantial, and I so find, on the facts.'[277]

While the substantial-equipment-or-machinery clause appears in a number of other treaties, it has remained subject to ad hoc interpretation as discussed supra in Chapter 2.1A, 2.1D.1 and 2.2K. It seems likely however that computer

274. Carroll, Part II, at 145.
275. Case No. H 106, 8 *Tax'n Bd. of Revsvs Cas.* 484 *(Bd. of Revsvs* No. 3, Sydney, Austl. 1957).
276. *Id.* at 486.
277. *Id.* at 488 (opinion of Member McCaffrey).

hardware of a sufficient size or entrepreneurial importance could be included, as summarized below.

2. *Computers and Servers*

In *ATO ID 2006/337*, the Australian Tax Office (ATO) ruled that the computer system of a NRE engaged in securities trading was not a substantial equipment PE. The equipment consisted on ten pieces of hardware weighing 164 kilograms and worth $200,000, including servers and routers and software used for market access and trading algorithms.[278]

Cases and rulings outside the Australian concept of 'substantial equipment' do not seem constrained by size. It is clear that automated vending machines can be a POB PE.[279] At least two cases have found source country servers to be a fixed POB PE provided they are under the control of an operated by a NRE and used in a core aspect of its business, a position which is also supported by the OECD Commentary e-commerce provisions.[280]

Finally, two Indian rulings have held that the promotional provision of some dumbed down computers to travel agents – as an alternative means – of accessing an offshore airline computer reservation system (CRS) constituted a fixed POB PE of an NRE owner of such system where the CRS mainframe servers and airlines were all offshore, where bookings and payments were

---

278. *See also Games Co*, Administrative Appeals Tribunal (Australia) Case U162 dated 5 August 1987 (87 ATC 942) (discussed in Mehta at 28) which involved the taxability of a loan out company of a US professional golf player who earned substantial endorsement fees by competing for 24 and 28 days in Australian golf events; the Tribunal held that 'substantial equipment' could not include a set of golf clubs or anything else associated with the taxpayers' activities in Australia; cf. Article 17, taxation of artists and athletes. *And see*, *Golf in Dubai LLC*, In re [2008] 174 Taxmann 480 (AAR – New Delhi), also discussed in Mehta at 32 and reproduced in Mehta, Appendix One, which held that 2 Indian golf courses rented by a UAE company for a weeks' tournaments did not constitute a fixed place of business for failure of the permanence test.

279. *See e.g., Reimer* at 42

280. Case No. II/1224/97 (6 Sep 2001, *Finanzgericht* of Schleswig Holstein) (German company's server on leased Swiss premises containing customer data relating to the company's core business in Switzerland was POB PE even though not maintained by Swiss employees). Discussed by Mehta at 50. Russo comments that the Italian tax authorities reached a similar conclusion in *Resolution 119* involving a French provider of online video games to Italian subscribers. Although it had no employees in Italy, the French company owned two servers through an Italian ISP. The French company configured the servers and their operation (including online delivery of game services to Italian customers) directly from France. The Italian tax authority's ruling holds that the servers could constitute a fixed place of business PE where the (1) servers were at the disposal of the NRE, (2) were located in the same place for a significant period and (3) were used to carry out the NRE's core business. R. Russo & E Pedrazzini, *Permanent Establishments under Italian Tax Law: An Overview*, European Taxation 289, at 393 (Aug-Sept 2007).

made offshore and where the NRE had no employees, offices or agents in India.[281]

In the author's view, the decisions in these two Indian cases were contrary to the OECD commentary since the provided computers were ancillary to the NRE's core CRS business, and were not necessary to it as travel agents could directly access the system through their own computers and a telecommunications node, were not kept at one fixed location of economic and commercial coherence and did not constitute a 'place of business' in any common sense of the words.

3. Logging and Other Equipment

The concept that personal property may constitute the fixed-place element of the permanent establishment formula under general treaty language may have originated in an American private letter ruling given in 1955.[282] It involved 'the inventor and manufacturer of special equipment which permits [the cutting of timber] on high and steep mountain slopes where ordinary methods cannot be employed.' This individual constructed a demonstration model of his invention which he brought to the United States for a series of demonstrations lasting 'up to two years.' In resolving the issue, the author of the ruling quotes from the applicable treaty the following provision:

> 'The maintenance within the territory of one of the contracting States by an enterprise of the other contracting State of a warehouse for convenience of delivery and not for purposes of display shall not of itself constitute a permanent establishment within that territory even though offers of purchase have been obtained by an agent of the enterprise in that territory and transmitted by him to the enterprise for acceptance.'[283]

Conceding that the taxpayer had no warehouse in the United States, the author observed that:

> 'he undeniably brought his machinery into this country "for purposes of display" with the hope and expectation of obtaining orders for such machinery. It is therefore held that he is engaged in trade or business within the United States through a permanent establishment located therein.'

---

281. *Amadeus* and *Galileo*, discussed at length supra under 2.02 (A).
282. Ltr. Rul. 5501105410A.
283. The treaty involved has been deleted from the ruling.

Rev. Rul. 56-165[284] appeared the following year. It was a re-run of the earlier ruling. The inventor had become a manufacturer, the machinery was identified as logging equipment, and the treaty involved became the Swiss convention. The crucial treaty term involving warehousing-for-display was paraphrased. The conclusion was as follows:

> 'Although the enterprise under consideration has no warehouse or other type of building in the United States in which or from which it is conducted, the equipment involved is logging equipment which is necessarily demonstrated in particular forest areas and was brought here for purposes of such demonstration with the expectation that orders would be obtained for such equipment. It is anticipated that the demonstration and sales activities will continue for approximately two years.
>
> Accordingly, it is held that a resident of Switzerland, who is engaged in the United States in demonstrating and selling logging equipment, together with the logs produced during such demonstrations, is carrying on an enterprise which is "engaged in trade or business in the United States through a permanent establishment situated therein" within the meaning of article III(1)(a) of the United States–Switzerland tax convention.'[285]

Because the applicable treaty did not specify the use of substantial equipment as a fixed-place permanent establishment, the ruling seems questionable on that ground. The result is possibly sustainable as a dependent-agency permanent establishment if the taxpayer, who was himself present in the United States for two years, may be regarded as a dependent agent of his own enterprise.[286]

4. *The Race Horse Rulings*

Six American rulings involving racehorses have contributed substantially to the confusion in the area.[287] The first was a private ruling dated in 1957. There, the issue was whether a $70,000 purse won by a horse owned by an unnamed alien individual was taxable in the United States. The author of the ruling recited the permanent establishment and business profits provisions of an unnamed tax treaty, and concluded that:

284. 1956-1 *C.B.* 849.
285. *Id.* at 850.
286. *See howevser* § 5.11, which deals with a proprietor as agent of his own enterprise.
287. *See*, R. Preston, *Race Horse Permanent Establishment* (1985) (available in Marian Gallagher Law Library, University of Washington, Seattle).

> 'The owner is not considered to have a permanent establishment in the United States merely by reason of bringing his horse to this country nor because he came here to view the race and participate in the social events connected therewith. Accordingly, the purse of $70,000 ... is exempt from United States income tax ...'[288]

No mention of the size of the purse appeared in a Revenue Ruling published the following year.[289] The conclusion was the same. But a significant change appeared in the statement of the holding:

> 'Accordingly it is held that a nonresident alien individual does not have a permanent establishment in the United States merely by entering a race horse in a single race in the United States and coming to the United States to view the race and to participate in the social events connected therewith.'[290]

If one race is exempt, what about four? The answer came in 1959, in a private letter ruling concerning entering a trotting horse in 'about four races.'[291] Apparently on the sole basis that four races 'would require stabling and related activities in the United States,' the author ruled that the horse-owner would have a permanent establishment in the United States. However unlikely that the horses mentioned in the earlier rulings were deprived of 'stabling and related activities,' these activities form the basis of this ruling. Is the author concerned about the absence of a fixed place of business? Is this an oblique ruling that the racing business is being conducted in these stables? As in the earlier instance, a Revenue Ruling[292] followed. But this one approached the problem from a different angle. The winner's purse was now subject to withholding.

> 'Accordingly, it is held that in the absence of definite information that a nonresident alien individual does not intend to enter a horse in another race in the United States during the taxable year, tax must be withheld from the winnings received by such nonresident alien individual from the entry of a horse in a race in this country, even though such winning may be exempt from Federal income tax from the provisions of a tax convention.'

288. Ltr. Rul. 5701094530A.
289. Rev. Rul. 58-63, 1958-1 *CB*. 624.
290. *Id*. at 625.
291. Ltr. Rul. 5910025160A.
292. Rev. Rul. 60-288, 1960-2 *C.B*. 265.

The safe area seems to have been narrowed to one race. And the rationale had shifted. The ruling asserts that:

> 'a "permanent establishment" may be acquired by the nonresident alien's entering his horse, or other horses owned by him, in other races in the United States during the taxable year.'[293]

The field was quiet for a score of years. A 1981 private letter ruling[294] reopened the inquiry. There the issue was whether racing personnel were required to withhold when a winner's purse was paid to a nonresident alien horse-owner who filed an official form denying the existence of a permanent establishment.[295] The ruling is less significant for taking four pages to produce a negative answer to the question than it is for the following classic dictum:

> 'The entering of a horse in more than one race, which may constitute a permanent establishment, is a rule designed to prevent a misapplication of treaty benefits. The substantive application of this rule is governed by the principle that the entering of a horse in more than one race does not in and of itself constitute a fixed place of business, but because of the underlying activities conducted in respect to the racing of the horse, a permanent establishment could arise. The Service will consider, in part, activities such as an owner or agent, with general contracting authority, concluding contracts within the United States with respect to the entry of the horse in a race, the stabling or training of the horse and his length of stay with the United States, as factors that may constitute the nonresident alien owner having a permanent establishment in the United States.'

Rev. Rul. 85-4[296] covers substantially the same territory, concluding that withholding must occur, despite the foreigner's filing the official form, if the race track operators have:

> 'information that the owner has raced a horse in another race during the taxable year (e.g., from the racing history papers provided [race track personnel] upon entry of a horse in a race).'

---

293. *Id.* at 265. The ruling was later cited for the proposition that withholding was required 'where definite information does not exist that the nonresident alien will not enter horses in more than one race.' Ltr. Rul. 6704066110A.

294. Ltr. Rul. 8138020.

295. Specifically, IRS Form 1001.

296. 1985-2 *C.B. 6*. The ruling seems to dash the hopes that the position stated in Rev. Rul. 60-249 had been abandoned. *See* Vogel, at 288, para. 28a.

What these six rulings seem to hold is that a permanent establishment may ensue from entering a horse in two or more races during the year in either of two factual circumstances. In the first, the owner has leased or operated a fixed place of business (stables and training facilities) in connection with the racing activity over a continuous period of time. In the second, the owner has himself been physically present and has concluded contracts (personally or through a dependent agent) regarding the maintenance and racing of the horse.[297]

What the rulings do not hold is that the horse itself constitutes a personal-property permanent establishment. Nor do the rulings equate permanent establishment status with certain activity level (entering two or more horse races, for example) independent of either a fixed-place or a dependent-agent permanent establishment.[298]

5. *Net Leasing of Containers*

The net leasing of containers is a particular case which is discussed in the OECD's 1983 Report on *The Taxation of Income Derived from the Leasing of Containers*.[299] Container leasing companies rent containers all over the world. A lessee may surrender his container to any one of more than 100 depots in 40 countries. Most depots are owned and operated by independent companies which receive the containers, inventory and inspect them and deliver them to their new customers. The agent will charge a fee to the leasing company for the use of the warehouse and for its services provided.

The OECD Report Guidelines state that such a simple independent agent depot does not constitute a PE of the lessor being exempt under Article 5(4). Where the lessor has contractual depot agents (*depot-agence*), no PE is suggested if the agent serves other leasing companies. If the *depot-agence* is owned and operated by the lessor however, a PE exists. Finally, the Report states that repair and maintenance activities will normally be considered PE-free preparatory and auxiliary activities.

Rents from the leasing of containers should also be exempt from withholding tax imposed on royalties under article 12 of the OECD Model, as 'royalties' are limited to intangible property and do not include rents from tangible

297. The ruling that withholding is due in single-race situations – Revs Rul. 60-288,1960-2 *C.B.* 265 – must be viewed as a tax official's attempt to protect the fisc. It should cast no inference as to the existence of a permanent establishment.
298. The horse-race rulings and the Swiss logging ruling constituted the bases for the conclusion, on the part of the author, that an 'activities' type of permanent establishment existed independently of the fixed-place and dependent agent types of permanent establishment. *See* Williams, 'Permanent Establishments in the United States,' in *Income Tax Treaties* 189, 310 (J. Bischel ed. 1979).
299. OECD Model Tax Convention 2010, Appendix II Report 3

property, which are only taxable if connected to a permanent establishment. Satellite transponder leasing and telecom roaming payments received by an NRE from a source country lessee are also exempt from source country taxation under the above principles.[300] Article 8 allocates exclusive taxation of shipping and air transportation profits to the country of effective management of the craft.

6. *Vending Machines, Servers and Other Automated Equipment*

Vending machines, like servers and other automatic equipment, may constitute a fixed POB PE if managed and operated by the owner. See the discussion in Chapter 2.1.E.1 above.[301]

7. *Semisubmersible Drilling Vessels*

A letter ruling published in 1985 concludes that a 'semi-submersible drilling vessel, conducting oil and gas exploration activity on the outer continental shelf (OCS) of the United States' constitutes a permanent establishment under the United States–Netherlands tax convention.[302] Having withdrawn an earlier ruling[303] in which it had held that the vessel was a 'place of extraction of natural resources' the Internal Revenue Service proceeded to rule that it was a 'construction project.'[304] Then, stating that it recognized 'the possible argument that such drilling activity is outside the scope of that provision,[305] the Service ruled 'as an alternative basis' that the vessel was a fixed place of business. Drawing an analogy to the construction-project for the geographic aspect and importing the construction-project time period as an indication of the temporal aspect, the Service concluded that the vessel operator had a fixed place of business.[306]

---

300. OECD Model Commentary, Art. 12, paras 9-9.2
301. *See* Vogel, at 290, para. 35 ('Vending machines and other automated devices may very well be permanent establishments if the enterprise engages in business beyond the mere installation of such machines.').
302. Ltr. Rul. 8426005. See S. Eskenazi, PLR 8526005: 'Permanent Establishment Defined?' (1985) (available in Marian Gallagher Law Library, University of Washington, Seattle).
303. Ltr. Rul. 8424007.
304. *See* section 3.8, *infra*.
305. As well it might. The term 'places of extraction of natural resources' does not include the exploration of such resources. If not specially dealt with, it must be governed by general fixed-place-of-business principles. OECD Model Commentary, Art. 5(2), para. 14. Such special provisions appear, *inter alia*, at United States–Canada V(4) and Norway–United Kingdom 23.
306. *See* Section 4.6, *infra*, 'Operations in Contiguous Waters.'

8. *Other Ships*

While the taxation of ships or aircraft used in the international transportation of cargo or passengers is generally exempt from source country taxation,[307] other uses of ships raise the issue whether a ship can ever be regarded as a POB permanent establishment. If a permanently-docked ship is used for commercial purposes – as a hotel, a restaurant, or a shopping site – the conclusion seems easy to reach. Such ships – the largest of which is the Queen Mary, permanently docked at Long Beach, California – have become features of urban waterfronts around the world. They should be treated as any other items of personal property that is permanently affixed to the land.

But permanent establishments have attached to ships that were actually moving in international traffic. A German ruling[308] finds a permanent establishment with respect to a restaurant concession on a ferry operating between Germany and Denmark. And in *Fugro Engineers BV vs ACIT*[309] and Indian Tax Tribunal held that a moving ship doing underwater geotechnical exploration was a 'fixed' place of business. The German ruling can be explained as based on a dependent agency conducted within German flag jurisdiction, and not upon a fixed-place-of-business finding. The Indian ruling is highly questionable.

2.3 BUSINESS ACTIVITY – WHAT IS IT?

> '[t]he term "permanent establishment",' asserts the OECD Model Convention, 'means a fixed place of business through which the business of an enterprise is wholly or partly carried on.'[310] The business need not be productive, adds the Commentary, although it is 'surely axiomatic to assume' that it will be.[311]

Business activities must be continuous, regular, and 'considerable,'[312] if they are to fill out the business-activity element of permanent establishment. And carrying on the day-to-day, ordinary routine business usually requires staff.[313]

307. *See*, e.g., OECD MC Article 8.
308. Judgment of 13 February 1974, BFH, West Germany, *IR* 219/71, discussed *infra* at section 5.01(h). See also the questionable *French Canal Boat* and *Turkish Yacht* case decisions discussed *supra* at fnn. 85 and 86.
309. (2008, Delhi), 26 SOT 78, discussed in Mehta at 77 and reproduced at Mehta, Appendix One
310. OECD Model 5(1).
311. OECD Model Commentary, Art. 5(1), para. 3.
312. *Herbert vs Commissioner*, 30 *T.C.* 26, 33 (1958).
313. *Consolidated Premium Iron Ores, Ltd. vs Commissioner*, 28 *T.C.* 127, 152 (1957).

Everyone in the area wants to talk about 'business' or 'enterprise.' Few seem to have undertaken to define just what is meant by the term. One case however, *Inverworld vs Commissioner*,[314] contains a comprehensive discussion of the US law concerning what constitutes a 'trade or business.'

The US and other country[315] concepts are broadly similar to the treaty term, but in the treaty sense the main function of the terms 'enterprise' and 'business' is to distinguish 'business' from 'passive' income.[316] Passive income in common law jurisdictions is commonly referred to a 'property income,' that is income from financial assets, but also includes passive income from physical assets such as rental income and from intangible assets such as royalties, provided it is not effectively connected with a PE.[317] Thus, mere investment or leasing or hiring or assets would not be a 'business'; however, active trading for others in securities or management of a collective investment fund would be.

In this broad sense, income from farms, agriculture and forestry would be included,[318] although sharecropping and the sale of timber cutting rights might come closer to the line of passive investment.[319] Income from real property is of course source country taxable under article 6 OECD MC, but the significance of including such income on an operational PE level would be relevant to attract taxation of effectively connected income (e.g., interest and royalties).[320]

---

314. T.C. Memo 1996-301, T1 TCM 3231, 3237-28 to 3237-30 (1966) contains the most complete definition of 'trade or business' and what constitutes a US taxable trade or business in the US lexicon.
315. *See Thiel vs FCT (Fed. Comm'r of Taxation)* 171 CLR 338, 90 ATC 4717 (1990 High Court of Australia; Reimer at 38
316. Reimer at 37
317. *See e.g.* Treaty articles 10(4) (EC dividends), 11(4) (EC interest), and 12(3) (EC royalties) of OECD MC
318. Reimer at 40; *contra,* Vogel, K in Vogel & Lehner (ed.), *Doppelsteuerungsabkommen. Kommentar.* 5th ed. 2008, Art 3 at m.no. 41a; per Reimer at 40.
319. Forestry income is concessionally taxed as capital gains in the United States and generally exempt in the UK.
320. OEC 2012 Revised Discussion Draft, which includes farms as potential PEs

Chapter 3

Building Sites and Construction or Assembly Projects

3.1 BACKGROUND

The OECD Model creates a special category of permanent establishment for 'a building site or construction or installation project' – referred to herein as a 'construction assembly site' or 'CAS' PE. Such site or project constitutes a permanent establishment under a single set of circumstances: 'if it lasts more than twelve months.'[1] The provision is not of recent fabrication. The Finnish treaty with Sweden, signed in March of 1931, states:

> 'The site of a building, the construction of which has exceeded or, as far as can be estimated, will exceed a period of 12 months, and shall be regarded as a permanent business establishment within the meaning of the Convention.'[2]

The provision failed to be included in League of Nations draft conventions prior to 1943. It emerged, in both the Mexico Draft and the London Draft,[3] in language almost identical to that of the Finland–Sweden Convention.[4] It was confined, as was its predecessor, to the construction of buildings. The construction of roads, bridges, dams, power lines and all of the rest were plainly outside of its coverage.

As late as 1965, the issue whether, in the absence of specific treaty provisions, construction or assembly projects were permanent establishments was discussed in a major American journal.[5] The article detailed the controversy that had produced a 1962 protocol to the United States–Japan treaty then in

---

1. OECD Model 5(3).
2. Finland–Sweden (1931) Protocol 10.
3. London Draft V(2); Mexico Draft V(2).
4. League of Nations Fiscal Committee, London and Mexico Model Conventions, Commentary and Text, Official No. C.88.M.88. 1946.2.A. (1946); 4 *LHUSTC* 4321.
5. *See* Roberts, Goldberg & Mallin, 'Are Construction Projects "Permanent Establishments"?,' 22 J. *Tax'n* 164(1965).

force. The protocol provided that an enterprise was to be deemed to have a permanent establishment if it carried out a construction, installation, or assembly project for more than 12 months or carried on supervisory activities in connection with such a project for more than 12 months.[6]

The OECD Draft Convention published the following year differed from the United States–Japan treaty in three important respects. First of all, the reference to supervisory activities was dropped. Secondly, the targeted activity became 'a building site or construction or assembly project.' Finally, the original freestanding provision was reduced to simply an example of a 'fixed place of business.[7]The 1963 Commentary is not in the least informative as to what may have motivated the creation of these differences:

> 'The terms "building site or construction or assembly project" cover constructional activities such as excavating and dredging. The provision that a building site or assembly project shall only be deemed to be a permanent establishment if it exists for more than twelve months is not intended to prevent a country from raising a tax assessment before a year has expired if it appears that the site or project is likely to last for more than twelve months. The period of twelve months may, of course, fall, in part, into more than one fiscal year.'[8]

Fourteen years later, the 1977 OECD Model Convention changed the crucial language to 'building site or construction or installation project.' More important, it restored the status of a free-standing provision that described a separate form of permanent establishment. No longer was it merely an example of a fixed place of business. The significance of the substitution of 'installation' for 'assembly' is unclear.[9] What is clear is that one of these 'sites' or 'projects' can constitute a permanent establishment irrespective of the presence or absence

---

6. United States–Japan, Protocol 1(1) (1962), reprinted at 7 W. Diamond & D. Diamond, *International Tax Treaties of All Nations* 204 (1976). 'This was supposed to reach a large United States corporation which maintained in Tokyo a staff of engineers and officers to supervise the installation of heavy equipment sold to a Japanese company.' Carroll, Part II at 146 (1968).
7. OECD Draft 2(g).
8. OECD Draft Commentary, Art. 5(2), para. 8 (8th, 9th, and 10th sentences). The true reason for moving them to a separate paragraph of the convention goes to the very nature of these sites and projects: they are almost never permanent. Their retention in the list of permanent establishment examples would have resulted in the view that they invariably constituted permanent establishments even when patently temporary. *See* Vogel, at 305, para. 72.
9. The inquiry is not assisted by the Fiscal Committee's dropping of the plural form of the word from the OECD Draft: '"Installations" has also been left out as being a term so general as to be virtually meaningless.' OECD Draft Commentary, Art. 5, para. 8 (fifth sentence).

of a fixed place of business. Hence, defining these terms and ascertaining how long each site or project 'lasts' (or is likely to 'last') become crucial tasks.[10]

Four years later, the 1980 UN Model Treaty included the 1977 OECD Model provision on construction projects, with the following changes:

- 'assembly' was included in the UN model, although it is debatable whether its omission from the OECD model has an substantive significance
- the time period is reduced to 6 months in the UN provision – from 12 months in the OECD provision
- UN Model article 5(3)(b) adds a 'Services PE' provision, which has never been accepted in the OECD model although the 2008 OECD Commentary offers an optional Services PE provision similar to the following UN provision:

> 'The furnishing of services, including consultancy services, by an enterprise through employees or other personnel engaged by the enterprise for such purpose, but only if activities of that nature continue (for the same or a connected project) within a Contracting State for a period or periods aggregating more than 183 days in any 12 month period commencing or ending in the fiscal year concerned.'

The OECD 2008 optional Services PE provision also offers an alternative Services PE category, which seems targeted at a self-employed individual who provides a principal part of his services in the source country over a 183-day period:

> 'a) through an individual who is present in that other State for a period or periods exceeding in the aggregate 183 days in any twelve month period, and more than 50 per cent of the gross revenues attributable to active business activities of the enterprise during this period or periods are derived from the services performed in that other State'[11]

This provision in effect extends source country taxation of an entrepreneur who provides services in the source country over a 183-day period though not through a fixed base (as fixed base services would be taxable under former OECD Article 14 (now repealed as duplicative of Article 5 taxation).

10. OECD Commentary, para. 16
11. OECD Commentary, para 42.23

3.2 BUILDING SITES

The 2010 OECD Commentary defines 'building site or construction or installation projects' as including:

> 'not only the construction of buildings, but also the construction of roads, bridges or canals, the renovation (including more than mere maintenance or redecoration) of buildings, roads, bridges or canals, the laying of pipe-lines and excavating and dredging. Additionally, the term "installation project" is not restricted to an installation related to a construction project; it also includes the installation of new equipment, such as a complex machine, in an existing building or outdoors. On-site planning and supervision of the erection of a building are covered by paragraph 3.'[12]

A building site should be regarded as a single unit:

> 'even if it is based on several contracts, provided that it forms a coherent whole commercially and geographically. Subject to this proviso, a building site forms a single unit even if the orders have been placed by several persons (e.g., for a row of houses).'[13]

And finally, it asserts that a 'site' – presumably a building site – includes an on-site planning office for the projected construction.[14] Routine repairs are not considered to be a CAS project although the resurfacing of an entire road system might be.[15]

3.3 CONSTRUCTION PROJECTS

In his 1968 article, Mitchell B. Carroll explained the adoption of the 'novel provision' in the 1962 protocol to the United States–Japan treaty in the following language:

---

12. *OECD Model Commentary, Art. 5(3), paras 17, 19.1. Interestingly, the original Commentary provided* 'Moreover, planning and supervision of the erection of a building are covered by this term, *if carried out by the building contractor*.' (emphasis added)
13. *Id.* at para. 18.
14. *Id.* at para. 17.
15. *Id.* at paras 17; *See generally*, Conger, *Doing Business in Japan: Permanent Establishment through Construction Projects*, available at Marian Gallagher Law Library, University of Washington, Seattle.

> 'This was supposed to reach a large United States corporation which maintained in Tokyo a staff of engineers and officers to supervise the installation of heavy equipment sold to a Japanese company.'[16]

The language of the treaty provision has no parallel in United States tax law. It closely parallels the language of the Japanese statutes.[17] Japanese domestic materials might contribute materially in delimiting the concept. It is unfortunate that they do little more than restate the rules in the statute.[18]

The OECD 1963 Draft Commentary added little. The statement that the terms in the treaty 'cover constructional activities such as excavating or dredging'[19] is informative, although hardly comprehensive.

The OECD Model Commentary is more forthcoming. In attempting to define the term 'building site or construction or installation project,' the authors state that 'the construction of buildings'[20] probably occurs at a 'building site' but must be regarded as 'construction' as well. The 'construction of roads, bridges or canals'[21] is by definition 'construction,' as is 'excavation and dredging.'[22] Renovation of buildings, roads, bridges or canals is also covered by this provision, as long as such renovation involves more than maintenance or redecoration.[23]

In *Pastor Engineering*,[24] a Croatian company performed engineering works through its Moscow office (e.g. installation of fire alarm systems, electricity cables, air conditioning, etc.). Having relied on the domestic definition of 'construction works', the tax authorities argued that the engineering works did not qualify as 'construction', and that the CAS PE provision of the Russia–Croatia treaty was not applicable. The Court, however, held that engineering works were closely related to the construction and thus came within the scope of CAS PEs.

What happens when a construction project is ended prematurely? Is design work preceding construction within the scope of the term 'construction'?

---

16. Carroll, Part II at 146 (1968).
17. 'A foreign corporation ... that carries on, within this country, construction, installation, assembly, or other work, or the rendition of services to direct or supervise such work ...' Japan Corporation Tax Law, Art. 141(3), as translated in J. Huston, T. Miyatake & G. Way, *Japanese International Taxation* S-10.11 (1985).
18. *Id.* at § 2.02[3].
19. OECD Draft Commentary, Art. 5(2), para. 8.
20. OECD Model Commentary, Art. 5(3), para. 17.
21. *Ibid.*
22. *Ibid.*
23. *Ibid.*
24. MDFAC, 24 Nov. 2003, KA-A40/9307-03, discussed in O. Konnov, E. Smirnov & H. Smith, Russia – Permanent Establishments, Topical Analyses IBFD (accessed 29 June 2013).

In *Skanska East Europe Oy*,[25] a Finnish company was commissioned to build a church in Russia. After the completion of design works, the construction agreement was terminated by mutual agreement. The Court held that the Finnish company did not have a CAS PE because design works prior to the start of the construction itself did not qualify as 'construction'.[26]

3.4 INSTALLATION PROJECTS

The appearance of the term 'installation' in OECD tax treaties is traceable in part to the first United States–Japan treaty. As earlier mentioned,[27] the 'supervisory activities' term in that treaty targeted a particular American corporation supervising the installation of specific items of heavy equipment in Japan.[28]

The OECD Model Commentary confirms that installation of heavy equipment also comes within the purview of this provision:

> '... the term "installation project" is not restricted to an installation related to a construction project; it also includes the installation of new equipment, such as a complex machine, in an existing building or outdoors'[29]

3.5 ASSEMBLY PROJECT

The very short tenure of the term 'assembly' in OECD treaties requires explanation. Absent from the London and Mexico Drafts, the term appeared in the 1963 OECD Draft Convention in the phrase 'a building site or construction or assembly project.'[30] Beyond the statement that those words 'cover constructional activities such as excavating or dredging,'[31] the Draft Commentary is silent as to the meaning of the terms.

The term was summarily excised from the 1977 OECD Model Convention. The phrase became '[a] building site or construction or installation project.'[32] One would think that some explanation for the excision and substi-

25. NWDFAC, 3 Mar. 2005, A56-24202/04, *Id.*
26. In addition, the conditions for the existence of a POB PE were not met due to lack of permanency.
27. In text at Section 3.02 *supra*.
28. Carroll, Part II at 146.
29. OECD Model Commentary, Art. 5(3), para. 17.
30. OECD Draft 5(2)(g).
31. OECD Model Commentary, Art. 5(1), para. 8.
32. OECD Model 5(3).

tution might appear in the Model Commentary. After all, 'installation' and 'assembly' are hardly synonymous. More important, an assembly project that did not fall within either of the other terms of this provision would be a permanent establishment under the Draft but would not be a permanent establishment under the Model.

The OECD Model Commentary includes no reference either to the original adoption of the term or to its demise. One can only speculate that the change was motivated by the possibility that 'assembly' occurred in the exempt activities of storage, display, processing, or delivery.

Indeed, the resurrection of the term in the 1980 United Nations Model Convention may be attributable to the deletion, in that Convention, of 'delivery' from the list of auxiliary and preliminary activities – i.e., to make it clear that in the UN Model, on site assembly could not be considered exempt processing or manufacturing.[33] The 2011 UN Model does not define 'assembly' either.

There are occasional references in the literature to 'assembly projects.'[34] The term appears in numerous treaties but precisely what the term 'assembly' means in the treaty context remains unresolved.[35]

3.6 SUPERVISORY ACTIVITIES

The guise in which the term 'supervisory activities' is most easily recognized is that of the UN Model, which states that the term permanent establishment 'likewise encompasses':

> 'A building site, a construction, assembly or installation project or supervisory activities in connection therewith.'[36]

The supervisory-activities provision is a popular one. Although it is usually to be found in treaties between developing and developed countries, it is not so confined. The current treaty between Australia and the United States contains a special provision to this effect,[37] as does its treaty with New Zealand[38]

33. UN Model 5(4)(a) and (b). *See* UN Model Commentary, Art. 5, para. 4.
34. *See,* e.g., Parliamentary Question, 12 June 1979, Belgium, p. 874 *Vragen en Antwoorden van de Kamer van Volksvertegenwoordigers,* 3 July 1979, summarized in 1 *International Tax Treaties,* Art. 5, p. 28 (Edwardes-Ker ed. 1979) (German enterprise delivering and assembling machinery in Belgium).
35. As to analogous interpretation of these provisions, *see* Skaar at 214.
36. UN Model, Art. 5(3) (f).
37. United States–Australia 5(4)(c).
38. United States–New Zealand 5(4). The provision appears also at Sweden–New Zealand 4(4)(a) and New Zealand–Switzerland 5(5)(a).

Adoption of the term has as its purpose the shifting of the taxes earned by supervisory activities from the country of residence of the foreign supervisor to the country of source.[39] Its appearance in the UN Model constitutes one facet of the compromise of competing interests represented by that Model[40]

The first appearance of the term seems to have occurred in the 1962 Protocol to the former United States–Japan convention.[41] Its purpose was that of resolving a controversy concerning a 'large United States corporation which maintained in Tokyo a staff of engineers and officers to supervise the installation of heavy equipment sold to a Japanese company.'[42] The United States had maintained that, without more, supervisory activities do not amount to a permanent establishment.[43] In the 1962 Protocol, the Japanese view prevailed (and the separate construction-project category was born).[44]

The United States maintained its original posture in an exchange of notes regarding the 1962 United States treaty with Luxembourg. The outcome is somewhat equivocal, but unique nevertheless. The Luxembourg tax director asserts, in response to an American hypothetical question regarding technicians supervising the installation of equipment delivered by a Luxembourg enterprise, that their 'directing and supervising installation of the equipment' would constitute 'a building site, or construction or assembly project' under the treaty were it to last for more than six months.[45] No reply to the assertion is recorded.

The United States Internal Revenue Service reiterated its view in a 1977 Revenue Ruling,[46] in which it held that supervisory activities were exempt under the United States–Canada tax convention which, at the time, contained no special provision for building sites or construction projects, much less supervisory activities. Stated the author of the Ruling:

---

39. *See* Moore, 'The Permanent Establishment Concept in Tax Treaties: Old Bottles for New Wine?,' 6 *Queen's L. J.* 483 (1981).
40. *See* Michaels, *Interpretation of the Use of the Term 'Supervisory Activities' in Recent United States Tax Treaties* (unpublished manuscript, available at Marian Gallagher Law Library, University of Washington, Seattle).
41. United States–Japan, Prot. I(1) (1962). The Memorandum of the Joint Committee on Internal Revenue Taxation accompanying that treaty summarizes the provision. 2 *Tax Treaties* (P-H) 54,146. Thereafter it asserts that 'this method of treatment is consistent with' the United States treaties with Austria, West Germany, and Luxembourg, as well as the OECD Model. None of these conventions contain a supervisory-activities provision.
42. Carroll, Part II at 146 (1968).
43. Memorandum of the Joint Committee on Internal Revenue Taxation, 2 *Tax Treaties* (P-H) 54,146, 2 *Tax Treaties* (CCH) 5640.
44. *Ibid.* The 'supervisory activities' language does not appear in the current United States–Japan convention. *See* Huston, Miyatake & *Way, Japanese International Taxation* § 2.03[4] n. 56.
45. *See* 'Exchange of Correspondence Clarifying the Interpretation of the Term "A Place of Management",' 2 *Tax Treaties* (P-H) 60,124 (Letters of Surrey and Schaus).
46. Rev. Rul. 77-45, 1977-1 *C.B.* 413.

> 'Planning and supervision of construction work do not of themselves ... make a construction site a construction site of the enterprise that plans and supervises construction. Thus, since [the Canadian firm's] activities are restricted to supervision and planning, whether they constitute a permanent establishment must be considered without regard to determinations applicable to construction sites.'[47]

Concluding that the firm had neither a fixed place of business nor a dependent agent, the author ruled that it had no permanent establishment in the United States.

Similarly, in *Chupin*,[48] the French *Conseil d'Etat* seemed to suggest that a mere supervisory activity in respect of construction sites should not lead to a CAS PE. The case concerned a French taxpayer supervising the construction of a hotel and a place of extraction of natural resources in Togo and Benin. The Court held that the activity in question was not attributable to a PE, and was thus taxable in France.[49]

A similar result was reached by an Indian High Court[50] involving a German engineer who supervised the installation of a 'bucket-wheel reclaimer.' The court, after examining European and Indian authorities, concluded that the engineer's activities did not constitute a permanent establishment under the general construction-project language of the applicable tax convention:

> 'He was only delegated to India for supervision... [T]he work of construction, installation or assembly was actually done by the Port Trust and not by the German engineer.'[51]

The 1977 American ruling[52] offers some specificity regarding what constitutes 'supervision.' The Canadian corporation in question was a consulting engineering firm. It planned and designed manufacturing plants. It evaluated

47. *Ibid.*
48. *Conseil d'Etat*, 30 December 2002, No. 229072, *Chupin*, RJF 3/03 No. 261. Discussed in Deltour, France – Permanent Establishments, Topical Analyses IBFD (accessed 29 June 2013) and Gouthière, Key Practical Issues in Eliminating the Double Taxation of Business Income, 65 Bull. Intl. Taxn. 4/5 (2011), Journals IBFD (accessed 29 June 2013).
49. In contrast, the German *Bundesfinanzhof* held that a non-resident general contractor who had carried out only supervisory activities in respect of a complex construction project, but had subcontracted the actual construction work, had a CAS PE where the duration requirement was met. *See* BFH, 13 Nov. 1962, BStBl III 1963, p. 71, discussed in Lewicki, A Construction Consortium as a Permanent Establishment from an International Tax Law Perspective: Inconsistencies and Deficiencies in Article 5(3) of the OECD Model and Commentary, 66 Bull. Intl. Taxn. 1 (2012), Journals IBFD (accessed 29 June 2013).
50. *Commissioner vs Visakhapatnam Port Trust*, 144 *Income Tax Kept*. (India) 146 (1983).
51. *Id.* at 166.
52. Rev. Rul. 77-45, 1977-1 *C.B.* 415.

actual sites and modified its plans to accommodate on-site conditions. It sent employees who inspected contractor work performance and the quality of materials, made minor changes in plans and specifications, checked contractor billings, kept account of job progress, and reported to their home office. These employees worked either in a construction shed or in a warehouse or workshop provided by the client. Their work space was furnished with the client's furniture and equipment. The Canadian firm bargained separately for neither work space nor equipment. Given facts paralleling the foregoing pattern, one can state with confidence that the activity is 'supervision.'

Up until 2003, the OECD seems to have concurred with respect to planning and supervision undertaken by a non-construction contractor. Moreover, the workplace of such a third party supervisor was sheltered:

> 'However, planning and supervision is not included [within the term "building site or construction or installation project"], if carried out by another enterprise whose activities in connection with the construction concerned are restricted to planning and supervising the work. If that other enterprise has an office which it uses only for planning or supervision activities relating to a site or project which does not constitute a permanent establishment, such office does not constitute a fixed place of business within the meaning of paragraph 1, because its existence has not a certain degree of permanence.'[53]

However the current version of the Commentary, as proposed to be amended by the 2012 Revised Discussion Draft, only refers to the inclusion of onsite planning and supervision from the commencement of work.[54] Whether third party supervision and planning is still excluded is therefore subject to some variables, e.g., the date of the applicable treaty (as well as its precise language), whether the third party is independently contracted by the property owner or instead by the general contractor, whether there is a nonprofit sharing joint venture, and so forth. As stated by Reimer in his 2009 treatise:[55]

> 'A dispute has arisen on whether a PE can be constituted by the on-site planning and on-site supervision of the erection of a building. While there is no doubt that situations in which the enterprise carries on both supervisory and proper building activities qualify, the mere supervi-

53. OECD Model Commentary, Art. 5, para. 17 (prior to 2003).
54. Revised Commentary Article 5(3), para. 19.
55. Reimer at 75, citing Baker, P, *Double Taxation Conventions*, loose-leaf ed. Art 5 at m.no. 5B.16, referring to *Cour Administratif d'Appel de Nancy* decision of 9 May 1996, Case No. 94-914, RJF 6/97, no 604.

> sion or planning has been regarded as insufficient under Article 5(3) OECD MC by some authors (which makes the twelve-month period inapplicable so that Article 5(1) and (2) OECD MC apply). Where the taxpayer is involved in planning and/or supervision, and the contractor functions as the main contractor but has transferred the entire 'real' work to subcontractors, prominent scholars have held that the taxpayer did not meet the requirements of Article 5(3) OECD MC.'

Absent a specific treaty provision including 'supervisory' activities, the better view would seem to be that planning and supervisory activities independently undertaken by a third party contractor should not be within the CAS type PE.[56]

3.7 THE TIME LIMIT EXEMPTION

The grace period in treaty CAS provisions is usually 6, 9, or 12 months[57] with a top limit of 24 months.[58] The time provisions seem to be growing progressively more elaborate, for example:

> 'a building site or construction, assembly or installation, or drilling rig or ship used for the exploration or development of natural resources within a Contracting State, but only if such site, or activity continues within the State for a period or periods aggregating more than 183 days in any twelve month period (including the period of supervisory activity connected therewith), provided that a permanent establishment shall not exist in any taxable year in which such site or activity continues within that State for a period or periods aggregating less than 30 days in that taxable year.'[59]

A. Stand-Alone Status of CAS PEs

The time limit provision must be recognized, first of all, as an exemption of sites and projects lasting less than the critical period. The OECD Model Commentary is quite specific:

56. *But cf.* Vogel, at 306, para. 74 (some commentators argue that mere planning and supervision of building works constitutes a 'building site').
57. Mehta at 284-299; 10 W. Diamond & D. Diamond, *International Tax Treaties of All Nations* 67, 74 (Series B, 1986). A few rare treaties limit the period to 3 months and some offshore oil countries, including the United States, have a 30-day provision applicable to natural resource exploration or exploitation.
58. Mehta at 284-299).
59. United States–Barbados 5(2)(i) (note the absence of the word 'project'); United States–Jamaica 5(2)(i) (adds 'dredging project'); United States–Malta 5(3) (adds 'project').

> 'This paragraph provides expressly that a building site or construction or installation project constitutes a permanent establishment only if it lasts more than twelve months. Any of those items which does not meet this condition does not of itself constitute a permanent establishment, even if there is within it an installation, for instance an office or workshop within the meaning of paragraph 2 [which sets out examples of fixed places of business], associated with the construction activity.'[60]

What this means is that an Article 5(3) CAS PE operates independently of an Article 5(1) POB PE to the extent the time requirement is concerned (i.e. it must be operational for more than 12 months). The OECD Model Commentary does not, however, provide a clear guidance as to whether or not the existence of a CAS PE is subject to the other conditions of Art. 5(1), e.g. geographical fixedness. There are differing opinions on this in literature.[61]

If a CAS does contain a POB which serves several CASs, the POB can itself be a PE, but only if it meets the fixedness and time requirements of an Article 5(1) POB PE, and only the functions carried out through such a POB (e.g. catering) will be attributable such a POB PE:

> 'Where, however, such an office or workshop is used for a number of construction projects and the activities performed therein go beyond those mentioned in paragraph 4, it will be considered a permanent establishment if the conditions of the Article are otherwise met even if none of the projects involve a building site or construction or installation project that lasts more than 12 months. In that case, the situation of the workshop or office will therefore be different from that of these sites or projects, none of which will constitute a permanent establishment, and it will be important to ensure that only the profits properly attributable to the functions performed through that office or workshop, taking into account the assets used and the risks assumed through that office or workshop, are attributed to the permanent establishment. This could include profits attributable to functions performed in relation to the various construction sites but only to the extent that these functions are properly attributable to the office.'[62]

---

60. OECD Model Commentary, Art. 5(3), para. 16.
61. For a detailed discussion of the arguments for and against these approaches, *see* Pijl, The relationship Between Article 5, Paragraphs 1 and 3 of the OECD Model Convention, 33 *Intertax* (International Tax Review), 4 (2005), pp. 189-193. The article includes references to works by authors who disagree with the view that Art. 5(3) PEs are subject to the conditions of Art. 5(1), e.g. by prominent Dutch scholar van Raad.
62. OECD Model Commentary, Art. 5(3), para. 16.

The UN Model 2011 recognizes that there are differing views on the relationship between Art. 5(1) and 5(3), but does not offer a solution:[63]

> 'The Committee notes that there are differing views about whether subparagraph (a) of paragraph 3 is a "self-standing" provision (so that no resort to paragraph 1 is required) or whether (in contrast) only building sites and the like that meet the criteria of paragraph 1 would constitute permanent establishments, subject to there being a specific six-month test. However, the Committee considers that where a building site exists for six months, it will in practice almost invariably also meet the requirements of paragraph 1. In fact, an enterprise having a building site, etc., at its disposal, through which its activities are wholly or partly carried on will also meet the criteria of paragraph 1.'

Indeed, the new UN Model Commentary language fails to acknowledge that the CAS PE provision does not apply exclusively to building sites, in which case the conditions of Art. 5(1) would have to be met. The relationship between Articles 5(1) and 5(3) is critically important in the case of assembly projects (which are covered by UN-type CAS PE provisions) and installation projects which are not related to building sites or construction projects.

Despite the differing views, it would be difficult to argue that the UN Model CAS PE provision is not 'stand-alone' – while the Services PE provision which appears under the same heading clearly is. This CAS 'stand-alone' status is generally accepted by case law and rulings. Thus, in Petition No. 24 of 1996,[64] the AAR held that the submersible diving vessel used by two Dutch companies for construction of an offshore Indian pipeline could be viewed as a POB, but since the activity fell under the CAS project PE and was less than the treaty required 6 months duration, it did not constitute either PE.

An AAR ruling in *Cal Dive Marine Construction (Mauritius) Ltd vs DIT*,[65] similarly held that a barge used by a Mauritian company in under-sea pipeline construction was involved in a CAS project and even if the barge were viewed as a POB, it would have to be operational for more than the same 9-month period as required for CAS projects by the Indian–Mauritius Treaty.

A similar holding was made in *DCIT vs Hyundai Heavy Industries Co. Ltd.*[66] where ITAT ignored an Indian project office since the 9-month requirement of the treaty CAS PE provision was not met. The CAS provision being a

63. UN MC Commentary Article 5(3), para. 7
64. Indian Advance Ruling Petition No. 24 of 17 Oct 1996, Mehta at 239.
65. 182 Taxman 124 (2009 AAR – New Delhi) reproduced in Mehta Appendix One and summarized at 240.
66. 31 SOT 482 (2009 Delhi) reproduced in Mehta Appendix One and summarized at 242.

lex specialis rule, it prevailed over the *lex generalis* rule of Article 5(1) POB PEs.

The use of the *lex specialis* rule of statutory construction is fairly common in Indian PE decisions, as in *CIT vs M/s BKI/HAM v.o.f.*[67] and *Brown & Root, Inc,*[68] which both ruled that the Indian CAS provision took precedence over Article 5(2) enumerated examples of a fixed POB PE (namely a project office and a support office in *BKI/HAM* and in *Brown & Root* an oil and gas well).

To similar effect is a *German Construction Project*[69] case, which ignored containers provided for construction workers' accommodation in a number of projects constructed by a Hungarian company in a German town. Since the 12 months threshold of the Hungarian–German treaty had not been exceeded, the Article 5(3) PE provision took precedence over the Article 5(1) PE provision.

As discussed in Chapter 7 (Services PE and Secondments), the OECD Commentary offers alternative Service PE provisions. The Commentary cautions however that if the alternative Service PE is used, the specified minimum time period should not be less than that specified in the CAS time period (e.g., 3 months, instead of 6 months). Otherwise, the Services PE provision could engulf CAS projects and be subject to the lesser Services PE time period.[70]

B. Beginnings

In apparent contrast to the rule governing fixed places of business,[71] the time period begins to run from the date at which planning for the site or project begins 'if carried out by the building contractor.'[72] More specifically:

> 'A site exists from the date on which the contractor begins his work, including any preparatory work, in the country where construction is to be established, e.g. if he installs a planning office for the construction.'[73]

The statement contains two rules. In the first place, the OECD Fiscal Committee states that the clock begins running on the day of beginning of work

67. 15 taxmann.com 102 (2011 *Uttarakhand*) discussed in Mehta at 348 and reproduced in Mehta Appendix One.
68. 103 Taxman 515 (AAR – New Delhi) summarized in Mehta at 249 and reproduced in Mehta Appendix One.
69. Case no. IR 47/00 (16 May 2001 *Bundesfinanzhof*).
70. OECD Commentary, Article 5, paragraph 42.27 (last sentence).
71. 'The period of time during which the fixed place of business itself is being set up by the enterprise should not be counted, provided that this activity differs substantially from the activity for which the place of business is to serve permanently.' OECD Model Commentary, Art. 5, para. 11.
72. OECD Model Commentary, Art. 5(3), para. 16.
73. OECD Model Commentary, Art. 5(3), para. 19.

in the source country.[74] This day may occur long before the day on which work begins at the construction site. Some commentators appear to disagree, arguing that the time period does not begin to run until activities begin 'on the spot.'[75]

Secondly, preparatory work sheds its usual guise as exempt activity and marks the beginning of the time period provided it occurs in the source country. Here again, not all commentators are in agreement.[76] However, case law does generally support the OECD position for the inclusion of preparatory activity where commenced within the source country.[77]

C. Pre-design and Fabrication Outside the Source Country Does Not Count

However actual project design and construction conducted outside the source country before the start of source country installation will not be counted within the grace time period, as held in *DCIT vs Hyundai Heavy Industries Co. Ltd.*[78] The South Korean manufacturer also had a limited Indian project co-ordination office, but since its project design and construction was completed offshore before commencement of installation in India, it was excluded.

As a result, the time spent during the Indian installation phase did not exceed the required 9 months CAS period and no CAS PE was found. ITAT held that the Article 5(3) type PE was a *lex specialis* provision which took precedence over the *lex generalis* POB PE provision of Article 5(1) and that the Indian sited activities having not exceeded the treaty required 9 months, the Indian co-ordination office itself could not be a POB PE.

How is the source-country to behave prior to the expiration of the time period? Some earlier treaties provided for a reasonable-estimate rule. For example:

---

74. *Accord, Cal Dive Marine Construction (Mauritius) Ltd. vs DIT,* 182 Taxman 124 (2009 AAR – New Delhi) (preparatory activities conducted outside India are not counted), summarized in Mehta at 230 and reproduced in Mehta Appendix One; *Air Drilling* Case No. 16,095 (29 Jun 1981 *Conseil d'Etat*) (Algerian PE found for French oil well drilling project in Algeria – drilling lasted two months, but staff and equipment were in Algeria for one year prior to drilling), Mehta at 233; *Czech Construction Project* Case No. 2004/15/0001 (22 Apr 2009 Austrian *Verwaltungsgerichtshof*) (preparatory activities conducted outside the Czech Republic not counted) Mehta at 235; *Turnkey Contracts* Case No. IR 99/97 (21 Apr 1999) (Czech construction project commenced with NRE's first employee to arrive on Czech site even if employee only engaged in preparatory activities) Mehta at 235; *Accord, Belgian Construction Project* 19 AFT 12, p. 223 (12 April 1984 Antwerp Court of Appeals Decision) Mehta at 237.
75. *See* Vogel, at 307, para. 77.
76. *Ibid.*
77. *See* Section B above at note 72 this chapter.
78. 31 SOT 482 (2009 Delhi) reproduced in Mehta Appendix One and summarized at 242.

> 'A site used for building work, the execution of which has exceeded, or, as far as can be estimated, will exceed a period of twelve months, shall be regarded as a permanent place of business within the meaning of the Agreement.'[79]

The OECD Draft seems to adopt an 'appears ... likely' test – the host-country can assess a tax before the one-year period prescribed by the Draft has expired 'if it appears that the site or project is likely to last for more than twelve months.'[80] Presumably, a refund is appropriate if the likelihood does not eventuate in fact, although the Draft Commentary fails to say as much. The OECD Model Commentary's greatly expanded discussion declines comment on the problem.

D. Tacking of the Time Spent by Subcontractors

The OECD applies the time line grace period in another dimension – tacking on the time spent by subcontractors:

> 'If an enterprise (general contractor) which has undertaken the performance of a comprehensive project sub-contracts parts of such project to other enterprises (sub-contractors), the period spent by a sub-contractor working on the building site must be considered as being time spent by the general contractor on the building project. The sub-contractor himself has a permanent establishment at the site if his activities there last more than twelve months.'[81]

The OECD 2012 Revised Discussion Draft proposes to modify this language to tack on the time period spent by a subcontractor even where the entire CAS project is subcontracted out. Moreover, the Revised Draft goes on to state that such a fully contracted out site is also 'at the disposal' of the general contractor.[82]

> 'where circumstances indicate that, during that time, the general contractor clearly has the construction site at its disposal by reason of factors such as the fact that he has legal possession of the site, controls

79. Denmark-Finland 10 (third unnumbered paragraph) (1937).
80. OECD Commentary, Art. 5(3), para. 18.
81. OECD Model Commentary, Art. 5(3), para. 19. One hastens to point out that the rule just stated ought not be applied if the subcontract involves planning or supervision.
82. OECD 2012 Revised Draft, para 19.

access to and use of the site and has overall responsibility for what happens at that location during that period.'

This language has been criticized as an ineffectual and unwarranted extension of limited German and Austrian precedent to create a NRE PE where the entire project has been contracted out to one or more subcontractors. It is also inconsistent with the exception of Article 5(6) that an NRE does not acquire a source country PE by merely doing business there through an independent contractor which is carrying on its own business, e.g., as a caterer, hotel manager, etc.

Admittedly, some German and Austrian precedential rulings have recognized that the time spent on a CAS by a sub-contractor can be aggregated with the time spent on the site by the NRE general contractor in determining whether the OECD 12-month minimum period is met for a CAS PE. This authority is however limited to where only a 'part' of the CAS work is contracted out to subs, and the general remains actively involved at the site with 'boots on the ground.' With limited exceptions discussed below this concept has not been extended to POB or CAS PEs.

An exceptional ruling involving the role of independent contractors is the *Norwegian Safe Service*[83] case. That case involved a Swedish supplier of catering services to offshore Norwegian oil well drilling platforms. The Swedish company subcontracted this contract to an unrelated independent Norwegian catering company. The Swedish company had no employees on the rig and conducted no business there. Under a unique provision of the Nordic Treaty (between Denmark, Iceland, Norway, Sweden and Finland), the provision of services relating to offshore natural resource exploration or development for a period of 30 days constitutes a PE. Relying on this Nordic Treaty provision,, the Court found that the Swedish contractor had a Norwegian PE even though it fully contracted out the project to an unrelated Norwegian caterer.

Apparently relying on this case and although no comparable provision or precedent exists in the OECD or the UN Models, the OECD 2012 Revised Discussion Draft states that an NRE can have not only a fixed POB PE, but also a CAS PE by dealing in a source country entirely through independent agents:[84]

> 'An enterprise may also carry on its business through subcontractors, acting alone ... [provided that the enterprise clearly has the effective power to use that site, e.g. because the enterprise owns or has legal possession of that site and controls access to and use of the site. Para-

83. Case No. 327/2001 (4 April 2001 Norwegian Supreme Court).
84. OECD 2012 Discussion Draft, revised paragraph 10.1

graph 19.1 illustrates such a situation in the case of a construction site; this could also happen in other situations. An example would be where an enterprise that owns a small hotel and rents out the hotel's rooms through the internet has contracted the on-site operation of the hotel to a company that is remunerated on a cost plus basis.'

The above principle plus the hotel example was criticized in 2011 comments on the Draft – for the following reasons:

- The German/Austrian subcontractor CAS precedent is specifically limited to meeting the CAS time period by tacking on the time spent by a sub engaged *for only a part* of the project where the general is on-site and actively supervising the sub while carrying out it own functions on-site. Such precedent does not establish a POB through the premises used by a sub
- The *Norwegian Safe Service* case is not in point. It is based on a unique offshore Nordic Treaty provision which is not in the OECD or the UN Models
- The OECD hotel example *ignores* two lines of case precedent discussed above: (1) the mere leasing or renting of source country real property through offshore personnel does not constitute a fixed POB of the lessor; and (2) if the lessor has no employees or dependent agents at the leased premises, it conducts no business there and the premises are the POB of the lessee or operator
- Under Article 5(6) similarly no CAS PE can exist merely through source country services provided by an independent contractor acting in the ordinary course of its business even if it takes directions from the general contractor

Totally contracted out projects do not constitute a PE under Canadian practice. As stated in public comments to the OECD 2011 Discussion Draft:[85]

'The confusion is apparent in the international tax community as, for example, the Canada Revenue Agency ("CRA") has publicly stated that, with respect to Article V(9) of the Canada–United States Treaty which is essentially a modified version of the alternative provision of the Commentary, where an enterprise of the United States subcontracts an entire contract, for which the services are to be performed in Canada, to a local subcontractor (i.e., a subcontractor in Canada), this will not

---

85. OECD 2011 Discussion Draft Comments at p. 88, Comments of Taxand Luxembourg, Taxand is of the view that a similar restriction should apply to the Services PE provision.

create a PE even if the services are performed for an aggregate of 183 days or more over any twelve month period.'

There is other case law which is contrary to the 2012 OECD Draft's proposal to attribute POB and CAS PEs to a NRE contractor which is present in the source country only through subcontractors. In *Pintsch Bamag*[86] a German company won a contract for the design, supply, fabrication, transportation and maintenance of steel navigational buoys and solar lighting equipment for an Indian ship channel project. Pintsch Bamag subcontracted most of the work to a third party sub-contractor, retaining the provision of technical study requirements, the design of buoys, mooring gears and solar operated navigational equipment as well as the supply of critical components required by subcontractors – all from its office in Germany. Pintsch Bamag supervised the onsite installation of the equipment through two of its engineers seconded for 60 days to subcontractors in India, the entire project lasting 16 months.

The AAR rejected the Indian tax authority's contention that all the activities of the subcontractor should be attributed to Pintsch Bamag and that since those activities exceed the treaty required 6-month period, Pintstch Bamag had an Indian CAS PE. Such an attribution would only be tenable if the subcontractor were viewed as a dependent agent of Pintsch Bamag. Since it was an independent contractor engaged in its own business, it was not a dependent agent and hence its subcontracted work could not be attributed to Pintsch Bamag. In the AAR's view attribution of a subcontractor's activities to the main contractor could only occur if the building site had been set up by the main contractor and the services of the sub were also employed in a conjoint effort of the main and the sub. But this was not the case in *Pintsch Bamag*.

In *Hyosung Corporation vs DIT*[87] a Korean company was awarded a contract for the construction of a power station in India. As permitted by the contract, Hyosung split the project into offshore and onshore components and assigned the latter to an Indian company ('L&T'). Hyosung was responsible for the offshore design, engineering and supply of equipment with L&T being responsible for plant supply and services in India. Pursuant to a memorandum of understanding, Hyosung and L&T assumed joint and several responsibilities for execution of the onshore part. The AAR held that Hyosung did not have a CAS PE because all of the onshore work was undertaken by L&T, despite the fact that Hyosung retained joint and several responsibilities for the execution of the onshore work.

---

86. 184 Taxman 122 (2009 AAR – New Delhi) discussed in Mehta at 257 and reproduced in Mehta Appendix One.
87. 18 Taxman 270 (2009 AAR – New Delhi) discussed in Mehta at 259 and reproduced in Mehta Appendix One.

In two Russian cases, the courts seemed to take into consideration whether or not the NRE had an office in Russia, although the income of the CAS PE was then computed separately. In *Velmont Enterprises*,[88] a Cypriot company with a registered office in Moscow had fully subcontracted construction works in Russia to a local company. The Court held that Velmont had a CAS PE as the 12-month duration test under the Russia–Cyprus tax treaty was met. The CAS PE income was not aggregated with the income derived through the Moscow office.

By contrast, in *Stora Enso*,[89] Finnish company which had no office in Russia which had entirely subcontracted an entire project to other Finnish companies. It was held the Finnish company did not have a CAS PE in Russia. However, the subcontractors themselves had CAS PEs.

E. When Do Projects End? Interruptions and Post-Completion Work

The OECD Model seems adamant on one point – once a project begins 'seasonal or other temporary interruptions'[90] are to be included in determining the life of a project. Be it weather, on the one hand, or materials shortages or labor troubles, on the other, the clock continues to run.

> 'In general, a site continues to exist until the work is completed or permanently abandoned.'[91]

But 'seasonal and temporary interruptions' and 'work completed or permanently abandoned' do not exhaust all of the possibilities. The Fiscal Committee's use of these terms suggests that Acts of God or the Public Enemy may yet have a role to play. An involuntary termination for a reason other than weather, materials shortages, or labor difficulties may well cause the clock to pause.

The OECD Commentary includes in the 12-month timeline a 3-month winter caused stoppage of work. However in shorter timeline scenarios, such interruptions might not be ignored. In *R & B Falcon Offshore Ltd vs Addt'l CIT*[92] ITAT accepted the taxpayer's argument that stoppage of work for a few days repair should not be counted with respect to the 120-day timeline provided in the Indian–US treaty for offshore exploration or exploitation activities.

88. MFDAC, 20 May 2010, KA-A40/4739010f, discussed in Konnov, Smirnov & Smith, Russia – Permanent Establishments, Topical Analyses IBFD.
89. NWDFAC, 8 July 2003, A26-6181/01-02-03/380; *Id.*
90. OECD 2012 Revised Draft, Art. 5(3), para. 19.1.
91. *Id.* (first sentence).
92. 42 SOT 432 (2010 Delhi) reproduced in Mehta Appendix One.

The Model Commentary defines when the clock has finished running as when the project or machinery is delivered and finally accepted by the customer. Post acceptance guarantee work is not counted. Relying on Dutch and Belgian authority, one commentator stops the clock when, after the testing of the device assembled, or the inspection of the building or construction project (and the finding that it is free of defects), the fully completed project is accepted.[93] This view seems accepted by case law.[94]

3.8 THE GEOGRAPHIC LIMITS – STAND-ALONE PROJECTS VS AGGREGATION

As a general rule, CAS projects are considered on a 'stand-alone' basis with respect to the 6-, 9- or 12-month timeline usually required.[95] Projects conducted in the same country by the same NRE are not aggregated to meet this timeline unless there is both unity of execution and a common geographic area – what the OECD Commentary refers to as 'coherent whole commercially and geographically.' Thus, a building site could be regarded as a single geographical PE even if based on contracts with different persons e.g. construction of a row of houses, provided it has commercial unity as well (unity of execution).[96]

In a 1982 Belgian court decision,[97] a Dutch building contractor undertook several construction projects on different sites in Belgium for the same client, but under different contracts. Each project was accomplished in less time than the treaty period,[98] although the period was exceeded in completing all of the contracts. The court dismissed an elaborate agreement entered into between the taxing authorities of Belgium and the Netherlands (arguably reaching the same result on the facts),[99] and concluded that the taxing authorities were not entitled to aggregate building sites in different places to determine whether

93. Vogel, at 308, para. 78.

94. *Turnkey Contracts* Case No. IR 99/97 (21 Apr 1999) (Czech construction contract completed on customer acceptance; post installation testing included; if no acceptance process, completion on contractor's leaving site; generally project interruptions included, except where caused by customer) Mehta at 237; *Accord, Belgian Construction Project* 19 AFT 12, p. 223 (12 Apr 1984 Antwerp Court of Appeals Decision) (completion when contractor permanently left the site) Mehta at 237

95. OECD Model Commentary, Art. 5(3), para. 18.

96. *Id.*

97. Decision of 29 June 1982, Lower Court of Antwerp, Belgium, *Jurisprudence Fiscale 2* (1983), No. 20 p. 4, summarized at 1 *International Tax Treaties Service,* Art. 5, page 28.5001 (Edwardes-Ker ed. 1986).

98. The period for *'the place* of performance of a building site or construction project' is 'more than 9 months' under Belgium–Netherlands 1970 5(2)(g).

99. *Bulletin der Belastingen* No. 2533, at 1790 (1975), summarized at 1 *International Tax Treaties Service,* Art. 5, page 28.5001 in the opinion of the case last cited (Edwardes-Ker ed. 1986).

the time spent exceeded the treaty period. A Belgian Court of Appeal reached the same result two years later.[100] The taxing officials' agreement was not mentioned. The Netherlands High Court reached a comparable result in a 1970 decision.[101]

The agreement that figured into the first Belgian case provides insight into what tax officials in two important jurisdictions regard as a 'coherent whole.' The agreement sets down two rules. Under the first, construction activities engaged in different places or at different times by the same contractor are to be deemed a single construction project if they are performed under a single contract. Under the second rule, projects separately contracted for are to be deemed a single construction project if there is 'unity of execution.' This characterization may apply if the projects are executed in series without interruption or in parallel. It may apply as well if separate projects are conceptually parts of a single whole (a highway, for example) and are carried through without significant interruption.

The French *Conseil d'Etat* has on occasion seemed to ignore the requirement of 'coherence' for aggregation of building sites, holding that:

> 'the writers of the treaty did not intend to exclude from the permanent establishment category an activity undertaken by a company for more than 12 months in one country but spread over several successive construction sites.'[102]

Several cases illustrate the requirement of commercial and geographic coherence, in particular involving offshore natural resource exploration or drilling. In *J Ray McDermott Eastern Hemisphere Ltd vs JCIT*[103] McDermott was a Mauritian corporation engaged in the business of installing offshore platforms, decks, pipelines and jackets for oil exploration projects. It had 3 such projects on the Indian continental shelf lasting 8 months, 10 days and 3½ months respectively. Each project was independent from the other and had a different scope of work. ITAT observed that certain Indian treaties (such as with Belgium, Canada, Denmark and the US) permitted aggregation of disparate

100. Judgment of 12 April 1984, Antwerp Court of Appeal, Belgium, 1984 *AFT* 12 p. 223, summarized at 1 *International Tax Treaties Service*, Art. 5, page 28.5002 (Edwardes-Ker ed. 1989).
101. Judgment of 4 February 1970, H.R., Neth., No. 16,305, summarized at 1 *International Tax Treaties Service*, Art. 5, pages 53-54 (Edwardes-Ker ed. 1986). The decision is probably dictum as applied to the construction-project point. The taxpayer was essentially a supplier of skilled labor to a German shipyard.
102. *See* Cordier Deltour, France – Permanent Establishments, Topical Analyses IBFD (accessed 30 June 2013).
103. 39 SOT 240 (2010 Mumbai) discussed in Mehta at 213 and reproduced in Mehta Appendix One.

CAS projects to determine if the requisite timeline were met (not counting more than one project on the same day).

Noting that the treaty between India and Mauritius did not provide for such aggregation, ITAT found that aggregation would be permitted only in the (1) case of an NRE's artificially splitting the same project between two or more different entities or (2) a showing that the 'projects were so inextricably interconnected or interdependent that they were essentially required to be viewed as a coherent whole'[104] Finding neither exception applicable, ITAT ruled that McDermott's projects had to be viewed on a 'stand-alone' basis and that it had no Indian PE.

In *Transco-Invest,*[105] two related Polish companies were commissioned to build in Russia a commercial building and a multifunctional entertainment center located on two connected plots of land. Construction works on each of these sites had lasted for less than 12 months, and the taxpayers claimed that no CAS PE was constituted as the time limit should be assessed separately in respect of each site. The Court ruled in favor of aggregation of the two sites, because (1) the two plots of land were consolidated after the completion of the construction, (2) the two buildings were connected (e.g. joint engineering networks), and (3) unjustified tax benefit was obtained as a result of the involvement of two associated enterprises (anti-avoidance considerations).

ADIT vs Valentine Maritime(Mauritius) Ltd[106] involved a Mauritian company engaged in marine and general engineering and construction which had 3 separate projects relating to barges for the same customer. ITAT noted that even if these projects were all in the same geographic area, their time periods could not be aggregated unless the tax authorities showed that the projects 'inextricably' had an 'interconnection' and 'interdependence' in addition to being economically and geographically coherent. For failure to make such showing, ITAT held Valentine had no PE.

In *Gurtler, Herbert & Co. Inc vs Stavanger*[107] a US company undertook 9 oil drilling projects on offshore Norwegian oil platforms for a few unrelated customers none lasting longer than 12 months. The Court found no PE stating that aggregation would be permissible only if the projects were carried out for the same customer in the same geographic area.

A US *IRS* private letter ruling[108] involved a Dutch company which used a semi-submersible vessel in drilling oil wells over sequential two year periods

---

104. Mehta summarizing at 214.
105. VVDFAC, 22 Oct. 2008, A82-6882/2007-27, discussed in Konnov, Smirnov & Smith, Russia – Permanent Establishments, Topical Analyses IBFD (accessed 30 June 2013).
106. 45 SOT 34 (2011 Mumbai) summarized in Mehta at 214 and reproduced in Mehta Appendix One.
107. Case No. 00 260A ((18 Sep 1980 Stavanger County Court).
108. Summarized in Mehta at 226.

for two apparently unrelated US customers in different 'oil blocks' on the US outer continental shelf. The Dutch company did not control the drilling exploration sites and each drilling project lasted only a few months. Each oil block consisted of 9 square miles and the drilling project did not exceed 3 months in any one block and no more than 5 months in any two adjacent blocks. Drilling in non-adjacent blocks was separated by a distance of at least 5 miles and the blocks drilled for the two US companies were at least 150 miles apart:

- For US Company 2, 17 wells were drilled over a 2 ¼ year period from August 1975 to October 1977 for a pre-determined contract price payable regardless of whether the Dutch company actually drilled the oil wells in a certain geographic area of the Shelf
- For US Company 1, three wells were drilled over a 2 ½ year period commencing November 1977

The ruling holds that the Dutch company's activities for *US company 2* constituted a construction or installation site PE as the drilling projects had commercial coherence since all 17 projects were pursuant to one contract with the same customer and also had geographic coherence since the same predetermined contract price was due regardless of whether the Dutch company actually drilled wells in a certain geographic area. Drilling projects for US company 1 were not aggregated and apparently did not create a PE.

The above case and ruling precedent thus holds that apart from a few treaties allowing aggregate treatment (timeline could be met by multiple projects),[109] 'stand-alone' treatment would prevail unless there were (1) geographic coherence (same site, e.g. row of houses, canal, pipeline, roads), (2) commercial coherence (same customer or same construction on a continuous site) and (3) unity of execution (same contract, the projects involved similar functions and were chronologically interdependent).

This view was also taken in a *German Turnkey Construction case*[110] which involved 4 turnkey projects for the same customer which were at the same site and chronologically interdependent. The absence of such interdependent

109. *See also* the *Dutch Contractor* case dated 29 June 1982 discussed above in which the Antwerp Court of Appeals ignored a Belgian–Dutch competent authority interpretative agreement allowing aggregation of contracts for the same customer if carried out simultaneously or consecutively or in various places as part of the same contract – i.e., lacking geographic or commercial coherence, holding that the treaty reference adopted a 'stand-alone' approach. *But cf.* a French Case No. 16,095 (29 Jun 1981 *Conseil d'Etat*) holding that the Spanish-French treaty intended to aggregate drilling projects in Spain and hence the French company had a Spanish PE exempting it from French taxation discussed in Mehta at 18.

110. Case No IR 99/97 (21 Apr 1999 *Bundesfinanzhof*) summarized in Mehta at 221.

commercial and geographic coherence will lead to 'stand-alone' treatment as held in several other German Federal Tax Court decisions.[111]

3.9 CONSTRUCTION PROJECTS ABSENT TREATY PROVISIONS

There are still treaties in force which antedate the widespread adoption of special clauses making building sites and construction projects lasting for this or that time period permanent establishments. In dealing with one of these, the American tax authorities stated in 1977:

> 'It is the view of the Internal Revenue Service that, in the absence of specific treaty language to the contrary, a construction site of any significant duration is generally considered to constitute a permanent establishment even if a treaty's permanent establishment article is silent as to such site. It is also the view of the Service that planning and supervision carried on by a building contractor are part of the activity allocable to its construction site permanent establishment.'[112]

There seems little authority on the issue. The only other pronouncement in the area is a German state ruling, under an old treaty[113] in which permanent establishment was defined simply as 'a permanent business organization in which the activity of the enterprise is wholly or partly carried on.' Purporting to follow an earlier ruling said to have been agreed on by German and Swiss authorities, the competent Minister ruled that a permanent establishment would be assumed to exist in the case of a construction or assembly project that existed for more than 24 months.[114]

---

111. *Case No. IR 47/00 (*16 May 2001 *Bunderfinanzhof*) (Hungarian contracts in German town were unrelated and could not be aggregated); *Case No. IR 3/02* (19 Nov 2003 *Bundesfinanzhof*) (German resident engaged in constructing telephone lines at various locations in Luxembourg over a two year period, each contract being awarded under a tendering process and independent of all others, the taxpayer's work at a particular time or location dependent upon the progress of unrelated contractors and hence extended over a two year period rather than sequentially; held the taxpayer did not have a PE since the projects were independent and not interdependent, were not geographically coherent and were not commercially coherent); *Case IR 87/04* (3 Aug 2005 *Bundesfinanzhof*); *See also, Belgian Construction Projects* Antwerp Court of Appeals decision 1984 AFT 12 (12 April 1984, p. 223) (unrelated projects could not be aggregated);discussed in Mehta at 225-226.
112. Rev. Rul. 77-45, 1977-1 *C.B.* 313.
113. Germany–Italy (1925).
114. Ruling of Finance Ministry, North Rhine Westphalia, 8 January 1974 (No. S 1201, Italien-I-VB 2), summarized at 1 *International Tax Treaties Service*, Art. 5, page 39 (Edwardes-Ker ed. 1986).

Given the existence for many years of the building site and construction project as just another example of a fixed place of business, the American view is probably the better of the two. In the absence of the time period that really delimits an exemption, the construction project is a fixed place of business, and should respond to the rules governing all fixed places of business.

Chapter 4
Special Provisions for Mineral Extraction

4.1 'MINE'

It may not be possible to place just when the term 'mine' first found its way into the permanent establishment provisions of tax treaties. Its entrance was apparently late. Its earliest appearance may be that found in the commentary accompanying the 1927 League of Nations Draft Convention.[1] The Fiscal Committee seems by then to have tumbled to the fact that the examples of permanent establishment applied to mercantile and manufacturing enterprises, and little else. 'The word "undertakings" must be understood in its widest sense,' asserts the Committee's Commentary, '*so as to cover all undertakings, including mines and oilfields*, without making any distinction between natural and legal persons.'[2]

The text of the revised Commentary published during the following year deleted the italicized clause.[3] Now, instead of appearing in the treaty Commentary, the words 'mining and oilfields' appeared in the list of agreed examples of permanent establishments in the revised treaty itself.[4] Mines and 'oil-wells' appeared in the later League Draft Conventions.[5] Changed to the singular, 'a mine' appeared in the OECD Draft[6] and Model[7] and also in the UN Model.[8]

The commentaries accompanying these conventions make no attempt to define the term. Neither courts nor administrative agencies have undertaken to fill the void. Hence, the parties to double-taxation conventions will have the task of answering a number of questions themselves. For example, do

1. 4 *LHUSTC* 4129. The term found its way into treaties shortly thereafter. *See*, e.g., Yugoslavia–Romania 3 (1st paragraph) (1933); Finland–Germany 5 (1935).
2. 4 *LHUSTC* 4129. Emphasis supplied.
3. 4 *LHUSTC* 4166.
4. 4 *LHUSTC* 4162.
5. Draft Plurilateral 4 (3d paragraph), 4 *LHUSTC* 4235, 4239, 4240; Revised Draft Business Income Allocation Convention, Prot. 2(c), 4 *LHUSTC* 4255; London Draft, Prot. V(l), 4 *LHUSTC* 4394; Mexico Draft, Prot. V(l), 4 *LHUSTC* 4395.
6. OECD Draft 5(2)(f).
7. OECD Model 5(2)(f).
8. UN Model 5(2)(f).

operations for the extraction of such minerals as rock phosphate, quartz, or silica constitute 'mines'? Are people engaged in recovering metal from mine tailings operating 'mines' for treaty purposes? And people engaged in exploiting geothermal deposits? Are clay-pits 'mines'? Are gravel pits? Given an enterprise engaged in the conventional recovery of metals, coal, or precious stones, what portion of that enterprise is a 'mine'?[9] Would an office situated in the city nearest the actual mining operation be a part of the 'mine?'

These questions and others like them may be resolved under the domestic tax law definitions of the parties to each particular treaty.

4.2 'OIL OR GAS WELL'

'Oilfields' appear for the first time in the League of Nation Fiscal Committee documents in the 1928 revision of the Draft Convention published a year earlier.[10] The first French-American treaty lists 'oil wells' among its agreed examples of permanent establishments.[11] 'Oil wells' are so listed in the Mexico and London Drafts.[12]

The elimination of term 'from OECD Draft' and the substitution of 'other place of extraction of natural resources'[13] occurred without explanation. The explanation for its restoration in the OECD Model is hardly better:

> 'Sub-paragraph f) provides that mines, oil or gas wells, quarries or any other place of extraction of natural resources are permanent establishments. The term "any other place of extraction of natural resources" should be interpreted broadly. It includes, for example, all places of extraction of hydrocarbons whether on or off-shore.'[14]

The OECD Fiscal Committee's treatment of 'oil wells' seems curious. One doubts that, by means of these language changes, the Fiscal Committee intended to exempt oil wells from the permanent establishment classification. It is far more probable that the shift in terms reflects the Committee's increasing understanding of the process by which petroleum is extracted.

9. *See*, e.g., I.R.C. §§ 613(c)(4) 'Treatment Processes Considered as Mining'; 613(3) 'Percentage Depletion.'
10. LON 1928 Draft 5 (2d paragraph).
11. United States–France (1932), Prot. 3(a) (1st paragraph).
12. Mexico Draft Prot. V(l); London Draft Prot. V(l).
13. OECD Draft 5(2)(f).
14. OECD Model Commentary, Art. 5(2), para. 14.

4.3 'QUARRY'

The term 'quarry' made its first model-treaty appearance in the OECD Fiscal Committee's first report in 1958.[15] The event did not strike the authors of the accompanying commentary as remarkable enough to mention.[16] The term was generally accepted. It was adopted in the United States treaties and protocols submitted to the Senate in 1964.[17] Its inclusion was not commented on. The term probably means for tax purposes what it means in common parlance – an open excavation made for the purpose of extracting building stone, slate, limestone, marble, and the like. Its meaning seems never to have been called into question.

4.4 'OTHER PLACE OF EXTRACTION OF NATURAL RESOURCES'

The shift between the 'mines and oil wells' of the Mexico and London Drafts[18] and the 'mine, quarry or other place of extraction of natural resources' of the OECD Draft[19] has not been explained in the commentaries accompanying these documents. Just a hint of uncertainty arises in comparing the earlier language to that of a 'mine, an oil or gas well, a quarry or any other place of extraction of natural resources' of the OECD Model.[20]

In some hypothetical controversy that turns on whether a natural-gas well is covered by either of the older formulae (or whether a gravel pit is an 'other place of extraction') these concerns might be important. In terms of the general theory of permanent establishment it is clear that they are not. Given a gravel pit, a clay pit, an excavation for semi-precious stones, or any other operation that falls just outside of the parameters of the standard categories, one finds it easy in this area simply to return to the basic formula. If minerals are being torn from the earth, the tearing occurs at a particular place. It is being conducted by individual workers. They are engaged in their businesses respectively and in the business of their employer. However denominated, there is a fixed place through which the business of an enterprise is wholly or partly carried on.

15. 'The Elimination of Double Taxation,' Report of the Fiscal Committee of the OECD 33 (1958), 4 *LHUSTC* 4477.
16. *See id.* at 48, 4 *LHUSTC* at 4492.
17. Exec. Rept. No. 10, 88th Cong., 2d Sess., 27 July 1964, reprinted in 10 *Legislative History of United States Tax Conventions*, Japan 135.
18. Mexico Draft Prot. V(l); London Draft Prot. V(l).
19. OECD Draft 5(2)(f).
20. OECD Model 5(2)(f).

4.5 RELATION TO BUSINESS ACTIVITY REQUIREMENT

The OECD Model Commentary sets out the business-activity requirement of the permanent establishment concept in the following terms:

> '[This definition ... contains the following conditions:] – the carrying on of the business of the enterprise through this fixed place of business. This means usually that persons who, in one way or another, are dependent on the enterprise (personnel) conduct the business of the enterprise in the State in which the fixed place is situated.'[21]

The extractive industries typically require large numbers of individuals employed as skilled and semi-skilled workers to carry on their activities. Most of these industries are highly labor-intensive. One could hardly assert that business activities were not occurring in the mine or quarry. But in two situations, the requirement is harder to regard as fulfilled.

Petroleum extraction seems considerably less labor-intensive once the well has been drilled and the equipment is in place. (It conjures up a picture of an oil well somewhere in the Texas or California, alone and unattended, pumping up black gold, hour after hour.) Is an unattended operating oil well a 'place of businesses?

The OECD conventions seem to assume that fixed places of business operate continuously without pause. The extractive industries, in contrast, seem especially subject to boom-and-bust economic conditions. Is a mine a permanent establishment when it is shut down? What of an oil well that has been capped to preserve its product for a more profitable future market?

4.6 OPERATIONS IN CONTIGUOUS WATERS

The OECD Model Convention converted 'a building site or construction or installation project' from simply an agreed example of a fixed place of business[22] into a free-standing category of permanent establishment.[23] The first United States Model added to that language:

> 'or an installation or drilling rig or ship used for the exploration of natural resources.'[24]

---

21. OECD Model Commentary, Art. 5(1), para. 2.
22. *See* OECD Draft 5(2)(g); OECD Draft Commentary, Art. 5(2), para. 7.
23. *See* OECD Model 5(3).
24. United States 1977 Model 5(3).

If a site, project, installation, rig, or ship 'lasts for more than 24 months,' it is a permanent establishment (asserted the Model.) The revised United States Model cut the time period in half.[25] In United States treaties with the Netherlands, and Norway the timeline is reduced to 30 days for a rig or ship used in territorial waters for the exploration or exploitation of natural resources.

A. Area of Operations

The added language is obviously targeted at offshore petroleum operations. Yet neither United States model purported to include continental-shelf areas within their geographic coverage.[26] American officials seem to have assumed that the domestic definitions would be imported via the undefined terms provision:

> 'As regards the application of the Convention by a Contracting State, any term not defined therein shall, unless the context otherwise requires ..., have the meaning which it has under the laws of that State concerning the taxes to which the Convention applies.'[27]

The domestic definitions are to be found in section 638 of the United States Internal Revenue Code,[28] adopted in 1969, and in three pages of Treasury Regulations interpreting that section.[29]

---

25. United States 1981 Model 5(3) ('only if it lasts more than twelve months').
26. *See* Patrick, 'A Comparison of the United States and OECD Model Income Tax Conventions,' 10 *Law and Policy in International Business* 613, 625 (1978) (discussing the first United States Model – the revised Model is identical in this respect).
27. United States 1977 Model 3(2) ('unless the context otherwise requires and subject to the provisions of Article 25 (Mutual Agreement Procedure)'); United States 1981 Model 3(2) ('unless the context otherwise requires or the competent authorities agree to a common meaning pursuant to the provisions of Article 25 (Mutual Agreement Procedure)').
28. 'Section 638. Continental Shelf Areas

    For purposes of applying the provisions of this chapter (including sections 861(a)(3) and 862(a)(3) in the case of the performance of personal services) with respect to mines, oil and gas wells, and other natural deposits –

    (1) the term "United States" when used in a geographical sense includes the seabed and subsoil of those submarine areas which are adjacent to the territorial waters of the United States and over which the United States has exclusive rights, in accordance with international law, with respect to the exploration and exploitation of natural resources; and

    (2) the terms "foreign country" and "possession of the United States" when used in a geographical sense include the seabed and subsoil of those submarine areas which are adjacent to the territorial waters of the foreign country or such possession and over which the foreign country (or the United States in case of such possession) has exclusive rights in accordance with international law, with respect to the exploration and exploitation of natural resources, but this paragraph shall apply in the case of a foreign country only if it exercises, directly or indirectly, taxing jurisdiction with respect to such exploration or exploitation.

As early as 1970, in its tax treaty with Trinidad and Tobago, the United States adopted a treaty coverage formula that incorporated the essence of the domestic definition.[30] Versions of that formula have appeared in nearly all of the United States treaties that have been ratified since that time.

B. Subjects of the Provision

An 'installation or drilling rig or ship' is the target of the treaty provision. One such apparatus is described in the letter ruling earlier discussed:

> 'The vessel has an upper deck that serves as the drilling platform. In deep water the vessel is operated from a floating but semi-submersible position, in which the lower hull assembly is about 80 feet below the water surface and the upper deck approximately 80 feet above the water surface. The vessel is held in the drilling position by a number of large anchors and heavy chains. It is not self-propelled.'[31]

How the apparatus behaves is described in another letter ruling, apparently involving the same taxpayer:

> 'To perform exploratory drilling services at the various exploration sites, the Taxpayer and its subcontractors constructed a vertical pipeline (the well) through the earth's crust. To do this, a drill bit was rotated vertically from the drilling vessel down through the soil. The drill bit would descend to a predetermined depth into the seabed, and then be withdrawn. The Taxpayer would install pipe casing, cementing it into place in the hollow space created by the drill bit. The drill bit would be reinserted and this process would be repeated until the well had been drilled to the desired depth. Although only approximately one

---

No foreign country shall, by reason of the application of this section, be treated as a country contiguous to the United States.'

29. U.S. Treas. Reg. §§ 1.638-1 and 1.638-2 (1973).
30. United States–Trinidad and Tobago, Article 2:
    '(1) In this Convention, unless the context otherwise requires:
    (a)(i) The term "United States" means the United States of America; and
    (ii) When used in a geographical sense, the term "United States" means the States thereof and the District of Columbia. Such term also includes: (A) the territorial seas thereof; and (B) the seabed and subsoil of the adjacent submarine areas beyond the territorial sea over which the United States exercises rights, in accordance with international law concerning the continental shelf, for the purposes of exploration for, or exploitation of, the natural resources of those areas, but only to the extent that the person, property, or activity to which this Convention is being applied is connected with such exploration or exploitation.'
31. Ltr. Rul. 8424007.

> in ten exploratory wells wind up producing oil or gas, if the Taxpayer discovered oil, the well was plugged and the Taxpayer's drilling rig was moved to another site.'[32]

In view of the peculiarly American nature of this particular formula, the description is especially useful. This sort of vessel must be within the treaty terms, although it appears to be both a 'drilling rig' and a 'ship.'

What 'installation' means is unclear. The second of the letter rulings goes on to describe the practice of oil companies in exploiting oil discoveries. In the depths in which the taxpayer was drilling, 'the oil company would typically have to construct a production platform to extract such oil and gas.'[33] The production platform is not an 'installation' engaged in 'exploration,' in any sense. It seems instead to constitute the above-ground portion of 'an oil well.' An 'installation' appears to have special significance – at least in the minds of some. The First Protocol to the current United States–Canada tax convention[34] changed the term 'the use of a drilling rig or ship' in the proposed treaty to 'the use of an installation or drilling rig or ship.' The Joint Committee Staff Explanation noted the foregoing facts without any sort of explanation.[35] Perhaps the addition of 'installation' reminds one that the exploration and, under some treaties,[36] the development of natural resources are activities that occur on land and with respect to solid minerals. It is possible that 'installation' bears the same relation to 'mine' as 'drilling rig bears to 'oil well.'

C. Stand-Alone vs Aggregated Offshore Drilling Projects

As discussed above in Chapter 3 – Construction Projects, several cases illustrate the requirement of commercial and geographic coherence, in particular involving offshore natural resource exploration or drilling. In *J Ray McDermott Eastern Hemisphere Ltd vs JCIT*[37] McDermott was a Mauritian corporation engaged in the business of installing offshore platforms, decks, pipelines and jackets for oil exploration projects. It had 3 such projects on the Indian continental shelf lasting 8 months, 10 days and 3 ½ months respectively. Each project was independent from the other and had a different scope of work.

---

32. Ltr. Rul. 8526005.
33. *Ibid.*
34. United States–Canada, Prot. II.
35. Joint Committee Staff, Explanation of Proposed Income Tax Treaty (and Proposed Protocols) between the United States and Canada (25 April 1984), reported in 1 *Tax Treaties* (P-H) 22,070, at page 22,100-Z.7 (1984). The Treasury Technical Explanation adds nothing. *See id.* at 22,065, page 22,072 (1984).
36. *E.g.*, United States–Tunisia 5(3).
37. 39 SOT 240 (2010 Mumbai) discussed in Mehta at 213 and reproduced in Mehta Appendix One.

ITAT observed that certain Indian treaties (such as with Belgium, Canada, Denmark and the US) permitted aggregation of disparate CAS projects to determine if the requisite timeline were met (not counting more than one project on the same day).

Noting that the treaty between India and Mauritius did not provide for such aggregation, ITAT found that aggregation would be permitted only in the (1) case of an NRE's artificially splitting the same project between two or more different entities or (2) a showing that the 'projects were so inextricably interconnected or interdependent that they were essentially required to be viewed as a coherent whole'[38] Finding neither exception applicable, ITAT ruled that McDermott's projects had to be viewed on a 'stand-alone' basis and that it had no Indian PE.

ADIT vs Valentine Maritime (Mauritius) Ltd[39] involved a Mauritian company engaged in marine and general engineering and construction which had 3 separate projects relating to barges for the same customer. ITAT noted that even if these projects were all in the same geographic area, their time periods could not be aggregated unless the tax authorities showed that the projects 'inextricably' had an 'interconnection' and 'interdependence' in addition to being economically and geographically coherent. For failure to make such showing, ITAT held Valentine had no PE.

In Gurtler, Herbert & Co. Inc vs Stavanger[40] a US company undertook 9 oil drilling projects on offshore Norwegian oil platforms for a few unrelated customers none lasting longer than 12 months. The Court found no PE stating that aggregation would be permissible only if the projects were carried out for the same customer in the same geographic area.

A US *IRS private letter ruling*[41] involved a Dutch company which used a semi-submersible vessel in drilling oil wells over sequential two year periods for two apparently unrelated US customers in different 'oil blocks' on the US outer continental shelf. The Dutch company did not control the drilling exploration sites and each drilling project lasted only a few months. Each oil block consisted of 9 square miles and the drilling project did not exceed 3 months in any one block and no more than 5 months in any two adjacent blocks. Drilling in non-adjacent blocks was separated by a distance of at least 5 miles and the blocks drilled for the two US companies were at least 150 miles apart:

38. Mehta summarizing at 214.
39. 45 SOT 34 (2011 Mumbai) summarized in Mehta at 214 and reproduced in Mehta Appendix One.
40. Case No. 00 260A ((18 Sep 1980 Stavanger County Court).
41. Summarized in Mehta at 226.

- For US Company 2, 17 wells were drilled over a 2 ¼ year period from August 1975 to October 1977 for a pre-determined contract price payable regardless of whether the Dutch company actually drilled the oil wells in a certain geographic area of the Shelf
- For US Company 1, three wells were drilled over a 2½ year period commencing November 1977

The ruling holds that the Dutch company's activities for US company 2 constituted a construction or installation site PE as the drilling projects had commercial coherence since all 17 projects were pursuant to one contract with the same customer and also had geographic coherence since the same predetermined contract price was due regardless of whether the Dutch company actually drilled wells in a certain geographic area. Drilling projects for US company 1 were not aggregated and apparently did not create a PE.

The above case and ruling precedent thus holds that apart from a few treaties allowing aggregate treatment (timeline could be met by multiple projects),[42] 'stand-alone' treatment would prevail unless there were (1) geographic coherence (same site, e.g. row of houses, canal, pipeline, roads), (2) commercial coherence (same customer or same construction on a continuous site) and (3) unity of execution (same contract, the projects involved similar functions and were chronologically interdependent).

D. Bareboat Leasing and Renting

In the case of ships, and water-borne drilling rigs, the bare words of the treaty might seem to create a permanent establishment for the owners thereof, irrespective of whether it was they or others were 'using' the ships or rigs for the purposes mentioned. However, by analogy to fixed places of business, the owner who simply leases these vessels to persons who operate them will not have a permanent establishment by reason of that ownership alone. 'Using' these vessels also means carrying out the core business activities of the NRE, as discussed supra in section 2.1 E 3.

42. *See also* the *Dutch Contractor* case dated 29 June 1982 discussed above in which the Antwerp Court of Appeals ignored a Belgian–Dutch competent authority interpretative agreement allowing aggregation of contracts for the same customer if carried out simultaneously or consecutively or in various places as part of the same contract – i.e., lacking geographic or commercial coherence, holding that the treaty reference adopted a 'stand-alone' approach. *But cf.* a French Case No. 16,095 (29 Jun 1981 *Conseil d'Etat*) holding that the Spanish-French treaty intended to aggregate drilling projects in Spain and hence the French company had a Spanish PE exempting it from French taxation discussed in Mehta at 218-19.

In *DDIT (International Taxation) vs Dharti Dredging & Infrastructural Ltd*[43] an Indian company hired a dredger from a Dutch company which also provided crew. However, the crew was under the direction of the Indian lessee, which also paid their salaries, food, accommodation and insurance on the dredger. ITAT held that the dredger was only let for hire and did not conduct any business of the Dutch lessor. Hence, there was no PE. Similarly, *Nederlandsche Overzee Baggermaatschappij BV vs DDIT* held that bareboat leasing of a dredging vessel did not constitute a POB PE of the lessor.[44]

43. 44 SIT 586 (2011 Hyd) discussed in Mehta at 136 and reproduced in Mehta Appendix One.
44. (14 May 2010) (bareboat lease charter of dredger was not an Indian PE of the lessor) discussed in Mehta at 138.

Chapter 5
Agency Permanent Establishments

5.1 AGENCY PERMANENT ESTABLISHMENTS – THE PARAMETERS

The form and content of most existing double taxation conventions generally follow the OECD 1963 Draft and 1977 Model Treaties.[1] The most common definition of an agency permanent establishment appears in Article 5 of the (currently 2010) OECD Model Double Taxation Convention on Income and on Capital:[2]

> '5. Notwithstanding the provisions of paragraphs 1 and 2, where a person – other than an agent of an independent status to whom paragraph 6 applies – is acting on behalf of an enterprise and has, and habitually exercises, in a Contracting State an authority to conclude contracts in the name of the enterprise, that enterprise shall be deemed to have a permanent establishment in that State in respect of any activities which that person undertakes for the enterprise, unless the activities of such person are limited to those mentioned in paragraph 4 which, if exercised through a fixed place of business, would not make this fixed place of business a permanent establishment under the provisions of that paragraph.
>
> 6. An enterprise shall not be deemed to have a permanent establishment in a Contracting State merely because it carries on business in that State through a broker, general commission agent or any other agent of an independent status, provided that such persons are acting in the ordinary course of their business.
>
> 7. The fact that a company which is a resident of a Contracting State controls or is controlled by a company which is a resident of the

1. See Appendix A.
2. OECD Model 5(5), (6) and (7).

> other Contracting State, or which carries on business in that other State (whether through a permanent establishment or otherwise), shall not of itself constitute either company a permanent establishment of the other.'

The current 2006 United States Model Treaty contains identical provisions.[3] The 2011 United Nations Model Double Taxation Convention between Developed and Developing Countries contains substantially identical language, but adds three significantly different provisions.[4]

First, the United Nations Model deems 'a person other than an agent of an independent status to whom paragraph 7 applies – [who] is acting in a contracting state on behalf of an enterprise of the other,' who has no authority to conclude contracts in the name of enterprise, 'but habitually maintains in the first mentioned state a stock of goods or merchandise from which he regularly delivers goods or merchandise on behalf of the enterprise' to be a permanent establishment of that enterprise.[5] This 'delivery agent' provision appears in some contemporary treaties between developed and developing countries; it was more common in treaties predating the 1963 OECD Draft.

Second, the United Nations Model, while defining an independent agent in substantially the same language as that of the OECD and United States Models, adds the following:

> 'However, when the activities of such an [independent] agent are devoted wholly or almost wholly on behalf of that enterprise, he will not be considered an agent of an independent status within the meaning of this paragraph.'[6]

Finally, the United Nations Model has a special provision dealing with insurance agents not found in either the United States or OECD Models:

> '6. Notwithstanding the preceding provisions of this article, an insurance enterprise of a Contracting State shall, except in regard to reinsurance, be deemed to have a permanent establishment in the other Contracting State if it collects premiums in the territory of that other State or insures risks situated therein through a person other than an agent of an independent status to whom paragraph 7 applies.'[7]

---

3. United States Model 5(5), (6) and (7).
4. United Nations Model 5(5), (7) and (8).
5. United Nations Model 5(5)(b).
6. United Nations Model 5(7).
7. United Nations Model 5(6).

A. Exempt Preparatory and Auxiliary Activities

With developing country exceptions, most new treaties adopt the OECD Model exceptions to a dependent agency (and fixed place of business) used for activities which are preparatory or auxiliary to the direct realization of profit. These include contract processing, warehousing, storage, display, delivery, purchasing, information gathering, and representative office functions.[8] These exceptions allow, *inter alia,* host country contract manufacturing to be generally combined with host country purchase or consignment sales structures. Combinations of a representative office and independent agency functions should also be possible.

B. No Fixed Place of Business Needed

Under the 1977 OECD and later Model Treaties the dependent agent is an alternative permanent establishment which does not require a fixed place of business, either of the foreign principal or of the agent. Indeed, if there is a fixed place of business of the foreign principal, it is irrelevant whether the persons using it are dependent or independent or have the requisite contractual authority. A permanent establishment already exists to which all of their activities will be attributed.[9]

Not only can a dependent-agency permanent establishment be acquired even though the agent himself has no fixed place of business, but the agent need not be a resident of the source country.[10] All that is required is that one or more persons exercise the requisite contractual authority within the source country

8. *See* Chapter 6, infra.
9. Skaar at 463, 467 (citing German and Norwegian precedent). Vogel also discusses the sequentiality of the permanent establishment tests at page 333 and para. 144. The independent-agency concept is only an exception to a dependent-agent permanent establishment, which itself applies only if there is no fixed-place-of-business permanent establishment. The point is significant, since if the foreign enterprise itself has a fixed place of business, staffing it with 'independent agents' will not exempt their activities from taxation.
10. *See* Vogel, at 333, para. 143; Skaar at 484-85. Skaar considers three criteria potentially applicable to the agents' attachment to the source country: (1) residence, (2) place of abode, and (3) transient presence – concluding that residence is not required, that a place of abode is, and that mere transient presence is not enough (even if salesmen makes regular and repeated visits). While 'mere transient' presence may be insufficient, the requisite permanent establishment presence should be found to exist, provided that one or more agents have power to conclude contracts and regularly exercise such authority in the source country. *Cf* Roberts & Warren at IX-163-164 and Williams, 'Permanent Establishments in the United States,' 29 Tax Law. 277 (1976), reprinted as updated in Income Tax Treaties 218 (Bischel ed. 1978). Contrast German domestic law, which, according to Skaar, held in a 1934 case that while 'residence' was not required, occasional dispatching of traveling agents was not enough. Further, Skaar states at 484 and n. 5 that under 'German domestic laws until 1977 ... only agents with a fixed place of business constituted a PE, cf 16 St Anp G.' Skaar 484-485.

with a sufficient degree of 'permanence' (the 'habitual' exercise of authority).[11] Such authority can be exercised successively by different persons.[12] Thus a software company which regularly sends its home country salesmen into a country with software packages which are sold there has a dependent-agency permanent establishment.

Nonetheless the treaties require something more than the mere transient presence of an agent in the taxing State.[13] Even if the requisite contractual authority exists, no permanent establishment exists if such authority is (1) exercised by an independent agent acting in the ordinary course of his business; (2) the authority is limited to the type of preparatory or auxiliary activities which may be conducted through a fixed place of business without creating a permanent establishment; or (3) the agent is a purchasing agent.

The United States has engrafted the permanent establishment concept onto its statutory rules defining the source of income and income effectively connected with a United States trade or business conducted by a foreign person.[14] These rules apply only if a United States fixed place of business exists – either of the foreign principal or of its dependent agent.

In sum, it is clear nonetheless that for the purpose of treaties based on the OECD, United States, or United Nations models, a dependent agent need not have a fixed place of business.[15] This follows logically from the inapplicability of the dependent agency type of permanent establishment where a fixed-place-of-business permanent establishment already exists. As stated by Vogel:

> 'Contrary to a permanent establishment of the kind envisaged in Art. 5(1) to (4), that constituted by an agent is not *locality related*.'[16]

Vogel illustrates the point with a significant example:

---

11. Skaar applies the temporal test of 'permanence' for a fixed-place-of-business permanent establishment to the dependent-agency permanent establishment, concluding that an agency of less than 6 months' duration will not normally be enough but 18-24 months will always be sufficient. Skaar 469. In practice, the 'habitual' requirement may connote an agency relationship of some duration, but the duration required will likely depend on the nature of the goods or services being sold. While some pre-OECD treaties require that a nonresident agent be 'established' in the source country, Roberts & Warren find this requirement satisfied by an agent who operates in the source country 'on a regular and continuing basis' without having a fixed place of business. Roberts & Warren X-156-157. A different result may obtain in some older German and other treaties which refer to 'permanent agencies.'
12. Vogel, at 333, para. 143.
13. *See* Roberts & Warren IX-138, and IX-156/157.
14. I.R.C. §§ 864(c)(4)(B), (c)(5)(A), and 865(e)(2) and (3).
15. Vogel, at 334, para. 146, 340, para. 153; Skaar at 463-464; Roberts & Warren at IX-156.
16. Vogel, at 334, para. 146 (emphasis in the original); see also *id.* at 340, para. 153 and, with regard to special German treaty provisions, *id.* at 341, para. 160.

> 'A permanent establishment may also be deemed to exist where an enterprise is represented by an agent on board a ship entered in a State's ships register or flying that State's flag on the high seas. In such an event, the ship itself would not be a permanent establishment since it has no link with a specific geographical point, but the manager of a restaurant or the salesman in a kiosk on board, for example, may be deemed a permanent establishment if authorized to conclude contracts for an enterprise.'[17]

The example is significant because absent a permanent mooring,[18] a ship cannot be a fixed-place-of-business permanent establishment. However, a ship can provide a dependent-agency permanent establishment if it has an agent(s) with the requisite contractual authority on board and it regularly plies territorial waters.[19] This was the basis for the ruling which held that a German permanent establishment existed with respect to a restaurant on board a ferry which regularly traveled between Germany and Denmark.

5.2 AGENCY DISTINGUISHED FROM PRINCIPAL TO PRINCIPAL DEALINGS

For another person to be considered a dependent agent PE they must *act as an agent* for its NRE principal rather than as a principal. This means the agent is acting for the principal and not for himself. Recognition of the 'principal to principal' principle is found in the OECD 2012 Discussion Draft 'CARCO' contract manufacturing example, which states that a toll manufacturing affiliate's operations are not attributable to the business of the parent which supplies the raw materials and retains ownership of WIP and finished goods.[20] Similarly with respect to horizontal relationships, the OECD Commentary states that reciprocal 'roaming' agreements of telecom companies are principal to principal dealings and not dependent agencies.[21]

Consignment sales arrangements similarly involve principal to principal relationships and not agencies. For example, in *Rev. Rul. 63-113*, a Canadian

17. BFH BStBl II 361 (1974): Germany–Denmark. Vogel at 334, para. 146.
18. Such as the Queen Mary at Long Beach, California.
19. Although under international law, a ship is a part of the territory of the country under whose flag it is registered, 'the vessel itself, however, is not a PE.' Skaar at 464. The point was essential to the Supreme Court's decision in BFH BStBI II 361 since an agent is only a dependent agent if it operates within the 'territory' of the taxing State.
20. In *Roche Vitamins* the Spanish Supreme Court appears to overlook this example, discussed in Chapter 9 B 3.
21. OECD Commentary, article 5(1), para. 9.1, that a telecom roaming agreement is a contract with an independent contractor and does not constitute a PE.

company shipped its products to a US company on a consignment basis title remaining in the Canadian company until the moment before the US company sold them. The US company controlled the movement and storage of the goods. The IRS held that the arrangement was one of seller and purchaser and did not create a dependent agency or an agency PE. In *Rev. Rul. 76-322*, the IRS similarly concluded that the arrangement was one of principals dealing with one another. Because the relationship was a buy-sell arrangement between principals and not a sales agency, the independent-agency exception was not relied upon.[22]

Similar consignment cases can be found in Australia, for instance *Cases No. F85*[23] and *No. 110*.[24] In F85 an Australian subsidiary of a United Kingdom supplier ordered the Australian contract manufacture of goods for the United Kingdom supplier which it then resold to third parties as an exclusive distributor for New South Wales and elsewhere. The Board held that the New South Wales distributor was not an agent for the United Kingdom company. Although the United Kingdom parent in effect set the retail price, the provision that the New South Wales company was to sell all goods purchased from the United Kingdom company on its own account and not that of the United Kingdom company appeared in a 1937 distribution agreement. The New South Wales company agreed not to sell at prices other than those set by the United Kingdom company. Although technically not relevant it may have been helpful may that these agreements were entered at the time that the UK company and the Australian company were unrelated. Five years later, the United Kingdom company acquired a 10% interest in the Australian contract manufacturing company. In 1947, the United Kingdom company acquired the New South Wales distributor.

In *Airline Rotables Ltd vs IDIT*[25] a UK aircraft repair company contracted with the Indian Jet Airways to repair its aircraft and comply with air worthiness directives. To keep the aircraft constantly in service, Jet Airways maintained at its Indian base a stock of Airline Rotables' replacement parts which could be immediately used while Jet Airways parts were being repaired or overhauled

---

22. *Accord* Ltr. Rul. 8318010 (applicable to the 1945 former United States–United Kingdom treaty) (United States subsidiary which represented only its United Kingdom parent supplier regarding United States consignment sale distribution held not a permanent establishment; United States subsidiary had no power to contract on behalf of foreign parent and sold on its own behalf, in its own name to its customers at prices determined by it). *See* Ltr. Rul. 7816031 (former 1942 United States–Canada treaty) (Canadian manufacturer sending goods into United States on consignment, has no permanent establishment; follows Rev. Rul. 63-113, 1963-1 C.B. 410).
23. 6 T.B.R.D. (n.s.) 483 (Australia 1955).
24. 5 CTBR NS 656, discussed in Tan How Teck, Some Aspects of a Permanent Establishment in Australia, Journal of Australian Taxation Sept/Oct 1998 at 152 (Teck) at http://www.buseco.monash.edu.au/blt/jat/1998-issue2-teck.pdf (last viewed May 26, 2013).
25. 44 SOT 368 (2011 Mumbai) Mehta at 372 and Appendix One.

by Airline Rotables. The replacement parts were kept by Jet Airway's stores staff under a separate bin identification system and remained the property of Airline Rotables but could be removed by Jet Airways as needed. ITAT held that although Jet Airways acted as a consignment warehousing 'agent', it did not conduct the business of Airline Rotables as such agent and could not be viewed as an agent PE. The relationship was one of principal to principal.

A. Principals and Their Activities

As briefly mentioned above, the concept of 'agent' requires a transactional relationship with another party. This needs to be well distinguished from dealings by the Principal himself or employees of the Principal. Some older treaties provide that an individual principal can be his own permanent establishment given substantial trading presence in the host country without regard to the existence of a fixed-place-of-business or dependent-agency permanent establishment. For instance the 1946 treaty between the United States and Republic of South Africa, includes principals within the definition of permanent establishments:

> 'When an enterprise of one of the contracting States carries on business in the other contracting State, whether personally, directly or through a nominee or through an employee or agent there who has authority to contract for his employer or principal or has a stock of merchandise from which he regularly fills orders which he receives, such enterprise shall be deemed to have a permanent establishment in the latter State.'[26]

The early treaties indicated that the mere presence of employees in the host country for delivery of goods and other purposes could constitute a permanent establishment. Thus the Polish-Czechoslovak treaty of 1925 states:

> 'For the purposes of this Convention the expression "working establishment" shall not include the following: journeys made by the head of the undertaking to obtain orders, delivery of orders, delivery of goods on commission to an established dealer, delivery to customers of goods transported from one country to the other or of goods lying in warehouses belonging to a transport undertaking or to a forwarding agent, providing that such transactions are not carried out by offices or employees of the undertaking.'[27]

---

26. United States–South Africa 2(II)(d). (This treaty is no longer in force.)
27. Poland–Czechoslovakia, 1925, 44 L.N.T.S. No. 1091.

It seems probable that employees were considered to be included within the generic term 'agencies' to which earlier treaties made reference. In any event, the 1943 Mexico Draft League of Nations Treaty made the point clear:

> '4. When an enterprise of one of the contracting States regularly has business relations in the other State through an agent established there who is authorized to act on its behalf, it shall be deemed to have a permanent establishment in that State. A permanent establishment shall, for instance, be deemed to exist when the agent:
> A. Is a duly accredited agent (*fondé de pouvoir*) and habitually enters into contracts for the enterprise for which he works; or
> B. Is bound by an employment contract and habitually transacts business on behalf of the enterprise in return for remuneration from the enterprise; or
> C. Is habitually in possession, for the purpose of sale, of a depot or stock of goods belonging to the enterprise.
>
> 5. As evidence of an employment contract under the terms of B above may be taken, moreover, the fact that the administrative expenses of the agent, in particular the rent of the premises, are paid by the enterprise.'[28]

While employees were clearly included within the definition of agency permanent establishments in the 1943 Mexico Draft, it was not until the publication of the OECD Models that it became clear that employees must not only regularly transact some aspect of the business proper, but must also have authority to do so. An employee without regularly exercised authority to bind the enterprise will not constitute a dependent-agency permanent establishment.

With the advent of the OECD, United Nations and United States Model Treaties the concept of a principal as permanent establishments seems clearly displaced by the alternative 'fixed-place-of-business' and 'dependent-agent' types of permanent establishments. Hence principals should not be his own permanent establishment in the absence of a dependent agency or fixed place of business, no matter how substantial his trading activities in the host country. And while an employee can create a permanent establishment for his principal, the conventional wisdom is that an employee cannot be his own permanent establishment.[29] In fact, the issue would seem preempted in the income tax trea-

28. Mexico Draft Prot. V(4) and (5).
29. Roberts and Warren, at IX-12, note 161 (citing Rev. Rul. 55-508, treaty legislative history, and treaty regulations). Roberts and Warren state: 'The obverse question, when does the fixed place of business of the principal qualify as a permanent establishment of his agent, arises commonly where an employee regularly works at the office of his employer. It has generally been assumed

ties by the usual 'commercial travelers' provision under which a nonresident employed by a foreign employer for (usually) less than six months in the host country is not taxable.[30]

5.3 DEPENDENT VS INDEPENDENT AGENTS

Since both dependent and independent agents can have authority to bind a foreign principal, the crucial distinction between the two lies in an area other than that of authority.[31] The distinction basically lies in whether the agent has his own business and is conducting his own business ('in the ordinary course') and not that of his foreign principal when acting on his behalf. The 1977 OECD Model Commentary adds:

> 'it stands to reason that such an agent, representing a separate enterprise, cannot constitute a permanent establishment of the foreign enterprise.'[32]

In *Morgan Stanley & Co., International Ltd*[33] Morgan Stanley traded in the Indian derivatives market through a number of independent brokers, bankers and custodians. Although the brokers worked for Morgan Stanley in separate enclosures and almost *exclusively* for Morgan Stanley, the AAR[34] said this did not make them dependent agent PEs of Morgan Stanley.[35]

---

that the employer's fixed place of business does not constitute a permanent establishment of the employee.'

30. OECD MC, Article 15.
31. Nitikman takes a different view, stating 'The independent agent has no power to bind a principal to a contract.' Nitikman at 259. But, while an independent agent need not have such power, he clearly can have it without losing independent-agency status. One has no further to look than the wording of the OECD-influenced treaties. They define a dependent agent as one, having contractual authority to bind a foreign principal, 'other than an agent of independent status … acting in the ordinary course of [his] business.' See OECD Model 5(6). See also *Secretary for Inland Revenue vs Downing*, 37 S. Af Tax Cas. 249 (1975) (holding that a South African stock broker with discretionary power to buy and sell securities in the name of the Swiss client was an independent agent acting in the ordinary course of his business). And *see* Skaar at 515, 'clearly, the mere fact that an otherwise independent agent is authorized to conclude contracts on behalf of another enterprise is not sufficient for deemed dependency.' For a historical analysis of the relationship between Arts. 5(5) and 5(6), see H. Pijl, Agency Permanent Establishments: in the name of and the Relationship between Article 5(5) and (6) – Parts 1 and 2, Bulletin of International Taxation, Nos. 1 and 2 (2013).
32. 1977 OECD Model Commentary, Art. 5(6), para. 35.
33. 142 Taxman 630 (2005 AAR – New Delhi) Mehta at 369 and Appendix One.
34. The Indian Tax Authority for Advance Rulings (AAR).
35. In contrast, the AAR ruled in *Seagate Singapore International Headquarters (Pty) Ltd*, 189 Taxman 181 (AAR – New Delhi) Mehta Appendix One that Seagate had a POB PE on just such a basis, i.e., that Seagate had an Indian PE through the separate warehouse space and booking facilities provided by independent warehouse agents for Seagate's deliveries to its

The AAR ruling also disagreed with the decision of ITAT[36] in *ACIT vs DHL Operations BV Netherlands*[37] which held that the DHL parent company's agreement with its Indian affiliate for the reciprocal forwarding of international courier deliveries resulted in the Indian affiliate's being an agency PE of DHL. DHL had no offices or employees in India and claimed its dealings were strictly principal to principal. The Indian DHL affiliate was free to set its own prices to be charged to Indian customers, carried out the outbound consignments entirely on its own account and had no authority to bind DHL.

Nonetheless, ITAT ruled that the Indian DHL affiliate *did create* an agency PE of the parent since the affiliate was carrying on the entire DHL business within India under the prestigious brand name of 'DHL Worldwide Express.' That factor may create a 'business connection' under Indian domestic law but would hardly appear relevant to a PE treaty determination. Indeed the same 'connection' could exist between any parent and a source country manufacturing affiliate or sales affiliate. In such cases the source country party is acting as a principal and not as an agent of the NRE principal with authority to bind it.

More appropriately, on somewhat similar facts in *Western Union Financial Services Inc vs ADIT*,[38] ITAT found no agency PE in Western Union's Indian agents for the transmission of money, finding they were independent agents with no authority to bind Western Union.[39] So what defines the dependent vs the independent agent?

A. Historical Evolution of the Concept

At the outset, treaty makers believed that domestic agents would constitute the permanent establishments of foreign persons. The 1899 treaty between Austria–Hungary and Prussia included 'other business facilities by which the owner, partner, manager, or other permanent representative carries on his normal business activities.' The 'dependent' agent (*ständiger Vertreter*) appears to have originated in German case law and legislation of the nineteenth century as an alternative to the fixed-place-of-business permanent establishment (*Betriebsstätte*).[40]

OEM customers. This ruling is contrary to the weight of precedent and the principles of an agency PE.

36. The Indian Income Tax Appellate Tribunal (ITAT).
37. 142 Taxman 1 (2005 Mumbai) Mehta at 370 and Appendix One.
38. 104 ITD 34 (Delhi) Mehta at 395 and Appendix One.
39. *See also* Australian Tax Authority *T.D. 2005/2* (NRE sale of products through a website hosted by an Australian Internet service provider did not create an agency PE.
40. Skaar at 471-472,506. Skaar indicates that prior to 1977, the German domestic concept of a dependent agent required that the agent have a fixed place of business at its disposal.

While the dependent agency derived from German domestic law, the independent-agent clause derived from British domestic law. Specifically, the model treaty prototype is Section 17(1) of the Finance Act of 1925, which exempted from United Kingdom tax nonresidents who confined their dealings to a qualified 'broker [acting] in the ordinary course of his business as such.'[41] The distinction between dependent and independent agents was made in the 1927 League of Nations Model Treaty[42] and appeared the same year in the Austrian–Swiss treaty of 1927, which provides an exemption from permanent establishment status:

> 'Where an independent agent merely negotiates business for the firm he represents, without maintaining on its behalf any warehouse, and without being authorized to conclude on its behalf any transactions ...'[43]

Two years later the treaty between Poland and Danzig of 1929 provided:

> 'The fact that an undertaking maintains business connections with the other territory through a really independent representative (broker, commission agent, etc.) shall not, however, be taken to mean that the undertaking maintains a business establishment (*Betriebsstätte*) in such territory.'[44]

This basic exemption for independent agents (including brokers, commissions and other agents of independent status) was retained by subsequent model treaties, which attempted to define the 'other' category in terms of legal and economic independence from a foreign principal. As stated by the 1928 Fiscal Committee Report of the League of Nations (and appearing in the 1930 Draft Commentary):

The words 'bona-fide agent of independent status' are intended to imply absolute independence, both from the legal and economic points of view.'[45]

---

41. Skaar at 474-475. The legislation responded to the British Board of Internal Revenue's attempt during the 1920s to tax nonresidents who sold goods through a local broker or commission agent, if the contracts were concluded in the United Kingdom. Carroll, 'United States Tax Treaties with the European Community Member Countries: Corporate Aspects,' 41-3rd Tax Mgmt. at A-3 (1975) (discarded).
42. Skaar at 475.
43. Austria–Switzerland, 1925,III(2), League of Nations Doc. C.345.M.102.1928.II, at 61.
44. Danzig–Poland (29 May 1929) Art. III, League of Nations, 'Double Taxation and Fiscal Evasion,' Supplement No. 1 to the Collection of International Agreements and Internal Legal Provisions for the Prevention of Double Taxation and Fiscal Evasion, League of Nations Doc. No. C.345.M.102.1928.11, at 10.
45. 'Double Taxation and Tax Evasion,' League of Nations Doc. No. C.562.M.178. 1928.II, at 12.

The concepts of legal and economic independence appear to derive from German court decisions which refer to 'legal' dependence (the power to instruct an agent), and 'commercial dependence' (the merging of the business interests of agent and principal).[46] The League of Nations Mexico Draft of 1943 illustratively defined 'economic independence' in terms of two concepts: (1) representation of several principals and (2) acting as a broker or intermediary between principals:

> 'The fact that a broker places his services at the disposal of an enterprise in order to bring it into touch with customers does not in itself imply the existence of a permanent establishment for the enterprise, even if his work for the enterprise is, to a certain extent, continuous or is carried on at regular periods, and even if the goods sold have been temporarily placed in a warehouse. Similarly, the fact that a commission agent (*commissionaire*) acts in his own name for one or more enterprises and receives a normal rate of commission does not constitute a permanent establishment for any such enterprise, even if the goods sold have been temporarily placed in a warehouse.'[47]

The definition of independence from a foreign principal in a legal and economic sense has carried through to the 1963 OECD Draft and 1977 OECD Model Commentaries, as well as the United States and United Nations Model Treaties, all of which define independence in terms of an agent's (1) legal and economic independence from a foreign principal[48] and (2) the agent's acting in the 'ordinary course of his business' as a specified type of independent agent. As stated by the OECD Model Commentary:

> '36. Where an enterprise of a Contracting State carries on business dealings through a broker, general commission agent or any other agent of

46. Skaar at 465.

47. Mexico Draft Prot. V(6).

48. Nitikman points out that the 1963 OECD Commentary got turned around because it applied a test of economic and legal dependence to dependent agents with anomalous results. Thus, an agent who was not 'independent,' because legally or economically dependent, would also not be dependent under the conjunctive dependency requirement of the 1963 OECD Model Treaty. The 1977 OECD Model Commentary corrects the inadvertence by applying the legal and economic independence test to independent agents. OECD Model Commentary, Art. 5(6), para. 36. A dependent agent is therefore one who is legally or economically dependent or who is an independent agent not acting in the ordinary course of his business. In both cases, to be a permanent establishment, the agent would have to be authorized to conclude contracts and regularly do so in the name of the foreign principal. In the case of the independent agent acting outside the ordinary course of his business, such authority would have to exist for such extraordinary transactions. *See* Vogel, at 345, para. 170 and at 346, para. 174.

> an independent status, it cannot be taxed in the other Contracting State in respect of those dealings if the agent is acting in the ordinary course of his business (cf. paragraph 32 above). Although it stands to reason that such an agent, representing a separate enterprise, cannot constitute a permanent establishment of the foreign enterprise, paragraph 6 has been inserted in the Article for the sake of clarity and emphasis.
>
> 37. A person will come within the scope of paragraph 6 – i.e. he will not constitute a permanent establishment of the enterprise on whose behalf he acts – only if
> a) he is independent of the enterprise both legally and economically, and
> b) he acts in the ordinary course of his business when acting on behalf of the enterprise.'[49]

Thus, permanent establishment status attaches to the principal if the agent of that principal is, first of all, either (1) 'dependent' (legally or economically) or (2) 'independent' but not 'operating in the ordinary course of business.' If the agent falls into either category, he will be a permanent establishment if he 'has and habitually exercises in a contracting State an authority to conclude contracts in the name of the enterprise,' according to the OECD Model Convention. If an agent is both independent (legally and economically) and is acting within the ordinary course of business, he will not constitute a permanent establishment even though he has contractual authority to bind a foreign principal.

B. Legal Independence

Legal independence of a foreign enterprise is a more uncertain concept than economic independence but essentially relates to the status of the agent as an independent contractor. The OECD Model Commentary defines legal independence both in terms of entrepreneurial risk borne by the independent agent and in terms of control over the agent's activities assumed by the foreign enterprise:

> 'Whether a person is independent of the enterprise represented depends on the extent of the obligations which this person has *vis-a-vis* the enterprise. Where the person's commercial activities for the enterprise are subject to detailed instructions or to comprehensive control by it, such person cannot be regarded as independent of the enterprise. Another

49. OECD Model Commentary, Art. 5(6), paras. 36 and 37.

> important criterion will be whether the entrepreneurial risk has to be borne by the person or by the enterprise the person represents.'[50]

Consistent with the treaty's presumptive recognition of related parties as separate entities, the control exercised by a parent over its subsidiary by reason of its share ownership is not considered in determining the status of the subsidiary as an independent agent.

The requirement of legal independence is evidenced in a Belgian ruling holding that a purchasing and canning agent is a permanent establishment of its foreign principal[51] because the agent had assumed no entrepreneurial risk.[52] Construing an older, non-OECD treaty, the ruling found that the agent was dependent because it used the principal's canning equipment and all of its expenses, purchases and credit line were covered by its Dutch principal (although the agent had its own staff).

An agent's freedom from 'control' by the foreign enterprise is a less certain test of legal independence than is the financial risk test. The 'lack of control' test appears to relate to the legal factors which distinguish an independent contractor from a common law employee.[53]

As stated in *Donroy, Ltd. vs United States*:[54]

---

50. OECD Model Commentary, Art. 5(6), para. 38.
51. Court of Appeal of Ghent, in 6 Revue Generale de Fiscalite 169 (1969) (1933 Dutch-Belgium treaty), also discussed in Skaar. Skaar states: 'In general, the principal's ownership of equipment or facilities used by the agent, as well as other substantial support of the agent's activities, indicates that the agent is "personally" dependent upon the principal. A strong indication of dependence also exists if the principal has a right to take over the premises of the agent when the assignment is ended.' Skaar at 512.
52. Skaar notes that the sharing of entrepreneurial risks can establish independence, citing a decision (BFH in BFHE Bd 139 (1984) 411), in which a container leasing agent was responsible for fifty percent of losses, and no permanent establishment was found. The point seems well taken, provided there is not a sharing of profits and losses occasioned by a joint contribution of property sufficient to constitute partnership status. Skaar at 513. See the discussion in Chapter 10, *infra*.
53. A different view is held by Nitikman, who takes issue with the relevance of distinguishing independent contractors from employees. Nitikman describes the relevant employee-independent contractor tests as follows: 'These comments by the OECD on how to determine whether the agent is independent are directly related to the issue of whether a person is an employee or independent contractor, and, in that sense, seem inappropriate. Control and financial risk are two key factors courts use to determine whether a person is an employee or an independent contractor. Other factors are also important, the degree to which the person is integrated into the principal's business, whether the agent is engaged in a distinct occupational business, the length of time a person is engaged, who supplies the tools (which is actually part of the financial risk factor); whether the type of work being doing is generally done by a specialist without supervision or by an employee with supervision and whether payment is by time or by job done.' Nitikman at 266. However, Vogel notes that employees and self-employed traders are polar examples of dependent and independent agents. Vogel, at 331, para. 138.
54. 301 F. 2d 200, 206 (9th Cir. 1982).

> 'An independent agent ... generally means one who, exercising an independent employment, contracts to do a piece of work according to his own methods and without being subject to control of his employer except as to the result of the work ...'

While the OECD Commentary includes 'detailed instructions' within the concept of control over a dependent agent, the *Donroy* court clearly recognizes that a principal's control over the result of the agent's activities is entirely consistent with independent-agent status. A foreign principal can give detailed instructions concerning the results to be achieved (as opposed to the means of accomplishing them) without denying the agent independent status.[55]

The cases and rulings in fact find independent status, if it exists economically and the agent is acting in the ordinary course of his business, whether the agent is subject to detailed instructions or is loosely supervised.[56] Thus, in *Secretary for Inland Revenue vs Downing*,[57] the court found that a South African broker was not dependent because management of a client's portfolio was a part of his normal occupation as a stockbroker. The real estate brokers employed in *De Amodio vs Commissioner*[58] to lease, manage and sell the United States commercial properties of a Swiss resident were found to be independent agents even though they only acted on the taxpayer's instructions as to which properties to sell or lease.

Skaar[59] observes that German case law distinguishes between 'objective' instruction (expected in an agency relationship) and 'personal' dependence. The latter, if a corporate agent is involved, is evidenced by a merging of the business interests of agent and principal. In this respect, the broader the agent's discretionary powers, the less his personal dependence (i.e., the less the agent is subject to detailed instructions) and also the less likely his business will merge with that of its principal.[60] Nonetheless, an agent subject to complete instructions (such as a real estate broker) is independent provided his business as a broker is not merged with that of his foreign principal.

Vogel distinguishes the permissible degree of control over independent as opposed to dependent agents in terms of 'material' as opposed to a 'personal' dependence. Any agent, including an independent agent, is 'materially' dependent on another person if bound to follow his instructions. It is only if an

---

55. *Accord*, Skaar at 508 ('the power to instruct the agent is a characteristic feature of the agency itself.').
56. *Accord*, Nitikman at 267.
57. 37 South African Tax Cas. 249 (1975).
58. 34 T.C. 894 (1960) aff'd, 299 F.2d 623 (3rd Cir. 1962) (United States–Switzerland treaty).
59. Skaar, at 510.
60. *See* the German Supreme Court decision in Insurance 1975 (BFH in BStBl 1975 II 626) discussed in Skaar at 510.

agent is also 'personally' dependent that a dependent agency exists.[61] An agent becomes personally dependent 'when his obligation to obey instructions is not merely related to specific transactions, but is of a comprehensive nature, such as by virtue of the power an employer has under labour law to give orders to his employees.'[62]

The 'comprehensive control' contemplated by the OECD Model Commentary thus appears limited to the means and resources by which the agent represents a foreign principal. At one end of the legal dependence spectrum, the foreign principal in effect establishes an agent by reimbursing all of his expenses and directing all of his activities. Such an agent resembles (or in some cases perhaps even is) in fact a common law employee and will not be an independent agent. At the other end of the spectrum, the agent who incurs entrepreneurial risk and has his own business, generally representing several principals, clearly is an independent contractor and is 'legally' independent of his foreign principals.

C. Economic Independence

Economic independence refers to the agent's relative independence of the foreign enterprise as a source of business, generally shown by the agent's (lack of) representing or dealing with several principals.[63] Service businesses can be mercurial: a consultant can at one time or another have one large client which consumes all of his time.[64] It would appear that if an agent consistently represents one large client, there is a risk of failing the economic independence test.

Thus, in *Fleming vs London Produce Company Ltd*[65] a British court held that a United Kingdom meat sales broker, 95% of whose sales were effected on behalf of a commonly-owned South African subsidiary was neither a commission agent nor a broker due to the lack of 'generality of its custom' and its

61. Vogel, at 344, para. 169.
62. Vogel, at 344, para. 169.
63. Skaar finds historical roots of the economic dependence test in a 1926 German Supreme Court Case (RFH in RST Bl 1926, at 161) finding that a company could be an agency permanent establishment (*ständiger Vertreter*) if it depended on a foreign principal as an 'employee,' subsequently interpreted by the Supreme Court to refer to a merger of the business of the agent with its principal. *See* Skaar at 507.
64. *See e.g.*, Nitikman, at 268, discussing the case of a lawyer whose major client consumes all of her time. The point would appear generally moot with respect to lawyers, accountants, and other consultants because they generally lack contractual authority to bind their foreign clients in their business 'proper,' and thus will not constitute a permanent establishment in any event. *See Capitol Life Ins. Co. vs The Queen*, [1984] Canada Tax Cases 141, 143.
65. 44 Tax Cases 582 (High Court, Chancery Div. 1968).

acting for the South African affiliate[66] outside the normal course of the business of a sales broker.

Generality of custom, or the lack of it, is clearly one factor to be considered in determining whether an agent is a bona fide independent agent.[67] Generality of custom refers to the number of principals an agent has, or is willing to have. It does not depend solely on whether the broker trades on an established commodity market (like the coffee market), although such markets clearly provide generality of custom on the purchaser side if the broker holds himself out to all customers. However, generality of custom also refers to an agent's holding himself out to the public in terms of representing several principals.

A classic example is *Taisei Fire & Marine Ins. Co. Ltd et al vs Comm'r of Internal Revenue*,[68] where 4 Japanese insurers gave discretionary authority to a US broker to book reinsurance business on their behalf. The US broker maintained a US office of 20 people and had complete discretion over its activities, subject to restrictions imposed by the insurers for risk management purposes. The broker had several unrelated principals, was not economically dependent on the insurers and acted in the ordinary course of its business. Its discretionary authority to book reinsurance business is typical of the insurance industry. An insurance company will routinely 'trust' a broker to buy or sell appropriate reinsurance cover to mitigate the insurer's primary exposure – without ever itself actually 'seeing' the total business booked. This is the usual way of participating in the law of large numbers risk exposure, which is the first rule of insurance risk management.[69]

---

66. The source of ninety-five percent of the sales represented meat contracts obtained by a commonly controlled New Zealand affiliate. The source of the remaining five percent was some 50 New Zealand farmers who wished to take the risk of profit or loss on the London Market.
67. Edwardes-Ker, Art. 5, page 36 cites a German–Dutch ruling 'holding that German shipping agents are PEs, despite being independent.' Was independence lost through a lack of generality of custom or due to agent activities outside the normal course of business?
68. 104 T.C. 535, (1995) Acq. AOD CC-1995-012
69. *See also, Recruitment Agency*, Case BK 07/00604 (15 Jul 2008 Hague Court of Appeal) (Dutch partnership negotiated contracts with a UK recruitment agency, with its approval, although the partnership did not sign the contracts; held an agency PE existed) discussed in Mehta at 422; *Australia Interpretative Decision 2004/546* (Australian distributor of South African magazine distributed to news agents and retail outlets on a commission basis; held independent agent and no PE), discussed in Mehta at 421; *German Insurance Agent*, Decision IR 152/73 (30 Apr 1975, Federal Tax Court) (insurance agent booked insurance contracts for Dutch insurer on standard terms of Bremen Sea Transport Insurers Association; held independent agent acting in ordinary course of its business and no PE), *Secretary for Inland Revenue vs Downing*, 18 taxmann.com 207 (South Africa) (discretionary portfolio management by SA agent was in ordinary course of his business, no PE); *Container Leasing*, Case No. III R 76/81 (22 Sep 1983 German Federal Tax Court) (use of local shipping agent by container leasing company was in ordinary course of agent's business, no PE); *Warehouse Delivery Agent* Case No IR 116/93 (14 Sep 1994) (German company made deliveries to customers of UK company's stock warehoused with the German company, such stock being in the name of the UK company, held no dependent agent

Depending on the functions performed for a foreign principal, by accepting an exclusive sales agency (refusing to deal with competitors of a particular principal), an agent could risk losing independent-agency status. In *Balfour vs Mace*,[70] Justice Rowlatt referred to an early English statute[71] paralleling the tax treaty independent-agency exception in addressing the generality of custom' issue in relation to a firm called Messrs. Bernasconi:

> 'I think this agent is assessable – he is not in receipt of the [total] profits or gains, but I do not think he is a general commission agent within the meaning of this Sub-section (6). He is doing Messrs. Bernasconi's entire business in most of their goods; he only has six other employers, and he has precluded himself from acting for any other manufacturer in goods that compete with Messrs. Bernasconi; and he gets his commission, as was pointed out to me (and really is not immaterial) from Messrs. Bernasconi on orders which customers place with Messrs. Bernasconi by going to Cernobbio where they live and giving these orders there. He is not a general commission agent. He is Messrs. Bernasconi's agent, I think, clearly within the meaning of this Sub-section and it seems to me that he is also an agent and an authorised person carrying on the non-resident's regular agency. I do not quite know what that means, but so far as Messrs. Bernasconi want things done in this country, this gentleman does them all including the posting on of the acceptances of the orders.'[72]

The 1980 United Nations Model Treaty provided that an agent will not be independent if its activities are wholly or almost wholly devoted to one client. That provision was subsequently amended and restricted in scope, as part of the 2001 update of the UN Model. It currently reads:

> 'However, when the activities of such an agent are devoted wholly or almost wholly on behalf of that enterprise, and conditions are made or imposed between that enterprise and the agent in their commercial and financial relations which differ from those which would have been

---

PE as German company acting in ordinary course of its business); *Sten E Rasmussen*, Case dated 25 June 1996) (management of leased Danish properties by lawyers held in ordinary course of their business and no PE, even though one of the lawyers was a partner in the leasing partnerships)

70. 13 T.C. 539, at 552 (1928) (construing S373(l) of the United Kingdom Income Tax Act, 1952), discussed in *Fleming vs London Produce Co. Ltd.*, 44 Tax Cas. 582 (High Court Chan. Div. 1968).
71. Section 31(b) of a 1915 United Kingdom Tax Act, discussed in *Fleming vs London Produce Co. Ltd.*, 44 Tax Cases 584 (High Court, Chan. Div. 1968).
72. This decision was affirmed on appeal, where this point did not arise. See 13 T.C. at 560.

made between independent enterprises, he will not be considered an agent of an independent status ....'[73]

The UN Model Commentary explains the logic behind this change as follows:

> '32. It was subsequently recognized that this sentence had given rise to anomalous situations. The concern was that if the number of enterprises for which an independent agent was working fell to one, the agent would, without further examination, be treated as dependent. In the 1999 revision of the Model, the wording was therefore amended as follows:
>
> However, when the activities of such an agent are devoted wholly or almost wholly on behalf of that enterprise, and conditions are made or imposed between that enterprise and the agent in their commercial and financial relations which differ from those which would have been made between independent enterprises, he will not be considered as an agent of an independent status within the meaning of this paragraph.
>
> 33. The revised version makes clear that the essential criterion for automatically treating an agent as not being of "an independent status" is the absence of the arm's-length relationship. The mere fact that the number of enterprises for which the independent agent acts has fallen to one does not of itself change his status from independent to dependent, though it might serve as an indicator of the absence of the independence of that agent.'[74]

Then finally, what is the relevance of (guaranteed) remuneration in assessing the economic dependence of the agent? The 2012 OECD Discussion Draft[75] failed to establish a clear link between the agent's remuneration and assumption of entrepreneurial risks by the agent, in the one hand, and the agent's independence, on the other. The OECD Working Party, however, acknowledged that bearing of entrepreneurial risks is an important criterion to identify an independent agent.[76]

D. The Clause 5 vs 6 Gap

A reasoning trap applicable to dependent agent rulings involving independent agents is the test of economic independence required for 'independent agents.'

73. UN Model, Art. 5(7), second sentence.
74. UN Model Commentary, Art. 5(7), paras. 32 and 33.
75. OECD 2012 Discussion Draft, paras. 120-123.
76. *Id.*, para 122.

This trap is magnified by the UN MC provision that an agent is not 'independent' if it performs most of its services for one principal and its fees are set at non-arm's length. This language has caused considerable confusion and resulted in findings of dependent agencies which are not supported by either the OECD or the UN MC provisions.[77] The trap is that there is a lacuna between:

- Article 5(5) which creates a dependent agent PE if, and only if, the agent has contractual authority to bind the NRE in the name of the NRE, and
- Article 5(6) which precludes an agency PE even if an agent has such binding authority provided it is legally and economically independent of its principal and acts in the ordinary course of its business

These are not mutually exclusive or interdependent provisions. It is not that hard to think of 'dependent' businesses or agencies which fall outside both provisions and hence cannot be an agency PE, because nothing in Article 5 makes them a PE – that is the lacuna and the trap is falsely tying the two provisions together –reasoning if it's not independent, it must be dependent, and if it's dependent, it must be a dependent agency PE.

What happens where a separate company lacks such authority but does almost all of its business with a NRE and pursuant to the NRE's direction and control? Both MCs tell us that it might not be an 'independent' agent but also that it is not an agency PE. That it is wholly or partly a dependent agent is only relevant if it also has the contractual power to bind its principal. If so, it is an agency PE only if it is also a dependent agent, or if an independent agent, it is acting outside the normal course of its business. Whether its fees are at arm's length or not is a function of the transfer pricing rules (if it is commonly controlled) and should not determine of whether a PE exists.

5.4 AUTHORITY TO CONCLUDE CONTRACTS

Permanent establishment status attaches to the principal if the agent of that principal is either (1) 'dependent' (legally or economically) or (2) independent *but not 'operating in the ordinary course of business'* of such independent agent. If the agent falls into either category, he will be a permanent establish-

77. For example, an ITAT ruling in Reuters Limited Construction House as discussed by Singhal at http://topcafirms.com/index.php/white-paper/201-dependent-permanent-establishment-under-indo-uk-treaty.

ment if he also 'has and habitually exercises in a Contracting State an authority to conclude contracts in the name of the enterprise.'[78]

There is a surprising lack of authority as to where the power to solicit orders ends and the power to enter into contracts begins. Soliciting orders at fixed prices subject to substantive home office approval is generally safe.[79]

The OECD Commentary, in response to the Italian *Philip Morris* decision,[80] has said that mere attendance of meetings or participation in negotiations is not enough.[81] Beyond that, there is considerable conjecture.

A. General vs Specific Authority

Aside from an agent for the delivery of goods from a host country stock of merchandise (an alternative type of dependent agency generally found in developing country treaties), a dependent agent must regularly exercise a degree of authority to bind the foreign principal in business dealings in the host country. In a tax treaty world, the required threshold authority of such agents is one of two types. In a number of earlier treaties (negotiated prior to the 1963 OECD Draft), the dependent agent had to have 'full or 'general' authority to negotiate and conclude contracts which was habitually exercised in one host country. Later, OECD-influenced treaties require only an 'authority' to conclude contracts, which is regularly or habitually exercised in the host country.[82] Absent is the power to 'negotiate' and 'general' authority to conclude contracts.

The earlier 'general authority' approach seems to have reflected a commendable and exhaustive review by the League of Nations fiscal experts of the concepts of agency under the various tax regimes with which they were familiar.[83] In contrast, the 'authority to conclude contracts' of the OECD and later treaties and models appears to be an abstract, economic, and perhaps fabricated construct which may be divorced from local country practice and which recognizes that an agent would rarely have unfettered authority. Moreover, because the OECD, United States, and United Nations Model treaties do not explicitly

---

78. OECD Model 5(5)
79. A United Nations Model Treaty provision found in developing countries treaties lifting the exemption of an independent agent if 'he habitually secures orders ... wholly or almost wholly' for his principal may ensnare the traditional treaty trader. See Singapore-Taiwan, 5(5)(c).
80. *Ministry of Finance (Tax Office) vs Philip Morris (GmbH)*, May 25, 2002, no. 7682/ (Supreme Court of Cassation), unofficial English translation, *Ministry of Finance vs Philip Morris* (2002), 4 ITLR 903. Discussed *infra* at Chapter 5.15
81. OECD Commentary, Paragraph 5, page 33; if there at the disposal of the NRE, however, sales negotiation agents at that office may turn it into a POB sales outlet PE. Commentary, Paragraph 4, para 24.2
82. *See* Section 5.01 *supra*.
83. For example, the 1943 Mexico Draft provided as an example of a dependent agency 'a duly accredited agent (*fonde de pouvoir*).' *See* Skaar at 476-477.

require the power to negotiate such contracts, some uncertainty appears in the cases and rulings involving recent treaties over just how much authority (or how little) is required to constitute a dependent agency.

The earlier treaty requirement of broad authority might also reflect the early concept of a permanent establishment as a host country extension of the foreign enterprise. Accordingly, for the agency to be perceived as the foreign enterprise itself doing business in the host State, the agency had to have general authority both to negotiate and to conclude contracts for the foreign enterprise in the host country.

A corollary is that an agent's 'mere formal power to conclude contracts' (for example, to conclude contracts at specified prices and on pre-set terms only) may not be sufficient to create a dependent agency under some older treaties requiring general authority to negotiate and conclude contracts – those of the United States and the United Kingdom, in particular.[84] Thus, the former 1945 United States–United Kingdom treaty and the 1948 United States–Denmark treaty regulations provided that an agent having 'power to contract on behalf of his principal but only at fixed prices and under conditions determined by the principal does not necessarily constitute a permanent establishment of such principal.'[85]

On the other hand, 'general authority' does not mean that a dependent agent must have full or exclusive authority to act for the nonresident in all matters affecting it in the source country. It is sufficient if a dependent agent regularly acts for the corporation in a particular business capacity. Thus in *Rev. Rul. 55-282*[86] a Canadian investment company had a representative in the United States with discretionary power to buy and sell securities in the United States and to keep its records there. A permanent establishment of the Canadian company was found to exist.[87]

84. Rev. Rul. 56-594, 1956-2 C.B. 1126 (former 1945 United States–United Kingdom treaty); see also the former 1946 United Kingdom–Australia treaty; and see Roberts & Warren at IX-159; Vogel, at 339, para. 151; Skaar at 494, 496, and 497.

85. See T.D. 5569, Treas. Reg. § 7.515,1947-2 C.B. 100,110-11 (United Kingdom treaty); T.D. 5777, Treas. Reg. § 7.953, 1950-1 C.B. 76, 84 (United States–Denmark treaty). However, under the former (1948) United States–Netherlands treaty, the Dutch Supreme Court held in 1971 that a permanent establishment existed where Dutch agents of a United States insurer sold two standard non-negotiable insurance policies. The court held that negotiation was irrelevant as the agents did everything required to sell the contracts. Hoge Raad BNB (1971-143).

86. 1955-1 C.B. 634 (former 1942 United States–Canada treaty).

87. Under current United States statutory law (I.R.C. § 864(b)(2)) a permanent establishment would not exist if the Canadian company lacked a principal United States office through which such transactions were effected. Further, if the Canadian company had been a manufacturing firm rather than an investment company, query whether the United States agent's authority to invest excess working capital on the Canadian company's behalf would constitute a 'general' authority to conclude contracts on behalf of the Canadian company. Note that a discretionary

However, in *Rev. Rul. 80-15*[88] a grantor trust set up by an Italian corporate licensor to prosecute a United States lawsuit for failure to pay patent royalties was found not to be a permanent establishment because the trustee lacked 'general authority' to conclude contracts.[89] On balance, the newer treaty definitions appear to require less contractual authority than do the early treaties. But apart from variations in mere formal power to conclude contracts in practice there may not be much difference. As the 1963 OECD Draft Commentary suggests:

> 'Treatment as a permanent establishment should be limited to dependent agents of those enterprises which, in view of the scope of their agent's authority or of the nature of their agent's business dealings take part to a particular extent in business activities in the other State. Therefore, the Article proceeds on the basis that only persons having the authority to conclude contracts shall be treated as permanent establishments. The term "general authority" which has been commonly used in bilateral conventions has been abandoned and replaced simply by the term "authority." In practice, it seems unlikely that any dependent agents have a completely unfettered authority to conclude contracts... For administrative reasons, it seems advisable to avoid the difficulties which would inevitably arise if the question whether or not the dependent agent is a permanent establishment had to be decided by reference to the precise extent of his authority. When the agent has sufficient authority to bind the enterprise's participation in the business activity of the other country it is such that the agent should be deemed to be a permanent establishment. The use of the term "permanent establishment" in relation to a person, presupposes of course, that that person makes use of his authority repeatedly and not merely in isolated cases.[90]

In an older treaty case, *Lewenhaupt vs Commissioner*,[91] a nonresident alien effected substantial real estate transactions through a cousin who resided in the United States. The cousin, although he held a power of attorney, was to take no important action without first consulting the taxpayer's father in England. In fact, the cousin corresponded weekly with the taxpayer's father, who also held a power of attorney. Although the United States dependent agent's authority

---

investment authority can be protected under the independent broker exception. *Secretary for Inland Revenue vs Downing*, 37 S. Af Tax Cases 249 (1975); discussed infra, Section 5.08.

88. 1980-1 C.B. 365.
89. In practice, this ruling confirms the right of a nonresident treaty litigant to litigate contractual claims, without subjecting itself to host country tax jurisdiction.
90. OECD Draft Commentary, Art. 5(4), para. 16 (emphasis supplied).
91. 20 T.C. 151 (1953) affd, 221 F.2d 227 (9th Cir. 1955) (United States–Sweden treaty prior to its 1963 amendment to reflect OECD provisions).

was thus not unfettered, the court indicated that a permanent establishment existed (assuming *arguendo* a contention that it rejected).

Similarly, a Dutch insurance agent having the power to conclude 'coasters' insurance policies for a United Kingdom insurer was a permanent establishment. The power to conclude a limited range of contracts was held to be general authority.[92]

Whatever the scope of the agent's authority, it must have authority to bind the principal in some aspect of its core business. In *American Wheelabrator & Equipment Corporation vs MNR*,[93] a US manufacturing had a Canadian sales representative who interviewed prospective customers and worked up technical sketches of their requirements. He did not however provide quotes and was not authorized to conclude contracts. No agency PE existed.

In *Danish Distribution Service*,[94] a German supplier contracted with a Danish company to store goods for shipment to its customers after the Danish company received orders from them. The Danish company issued invoices to the supplier's customers, collected payments from them and satisfied the supplier's VAT liabilities. No approval was required for acceptance of the orders by the Danish company, but it was not authorized to conclude contracts binding on the supplier and did not provide marketing or sale promotion. The Court held no agency PE existed because the Danish company performed no sales function and was unauthorized to bind the supplier.

In *Grinsley Holdings*,[95] a Cypriot company represented a German company and another Cypriot company in Russia in respect of the sale and purchase of certain commodities. Grinsley negotiated and prepared the contracts with customers, which were subject to approval by the NRE principals. The Court held that Grinsley did not create a dependent agent PE for the NRE principals, because Grinsley did not have an authority to bind these principals.

In DDIT vs Daimler Chrysler AG[96] Daimler sold cars direct to Indian customers and knocked-down parts to its Indian subsidiary, both FOB Germany. The subsidiary assembled the parts in India and assisted in the sale but had no inventory of cars and no authority to bind Daimler. No agency PE was found.

Insurance agents will generally create an agency PE if they have even limited authority to bind insurance. In *Marine Insurance Agent*,[97] the Dutch Supreme Court held than an agency PE existed where a UK insurance com-

---

92. Judgment of 17 May 1961, HR, Netherlands, BNB 1961-196, summarized at 1 International Tax Treaties Service, Art. 5, page 54 (Edwardes-Ker ed. 1990).
93. 51 DTC 285 (Canadian Tax Appeal Board)
94. Case No 1988-4-565 (15 Dec 1988 Danish Admve Tax Court)
95. NWDFAC, 21 June 2005, A56-26540/04, discussed in O. Konnov, E. Smirnov & H. Smith, Russia – Permanent Establishments, Topical Analyses IBFD (accessed 1 July 2013).
96. 39 SOT 418 (2010 Mumbai) Mehta at 392 and Appendix One.
97. Case No. 14,458 (17 May 1961 Hoge Raad) discussed in Mehta at 385.

pany had authorized its Dutch agent to conclude contracts in some but not other categories of insurance.

In *Air Insurance Agent*,[98] a US insurance company sold life policies to airline passengers through an agent's kiosk at Schiphol Airport. An agency PE was found since the agent was authorized to sign the policies on behalf of the insurer.

The display of goods consecutively at different locations will not constitute a fixed-place-of-business permanent establishment, even if orders are solicited.[99]

B. Authority in Respect of Conduct of the Business Proper

Under the newer treaties, a power to conclude contracts in the name of the foreign enterprise is sufficient to create a permanent establishment if it applies to the conduct of the business proper of that enterprise. In contrast, mere administrative contractual powers (for example, the power to hire and fire employees, to order supplies and equipment, or to lease branch office space) do not create an agency permanent establishment. Such powers fall within the exception from permanent establishment status for agency powers used to conduct auxiliary or preparatory activities. Thus, the 1977 OECD Model Commentary states:

> 'The authority to conclude contracts must cover contracts relating to operations which constitute the business proper of the enterprise. It would be irrelevant, for instance, if the person had authority to engage employees for the enterprise to assist that person's activity for the enterprise or if the person were authorized to conclude, in the name of the enterprise, similar contracts relating to internal operations only.'[100]

If the agent's authority is limited only to a particular line of business, permanent establishment status only extends to that line of business. Direct transactions by the enterprise itself should be disregarded unless attributable to that permanent establishment.[101]

98. Case No. 16,445 (13 Jan 1971 Hoge Raad).
99. Vogel, at 320, para. 110. Vogel characterizes the famous Swiss logger case (Rev. Rul. 56-165, 1956-1 C.B. 849), which is contra, as 'definitely obsolete on account of what is stated in both OECD and United States MC.'
100. OECD Model Commentary, Art. 5(5), para. 32.
101. Vogel, at 331, para. 139.

C. Apparent and Implied Authority

The requisite authority need not be exercised only by the authorized conclusion of written contracts. The enterprise may be contractually bound by the agent's statements.[102] The 1977 OECD Model Commentary states that 'commercial realities' will govern:

> 'A person who is authorized to negotiate and determine all elements and details of a contract in a way binding on the enterprise can be said to exercise this authority "in that State", even if the contract is signed by another person in the State in which the enterprise is situated.'[103]

Several commentators have suggested that the regular exercise of apparent authority or authority implied in fact or created by estoppel can create a dependent-agency permanent establishment in the absence of written contractual authority.[104] Although an agent's authority by estoppel binds a foreign principal by its failure to repudiate unauthorized actions of the agent (rather than by an

---

102. *Ibid.* Can dependent agency be avoided if the agent concludes contracts in its own name but for account of an undisclosed foreign principal? Skaar states that the principal would be bound under a 1926 German decision (applying the agency clause of German domestic law, which does not require contractual authority) but states that under the OECD Model, the agent must have authority to bind the foreign principal. Skaar at 488. This would seem correct. If the agent is really holding himself out as a principal to the outside world, he is a principal and not an agent. See Rev. Rul. 76-322, 1976-2 C.B. 487 and the discussion of consignment sales schemes in Section 5.04. If this leaves the fisc at the mercy of undisclosed agencies, as Skaar implies, transfer pricing laws should prevent abuse. If such laws do not apply, due to the lack of a control relationship, arms-length pricing should result and abuse should be unobtainable. Nonetheless the status of '*commissionnaire*' (buy-sell) agents may be uncertain in some countries, e.g. the UK, particularly if the 'agent' represents only one principal.
103. 1977 OECD Model Commentary, Art. 5(5), para. 32. What happens when negotiations take place in one country and the contract is concluded in another source country? Skaar's view is that the permanent establishment, if it exists under commercial realities, should be in the country in which the major activities occur, i.e., the place of negotiation. Skaar at 494.
104. Vogel, at 331-332, paras. 139-140; Nitikman at 261 and n. 14 and 264 and n. 27; Skaar at 490-492. Skaar observes that whether apparent authority suffices depends on source country local law under the treaty renvoi clause (referring to local law for undefined treaty terms). Skaar at 490 and 500-502. He concludes that apparent or 'external' authority is sufficient in Germany, Holland, Canada, and Denmark and should apply in Norway, but finds the position unclear in common law countries. *Id.* at 498-500. In fact, there is ample authority in American and English common law for apparent authority, implied authority, and authority by estoppel. *See, e.g.*, Restatement (Second) of Contracts § 27. On this point, neither *Herbert vs Commissioner*, 30 T.C. 26, 29 (1958) nor Rev. Rul. 63-113,1963-1 C.B. 410, are in point, as Skaar observes. Herbert was dismissed for lack of a United States 'trade or business.' It was therefore irrelevant that an attorney possessed a general power of appointment but was to consult the taxpayer first. Rev. Rul. 63-113 found a consignment sales arrangement and not an agency. Because the consignee was found to be a 'purchaser,' the ruling holds that not even a 'limited agency' was involved. Cf. Roberts & Warren at IX-158 and n. 182.

agent's *de facto* authority), the distinction may not be relevant for purposes of agency permanent establishment status, which fundamentally looks to public perception of the agency as a host country trading presence of the foreign enterprise.[105]

The issue may arise in two contexts. First, if a manufacturer's representative purports to bind it without its authority, that authority will be implied in law if the principal knows of such representation and fails to disavow it.[106] The agent gains authority by estoppel.[107] For instance in a 1978 decision involving the Swiss treaty, a Dutch lower court held that a Dutch sales agent was a permanent establishment of a Swiss principal. Although his contract forbade him from accepting orders for the Swiss supplier, the Dutch agent did so in practice.[108]

Second, if a foreign supplier requires home office approval of orders solicited by source-country agents, but ignores the requirement in practice or treats it as a mere rubber stamp formality – approving all orders routinely without inquiry into price, terms, or customer creditworthiness – it may confer *de facto* or apparent authority.[109] There are a number of instances in common law where an agent can have implied authority, *de facto* authority of authority by *estoppel*, but all of these doctrines apply only to where the agent is attempting to act for the foreign principal or acts for it in practice, both overt agencies.

Such a result does not seem possible in civil countries with respect to commissionaires who sell in their own name as confirmed in *Dell* and *Zimmer*,

105. Skaar refers to the German concept of *Vollmacht*. He concludes where *Vollmacht* is used in treaties, it is likely that the reference is to external authority, 'i.e. the authority as it appears to a bona fide third party.' Skaar at 500. He refers to a German lower court decision (*Finanzgericht* Berlin in EFG 1970, at 327) holding that the binding effect of business arranged by an agent may constitute a permanent establishment 'even if the activity goes beyond the limits of his authorization in the internal relationship' with the principal. Skaar also cites German treaty commentators who include *Duldungsvollmacht* (pseudo-authorization) as a permanent establishment constituting agency. Under this doctrine, the principal must take action to inform possible third parties that an agent does not have authority to conclude contracts on his behalf, or accept the contracts as binding. For the Canadian position, see Nitikman at 261.

106. *TVM Limited vs CIT*, 102 Taxman 578 (1999 AAR – New Delhi) Mehta at 406 and Appendix One.

107. Nitikman at 261 and n. 14; Skaar at 500-501.

108. Judgment of 20 June 1978, GH, Netherlands, BNB 1979-190, summarized at 1 International Tax Treaties Service, Art. 5, page 58 (M. Edwards-Ker ed. 1990).

109. *See* Nitikman, who states: 'In other words, when the parties intend the signing to be a mere formality, a contract exists before and in the absence of a signing. When the parties so intend, no contract is created unless and until the signing occurs.' Nitikman 264 and n. 27, citing Restatement (Second) of Contracts § 27, Comment (b). *See also* Vogel, at 332, para. 140, citing several German commentators to the same effect. Skaar states that a permanent establishment exists 'when the approval of the contract is a pure formality, and not a real part of the negotiations.' Skaar at 492. Sound economic reasons should support the enterprise's reserving the right to conclude contracts offshore.

although similar arguments of 'de facto binding' were made by the lower courts.

D. Regular Exercise of Authority

The mere possession of the requisite authority is not sufficient. It must be exercised regularly or habitually. Even a general power of attorney is not sufficient if not regularly exercised. The relevant authority is that which is exercised, not that which is given. The authority must be exercised 'habitually.' The 1977 OECD Model Commentary states that this term 'presupposes, of course, that the person makes use of this authority repeatedly and not merely in isolated cases.'[110] However, individual acts of authority by several agents can be aggregated to determine whether authority is 'habitually' exercised on behalf of a foreign principal.[111] One commentator ventures the term should have its 'ordinary, grammatical meaning of "to become a habit".'[112]

Vogel, who states that the conclusion of a single contract would be insufficient, postulates that the required frequency will depend on 'what is normal in the actual line of business concerned.'[113] In cases of doubt, Professor Vogel states that reference should be had to the type of continuity applicable to the fixed place of business – the decisive factor being 'whether the activity was from the outset devised as a lengthy activity or only as a temporary expedient.'[114] Vogel's view has support in case law. In *Unisys Corp. vs Federal Commissioner of Taxation*,[115] the Australian court held a PE was not created by the signing of two license agreements by an employee in the US, such not being a habitual exercise of authority. Accordingly, the relevant authority is that which is exercised, and not merely that which is given.

The 'continuity' requirement has significant consequences for purveyors of non-standardized services and products as well as for major contractors. Does the continuity requirement exclude an agent with authority to conclude a construction contract for a large dam or a transatlantic telephone cable,[116] or

110. OECD Model Commentary, Art. 5(5), para. 31.
111. *Cf.* Vogel, at 333, para. 143.
112. Nitikman at 263.
113. Vogel, at 332, para. 142.
114. Vogel, at 332-333, para. 142. Vogel also equates the treaty terms 'regularly' and 'habitually' and defines both by reference to the object and nature of the transaction involved. *Id.* at 339, para. 151. A different view is said to be had by Debatin and Walter who 'think the term 'regularly' requires a comparison of the activities to be measured with other business handled by the agent.' Vogel, at 339, para. 151.
115. New South Wales Supreme Court, 4 December 2002, *Unisys Corp. vs Federal Commissioner of Taxation*, No. 1527/02, [2002] NSWSC 1115; IBFD Tax Treaties Case Law Database.
116. The 6- or 12-month construction project inclusion may be inapposite in view of the limited period of construction within territorial waters.

for the sale of a ship or an aircraft?[117] If only one contractual act were involved the answer should be 'Yes.' But because long projects may require license approvals, negotiations and a number of collateral agreements, large contracts, despite their singularity in occurrence, the answer is necessarily more subtle.

E. Non Authorized Employees and Representatives

If a foreign principal does not have a host-country fixed place of business or a dependent agent in that country, it can dispatch to or maintain in the host country employees and representatives who lack authority to bind the enterprise in its trading activities, without creating a permanent establishment. Thus, in *American Wheelabrator & Equipment Corporation vs MNR*,[118] a Canadian resident salaried engineer was held not to be a permanent establishment of his American employer even though he drew up sketches of the premises of prospective customers and proposed suggestions as to the kind and type of equipment which might be installed by his employer. The sketches and suggestions were subject to review by head office engineering. The local engineer did not quote prices or contract terms, operated out of his home (without employer reimbursement), and used (at his own expense) an answering service to which mail or telephone correspondence addressed to him or to the company was sent.[119]

Similarly, United States *Rev. Rul. 77-45*[120] holds that employees of a Canadian engineering company present in the United States for less than a year planning and supervising construction activities were not a permanent establishment where the employees were 'not authorized to make any major decisions concerning basic plan design.' Their employer was provided, as an

117. Some indication of the answer is provided in the Swiss logging equipment ruling (Rev. Rul. 56-165, 1956-1 C.B. 849) and the *Race Horse* rulings (Rev. Rul. 58-63, 1958-1 C.B. 624 and Rev. Rul. 60-249, 1960-2 C.B. 264). The former suggested that two years of sale demonstrations in the United States was clearly a sufficient continuous presence to create a permanent establishment even in the absence of a fixed place of business or a dependent agency. The race horse cases are a withholding tax anomaly which indicate that more than one big transaction is required to create a permanent establishment (on the theory that one race would not constitute a permanent establishment, thereby justifying withholding). Nitikman raises the issue whether 'habitually' is limited to the taxable year in question, for which the answer may be 'no,' in view of the 'at any time' rule. *See* Nitikman at 262. See Williams, 'Permanent Establishments in the United States,' 29 Tax Law. 277 (1976), reprinted as updated in Income Tax Treaties 256 (Bischel ed. 1978).
118. 51 D.T.C. 285 (Inc. Tax App. Bd., 1951) (1942 former United States–Canada treaty).
119. *Id.* at 286.
120. 1977-1 C.B. 413.

accommodation, an on-site office but this was held not to constitute a fixed place of business because no consideration was charged.[121]

A similar rationale should apply to exempt traveling salesmen, itinerant service and technical personnel, and even host country sales or manufacturers' representatives, whether salaried or on commission, provided there is no host country trading office and they possess no contractual authority, actual, apparent or implied, to bind the foreign enterprise.[122]

5.5 ACTING IN THE ORDINARY COURSE OF THEIR BUSINESS

In addition to economic and legal independence, the Model Treaties require that an independent agent represent the foreign principal in the 'ordinary course' of his business as an independent agent. In meeting this test, the degree and nature of the agent's contractual authority, if any, to bind a foreign principal is relevant not to distinguish an independent from a dependent agent, but to determine whether the agent is acting in the ordinary course of his business in representing a foreign principal.[123]

---

121. *See* OECD Model Commentary Art. 5(4), para. 24 (permanent establishment exists where the fixed place of business not only gives information, but also furnishes plans, etc. specifically developed for the purposes of the individual customer).
122. *See* Judgment of 10 October 1978, France, 7.0. Deb. AN, p. 5850 No. 1300, summarized at 1 International Tax Treaties Service, Art. 5, page 34.5009 (Edwardes-Ker ed. 1981) (France–Sweden treaty, sales representative not a permanent establishment, because activities preparatory or auxiliary); but cf. Judgment of 5 May 1937, Germany, *Reichsfinanzhof*, RStBl 1937 Vol. 41 p. 239, summarized at 1 International Tax Treaties Service, Art. 5, page 36 (Edwardes-Ker ed. 1989) holding that a traveling salesman can be a permanent establishment); 2 December 1972 Letter of Dept. of Fin., Skatte-Nytt A 1972 No. 12 at A72-305, summarized at 1 International Tax Treaties Service, Art. 5, page 61.5005 Edwardes-Ker ed. 1979) (Norway–Germany treaty; Norwegian tax authority said a representative with authority to conclude contacts was a permanent establishment; exercise of the power was unnecessary); Ltr. Rul. 5412225580A (United States salesman soliciting United Kingdom merchandise not a permanent establishment); Ltr. Rul. 5509205580A (United States commission agent soliciting orders approved in United Kingdom with a United States warehouse for small orders not a permanent establishment). Also see regulations under former United States treaties with Canada and the United Kingdom, which state that the 'mere fact that salesmen, employees of a [foreign] enterprise, promote the sale of their employer's products in the United States or that such enterprise transacts business in the United States by means of mail order activities, does not mean that such enterprise has a permanent establishment therein.' T.D. 5569, Treas. Reg. § 7.515,1947-2 C.B. 100,110-11, interpreting 1945 former United States–United Kingdom treaty; T.D. 5206, Treas. Reg. § 7.22, 1943 C.B. 526, 534-535, interpreting 1942 former United States–Canada treaty. Skaar cites a Norwegian administrative decision finding no permanent establishment where a traveling agent sought out prospective customers, demonstrated company's products and submitted orders for subsequent approval by the Danish principal. Skaar at 492.
123. *See* the discussion in section 5.13 *supra*. Nitikman argues that the distinction between general (dependent) and special (independent) agents made in the *Donroy* case (301 F.2d at 205-206) is

A. Degree and Nature of Agent's Authority

The degree and nature of authority exercised by an agent will vary with the nature of its business. For example, a commission sales agent may have authority to sell the goods of a foreign principal in the United States (typically at preset prices and terms),[124] or may have no authority to sell the goods, having authority merely to solicit orders for approval by the principal.[125] In contrast, a stock broker can have unfettered discretionary authority to manage a foreign client's stock portfolio.[126]

B. Acting in Ordinary Course

Where an agent acts in the name of foreign principal, what is relevant is whether, in representing the foreign principal, the agent is exercising the degree and nature of authority (1) it usually exercises in representing such principals in the ordinary course of his business and (2) whether such activity is customary in the trade for that type of agent.[127] A number of rulings reflect that both are

---

incorrect. *See* Nitikman at 266. The *Donroy* court was probably focusing on the 'general authority' required of a dependent agent under the old United States–Canada treaty. But Nitikman's point seems well taken. Dependent agents need not be general agents and independent agents can have full discretionary authority in certain areas (as in the case of a stock broker entrusted with portfolio management). Similarly, doctrines of agency under contract law, master-servant tort liability, and other principles of agency would appear irrelevant both as to the creation of a dependent agency and as to the distinction between dependent and independent agents. See Nitikman at 259 and fn. 5.

124. *See* Rev. Rul. 55-617, 1955-2 C.B. 774 (United States–Belgium treaty), which states: 'The corporation does extensive business in the United States through the medium of a commission agent and is thus engaged in trade or business within the United States as defined by section 871(c) of the Internal Revenue Code of 1954. However, the corporation has no permanent establishment in the United States.'

125. *See* Rev. Rul. 62-31,1962-1 C.B. 361, revoking Rev. Rul. 54-588,1954-2 C.B. 456 (former United States–United Kingdom treaty) suggesting that the sales solicitation office of one United Kingdom company is not that of a second United Kingdom company for whom orders were solicited.

126. *See Secretary for Inland Revenue vs Downing*, 37 S. Af. Tax Cas. 249 (1975).

127. *See* Skaar at 516-519. In case I R 116/93 (14 September 1994), the *Bundesfinanzhof* held that a legal entity with substantial business activities of its own is, as a matter of principle, to be regarded as independent. The Court found that the agent (a German GmbH) was acting in the ordinary course of business as his activities were typical for the business of a broker, general commission agent or other agent of an independent status. The Court refused to derive a definition of 'ordinary business activities' from the activities which were typical for this specific individual agent prior to the material time, because defining ordinary business activities on the basis of previous activities could lead to a questionable outcome. For example, a manufacturing enterprise would always be acting outside the ordinary course of its business during its first agency activity whereas further agency activities for other principals would be regarded within the ordinary course of its business. The fact that the GmbH was subject to the directions of its principal was not regarded as contradictory to it acting in its ordinary course of business

crucial factors in determining whether the agent is acting in the ordinary course of its business.

Thus, in *Secretary for Inland Revenue vs Downing*,[128] the court found that a South African stock broker was acting in the normal course of his business in managing the portfolio of a Swiss client. Finding that the broker received 'no remuneration over and above the normal brokerage payable to a broking member of the stock exchange,' the court found that the broker's exercise of a discretionary authority to conclude contracts in the name of foreign principal[129] was a part of his usual activities as a broker, even though the exercise of such authority might not be customary for other independent agents:

> 'There is nothing to contradict or to place in doubt Mr Smith's assertion that it was within the scope of his ordinary functions as a stockbroker to handle the appellant's portfolio as he did and to exercise authority to buy or sell equities in the interests of his client. It may be that the exercise of authority to conclude transactions on behalf of and in the name of a principal may fall beyond the scope of the ordinary business of certain types of agents or broker but that is not necessarily, nor even probably, so in the case of a stockbroker handling a portfolio for a client. It is of the very nature of his business, dealing as he does in shares which are bought and sold in a market where rapid and substantial fluctuations of price are not uncommon, to be able to deal expeditiously with situations which might suddenly arise. Nor does the circumstance that there was a degree of permanency in the management of the portfolio militate against a finding that the broker acted in the ordinary course of his own business; management of a portfolio of shares implies a degree of permanency.'[130]

---

because other agents are also bound to follow their principal's instructions. *See* IBFD Tax Treaty Case Law Database.

128. 37 S. Af. Tax Cas. 249 (1975).
129. Which authority the court assumed, *id.* at p. 258.
130. *Id.* at p. 259, quoting with approval the lower court's judgment. In approving this finding, the appellate court rejected an argument by the government that under the OECD Commentary, an otherwise independent agent with contractual authority to bind a foreign principal was a dependent agent. However, the OECD Commentary was consistent with the court's decision. The cited OECD Commentary states: 'Persons cannot be said to act in the ordinary course of their own business if, in place of the enterprise, such persons perform activities which, economically, belong to the sphere of the enterprise rather than to that of their own business operations. Where, for example, a commission agent not only sells the goods or merchandise of the enterprise in his own name but also habitually acts, in relation to that enterprise, as a permanent agent having an authority to conclude contracts, he would be deemed in respect of this particular activity to be a permanent establishment, since he is thus acting outside the ordinary course of his own trade or business (namely that of a commission agent), unless his

Curiously, the *Downing* court found that the broker's activity of deciding to which stocks to buy and sell fell outside the scope of his work as an 'agent,' perhaps because he was not compensated for making these decisions, but rather for effecting the purchase and sale transactions. Nonetheless, because it was customary to provide such services, including monitoring of the market in portfolio management, their provision did not taint the broker's status as a dependent agent.[131]

In a German ruling under the German–Dutch treaty it is held that an insurance agent could write policies, collect premiums, and represent the insurer in court without creating a permanent establishment. This was the normal custom in this line of business.[132] The agent had similar contracts with thirteen other insurers.[133]

However, insurance brokers which sold two standard flight insurance policies from a booth at Schiphol Airport were held to be a permanent establishment of the United States insurer. The brokers (and authorized travel agents who also sold such policies) were not acting in the ordinary course of their own businesses and hence did not qualify for the independent-agency exception. Because the policies were standard and sold at pre-set terms, home office approval was not required and hence the agents were acting as dependent agents.[134]

Activities may be within the normal custom of a given line of business even if carried on by only a few agents in that line (for example, by those within large capital or those who are innovation-minded). Vogel[135] and Skaar[136] both cite the example of container leasing by a shipping and air transport agent for a United States enterprise when containerization was just being introduced.[137] The agent was also a ship broker and travel agent and provided marketing support for the United States company in Germany. Under the container leasing arrangement, the agent received a ten percent commission on the leasing fees, bore fifty percent of the losses for which he was not responsible and

activities are limited to those mentioned at the end of paragraph 5.' OECD Model Commentary, Art. 5(6), para. 38.7.

131. *Id.* at 261.

132. Edwardes-Ker, Art. 5, P13.5004 (BFH BStBl II 626, 628 (1975)).

133. Similarly, a Dutch ruling under the same treaty holds that a Dutch real estate broker who 'administers' a building is a permanent establishment because it had the power to conclude contracts on behalf of the German resident owner. Customarily, brokers lease and manage real property only on specific instructions from the owner. Lower Court of the Hague, 10 November 1970 (Rolno. 16,528). *See also Cour de Cassation in Repertoire Fiscale* (1970-166), holding that a Belgium architect who handled the advertising and sale of apartments for a French company, was a permanent establishment.

134. Hoge Raad in *BNB* (1971-143) (1948 United States–Netherlands treaty).

135. Vogel, at 172, para. 172.

136. Skaar at 519-521.

137. BFH in BFHE Bd 94, 139 (1984) 411.

bore all of the losses for which he was. The agent was authorized to negotiate and conclude leasing contracts pursuant to a broad power of attorney but was authorized neither to buy or sell equipment. The court found that the activity could presently be performed by only a few well-financed, innovative agents, but could become customary in the industry in the future. As stated by Skaar:

> 'Lacking objective criteria the Supreme Court considered the "ordinary course of business test" individually, and an assessment of the total activities of the agent was decisive. The Court concluded that the hiring-out of container chassis was within the ordinary course of this particularly innovative agent's business. The agent was therefore an independent agent and no agency PE was found.'[138]

In *Fleming vs London Produce Co. Ltd.*[139] a United Kingdom meat commission sales agent was found to be the United Kingdom permanent establishment of a South African affiliate on whose behalf it made ninety-five percent of its sales. The meat was actually purchased from a New Zealand affiliate with five percent of sales made on behalf of 20 to 60 New Zealand farmers who wanted to take the risk of profit or loss on the London market. London Produce held itself out to the public as a commission meat salesman, its sales accounting for 1.7 percent of United Kingdom imported meat sales. The sales commission charged was usual for the trade.[140] The court found that London Produce was not an independent agent since it lacked generality of custom, paid insurance, collected accounts, acted as a factor and did other things meat brokers do not ordinarily do.

The opinion is actually based on English statutory law, which paralleled the independent-agency exemption in the United Kingdom–South African treaty (and was apparently dispositive of the treaty claim). This parallel statutory law first appeared in 1925 and had its substantive origins in a 1915 United Kingdom enactment:

> 'Provided that where sales or transactions are carried out on behalf of a non-resident person through a broker in the ordinary course of his business as such and the broker – (i) is a person carrying on bona fide the business of a broker in the United Kingdom; and (ii) receives in respect of the business of the non-resident person which is transacted through

138. Skaar at 520-521.
139. 44 Tax Cas. 582 (High Court, Chancery Div. 1968).
140. There was evidence that Kaiapoi was a fictitious principal, set up by a controlling family patriarch to siphon off profit from the United Kingdom tax base. The Revenue accordingly argued that all of the profit should be charged to London Produce as principal. This argument was rejected, Justice Megarry finding that London Produce acted as Kaiapoi's agent.

> him remuneration at a rate not less than that customary in the class of business in question, then, notwithstanding that the broker is a person who acts regularly for the non-resident person as such broker, the non-resident person shall not be chargeable in the name of that broker in respect of profits or gains arising from those sales or transactions. In this subsection, "broker" includes a general commission agent.'[141]

This statutory provision was the prototype on which the League of Nations fiscal experts crafted the independent-agency exception in the 1920s which provided:

1) representation by a 'broker' or 'general commission agent';
2) who is a bona fide agent (that is, who represents several principals);
3) acting 'in the ordinary course of his business as such';
4) at customary rates for that class of business.

It therefore becomes relevant to look at the English case law considered by Justice Megarry in construing this provision. In *Gavazzi vs Mace*,[142] Justice Rowlatt, considering the 1915 Act, held that a 'broker' or 'general commission agent' is an agent who is not an authorized person carrying on a regular agency of the non-resident person and therefore there was no need for a statutory exception for such independent agents. Interestingly, the same point is made in the OECD Commentary.[143] On the facts, Justice Rowlatt, found that the United Kingdom agents were neither brokers nor general commission agents because by accepting bills of exchange enabling their foreign seller to get its money in advance, they acted as factors. They did not act in the ordinary course of the business of a general commission agent.[144]

As stated in *Gavazzi*, to qualify for the independent-agent exception, an agent must (1) fit into a class of traders which have a defined role as intermediaries recognized by both the sellers and buyers in that service or product market and (2) act within that role and not some other role, apparently even if that other role would also qualify for exemption as an independent agency.[145]

---

141. § 373(1), proviso, which first appeared in the form considered by Justice Megarry in 1925, but which appears to clarify the 1915 statute substantively. Ibid.
142. 10 T.C. 698, 744 (1926).
143. *See* OECD Model Commentary, Art. 5(6), para. 35, last sentence.
144. *London Produce*, *supra*, at 594.
145. Thus, Edwardes-Ker, p. 13.5004 cites a German–Dutch treaty ruling holding that a Dutch agent is not a permanent establishment, even though it concluded contracts in the name of its foreign principal, because it was acting in the ordinary course of its business.

5.6 PARTICULAR AGENTS

A. Managing Agents

An agent in the host country managing the business proper of a foreign enterprise will be a permanent establishment if the agent has and exercises the required contractual authority (and is neither a purchasing agent nor independent agent acting within the ordinary course of its business).

The management of real property can usually be undertaken without creating permanent establishment status, either because leasing activities do not rise to the level of a trade or business[146] or because commercial lease management and sale activities are undertaken by independent real estate agents.[147] However, the income and gain from real property are typically subject to host country taxation under a treaty real-property income articles.[148]

In a 1972 French ruling,[149] a franchise operator of a French school was held to be a permanent establishment of the Swiss franchiser. The ruling found the school was operated by the Swiss owner through a managing agent even though the agent paid a royalty-like fee and assumed the risk of loss.[150]

B. Brokers and General Commission Agents

Brokers are fundamentally negotiators for the sale of property on commission.[151] They may operate in specialized markets – as do tea brokers and stock brokers – or they may be general commission agents.[152] To qualify as an inde-

146. *E.g.*, with respect to single properties or net leased properties. *Herbert vs Commissioner*, 30 T. C. 26 (1958) (former United States–United Kingdom treaty) held that the leasing of a single Washington D.C. men's clothing store did not constitute a trade or business even though checks were paid, tax returns made, and repairs were authorized through the office of a Washington D.C. holding company of which the taxpayer was a minority stockholder. In the United States, triple net leases are also sometimes used. In a triple net lease, the tenant assumes the cost of repair, insurance and local taxes on the property.
147. *See De Amodio vs Commissioner*, 34 T.C. 894 (1960), aff'd, 299 F.2d 623 (3rd Cir. 1962) (United States–Switzerland treaty). An independent real estate agent acting as a dependent agent will constitute a permanent establishment, Dutch Supreme Court, 21 April 1971, BNB 1971/110.
148. *See* OECD Model 6, 13(1).
149. Edwardes-Ker, Art. 5, page 13.5002.
150. *See* Edwardes-Ker, Art. 5, page 13.5003 (German–Dutch ruling, 3 December 1936, held a local manager can be a permanent establishment even though he owns the premises and business equipment therein); Skaar states that a series of German Supreme Court decisions have denied the existence of an agency permanent establishment (*ständiger Vertreter*) under domestic law where the whole business of the enterprise was rented. Skaar at 487 and note 41. *See* Leasing, BFH in BStBl 1960 III 468.
151. *See Fleming vs London Produce Co. Ltd.*, 44 Tax Cases 582, 595 (High Court, Chan. Div. 1968).
152. Discussed in the following section.

pendent agent for treaty purposes, a broker must hold himself out to the public, not only in terms of the market in which he deals, but also with respect to the number of principals he represents or is willing to represent.[153] Secondly, a broker must act in and be compensated in the ordinary course of his business.

In *London Produce*, the Chancery Division held that a United Kingdom meat sales broker was not acting in the ordinary course of its business, when ninety-five percent of its business was conducted in the name of a South African affiliate and the United Kingdom broker also acted as a factor, paid insurance, collected accounts, and conducted all of the United Kingdom business proper of its South African affiliate.[154]

Similarly, in a 1971 Dutch Supreme Court decision,[155] a Dutch insurance broker sold flight insurance policies at Schiphol Airport on behalf of an American insurer. The ruling holds that the broker was a permanent establishment of the United States company because the broker was not acting in the ordinary course of his business in selling insurance policies from an airport booth.[156] Since the policies were standard and sold at pre-set premiums, home office approval was not required and a dependent agency existed.

1. Securities Brokers

Trading in shares, securities and commodities through an authorized resident broker may constitute a permanent establishment only if the broker is not an independent agent or if the independent agent doesn't act in the ordinary course of his business. For instance an independent agent may be a permanent establishment if he exercises authority to buy and sell such securities on behalf of the foreign principal in an abnormal fashion or under an out-of-the-ordinary fee arrangement.

In the United States, a nonresident (other than a dealer) can engage in unlimited trading for his own account in stocks, securities and exchange-traded commodities 'whether by the taxpayer or his employees or through a resident broker, commission agent, custodian or other agent, and whether or not any such employee has discretionary authority to make decisions in effecting transactions'[157] The only exceptions apply to closely held[158] investment

---

153. The relevant principals will be sellers since dealings for buyers are protected under the purchasing agent exception to dependent-agency status.
154. *See* the discussion at footnote 139.
155. 13 January 1971, BNB 1971/143.
156. Perhaps similarly explained is a Dutch German treaty ruling, cited by Edwardes-Ker (¶13.5005), which holds that a Dutch broker administering a building owned by a German company is a permanent establishment in the Netherlands.
157. IRC Section 864(b)(2)(A)(ii).
158. That is, companies other than those more than 50% of the value of which is held directly or indirectly by five or fewer individuals.

companies[159] and partnerships which have 'principal offices' in the United States.[160]

In *Rev. Rul. 55-282*,[161] it was held that under the former 1942 United States–Canada treaty, a United States agent of a Canadian investment company with a discretionary power to buy and sell securities on its behalf was a permanent establishment. This status could be avoided under current United States law[162] if the Canadian company did not have its principal office in the United States or if the agent were independent and acted in the ordinary course of its business.

The wide scope permitted for securities management through an independent stock broker is illustrated in *Secretary for Inland Revenue vs Downing*.[163] There the court found that a South African broker, with discretionary authority to manage and trade his Swiss client's stock portfolio, was not a permanent establishment because such activities were customarily undertaken by stockbrokers for their clients.

2. *General Commission Agents*

'Brokers' and 'general commission agents' are terms commonly used together. In *Fleming vs London Produce Co. Ltd.*,[164] the court construed an English statute exempting nonresident dealings through a resident broker' (including a 'general commission agent'). The provision considered was the statutory prototype for the treaty 'independent-agent' exception.[165] Prevailing counsel argued that a 'general commission agent' is essentially a broker who does not deal with specific commodities or on a specific market:

> 'Mr. Goff forcefully urged that "general" is used in relation to markets. Brokers, he said, have recognised markets, such as wool brokers, tea brokers, rubber brokers and the like. In the end, however, he somewhat shifted his ground, without abandoning any territory, and contended that the term general commission agent was inserted to cover (a) those who would be brokers if there were a recognised market for the goods

159. Treas. Reg. § 1.864-2(c)(2)(ii), referring to a company the 'principal business of which is trading in stocks or securities for its own account.'
160. *See* Treas. Reg. § 1.864-2(c)(2)(iii) (defining foreign principal office). An exception also applies to trading activities (not for one's own account) conducted through independent United States agents where the taxpayer does not have a United States office through which such transactions are effected. *See* IRC § 864(b)(2)(e).
161. 1955-1 C.B. 634.
162. IRC § 864 discussed above.
163. 37 S. Af. Tax Cas. 249 (1975).
164. 44 Tax Cases 582, 595 (High Court, Chan. Div. 1968).
165. *See* the discussion at footnote 139.

in which they deal and (b) those who deal in a broker-like way with several commodities but because of the generality of their dealings are not usually described as brokers. Further or alternatively, he submitted that "general" was used as meaning that the agent must have generality of customers and not merely act for only one principal.'[166]

Without distinguishing 'brokers' from 'general commission agents' according to the products or markets in which they deal, the court found that a general commission agent must act as a broker and must hold himself out to the public generally as a commission agent:

> 'Accordingly, I consider that a "general commission agent" must have sufficient broker-like qualities to make it reasonable for Parliament to provide that "broker" should include him. After all, brokers are essentially negotiators for commission. Second, the general trend of the proviso is to confer exemption on non-residents who merely employ brokers for broking in the ordinary way, even if they regularly employ the same one. The words "ordinary course of his business," "carrying on *bona fide* the business" [*sic*] and "a rate not less than that customary in the class of business in question" seem to me to be significant: in relation to broking the proviso is redolent of ordinariness. Third, the word "general" in the phrase "general commission agent" itself must have some import; and in the context I think the most likely sense is that of a commission agent who holds himself out as being ready to work for clients generally, and who does not in substance confine his activities to one principal, or an insignificant number of principals. This, perhaps, is another facet of his broker-like qualities: He must be broker-like in his receipt of custom.'[167]

The rulings concerning general commission agents suggest the correctness of counsel's argument that commission agents are sales brokers not operating in established markets or selling specific commodities. Thus, in *Rev. Rul. 55-617*,[168] a Belgium seller was held not to have a United States permanent establishment even though it made substantial sales through a 'commission agent,' since such sales were made in the ordinary course of its business.

166. 44 Tax Cases at 595.
167. *Id* at 596.
168. 1955-2 C.B. 774. Similarly, Edwardes-Ker cites a German–Swiss treaty ruling. An agent can be independent even if he maintains a stock of merchandise which he normally sells on commission; this is how commission agents normally operate. Art. 5, p. 13.5003.

The examples of an independent agent cited in the model treaties are a broker and a general commission agent. Any other agent of independent status can also qualify provided his activities are sufficiently defined and perceived in the market that it can be said that he is acting in the 'ordinary course of his business.'[169] Other independent agents have been held to include the *Handelsvertreter* in Germany, the custodian in the United States[170] and shipping agents (*cargadoor*) in the Netherlands.[171]

C. Purchasing Agents

The general rule that maintaining a fixed place of business or maintaining an agent for the sole purpose of purchasing goods[172] – almost invariably 'the mere purchase of goods' – does not constitute a permanent establishment is well accepted by developed countries.[173] Its inclusion as an exempt permanent establishment in the United Nations Model[174] indicates broader acceptance of the principle.

The treaties generally provide that an office or fixed place of business used solely for the purchase of goods or merchandise for a foreign enterprise shall not constitute a permanent establishment.[175] In addition, the OECD-patterned treaties exclude from the definition of a dependent agent one whose authority is limited to the purchase of goods or merchandise for the account of the foreign enterprise. Thus, the newer treaties create a purchasing exception to both the asset and dependent-agency types of permanent establishments. It is possible that the older treaties, although exempting only purchasing 'offices,' may allow a mere purchasing 'agent' exception, as well.[176]

---

169. According to Vogel, however, an agent's 'independence' need not be necessarily apparent to outsiders since 'all that matters is the relationship between him and the enterprise.' Vogel, at 345, para. 169.
170. *See* Ltr. Rul. 5410065930A.
171. *See* authorities cited at Vogel 345, para. 169a.
172. *See* OECD Model 5(4)(d).
173. *See* Lenz, 'The Development in Different Countries of the Concept of a Permanent Establishment, Notably from the Point of View of Harmonization in Future Double Taxation Agreements,' General Report, 52 Cahiers 283, 298 (1967).
174. United Nations Model 5(4)(4).
175. A reference to purchasing activities may be omitted in some older treaties (e.g., the terminated United States–South Africa treaty).
176. Roberts & Warren at IX-159. Edwardes-Ker Art. 5, p. 13.5 cites a Belgium–Dutch ruling under an older (non-OECD) treaty which holds that a dependent purchasing and canning agent is a permanent establishment. Dependency was found because the foreign principal paid all of the agent's expenses and covered his credit line (See discussion in Section 5.3 under 'Legal Independence'). However, if his activities had been limited to purchasing, even an agent with general authority to negotiate and conclude contracts should not be a dependent-agency permanent establishment. *See* Vogel, at 339 para. 151.

In the United States, at least, the purchasing- and independent-agent exceptions have an historical and economic rationale deriving from the United States source of income rules relating to the import-export trade. Commencing with an early Attorney General's Opinion,[177] the United States Treasury has accepted the principle that no income is realized from the mere purchase and exportation of domestic goods for sale abroad. Similarly, the long-standing 'title passage' rule for determining international product sales income means that United States import sales can be structured not to result in United States source income.[178]

The purchasing-agent or office exception, like the independent-agency exception, confers an absolute exemption from taxation, *pro tanto* the exemption. While the exemption could be lost in either case if other activities are undertaken by the same agent (beyond mere purchasing, or the ordinary functions of an independent agent), there appears to be no prohibition against the combined use of different[179] agents and representatives (perhaps at separate locations), including, for example, a host-country purchasing agent, an independent agent, a representative office (under the OECD exemption for preparatory or auxiliary activities), and dealings with host-country principals.[180]

D. Insurance Agents

An insurance company can engage in substantial insurance business in a host country through dependent insurance agents who issue policies (subject to home office approval), collect premiums, and pay claims (as adjusted by third parties subject to the insurer's control) – all without creating a permanent establishment of the insurer.[181] Further, contractual authority to bind the insurer

177. Opinion of the United States Attorney General to the Secretary of the Treasury, 32 Op. Atty. Gen. 336 (1920) (export of logs purchased in the United States and of 'handle blanks' sawed from logs by two United States sawmills of Scottish corporation do not produce any income from United States sources when no products are sold in the United States).
178. From 1921 through 1953, the Code provided that income from the purchase and sale of personal property was to be considered as 'derived from the country in which sold.' Since 1954, gain from the sale of personal property generally has its source at the place of title passage, which can be contractually designated, i.e., property purchased without and sold within the United States (but with title passing abroad) is foreign-source income, the rule being limited to inventory property since 1986.
179. Both purchases and sales might be made by a purchasing agent, if the sales were ancillary. *See* Ltr. Rul. 7810010, holding that three United States coal purchasing agents were not a permanent establishment even though they also sold coal to United States purchasers.
180. Case No. F 85, Tax'n Bd. of Review Cas. (Australia) 483, discussed in Section 5.4 supra.
181. See *Capitol Life Ins. Co. vs The Queen*, [1984] Canada Tax Cas. 141 which involved an American insurer which was licensed to insure in Canada, where it had a registered agent and had made a $400,000 deposit. However, the court found no permanent establishment as the contracts were written through the Denver head office of the insurer.

can be granted to independent agents without creating a permanent establishment.

A 1920 United States Treasury ruling[182] holds that a United States insurance 'broker' who solicited and procured insurance for nonresident 'alien' corporations, collected the premiums thereon, and credited the account of the foreign insurers with the proceeds, net of losses, was a United States 'resident agent' with respect to such business. It would seem that the agent described could be an independent agent under current tax treaties with the United States. Article 5(6) of the United States–Philippines treaty indicates that such an insurance broker can be an independent agent, at least as to the collection of premiums, and possibly as to other activities with respect to reinsurance.[183] US The 1977 OECD Model Commentary makes the point clear:

> 'According to the definition of the term "permanent establishment" an insurance company of one State may be taxed in the other State on its insurance business, if it has a fixed place of business within the meaning of paragraph 1 or if it carries on business through a person within the meaning of paragraph 5. Since agencies of foreign insurance companies sometimes do not meet either of the above requirements, it is conceivable that these companies do large scale business in a State without being taxed in that State on their profits arising from such business. In order to obviate this possibility, various conventions concluded by OECD Member countries include a provision which stipulates that insurance companies of a State are deemed to have a permanent establishment in the other State if they collect premiums in that other State through an agent established there – other than an agent who already constitutes a permanent establishment by virtue of paragraph 5 – or insure risks situated in that territory through such an agent. The decision as to whether or not a provision along these lines should be included in a convention will depend on the factual and legal situation prevailing in the Contracting States concerned. Frequently, therefore, such a provision will not be contemplated. In view of this fact, it did not seem advisable to insert a provision along these lines in the Model Convention.'[184]

The United Nations 1980 Model Treaty has in fact added such a provision in response to concerns of the developing countries. The United Nations Model states:

182. O.D. 586, 3 CB. 284.
183. Senate Exec. Rept. No. 97-39, 1984-2 C.B. 398, 404.
184. 1977 OECD Model Commentary, Art. 5(6), para. 38.

'Notwithstanding the preceding provisions of this article, an insurance enterprise of a Contracting State shall, except in regard to re-insurance, be deemed to have a permanent establishment in the other Contracting State if it collects premiums in the territory of that other State or insures risks situated therein through a person *other than an agent of an independent status to whom paragraph 7 applies*.'[185]

Under this provision, a permanent establishment would exist if the insurer established its own agents or employees in the host country to collect premiums or to insure risks. No mention is made of claims adjustment and payment. However, any or all of these activities conducted by independent insurance agents or adjusters should not create a permanent establishment even under the United Nations provision if done in the ordinary course of such agent's business.[186] It is only the collection of premiums or insurance of risk by employees and dependent agents which can result in permanent establishment status under the United Nations version regardless of contractual authority. Note that reinsurance is unaffected by the UN MC provision.

E. Delivery Agents

The origin of another sort of agency permanent establishment is traced by one of the fiscal experts who participated in the drafting of the League of Nations Model Treaties: the distinguished American tax lawyer Mitchell B. Carroll. He states:

'Included within the 1932 Convention with France (Protocol Par. 3(a)) was a list of the establishments that give rise to taxation and also added to the definition a clause which provided in substance that carrying on business through a local agent who has a general authority to negotiate and conclude contracts for the account of the non-resident enterprise is considered as having a permanent establishment. The 1939 Convention with France added to the definition in the Protocol III (a) the maintenance of a stock of merchandise from which the employee or agent regularly fills orders which he receives.'[187]

---

185. 1980 United Nations Model 5(6) (emphasis added).

186. *See* Edwards-Ker, Netherlands–United States 13/1/1971 BNB 1971/43 No. 16.445, held a permanent establishment existed where brokers issued standard, non-negotiable policies. Home office approval was therefore irrelevant and the agents were held to be dependent agents, as not acting in the ordinary course of their business.

187. Carroll, Part II, 145.

This alternative 'delivery agent' type of permanent establishment appeared in a number of treaties predating the 1963 OECD Draft and appears in a number of subsequent treaties with developing countries. A typical formulation appears in the first-generation United States treaties with Austria, Greece, Ireland, New Zealand, Switzerland and Pakistan which provide that the term 'permanent establishment':

> 'does not include an agency, unless the agent has, and habitually exercises, a general authority to negotiate and conclude contracts on behalf of [the foreign] enterprise or has a stock of merchandise from which it regularly fills orders on its behalf.'[188]

This 'delivery agent' type of permanent establishment is a separate and distinct concept. The basic agency permanent establishment test refers to an agent in the contract law sense; the delivery agent test does not require any agency authority, but refers to mere business activity, viz., the regular filling of orders by a person in the taxing State from a stock of merchandise of the foreign principal located there.[189] Although the treaties generally refer to an 'agent' with regard to this alternative test of business activities, employees and other representatives who regularly deliver the taxpayer's goods from a stock of merchandise may constitute a delivery-agent permanent establishment although possessing no contractual authority (unless the authorization of delivery is so viewed). Indeed, the former United States–Austrian treaty (as well as former United States treaties with Canada and South Africa) specifically and disjunctively refer to an 'employee.'[190]

While the former United States–Canada treaty referred to an employee or agent 'established there,' it does not appear even under the pre-OECD treaties that the delivery agent must reside or have a fixed place of business in the taxing State. The presence of an agent or other person in the taxing State, who regularly makes deliveries from a stock of merchandise maintained there, will constitute a permanent establishment. An exception appears to exist for isolated or convenience deliveries from incidental stocks or deliveries from a public warehouse.[191]

188. Former United States–Ireland II(1)(l). The 1948 United States–Denmark treaty is identical but for the omission of 'habitually.' United States–Denmark II(1)(c). The other treaties have minor variations.

189. Vogel argues in a discussion of German treaties, some of which require a delivery agent to have contractual authority, that all delivery agent treaties require interposition of a delivery agent in the same manner as a contractual agent. Vogel, at 339-340, para. 152. If head office approval is routine, Vogel argues that the delivery agent is in substance a contractual agent.

190. Former United States–Austria II(f).

191. Thus United States regulations under the 1948 Danish treaty provide that the 'mere fact that an agent (assuming he has no general authority to contract on behalf of his employer or principal)

Meanwhile, the maintenance of stock for delivery or the use of a fixed place of business, operated by the foreign enterprise for delivery of its goods to its customers is by itself not a permanent establishment under treaties patterned after the OECD and United States models. The revised 2012 OECD Draft proposals amends the commentary in respect of Sub a) and Sub b) of art 5 (2) as follows;

> 'Subparagraph a) relates only to the case in which an enterprise acquires the use of facilities for storing, displaying or delivering its own goods or merchandise. Subparagraph b) relates to the stock of merchandise itself and provides that the stock, as such, shall not be treated as a permanent establishment if it is maintained for the purpose of storage, display or delivery. *Subparagraphs a) and b) apply regardless of whether the storage or delivery takes place before or after a contract for the sale of the goods or merchandise has been concluded provided that the goods or merchandise belong to the enterprise whilst they are at the relevant location (e.g. the subparagraphs would remain applicable if contracts for the sale of some of the goods that are stored at a location have already been concluded but the property title to these goods only passes to the customer after their delivery) …*'

This can be read to say that a facility where the foreign enterprise stores, displays and delivers its own goods does not create a PE. Goods at the location should remain for the title the enterprise. Storage, display or deliver of property of which the title has already passed to a third party causes a potential PE. However, delivery of goods in the possession of the enterprise will still constitute a permanent establishment under certain United Nations Model Treaties and treaties antedating the OECD Model by reason of the foreign principal having an agent for the regular delivery of goods in the host country.

---

maintains samples or occasionally fills orders from incidental stocks of goods maintained in the United States will not constitute a permanent establishment there.' Treas. Reg. § 7.953, T.D. 5777, 1950-1 C.B. 76, 84 interpreting 1948 United States–Denmark treaty; *see also* Treas. Reg. § 7.22, T.D. 5206, 1943 C.B. 526, 534 interpreting former 1942 United States–Canada treaty and Treas. Reg. § 7.515, T.D. 5569, 1947-2 C.B., 100, 110-11 interpreting former 1945 United States–United Kingdom treaty. *See also* Rev. Rul. 56-594,1956-2 C.B. 1126 (where the United States commission agent had no authority to deliver goods or commit orders) and Ltr. Rul. 5509205580A (delivery of small orders of shoes, out of a New York warehouse, not a permanent establishment where orders and delivery approved by United Kingdom supplier), Ltr. Rul. 7749009 (United Kingdom alcoholic beverage supplier maintained force majeure 3 months reserve supply in United States bonded public warehouse, with inventory turned over annually by sales to United States affiliate to prevent spoilage, held no permanent establishment).

The delivery-agent permanent establishment seems mainly a trap for the unwary as important limitations on its application are factored in. It does not apply to independent delivery agents, even under the older treaties. Thus it is possible to use public warehouses for storage and independent sales agents for sales and deliveries.

5.7 COMMISSIONAIRES AND THE RELATIONSHIP BETWEEN INDEPENDENT AGENTS AND AGENCY PEs

A 'commissionaire' is a European civil law entity which sells in its own name products of its supplier. The commissionaire has almost no inventory or credit risk. The commissionaire can accept orders, negotiate prices and conclude sales contracts for the supplier's products in its own name and without the supplier's approval. The supplier or another entity will generally be responsible for marketing in the sales area. A commissionaire does not legally bind its supplier to the sale.

In contrast, the common law view of agency (applicable in the Anglosphere, i.e., the UK and its former colonies) recognizes as legally binding on a principal, a contract effected by an agent with a customer on behalf of the agent's principal, even if the agency is undisclosed to the customer, provided there is an internal agreement between the agent binding the principal. This agreement can be actual, implied or ratified ex post facto.

Some historical background is useful. The concept of a 'person' PE – an Agency PE – was within the German concept of a PE from early years (as well as being within the German domestic concept of a 'permanent' agent habitually acting with authority over a period of at least 6 months). In contrast, the exception provided for 'independent agents' emerged later and derived from the English common law of agency as expressed in 1915 and 1925 English Acts.

Articles 5(5) and 5(6) of the OECD Model define respectively (1) an Agency PE and (2) exempt NRE dealings through a 'broker, commission agent or other agent of independent status.' Article 5(5) defines an Agency PE as follows:

> 'Notwithstanding the provisions [defining a fixed POB PE], where a person —other than an agent of an independent status to whom paragraph 6 applies —is acting on behalf of an enterprise and has, and habitually exercises, in a Contracting State an authority to conclude contracts in the name of the enterprise, that enterprise shall be deemed to have a permanent establishment in that State in respect of any activities which that person undertakes for the enterprise, unless the activities of such

person are limited to [exempt preparatory or auxiliary activities]. [emphasis added]'

Article 5(6) of the OECD defines the independent agent exception as follows:

> 'An enterprise shall not be deemed to have a permanent establishment in a Contracting State merely because it carries on business in that State through a broker, general commission agent or any other agent of an independent status, provided that such persons are acting in the ordinary course of their business.'

These provisions went through many iterations from their first appearance to the final form when approved in 1958 by the OEEC Council and later incorporated into the 1963 OECD Draft MC and the 1977/2010 OECD Models where it remains unchanged to this day. The OECD language appears in substantially the same form in the UN 1980/2011 Models and the US 2006 Model.

Pijl in his two part January-February 2013 article[192] meticulously traces the 'legislative history' of these iterations in order to divine the true intended meaning of 'in the name of' and the relationship of Article 5(5) and Article 5(6). As an integral part of his analysis, Pijl reviews, critiques and disagrees with the differing views of two giants in the field of PEs, Jones[193] and Roberts,[194] stated in their landmark 1993 articles on Agency PEs. Pijl's analysis is crucial to an understanding of the correct relationship of these pivotal agency provisions as well as the intended limits of the Agency PE concept. His treatise convincingly reveals both from the legislative history of the UN and OEEC Fiscal Committees, as well as the commissionaire court cases (which found no agency PE),

1) that Articles 5(5) and (6) were drafted to accommodate both civil and common law types of agencies according to a common measure of authority to legally bind a principal,
2) Article 5(6) is a clarification that independent agencies, including those with authority to bind a principal in the ordinary course of the agent's business, do not create a PE and

192. Pijl, Agency Permanent Establishments: 'in the name of' and the Relationship between Article 5(5) and (6) – Part I I.B.F.D. Bulletin for International Taxation, January 2013 pp 3-21 and Part II I.B.F.D. Bulletin for International Taxation, February 2013 pp 63-99 (the best history and analysis of Agency PEs).

193. Jones, J F & Ward, D A Agents as Permanent Establishments under the OECD Model Tax Convention, British Tax Review 341 (1993), Eur. Taxn 5, Journals IBFD 16.

194. Roberts, S I, The Agency Element of Permanent Establishment: The OECD Commentaries from the Civil Law View (Part One),__Intertax 9, pp. 396-420 (1993) and (Part Two),_Intertax 10, pp. 488-508 (1993). *See also* Robert's abstract posthumously published by his widow in 2007 by European Taxation, March 2007 at pp. 1-7

3) all other agencies, no matter how legally and/or economically dependent upon a principal, do not constitute an agency PE unless the agent has authority to legally bind his principal in the principal's core business and the agent regularly exercises such authority.[195]

Pijl notes that the Agency PE 'authority' clause started life as an authority to legally bind the NRE principal – referring to the conclusion of contracts 'on behalf of' or 'in the name of ' the principal – terms which were equally understood by common law and civil law members of the UN Fiscal Committee Reports in 1929, 1930 and 1931 as well as the OEEC Fiscal Committee in 1958 to refer to an agent's authority to legally bind its principal. However during the course of OEEC Fiscal Committee drafts in 1957 and 1958, a linguistic mismatch developed whereby the original English version 'on behalf of' was translated into the French 'au nom de.' Although the mismatch was noted by the drafters in February 1958, it appeared in the OEEC Fiscal Committee final French Report of May 1958 as 'au nom de' and 'in the name of' rather than 'pour le compte de' and 'on behalf of' – and was so accepted in the final version recommended by the Council on July 11, 1958.

Pijl could discern no reason in any contemporary papers for this change and concluded that civil law as well as common law delegates mutually understood both terms to refer to an agent's activities which 'legally bound' his principal,[196] an interpretation which has since been recognized in all four of the recent European 'commissionaire' cases in France, Norway, Italy and Spain.[197]

Although 'in the name of' was not a legal term cognizable in common law, it did resonate well with the legal status of a common law commissionaire, which did not sign contracts in the name of its principal.[198] More likely, Pijl

195. This discussion just focuses on the contractual dependent agent and not on dependent delivery agents or insurance agents found in some older or UN based treaties.

196. Pijl Part II at 72-73

197. *Societe Zimmer Ltd, Conseil d'Etat*, NNos. 304715 and 308525 (restructured French subsidiary could conclude contracts, negotiate discounts and payment terms without prior approval; no inventory and clients other than selling Zimmer products), *Dell Products (NUF) vs Tax East*, HR-2-11-2245-1(2011) (Norwegian subsidiary's only client was Dell Ireland, standard contracts used and approved, shared accounting systems and board members with parent; held commissionaire could not legally bind supplier parent; Pijl notes that in Norwegian 'in the name of' and 'on behalf of' are both translated by 'på vegne af'); Boston Scientific (*Corte Suprema di Cassazione*, No. 3769/2012 (Doc. 2012-7737) (despite the fact that the Italian subsidiary had only one supplier (its Dutch parent), the lower courts found independence in that the subsidiary bore entrepreneurial risk in the form of sales staff and fixed costs and handled a significant number of customer complaints and non-sales activities in the parent's name). In the fourth case, *Roche Vitamins Europe Ltd.*, No. 1626/2008 (2012), the Spanish Supreme Court also found that 'in the name of' meant legally binding on the principal, but found a PE on other grounds. See Pijl, Part I at 7.

198. Pijl Part I at 21 notes, according to the 1929 UN Fiscal Committee Report that the term 'commission agent' could refer both to a 'commissionaire' (which contracts in its own name) and

concludes, the Committee simply did not perceive a substantive difference and went along with 'in the name of 'to diplomatically avoid having to 'correct' in English, terms written in French as the original language of the 1958 draft.

No one objected to this change in terminology until 1992 when an English lower court (the High Commissioners) took a literal view of 'in the name of' as avoiding PE status for dealings conducted through an agent which did not have the literal power to conclude contracts 'in the name of ' the principal. The UK made an observation to the article 5(5) Commentary unless it were amended to provide, in the Anglosphere at least, that an Agency PE could exist even through an agent did not have the legal power to sign contracts 'in the name of' his principal.[199] This decision inspired the great debate about Agency PEs started by Roberts and Jones in their seminal but differing 1993 articles. In response the Commentary was amended in 1994 to allow the UK to remove its observation. The amended version provides:

> '... the phrase "authority to conclude contracts in the name of the enterprise" does not confine the application of the paragraph to an agent who enters into contracts literally in the name of the enterprise; the paragraph applies equally to an agent who concludes contracts which are binding on the enterprise even if those contracts are not actually in the name of the enterprise.'

The Commentary also gratuitously added:

> 'Lack of active involvement by an enterprise in transactions may be indicative of a grant of authority to an agent. For example, an agent may be considered to possess actual authority to conclude contracts where he solicits and receives (but does not formally finalize) orders which are sent directly to a warehouse from which goods are delivered and where the foreign enterprise routinely approves the transactions.'[200]

This second sentence has questionable application in civil law countries.[201] Pijl's analysis establishes that the OECD drafters included knowledgeable persons from both civil and common law countries who (contrary to Jones' assertion) were familiar with the different concepts of the two systems and integrated them with the requirement that the dependent agent must have actual authority

---

an agent which contracts in the name of its principal (agent a la commission). *Accord,* Jones (2011).

199. Pijl Part II at 82-83.

200. OECD Commentary Article 5(5) paragraph 32.1.

201. *See* Dell, supra, where the Norwegian Supreme Court held factually binding irrelevant, the treaty requirement being legal binding. Pijl, Part I, at 8

to legally bind its principal. Thus the drafters also ruled out any concept of an agency PE arising by reason of the agent's actions' 'economically' binding the principal.[202] Further, the Commentary itself dismisses any notion of an agency PE's being created by a dependent agent's activities short of having the legal authority to bind its principal:

> 'It would not have been in the interest of international economic relations to provide that the maintenance of any dependent person would lead to a permanent establishment for the enterprise. Such treatment is to be limited to persons who in view of the scope of their authority or the nature of their activity involve the enterprise to a particular extent in business activities in the State concerned. Therefore, paragraph 5 proceeds on the basis that only persons having the authority to conclude contracts can lead to a permanent establishment for the enterprise maintaining them.'[203]

The above phraseology – 'or the nature of their activity involve the enterprise to a particular extent in business activities in the State concerned' – is misplaced since an agent must first have authority regularly exercised to bind its principal. If so, an agency PE exists and attracts income not only attributable to the exercise of the agent's authority but also attributable to its other actions, as stated in the italicized language of Article 5(5) quoted above. The phraseology does not indicate that an agency PE can be created either through the regular exercise of the agent's authority or other activities of a dependent agent, as the Spanish Supreme Court assumed in the *DSM Roche Vitamins* case.[204] Finally, the 2012 OECD Discussion Draft further proposed to add the following sentence:

> 'For example, in some countries an enterprise would be bound, in certain cases, by a contract concluded with a third party by a person acting on behalf of the enterprise even if the person did not formally disclose that it was acting for the enterprise and the name of the enterprise was not referred to in the contract.'

It is doubtful that this language would have any application to civil countries since it is an obvious reference to English common law.

---

202. Switzerland and South Africa take a different view de lege ferenda. Pijl, Part I at 7.
203. OECD Commentary Article 5(5), para. 32.
204. *See* Pijl, Part I at 9.

A. The Stand-Alone Status of the Independent Agent Exception

According to Pijl's analysis, the independent agent exception was not an exception to Article 5(5), but clarified those persons and transactions which would not create a PE. It is thus the main principle and should be applied first, before reference to Article 5(5). In similar vein, the original reference to 'bona fide' independent agents was replaced with legally and economically independent agents acting in the customary course of business conducted by such 'broker, commission agent or any other agent of independent status.' As stated by the OECD Commentary:[205]

> 'Where an enterprise of a Contracting State carries on business dealings through a broker, general commission agent or any other agent of an independent status, it cannot be taxed in the other Contracting State in respect of those dealings if the agent is acting in the ordinary course of his business (see paragraph 32 above). Although it stands to reason that such an agent, representing a separate enterprise, cannot constitute a permanent establishment of the foreign enterprise, paragraph 6 has been inserted in the Article for the sake of clarity and emphasis.'

At this point, it is appropriate to refer to the great debate about Agency PEs which started with Jones' and Roberts' 1993 treatises on Agency PEs. As stated by Pijl, Jones took the view that Article 5(6) was an exception to Article 5(5) (and it is, in terms of the exercise of authority to bind a principal). But then Jones would apply Article 5(5) as the main principle, only referring to Article 5(6) to determine if the exception applied. Pijl notes that you could reach the correct answer under Avery Jones' approach, but it is not a logical approach as, e.g., it isolates brokers and commission agents who do not exercise authority to bind a principal and hence are only perceived through an independent reference to Article 5(6).

In contrast, Pijl's approach states the correct order of logical analysis and is supported by the OECD Model, the Commentary and the historical papers. If there is no physical PE, the first inquiry concerning Agency PEs is whether the agent is (1) legally independent, (2) economically independent and (3) acting in the customary course of its business. At this level, whether not the agent has authority or not to bind its principal is only relevant if it flunks one of the 3 tests. If so and it does not have such authority, it is a dependent agent (because it failed one of the tests and hence is not an independent agent), but it is not *ipso facto* an Agency PE. If it does have such authority, it is a dependent agent which may be an Agency PE. Reference is then made to the tests of an Article

205. OECD Commentary Article 5(6), para. 36.

5(5) Agency PE – i.e., does its authority relate to its principal's core business and is it regularly exercised in the source state.

In contrast to Avery Jones, Roberts viewed Articles 5(5) and 5(6) as independent provisions. Further, he reasoned, under the '*ejusdem generis*' principle, that since 'brokers' and 'commission agents' do not have authority to bind their principals,[206] that Article 5(6)'s inclusion of 'any other agent of independent status' meant that any other agent also could not have authority to bind a principal, or if did, it was an agency PE as such authority would be outside the customary course of such agent's business.

Pijl finds this quite a stretch. Pijl refers to it as a fallacious assumption that a particular characteristic of a class must be shared by all other members – in his analysis: dogs and cats are furry animals which make fine household pets; lions and tigers are also furry animals, but do they make fine household pets? (Only the Dutch can be so forthright). Further, it is clearly not the OECD view, as Article 5(5)'s exception of authorized agents who are legally and economically independent and operating in the customary course of their business, recognizes two postulates: (1) some independent agents can bind their principals and (2) if within the ordinary course of their business such an agent will not be an Agency PE.

Numerous cases discussed in this book support the proposition that an independent agent can bind its principal within the course of the agent's business and hence not create an agency PE. Perhaps the best known example is *Taisei Fire & Marine Ins. Co. Ltd et al vs Comm'r of Internal Revenue*,[207] where 4 Japanese insurers gave discretionary authority to a US broker to book reinsurance business on their behalf. The US reinsurance broker bound the Japanese principal insurer clients to blocks of reinsurance business which the Japanese insurers never saw or approved. That is just the way it is done in the reinsurance broker business – the object is to minimize underwriting risk by taking advantage of the law of large numbers to participate in as little risk across as broad a spectrum of the relevant market risks as possible. To that end insurance companies 'trust' a reinsurance broker to share their primary risks by reinsuring them with blocks of reinsurance within the risk parameters set by the insurer.

While Article 5(6) clarifies the principle that 'independent agents' cannot be an Agency PE, Article 5 has an unstated broader principle that any person which does not have authority to habitually bind its principal in some aspect of the principal's core business is not an agency PE, whether or not that person

206. In fact, according to Jones (2011) at 667, the difference was that a broker did not have possession of goods, whereas a commission agent did; a commission agent could also have power to contract in its own name or in the name of a principal. *See also* Pijl, part I at 4.

207. 104 T.C. 535, (1995) Acq. AOD CC-1995-012.

is an independent agent within the meaning or Article 5(6) or is legally and/or economically dependent on an NRE principal. Article 5(5) refers to a 'person' having authority to bind a principal. It does not refer to a 'dependent' agent. Further Article 5(7) and the OECD Commentary make it clear that a parent's control over its subsidiary does not ipso facto make the subsidiary an agent though it could make the subsidiary both legally and economically dependent on its parent.

The 2012 OECD Discussion Draft, recognizing the differences between common law and civil law versions of agency, ducks the issue whether and where a commissionaire could be a dependent agent PE.[208] However, three European courts have not. High Court decisions in 3 European countries (France, Norway and Italy) have uniformly held as matter of local law, that a commissionaire cannot act in the name of its principal and hence under the plain language of Article 5(5), English or French, cannot be a dependent agency PE.[209]

5.8 PARENT AND SUBSIDIARY

The older (pre-OECD model) treaties generally provide that ownership by a foreign enterprise of a subsidiary corporation which is a resident of, or has a permanent establishment in the host country, shall not constitute the subsidiary a permanent establishment of the parent enterprise. The OECD-patterned treaties similarly state that the fact that a company resident in one country controls or is controlled by a company which is a resident of the other country or which is engaged in business in the other country[210] shall not of itself constitute either company a permanent establishment of the other. The OECD Commentary extends this rule to brother-sister subsidiaries.[211]

---

208. 2012 OECD Discussion Draft Art. 5(5) at para 32.1.
209. *Societe Zimmer Ltd, Conseil d'Etat*, NNos. 304715 and 308525 (restructured French subsidiary could conclude contracts, negotiate discounts and payment terms without prior approval; no inventory and clients other than selling Zimmer products), *Dell Products (NUF) vs Tax East*, HR-2-11-2245-1(2011) (Norwegian subsidiary's only client was Dell Ireland, standard contracts used and approved, shared accounting systems and board members with parent); Boston Scientific (*Corte Suprema di Cassazione*, No. 3769/2012 (Doc. 2012-7737) (despite the fact that the Italian subsidiary had only one supplier (its Dutch parent), the lower courts found independence in that the subsidiary bore entrepreneurial risk in the form of sales staff and fixed costs and handled a significant number of customer complaints and non-sales activities in the parent's name).
210. *See* OECD Model 5(7).
211. *See* OECD Model Commentary 5(7), para. 41.1.

Recognizing subsidiaries as independent legal entities is consistent with general principles of taxation[212] and provides fundamental assurance to multi nationals that they can avoid host country taxation of home country activities by conducting foreign activities through host country subsidiaries.[213] The OECD Model Commentary states:

> '40. It is generally accepted that the existence of a subsidiary company does not, of itself, constitute that subsidiary company a permanent establishment of its parent company. This follows from the principle that, for the purpose of taxation, such a subsidiary company constitutes an independent legal entity. Even the fact that the trade or business carried on by the subsidiary company is managed by the parent company does not constitute the subsidiary company a permanent establishment of the parent company.
>
> 41. A parent company may, however, be found, under the rules of paragraphs 1 or 5 of the Article, to have a permanent establishment in a State where a subsidiary has a place of business. Thus, any space or premises belonging to the subsidiary that is at the disposal of the parent company (see paragraphs 4, 5 and 6 above) and that constitutes a fixed

212. Nitikman argues that the higher agency threshold standards of United States statutory law might be exploited by foreign enterprises resisting IRS-claimed agency permanent establishment status of their United States subsidiaries. Nitikman at 269-273. In the United States, it has long been held that a corporation will be respected as a taxpayer separate from its shareholder if the corporation serves any business purpose. *Moline Properties Inc. vs Commissioner*, 319 U.S. 436 (1948) (respecting corporation used to hold shareholder's property to avoid state usury law limit on loans to individuals). In effect, Moline Properties rejects shareholder arguments that a totally-owned company was a mere agent of the shareholder for tax purposes, where there is no actual contract of agency, nor the usual incidents of an agency relationship. Subsequently, *National Carbide Corp. vs Commissioner*, 336 U.S. 442 (1949), held that for a subsidiary to be a true agent, it must (1) act for and in the name of the parent as principal (2) bind the principal by its actions (3) transmit any income it receives to the parent, which income must be attributable to the parent's employees and assets, and (4) have a business purpose limited to acting as the parent's agent. Finally, *Commissioner vs Bollinger*, 485 U.S. 340, (1988) clarified the last National Carbide test by holding that a shareholder claiming agency status would have to show by unequivocal evidence set forth in a written agency agreement at the time a particular asset is acquired that the corporation functions with respect to the asset (1) as agent rather than principal for all purposes and (2) that the corporation is held out as an agent and not as principal in all dealings with third parties relating to the asset. However, as Nitikman points out, Bollinger may be limited to testing tax avoidance by taxpayers and hence may be viewed as an IRS sword and not a shield which could be used by taxpayers to resist IRS claims of agency status. Nonetheless, until the point is clarified, affected foreign enterprises might raise the 'Bollinger' defense.

213. The notable exception is unitary taxation in California and a handful of other American states, even if limited by a 'water's edge' election. See also Vogel, who cites internal 'look through' case law in the United States, France, and Germany to which the 'anti single-entity clause' is opposed. *See* Vogel, at 352, para. 191.

place of business through which the parent carries on its own business will constitute a permanent establishment of the parent under paragraph 1, subject to paragraphs 3 and 4 of the Article (see for instance, the example in paragraph 4.3 above). Also, under paragraph 5, a parent will be deemed to have a permanent establishment in a State in respect of any activities that its subsidiary undertakes for it if the subsidiary has, and habitually exercises, in that State an authority to conclude contracts in the name of the parent (see paragraphs 32, 33 and 34 above), unless these activities are limited to those referred to in paragraph 4 of the Article or unless the subsidiary acts in the ordinary course of its business as an independent agent to which paragraph 6 of the Article applies.

41.1. The same principles apply to any company forming part of a multinational group so that such a company may be found to have a permanent establishment in a State where it has at its disposal (see paragraphs 4, 5 and 6 above) and uses premises belonging to another company of the group, or if the former company is deemed to have a permanent establishment under paragraph 5 of the Article (see paragraphs 32, 33 and 34 above). The determination of the existence of a permanent establishment under the rules of paragraphs 1 or 5 of the Article must, however, be done separately for each company of the group. Thus, the existence in one State of a permanent establishment of one company of the group will not have any relevance as to whether another company of the group has itself a permanent establishment in that State.'[214]

Two significant points emerge from this Commentary excerpt. First, a subsidiary will apparently not constitute a fixed place of business of the parent with respect to the trade or business of the subsidiary even though that business is managed by the parent. In this respect, the OECD Model Commentary goes considerably beyond United States regulations which construe a parallel statutory reference to a fixed place of business as including a subsidiary whose trade is actively and continuously managed in the United States by the officers of the parent.[215] The rationale for the OECD exception is presumably that the subsidiary will be subject to full local country taxation with respect to its own trade, subject to appropriate transfer pricing adjustments. This rationale would not, however, extend to the parent's trade or business where such trade was managed by the subsidiary for the parent.[216]

214. OECD Model Commentary, Art. 5(7), paras. 40, 41, and 41.1.

215. Treas. Reg. § 1.864(c)-7, construing IRC § 864(c)(5).

216. Where the parent's trade is managed by the subsidiary, the subsidiary will usually be a dependent managing agent. The fixed place of business of the subsidiary will not generally be attributed to the parent unless facilities are actually leased or are made available to the parent's

Second, a subsidiary will constitute a permanent establishment of the parent if it is dependent agent, which means that it has failed to qualify for the independent-agent exception and regularly has and uses authority to bind the parent to some aspect of the parent's business proper in the host country,[217][218] of if the parent uses the premises of the subsidiary as a place of business through which it conducts it trade.

The principal exposure is therefore where the subsidiary is used to conduct the parent's business. Thus, in *Motorola Inc. vs DCIT*[219] Motorola's supply of telecommunication equipment to Indian customers was carried out partly by Motorola India. Motorola paid its own expatriate employees stationed at Motorola India's office to assist Motorola India in these activities. ITAT found that the employees worked for both Motorola and Motorola India through the latter's offices which they had a right to use, and that there was a projection of Motorola US in India through a dependent agent PE.[220]

Another example of this principle is *Inverworld vs Commissioner*[221] Although the case dealt with US domestic permanent establishment law in connection with the use of a US subsidiary to conduct the investment management business of a Cayman parent, the dependent agency PE principle considered is the same as the treaty concept. The US Tax Court found that not only was the US subsidiary economically dependent on the parent's business, but that its Texas offices were used to conduct the business of the parent and thus it was

---

employees and within their control. See Rev. Rul. 62-31. *Rolls Royce Plc vs DDIT* (ITAT Delhi, October 26, 2007) (online: http://www.itatonline.org/) (subsidiary's facilities must be subject to the control of the parent).

217. *Accord,* Vogel, at 352-353, para. 192. In the event of such taxation, the parent will be taxed on profits derived from contracts concluded by the subsidiary on behalf of the parent, while the subsidiary will remain taxable in respect of its own income – including a commission or fee element. Similarly, a parent can be a dependent agent of its subsidiary or an affiliate company a dependent agent of its sister company. Vogel, at 353, paras. 193-194.
218. *See Handfield vs Commissioner*, 23 T.C. 633 (1955, construing former United States–Canada treaty); *see also* Edwardes-Ker, Art. 5, p. 13,5004 (Greece–Germany treaty, 1989 Athens Court of First Instance, held subsidiary not a permanent establishment); ibid, page 13.5004 (Greece–Italy treaty, 1972 Greek Court of Appeals held subsidiary not a permanent establishment); *id.* p. 13.5005 (Netherlands–Belgium treaty, 5 December 1974, opinion holding that an individual does not have a permanent establishment, even though his company did and taxpayer furnished equipment in connection with the project: the taxpayer wanted permanent establishment status to claim Dutch tax exemption for his Belgium branch income); ibid, p. 13.5 (Belgium–United Kingdom treaty, 28 May 1968 ruling, holding subsidiary not a permanent establishment).
219. 95 ITD 269 (2005 Delhi SB) Mehta at 450 and Appendix One.
220. A contrary result was reached in *Ericsson Radio Systems AB vs DCIT* and *Nokia Networks OY vs DCIT* delivered in a companion judgment, the parent's employees traveling to India on business visits and not having the affiliate's offices 'at their disposal.' Mehta at 450. See similarly, the Indian Supreme Court decision in *DIT vs Morgan Stanley & Co*. 162 Taxman 165 (2007) Mehta at 455 at Appendix One. H Pijl, *Morgan Stanley*, Bulletin for International Taxation (May 2008) pages 174-82
221. 71 TCM (CCH) 3231 (1996)

an agency PE of the parent. This lengthy decision is notable for having the most comprehensive definition of what constitutes 'US trade or business' and the circumstances in which that business will be conducted through a US PE.

In *Nokia Networks OY vs DCIT*,[222] a Finnish mobile telephone provider sold telecommunication hardware in software in India with the assistance of its Indian affiliate. ITAT found that employees of the Finnish parent and Indian subsidiary worked together at the affiliate's offices under the same management and found a PE based on a dependent agent concept that regarded the Indian affiliate as a mere 'projection' of the Finnish parent. This finding was predicated on the subsidiary's lack of entrepreneurial risk with respect to its marketing activities, for which the parent compensated it on a cost plus basis and on the fact that the subsidiary had incurred installation losses, which ITAT attributed to the control over it exercised by its parent:

> 'In other words the installation charges received by NTPL [the Indian subsidiary] from the cellular operator in India were not commensurate with the costs and expenses incurred therefore and that is the reason why such a loss has been incurred. Now the other question is how does that result in NTPL being regarded as the PE of the assessee company. The answer is that since NTPL is a wholly owned subsidiary of the assessee in India and is consequently in a position to control and monitor its activities, the installation charges were directed to be so fixed that they were not commensurate with the services rendered by NTPL ... [T]here was [ample] scope for the assessee to control and monitor the activities of NTPL which, it should be remembered is a 100% subsidiary of the assessee, in such a manner that NTPL became a virtual projection of the assessed company in India.[223]

That ITAT reached a contrary conclusion in the companion Ericsson decision based on the government's failure to show that the Indian affiliate's offices were 'at the disposal' of the parent's employees, does not provide comfort for similar scenarios with subsidiaries with limited risk, if the subsidiary is shown to incur a loss (although one could argue that this is really a function of transfer pricing and should not be in the PE realm at all). Further, the ITAT ruling ignores the concept of stewardship and the irrelevance of parental legal control over a subsidiary, which are intended to have PE-free status. As stated by Nitikman with regard to a Belgian case:[224]

222. Delivered in a companion judgment with *Ericsson and Nokia Networks OY vs DCIT*, Mehta at Appendix One.
223. Nitikman at 229.
224. Nitikman at 230.

> 'the Supreme Court of Belgium on French-Belgium Treaty) has held that a Belgian subsidiary of a French parent company was not the parent's "permanent establishment," notwithstanding the very tight control exercised by the parent company over the sales-territory and product lines allocated to the subsidiaries notwithstanding the considerable amount of management and financial reporting which was required of the subsidiary'

The most criticized example of parent-subsidiary agency PE exposure is the *Philip Morris (GmbH)*[225] case. There, a German Philip Morris affiliate received royalties from its license of the Italian Tobacco Administration to manufacture and supply cigarettes under the PM label. Intertaba SpA was an indirectly owned Italian subsidiary primarily engaged in the manufacture and distribution of cigarette filters in Italy and abroad. Intertaba participated in the negotiation of this license, and provided agency and promotional support in duty free areas. Philip Morris GmbH had no place of business in Italy and Intertaba was not authorized to bind the German company in its business dealings. Reversing the lower court decisions finding no PE, the Italian Supreme Court held that the Intertaba was used to conduct a part of the parent's core business which went beyond the subsidiary's ordinary course of business and that Intertaba constituted a dependent agency PE of the Philip Morris *group* of companies due to its negotiation of the license and undertaking of certain 'management' activities for the group.

The OECD Commentary was subsequently amended[226] to provide that the mere attendance of negotiations or even participation in such negotiations did not create a dependent agent PE,[227] to which Italy entered an observation, stating it would follow its own precedent.[228] The Italian Supreme Court did just that in a subsequent case involving common directors and shareholders of Italian and Panamanian companies. The Italian company negotiated some contracts for the Panamanian company, whose books and records were kept at the offices of the Italian company.[229] A dependent agency PE was found.[230]

---

225. *Ministry of Finance (Tax Office) vs Philip Morris* (GmbH), May 25, 2002, no. 7682/ (Supreme Court of Cassation), unofficial English translation, *Ministry of Finance vs Philip Morris* (2002), 4 ITLR 903.
226. Nitikman at 230-31 cites numerous articles on the *Philip Morris* case. Following the Supreme Court's decision, Tax Executives Institute filed a complaint with the OECD which led to the amendment of the Commentary discussed in the text.
227. OECD Model Commentary, Art. 5(5), para. 33.
228. OECD Model Commentary, para. 45.10.
229. Russo and Pedrazzini, 'Permanent Establishments Under Italian Tax Law: An Overview' (2007) vol. 47, no. 8-9 European Taxation 389-97, at 395-96.
230. Supreme Court Decision No. 17206 of 28 July 2006, discussed in Russo & Pedrazzini, Permanent Establishments under Italian Tax Law: An Overview, European Taxation 289, at 396 (Aug-Sept 2007).

Chapter 6
Preparatory and Auxiliary Activities and Places

The OECD, United Nations, and United States Model Treaties all except from the permanent establishment definition a fixed place of business used for preparatory or auxiliary activities of the foreign enterprise. Moreover, host country activities of an employee or agent which are limited to preparatory or auxiliary activities for the enterprise are excluded from the definition. The purchase, contract processing, storage, display, or delivery of goods belonging to the enterprise are expressly enumerated as exempt preparatory or auxiliary activities. In addition, a representative office for the collecting of information or used for any other 'in-house' preparatory or auxiliary activity is also exempt. As stated by the OECD Model Treaty, the term 'permanent establishment' shall not include:

> 'a) the use of facilities solely for the purpose of storage, display or delivery of goods or merchandise belonging to the enterprise;
> b) the maintenance of a stock of goods or merchandise belonging to the enterprise solely for the purpose of storage, display or delivery;
> c) the maintenance of a stock of goods or merchandise belonging to the enterprise solely for the purpose of processing by another enterprise;
> d) the maintenance of a fixed place of business solely for the purpose of purchasing goods or merchandise or of collecting information, for the enterprise;
> e) the maintenance of a fixed place of business solely for the purpose of carrying on, for the enterprise, any other activity of a preparatory or auxiliary character;
> f) the maintenance of a fixed place of business solely for any combination of activities mentioned in subparagraphs a) to e), provided that the overall activity of the fixed place of business resulting from this combination is of a preparatory or auxiliary character.'

The United Nations Model is the same except that the word 'delivery' is omitted from subparagraphs a) and b) – with the result that a delivery agent, even without contractual authority, can constitute a dependent-agent permanent establishment. Thus in treaties with developing countries following the United Nations Model, the mere maintenance of a stock of goods of the foreign enterprise for delivery by an agent or a warehouse used for that purpose may constitute a permanent establishment.

The OECD Model Commentary (which is otherwise adopted at length by the United Nations Commentary) states that subparagraph e) serves two functions. First, this subparagraph makes it unnecessary to produce an exhaustive list of exceptions. It is therefore clear that the drafters in fact contemplated a number of unlisted preparatory or auxiliary activities, any or all of which may be pursued without creating a permanent establishment.

Secondly, subparagraph e) is described as a general limitation on the scope of both the fixed-place-of-business and dependent-agency types of permanent establishment. It is only the conduct of the business 'proper' of the foreign enterprise which creates a permanent establishment when conducted through a fixed place of business or by a dependent agent. The 1977 OECD Model, paragraph 4, enumerates the above four activities (a-d) which are not considered the business 'proper' of the enterprise if the use of the facility or the authority of an agent is limited to such activities. A number of other activities are clearly possible if 'preparatory' or 'auxiliary' to the enterprise's business 'proper.'

The OECD 2012 Revised Discussion Draft clarifies that the activities or uses specified in subparagraph a) through d) are conclusively deemed to be 'preparatory or auxiliary' and thus PE-free activities and uses irrespective of the core business of the user *provided*:

1) these activities are conducted for the NRE's transmission, storage, purchase, display, delivery or manufacture of *its own goods* and not of goods belonging to others[1] and
2) if combined with these four or other activities, the combination is preparatory or auxiliary, that is, not within the core activities of the NRE's business[2]

---

1. OECD 2012 Revised Discussion Draft, para. 21: '*Where the only activities carried on at a fixed place of business are activities to which one of subparagraphs a) to d) apply, the place is deemed not to constitute a permanent establishment.*' This is of course a proposed change (as of April 2014) which may not be made in view of the July 19, 2013 OECD BEPS Action Plans and specifically Action 1 proposals with the digital economy and issued March 24, 2014.
2. OECD Commentary, para. 24. In case No. 2005/AR/477 (16 January 2007), Court of Appeals of Ghent (*Hof van Beroep Gent*) implied that the exceptions mentioned in subparagraphs (a) and (b) of Art. 5(3) of the Netherlands–Belgium treaty also apply if they constitute the main activity of the company, which was at odds with the guidance found in the OECD Model Commentary (for details, see *IBFD Tax Treaty Case Law Database*).

Thus, an online retailer might utilize PE-free a source country warehouse for the storage, display and delivery of articles sold by it – provided no other functions are conducted through such warehouse and the goods remain titled in the retailer until delivered to customers. However an Indian ruling suggests that a courier could not *itself* maintain a PE-free source country depot for the collection and delivery of post and cargo of *its customers* for delivery since the goods would belong not to the courier but to its customers (although it could contract with an independent agent or affiliate to do so).[3]

Similarly, a pipeline owner could run PE-free a pipeline through Germany for transmission of its own oil, but could not do so for *customers* without having a POB PE.[4] Similarly, a bank could establish a source country representative office to *collect information* about its customers, reconciling correspondent banks and to research market conditions[5] without creating a PE.

However, a NRE owned public warehouse would have its own PE.[6] And a representative office of Bloomberg established to collect and process market information to be sold in bundled form to customers would not qualify for the PE free exception of subparagraph d).[7] In contrast, an Indian D&B affiliate which prepared its own Business Information Reports about Indian customers did not constitute a PE of the D&B parent company when such BIRs were uploaded onto an offshore computer platform for use for a fee by other D&B affiliates and where non-Indian BIRs were downloaded by an Indian affiliate for a fee and licensed by it at its own rates – such activities being within its own business as an independent contractor.[8]

Merely considering the activities enumerated, paragraph 4 creates several broad exceptions to permanent establishment status, which, if permitted in combination, could allow a foreign commercial or industrial enterprise to conduct several host-country activities up to the point of sale without creating a permanent establishment. Thus (subject to the combination clause) a foreign enterprise may itself engage in the purchase, storage, display, and delivery of

---

3. *Cf. ACIT vs DHL Operations BV Netherlands,* 142 Taman 1 (Mumbai Magistrate) Mehta at 424 and Appendix A, which appears to be wrongly decided on the basis of India's domestic "business connection" test rather than PE criteria.
4. *German Pipeline* Case no. II R 12/92 dated 30 Oct 1992; *Bundesfinanzhof* BStBl. II 111,112 (1978); Reimer states at 40: 'Nevertheless, many courts have held that the mere *transportation of oil or other substances through a pipeline* or similar installation as well as the conduction of electricity through cable would not qualify as the carrying-on of any activity, and would thus not constitute a PE.'
5. *UAE Exchange Centre Ltd vs UOI,* 139 Taxman 82 (2004 AAR – New Delhi) Mehta at 303 and Appendix One.
6. As it would be warehousing its customers' goods.
7. *Bloomberg LP vs Tax Inspectorate,* Case No. A40-94931/10-142-134 dated 8 Dec 2012, Mehta at 305.
8. *Dun & Bradstreet,* AAR No. 615 of 2003, at http://www.bcasonline.org/ContentType/Contentin.asp?828.

goods. It may contract out raw materials to third parties for manufacturing and processing. It may effect sales through consignment sales arrangements with affiliated sales companies.[9]

The PE-free activities of Article 5(4) generally override all four of the PE-creating provisions – including POB PEs, CAS PEs, Agency PEs and Services PEs.[10] The principal exceptions are activities which are preparatory or auxiliary to a CAS project which will be included in the CAS PE if undertaken after commencement of the project in the source country.[11]

6.1 'STORAGE'

Subparagraph (a) exempts the use of a facility for the storage, display, or delivery of goods or merchandise belonging to a foreign enterprise. This paragraph permits the use of a warehouse, warehouse space, or a lot (owned, rented or used by the foreign enterprise) solely for the storage of its own inventory. Under the OECD version, the same premises may also be used for the display and delivery of such goods.[12]

---

9. To appreciate the wide latitude afforded by the OECD 'permitted activities' one has only to look at treaties without it – for example, the old 1956 treaty between Austria and the United States. In Article II(f) of that treaty, a permanent establishment includes (1) a warehouse (other than one used for convenience of delivery and not for display, (2) an employee or agent without authority to conclude contracts but who regularly makes delivery from a host country stock of merchandise and (3) the storage of goods in a rented space or lot (other than the casual and temporary use of mere storage facilities or through bailment with a public warehouseman).
10. Although this is not always obvious from the text of the relevant provisions.
11. See Mehta at 205-68, who also discusses a ruling that the repair and maintenance of equipment did not count for purposes of the 120-day timeline provision in the US–India Treaty.
12. *See* Ltr. Rul. 7749009 (United Kingdom distillery warehousing inventory in the United States had no permanent establishment under the 1945 former United States–United Kingdom treaty); *Fish Wholesaler,* decision of Ghent Court of Appeal date 19 Jun 2002, Mehta at 310 (Dutch fish wholesaler's use of an Antwerp cold storage facility not a PE); *Airline Rotables Ltd vs IDIT,* 44 SOT 368 (2011 Mumbai) Mehta at 311 and Appendix One (Jet Airway's maintenance of UK aircraft repairer's consigned stock of replacement parts not a PE); *Danish Distribution Service,* Case No 1988-4-564 15 Dec 1988 (Danish company maintained consigned stock of German supplier and dispatched to customers upon receipt of orders, collected premiums and deposited same, held no agency PE or POB, as no sales functions were performed); *Spanish Distribution Case* No. 0657/2003 (2 Mar 2006 Central Economic Administrative Court) (Finnish supplier used Spanish third party storage and distribution facilities but also had a Spanish subsidiary which acted as its sales agent and marketed its merchandise in Spain – held a dependent agency PE although subsidiary did not have authority to conclude contracts) Mehta at 318; *Hungarian Storage Facility,* Case no Kfv.1.35.021/2007/8 (17 Jan 2008 Hungarian Supreme Court) (UK Company used Hungarian premises for storage of goods; premises also facilitated import, export and sales of goods to its customers; held a POB PE; decision complicated by fact that UK company had initially registered premises as a PE); *Hallminster Ltd vs Ministre de l'Economie, des Fainances et de l'Industrie,* Case No. 98BX0558 (9 Jul 2002, Administrative Court of Appeals, Bordeaux) (wine inventory not a place of business)

6.2 'DISPLAY'

The display of goods contemplates their exhibition at trade fairs, but contemplates showrooms as well, provided that sales are not solicited or affected from the premises.[13] However, merchandise displayed at a trade fair or convention may be sold at the termination of the trade fair or convention without creating a permanent establishment.[14]

In *Rev. Rul. 62-31*,[15] a United Kingdom corporation was held to have a 'fixed place of businesses by its 'maintenance of an office or showroom used by a group of salesmen for sales promotion' of the products of the corporation. The employees of the United States office – salesmen and general clerks – were empowered only to run the office, to arrange for the appointment of United States distributors subject to home office approval, and to solicit orders generally. The ruling turns on the mere business use of a fixed place of business, a sales solicitation and promotion office, since the employees did not have any authority to negotiate and enter into contracts on behalf of the corporation.

Rev. Rul. 62-31 revoked and re-decided *Rev. Rul. 54-588*,[16] which it considered analogous but improperly decided on the basis of agency rather than fixed place of business. In the earlier ruling, a United Kingdom corporation (the 'sales corporation') maintained a showroom in New York City from which its salesmen solicited orders from samples of the merchandise of another United Kingdom corporation (the 'manufacturing corporation'). Purchase orders were transmitted for acceptance directly by mail to the manufacturing corporation. That corporation shipped the merchandise directly to the customer and received payment directly from the customer.

Mehta at 322; *Group Distribution Centre*,Case No. 2005/AR/477 (16 Jan 2007 Ghent Court of Appeals) (Dutch group distribution center not a PE even though it stored merchandise for other members of the group to create supply chain efficiencies) Mehta at 323.

The enterprise storing, displaying or delivering the goods must be their owner (or have beneficial ownership). Vogel includes within this category a German *Kommissionär* (an agent who acts for a foreign principal but in his own name). *See* Vogel, at 319, para. 110.

13. *See* Edwardes-Ker Art. 5, p. 13.0008, former United States–United Kingdom treaty ruling holding that a showroom is a fixed-place-of-business permanent establishment. Carroll states, referring to the former 1951 United States treaty with Switzerland: 'The Convention with Switzerland adds to the standard terms a clause to the effect that the maintenance of a warehouse for convenience of delivery and not for purposes of display shall not of itself constitute a permanent establishment, even though offers of purchase have been obtained by an agent of the enterprise in that territory and transmitted by him to the enterprise for acceptance (Art. II(i)(c)).' Carroll, Part II, at 145.
14. OECD Model Commentary, Art. 5(4), para. 29.
15. 1962-1 *C.B. 367*, revoking Rev. Rul. 54-588,1954-2 *C.B.* 456 (former United States–United Kingdom treaty).
16. 1954-2 C.B. 456 (former United States–United Kingdom treaty).

The 1954 Ruling concluded there was no permanent establishment of the manufacturing corporation because the sales corporation merely used its own United States showroom to solicit sales for the manufacturing corporation in return for commissions for sales made, the sales corporation 'clearly' having a fixed place of business in the United States. While *Rev. Rul. 62-31* did not actually decide whether the manufacturing corporation had a fixed place of business, the implication is that it did not, because the showroom was the office of the sales corporation and the sales corporation had neither authority to conclude contracts for the manufacturing corporation nor a stock of its merchandise from which it regularly filled orders.

In sum, *Rev. Rul. 62-31* held that a sales solicitation office is a 'fixed place of business' if operated by a foreign corporation. Similarly, a 'fixed place of business' will exist if a 'sales showroom' is operated by one corporation to solicit sales for another, but the 'fixed place of business' will be that of the corporation which operates the sales showroom, not the one whose orders are solicited there (provided the soliciting agents have no authority to bind the supplier).[17] So the ruling concludes that the manufacturing corporation did not have a fixed place of business PE, while the sales corporation did.

The display of goods consecutively at different locations will not constitute a fixed-place-of-business permanent establishment, even if orders are solicited.[18]

6.3 'DELIVERY'

The use of a fixed place of business, operated by the foreign enterprise, for delivery of its goods to its customers is by itself not a permanent establishment under treaties patterned after the OECD and United States models. Such delivery will constitute a permanent establishment under certain United Nations Model Treaties and treaties antedating the OECD Model by reason of the foreign principal having an agent for the regular delivery of goods in the host country.

Because each of the functions of storage, display, and delivery is separately characterized by OECD Article 5(3)(e) as a preparatory or auxiliary

17. Special proscriptions may apply, particularly in developing countries. For example, the 1970 United States–Trinidad and Tobago treaty does not allow the use of a fixed place of business for the display of merchandise but does allow the use of a fixed place of business for 'processing [of the foreign enterprise's goods] by another person under arrangements or conditions which are or would be made between independent persons.' (Art. 9(3) and (4)).
18. Vogel, at 320, para. 110. Professor Vogel characterizes the famous Swiss logger case (Rev. Rul. 56-165, 1956-1 *C.B.* 849), which is *contra*, as 'definitely obsolete on account of what is stated in both OECD and United States MC.'

activity, the use of single premises for storage, display, and delivery satisfies the 'overall' preparatory or auxiliary character required by the OECD combination clause.

6.4 'GOODS OR MERCHANDISE'

'Goods' appears to refer to all manner of *tangible* personal property which can be sold, including raw materials, commodities, minerals, natural resources, agricultural produce, and manufactured, fabricated, produced and processed products and tangible software, such as CDs, DVDs sold as end user licenses.[19] It does not include *intangible* property such as software or intellectual property rights.[20] 'Merchandise' appears to refer to a narrower class of manufactured or industrial goods produced for public consumption.[21]

6.5 'MAINTENANCE OF A STOCK OF GOODS OR MERCHANDISE'

The mere host-country maintenance of a stock of goods or merchandise of the foreign enterprise will not constitute a permanent establishment in treaties patterned after the OECD, United Nations, and United States Model Treaties.[22] Article 5(4)(b) of each of these treaties seems to refer to the maintenance of goods in 'facilities' not owned, leased or used by the foreign enterprise. Involved might be the storage of raw materials or finished inventory on the premises of a contract manufacturer, or the storage of inventory on consignment to a distributor or sales agent.[23]

---

19. OECD 2012 Revised Discussion Draft, para. 22.
20. The IRS is to be commended for promulgation of Treas. Reg. 1.861-18, *Classification of Transactions involving Computer Programs*, resolving a long standing divergence of opinion between IBM and Microsoft as to the classification of software program income as royalties (retained property rights) and opposed to product sales (e.g., all substantial rights transferred or end user license sales of such items as CDs and DVDs).
21. Vogel, at 319, para 110, defines both terms as including all current or fixed assets, including associated services such as packaging or dispatching.
22. Even under the pre-OECD treaties, casual or limited warehousing would generally not create a permanent establishment. *See* Rev. Rul. 56-594,1956-2 *C.B.* 1126 (no permanent establishment under 1945 former United States–United Kingdom treaty despite having 'a small stock of merchandise at a New York warehouse') and Ltr. Rul. 7749009 (United Kingdom distillery warehousing inventory in United States lacked a permanent establishment under former 1945 United States–United Kingdom treaty).
23. *Cf.* Vogel, at 320, para. 111, who finds this provision a clarification, since the lack of a fixed place of business precludes a permanent establishment under the general rule.

6.6 'PROCESSING'

The maintenance of a host-country stock of merchandise for processing by another enterprise will not constitute a permanent establishment under treaties conforming to the OECD, United Nations, and United States Model Treaties. These treaties allow a foreign enterprise to have raw materials converted, processed, fabricated, or manufactured by another enterprise in the host country, and to store such materials in the host country with the contract manufacturer prior to processing.[24] Under the combination of OECD-permitted activities, the raw materials and finished inventory can be stored on premises operated by the foreign enterprise or with a toll manufacturer or may be consigned to a sales agent. In light of the parent-subsidiary paragraph,[25] it is possible to have the contract manufacturing done by a wholly-owned host-country affiliate.

For the exemption to apply, the foreign enterprise cannot participate in the processing. Otherwise, permanent establishment status will apply to all processing activity. For example, supervision by the foreign enterprise could disqualify it. However, it should be permissible for foreign enterprise employees to make periodic site visits to verify compliance with the processing contract.

Some treaties patterned after the OECD Model apply limitations to contract manufacturing with respect to host-country sales, and host-country purchase-and-sale operations. For example, the 1970 United States treaties with Belgium and with Trinidad and Tobago provide that a permanent establishment exists if merchandise stored in the taxing State is sold there, if such merchandise was purchased there and not subjected to substantial processing elsewhere, or if such merchandise is subject to substantial processing in the taxing State – whether or not purchased there.[26] Under the United States–Belgium treaty, a permanent establishment will not be deemed to exist unless the foreign enterprise also has a fixed place of business in the taxing State.[27]

Under the Trinidadian treaty, the mere turn-around purchase and sale of goods in the taxing State or the sale there of goods subjected to substantial

---

24. 'Processing' means the working of articles or products to change some of their essential features, or, if they are raw materials, to turn them into something different. Vogel, at 320, para. 113.
25. OECD Model 5(7).
26. United States–Trinidad and Tobago 9(4)(c).
27. United States–Belgium treaty Art. 5(2). The United States Technical Explanation interprets 'processing' as 'substantial processing.' In some (pre-OECD) treaties, there may be a limitation as to how long or how many goods can be stored for processing without creating a permanent establishment. Thus, Vogel cites a 1935 German decision (RFH *RStBl* 1399, 1401) finding a permanent establishment where, over a lengthy period of time, more goods were stored than needed for processing (the applicable treaty included as a permanent establishment, stocks of goods or merchandise). *See* Vogel, at 320, para. 112.

processing in the taxing State will result in a permanent establishment, even though no fixed place of business or dependent agency exists. In treaties without these proscriptions, the activities discussed above should be possible so long as they maintain an overall preparatory or auxiliary character.

6.7 'PURCHASING'

A pioneer of double-taxation conventions has recalled:

> 'In the 1920s and 30s attempts were made from time to time to subject a nonresident to tax on the presumed profits attributable to the act of purchasing, but progressively it was acknowledged that a so-called purchasing profit was usually fortuitous and was impossible to measure. Nevertheless some less developed countries still try to reach a foreign company which buys and exports locally produced goods, especially if they are processed and packed before shipment, and sell them at an establishment in its home country.
>
> Except for the [United States] Conventions with Austria and Pakistan, which said nothing on the subject, all the conventions categorically proscribed treating as a permanent establishment a mere office to purchase goods for export, or attributing any profit to the mere act of purchasing.'[28]

It has been held that the purchasing-agent exemption is exceeded where purchased hides were subject to salt curing in the host country for a period of 21 days prior to shipment where such curing, although accounting for only five percent of their value, was essential to their resale.[29]

In an American letter ruling,[30] it is held that, pursuant to a long-term coal supply contract with a foreign enterprise, the United States supplier's incidental sales of coal on behalf of the foreign enterprise did not constitute the supplier a permanent establishment of the foreign enterprises. Such sales

28. Carroll, Part II at 149. Mitchell B. Carroll states in his 1988 article: 'The Treaty with New Zealand removes from the definition of a fixed place of business [one used] exclusively for the purchase of goods or merchandise (Art. II(1) (0) [*sic*]. Carroll, Part II, at 145. Note also that the article contains a brief summary of the opposition of Spanish America to the exemption of purchasing operations from source-country taxation, as well as the difficulty-of-allocation justification for its existence.
29. *Transvaal Associated Hide and Skin Merchants vs Collector of Income Tax, Botswana* [1967] 3 *South Africa* 111 *(obiter dictum* regarding contended application of United Kingdom treaty to Botswana) *See also* Edwardes-Ker Art. 5 page 13.5004, Italy–France (purchasing office not permanent establishment).
30. Ltr. Rul. 7810010.

were authorized only when shipment was prevented by operation of law not affecting the supplier or where the foreign enterprise failed to accept delivery.

6.8 'COLLECTING INFORMATION'

The OECD Model Commentary asserts that use of a fixed place of business for 'collecting information' for the enterprise is no more than an extension of the 'mere purchase' exemption:

> 'The reference to the collection of information in subparagraph d) is intended to include the case of the newspaper bureau which has no purpose other than to act as one of many tentacles of the parent body; to exempt such a bureau is to do no more than to extend the concept of mere purchase.'[31]

While the collection of information is permitted for the enterprise, there is an apparent requirement, as in the subparagraph e) 'catchall' exception, that the enterprise show that the collection of such information is 'preparatory' or 'auxiliary' to the business proper of the enterprise. For example, the collecting information exception would not appear to protect data-base companies which collect financial and business information about host country firms which are then analyzed and compiled into reports which are sold to subscribers. On the other hand, the information-collection exemption should apply by analogy to a newspaper bureau which merely collects news and sends news dispatches for editorial compilation elsewhere.[32] Such information collection is analogous to the purchase of raw materials, which are processed elsewhere. Host country research activities appear to fall under the subparagraph (e) catchall exemption and are protected only if shown to be preparatory or auxiliary to the business proper of the enterprise.

The information-collection exemption would seem to apply generally to host country representative offices which exist to gather information about the

31. OECD Model Commentary, Art 5(5), para. 22 (fourth sentence).

32. Vogel finds the exemption lost if information is 'processed,' i.e., 'evaluated or edited in a fixed place of business.' Vogel, at 320-321, para. 114. *See also* Edwardes-Ker, BFH *BStBl* II417 (1985) (German treaties with France, Greece, Great Britain, and the United States held editorial offices may be permanent establishments, news bureaux are not). *See also* Ltr. Rul. 8442107 (United States–Japan treaty, held no permanent establishment where not-for-profit Japanese entity collected information on overseas economies and conducted comprehensive research and studies for dissemination to its members, and United States branch did not engage in entity's commissioned projects, and did not participate in the preparation of the entity's reports and publications other than by supplying information.)

state of the market, competitive factors, and customer needs.[33] A representative office which advertises for the enterprise, transmits customer complaints, and houses 'goodwill' staff to perform other functions short of direct solicitation may be exempt only if it could be shown that such activities are in fact 'preparatory' or 'auxiliary' to the business proper of the enterprise.[34] The Commentary states for example, that the furnishing of 'plans etc., specially developed for an individual customer' is not exempt.[35] Nor would the exemption apply 'if a research center were to concern itself with manufacture.'[36] Presumably however, basic research could be protected as a 'preparatory' activity.

6.9 'PREPARATORY' OR 'AUXILIARY' ACTIVITIES

Subparagraph (e) of the OECD Model exempts the maintenance of a fixed place of business maintained for the purpose of carrying on for the enterprise any other activities of a 'preparatory' or 'auxiliary' nature. Several points emerge from the OECD Commentary concerning this generic exception. First, this provision is thought to be potentially broad in scope. The Commentary says that its wording 'makes it unnecessary to produce an exhaustive list of exceptions.'[37] However, the foreign enterprise will have the burden of proving that unlisted activities are 'preparatory' or 'auxiliary' in character.[38] Second, the Commentary states that subparagraph e) represents a purposeful narrowing of the fixed-place-of-business type of permanent establishment:

> 'this sub-paragraph provides a generalized exception to the general definition in paragraph 1 and, when read with that paragraph, provides a more selective test, by which to determine what constitutes a permanent

33. United States Ltr. Rul. 8442107 (a United States branch simply supplying its home office with data does not constitute a permanent establishment).
34. *Sumitomo Corporation vs DCIT*, 114 ITD 61 (2008 Delhi) (Sumitomo had a substantial import export business with India, 3 project offices and a rep office which had substantial assets and expenses but was not allowed to engage in trading activities; held no PE); see also, *IAC vs Mitsui & Co. Ltd*, 39 ITD 59, *DCIT vs Tokio Marine & Fire Insurance Co Ltd*, Mehta at 363, which allowed rep offices in connection with joint ventures.
35. OECD Model Commentary Art. 5(4), para. 24. *See Metal Products Ruling*, Case No. 340/404-131 (30 Nov 1989 (Danish Assessment Board).
36. *Ibid. See Pioneer Overseas Corporation vs ADIT*, 37 SOT 404 (2010 Delhi) (conduct of agri-genetic research, production of hybrid parent seeds and sale of to a joint venture company was the core business of the US parent company and hence branch office was a PE) Mehta at 352; Metal Products Ruling, No. 340/4024-131 (30 Nov 1989 Danish Assessment Board) (Danish design and sales solicitation office was POB PE) Mehta at 355;
37. OECD Model Commentary, Art. 5(4), para. 23.
38. OECD Model Commentary, Art. 5(4), para. 24.

> establishment. To a considerable degree it limits that definition and excludes from its rather wide scope a number of forms of business organizations which, although they are carried on through a fixed place of business, should not be treated as a permanent establishments.'[39]

Third, preparatory or auxiliary activities may be a profit-contributing part of the business (such as scientific research, advertising or the furnishing of patent services) and yet still be excluded if sufficiently preceding the realization of profit as to be viewed as 'preparatory.' As stated by the OECD Commentary:

> 'It is recognized that such a place of business may well contribute to the productivity of the enterprise, but the services it performs are so remote from the actual realization of profits that it is difficult to allocate any profit to the fixed place of business in question. Examples are fixed places of business solely for the purpose of advertising or for the supply of information or for scientific research or for the servicing of a patent or a know-how contract, if such activities have a preparatory or auxiliary character.'[40]

Fourth, an activity which is a part of the business 'proper' of the enterprise will not be 'preparatory' or 'auxiliary.' Thus, host country patent servicing by a company licensing patents can create a permanent establishment:

> 'It is often difficult to distinguish between activities which have a preparatory or auxiliary character and those which have not. The decisive criterion is whether or not the activity of the fixed place of business in itself forms an essential and significant part of the activity of the enterprise as a whole. Each individual case will have to be examined on its own merits. In any case, a fixed place of business whose general purpose is one which is identical to the general purpose of the whole enterprise, does not exercise a preparatory or auxiliary activity. Where, for example, the servicing of patents and know-how is the purpose of an enterprise, a fixed place of business of such enterprise exercising such an activity cannot get the benefits of sub-paragraph e).'[41]

As an example of this 'business proper' limitation, the OECD Draft Commentary suggests that if the results of laboratory research are sold to third parties,

---

39. OECD Model Commentary, Art. 5(4), para. 23.
40. *Id.* (fifth and sixth sentences).
41. OECD Model Commentary, Art. 5(4), para. 24 (first through fifth sentences).

the laboratory may constitute a permanent establishment.[42] The OECD Draft Commentary reaches a similar conclusion if a research establishment 'were to concern itself with manufacture.'[43]

Fifth, to be preparatory or auxiliary in nature, activities must be carried on for the enterprise itself. A fixed place of business which renders services not only the enterprise but to other group companies could fall outside subparagraph e) – provided that such services were a core part of the provider's business enterprise and provided to a different enterprise with the group.[44] Similarly, with respect to a foreign advertising agency, a United States branch which performs functions related to providing advertising for other advertisers should be a permanent establishment.[45] Further, and as an illustration of the concept, the after-sale supply of spare parts and repair services provided customers will not qualify for exemption as these activities go beyond 'delivery' and constitute an essential and significant part of the services of an enterprise and are thus not auxiliary activities.[46]

Sixth, management activities are not preparatory or auxiliary activities, whether the management is concluded through a 'headquarters office' or regional office.[47] Thus, coordination centers and headquarters offices are permanent establishments as they constitute a 'place of management' under the basic rule.

Seventh, an activity qualifying for exemption from the fixed-place-of-business permanent establishment classification is exempt from a dependent-agency permanent establishment classification, as well.[48]

---

42. OECD Draft Commentary, Art. 5(3), para. 13.
43. OECD Draft Commentary, Art. 5(3), para. 12; *see* OECD Model Commentary, Art. 5(4), para. 24.
44. Vogel includes as prohibited activity a company which furnishes common facility services to consortium owners. Vogel, at 321, para. 116a. However, a non-recurring service for a third party will not result in permanent establishment status as 'permanence' does not exist. *Compare* Ltr. Rul. 8442107 (United States–Japan treaty, holding that a consortium-owned not-for-profit Japanese company which did prepare commissioned reports for third parties did not have a United States permanent establishment, where the branch merely collected information, for which it did not charge).
45. Roberts & Warren, at IX-145.
46. OECD Model Commentary, Art. 5(4), para. 25.
47. OECD Model Commentary, Art. 5(4), para. 24.
48. The OECD Model Commentary states: 'The employees of places of business within the meaning of paragraph 4 who are authorized to conclude such contracts should not be regarded as agents within the meaning of paragraph 5. A case in point would be a research institution the manager of which is authorized to conclude the contracts necessary for maintaining the institution and who exercises this authority within the framework of the functions of the institution. A permanent establishment, however, exists if the fixed place of business exercising any of the functions listed in paragraph 4 were to exercise them not only on behalf of the enterprise to which it belongs but also on behalf of other enterprises. If, for instance, an advertising agency maintained by an enterprise were also to engage in advertising for other enterprises, it would

An illustration of the type of permissible activities that may be carried on through a fixed place of business is provided by *Rev. Rul. 72-418*.[49] There, a German bank leased a United States office in the name of its representative for the purposes of:

1) obtaining information on various banking and financial matters including credit reports on American banks;
2) assisting the United States and German customers of the bank with information and letters of introduction to American banks and firms;
3) maintaining contacts with American banks and firms and providing the same with information on German financial conditions;
4) on rare occasions, communicating with United States debtors of the bank and obtaining information on repayment possibilities; and
5) advertising for the bank through the United States in newspapers, periodicals, and by personal contacts.[50]

In holding that this United States office was exempt under the United States–Germany treaty as a 'fixed place of business for the purpose of advertising, for the supply of information, for scientific research or for similar activities, if they have a preparatory or auxiliary character,' the ruling noted that no commercial banking activities were carried on by the United States office.

Finally, if a fixed place of business is used both for permitted and impermissible activities (as in the case of a place of business maintained for the delivery of goods that also engages in sales or sales solicitation), it is a permanent establishment with regard to all activities.[51]

6.10 REPRESENTATIVE OFFICES

A non-resident's enterprise's (NRE's) decision to establish a source country presence is usually a staged development, which reflects the interplay of the local country's rules with regard to income tax, VAT, visas and permits for NRE staff, rental of office space and required corporate and or tax registration where applicable to conduct commercial activity within the country through

be regarded as a permanent establishment of the enterprise by which it is maintained.' OECD Model Commentary, Art. 5(4), para. 28 (third through sixth sentences).

49. 1972 *CB*. 661 (United States–Germany treaty).

50. *Id.* at 661-662. *See also* Ltr. Rul. 7810010, held no permanent establishment where foreign enterprise financed long-term United States coal supplier and provided three on site liaison employees to observe construction of mine, sample minerals and examine United States supplier's books and records.

51. OECD Model Commentary Art. 5(4), para. 27.1.

a representative liaison or branch office. How and where PE status fits within this spectrum requires strategic advice from local professionals well before implementation.

Local laws will require tax or administrative registration at various phases of the entry process. Key amongst these are the definition of a 'non-commercial' representative office (RO) and the potential acquisition of PE status by such a local office. Delineating the two types of offices – one taxable, one not – is often a fine line exercise, which is complicated in Russia, for example, as the same word – '*predstavitel'stvo*' – is used for both the civil term 'representative office' and the treaty term 'permanent establishment,' although the two have very different meanings.[52]

Accordingly, in certain cases a first step might be to avoid both, and instead to appoint a local agent to represent the NRE as an 'independent contractor.'[53] A later step could involve establishment of a representative office (RO). Establishment of a RO generally requires registration with the tax authorities (if only for VAT and wage taxes etc.) and the Ministry of Justice or Chamber of Commerce but can in most cases avoid income tax exposure as a PE provided the RO carefully limits its activities to non-entrepreneurial activities. The following should be considered[54]:

- The NRE's property base in the host jurisdiction;
- Clarity in the objectives, authorities and functions of the RO and its employees ensuring their auxiliary and preparatory nature;
- The risks of entrepreneurial activity through that office either using its own or RO employees;
- Sending employees on business trips should be supported by documents showing the non-business nature of such trips.

Unlike an RO, a branch is authorized to engage in full commercial activity and like an RO will be a PE if it is engaged in entrepreneurial activity. The 2010 Bloomberg case illustrates some of the perils of RO vs PE classification. The noted US financial services provider produced and sold information products, including analytical databases. It had in 2006 and 2007 a Moscow RO where a number of employees gathered, correlated and analyzed information which was incorporated into its databases which were a part of financial

---

52. Roche & Duffay, Moscow, *Representative Office of a Foreign Company in Russia*, http://www.roche-duffay.ru/articles/representative.htm#1.
53. Danske Bank, Company Business Guides, *Russia*, at p. 10, http://www.danskebank.com/en-uk/ProdServ/corporate/country-business-guides/Documents/Business_Guide_Russia.pdf.
54. G Neverov. Director RTF-Audit, Moscow, 29.07.2011 *Foreign Representative Office: How to Confirm the Tax Status And Avoid Disputes with the Tax Inspectorate* http://rtf-audit.ru/eng/subscribe/20110827/01/

services sold by Bloomberg's UK affiliate to Russian purchasers on whom VAT was assessed. Bloomberg argued that such collection and assemblage of information was ancillary or preparatory to its core business services and that no charge was made for the databases. The Supreme Court of Moscow in a December 8, 2010 ruling found that (1) such information collection and analysis were part of Bloomberg's core business services and (2) assessed it income equal to the full amount of Bloomberg's Russian sales less some allocable expenses.[55]

6.11 COMBINATION OF ACTIVITIES

The 1977 OECD and the 1981 United States Model Treaties permit any combination of the listed or unlisted preparatory or auxiliary activities. The OECD and US Models require that the overall activity be of a preparatory or auxiliary character. The OECD Model exempts:

> 'f) the maintenance of a fixed place of business solely for any combination of activities mentioned in sub-paragraphs a) to e), provided that the overall activity of the fixed place of business resulting from this combination is of a preparatory or auxiliary character.'[56]

The United Nations Model and the 1963 OECD Draft both omit this 'combination' provision. The United Nations Commentary simply states that member countries felt that inclusion of subparagraph f) of the 1977 OECD Model should be left to bilateral negotiation. Thus, in developing-country treaties from which this subparagraph f) is absent, a combination of two or more listed or unlisted preparatory or auxiliary activities (for example, storage and processing) may create a permanent establishment.

The OECD Model Commentary states, in determining whether a combination of preparatory or auxiliary activities maintains such overall character,

> '[s]uch combinations should not be viewed on rigid lines, but should be considered in the light of the particular circumstances. The criterion

---

55. Schekin & Vakhitov, International Law Office, *Permanent establishment; court's warning for representative offices*, March 25, 2011, http://www.internationallawoffice.com/newsletters/detail.aspx?g=7918569d-2497-4770-8006-65f941241a6a.

56. OECD Model 5(4)(f). The OECD Model thus eliminated earlier confusion caused by the 1963 OECD Draft's reference to the use of facilities solely for one of five permitted categorical activities. *See* Vogel at 322, para. 117.

> "preparatory or auxiliary character" is to be interpreted in the same way as is set out for the same criterion of sub-paragraph e) ...'[57]

Thus, combined activities should be antecedent or auxiliary to the realization of profit, provided to the enterprise itself, not be part of its business 'proper,' and not be management.

Under the OECD provision, a leading commentator concludes that a combination of activities which are separately listed as 'preparatory or auxiliary' cannot constitute a permanent establishment 'unless and until it leads to the emergence of a facility which would be economically viable if separated from the enterprise to which it belongs.[58] Notwithstanding this separate economic entity limitation, it should be specifically possible under OECD-based treaties to combine activities within the same subparagraph (e.g., the storage, display and delivery of goods).

It would seem that the combination of activities within different subparagraphs should be subject to the separate economic entity rule. Thus, the use of the same facility to purchase, store, display and deliver goods, might result in a viable independent enterprise and hence permanent establishment status. Whether permanent establishment status existed would depend generally on the principal activity of the enterprise. If it is trading, for example, permanent establishment status might result. If an office is used for advertising and also stores goods for purposes of display of the range of the products of the enterprise, permanent establishment should not exist; the combination remains 'preparatory or auxiliary.'[59]

If doubt exists whether a combination fails these tests, comfort might be obtained by using separate premises for separate permitted activities. The OECD Commentary states:

> 'Sub-paragraph f) is of no importance in a case where an enterprise maintains several fixed places of business within the meaning of the sub-paragraphs a) to e) provided that they are separated from each other locally and organizationally, as in such a case each place of business has to be viewed separately and in isolation for deciding the question whether or not a permanent establishment exists.[60] ... States which want to allow any combination of the items mentioned in sub-paragraphs a) to e) disregarding whether or not the criterion of the preparatory or auxiliary character of such a combination is met, are

57. OECD Model Commentary, Art. 5(4), para. 27 (fourth and fifth sentences).
58. Vogel, at 322-323, para. 117a.
59. *Ibid.*
60. OECD Model Commentary, Art. 5(4), para. 27.1.

> free to do so by deleting the words "provided" to "character" in sub-paragraph f).'[61]

If a fixed place of business under paragraph 4 is deemed not to be a permanent establishment, this exception applies likewise to the disposal of movable property forming part of the business property of the place of business at the termination of the activity of the enterprise in such installation. Since, for example, the display of merchandise is excepted under sub-paragraphs a) and b), the OECD Commentary states that the sale of the merchandise at the termination of a trade fair or convention is covered by this exception.[62]

61. OECD Model Commentary, Art. 5(4), para. 27.
62. OECD Model Commentary, Art. 5(4), para. 29.

Chapter 7

Permanent Establishments – Services and Secondments

7.1 AN INTRODUCTION TO SERVICE PEs

In the original 1976 law review article which was the prototype of this book, the author concluded that there were basically 3 types of PEs – assets, agencies and activities, the last based on some rather far-fetched American rulings. Four years later, a Services PE provision was added to Article 5(3)(b) of the UN MC at the request of source country members. In 2008 the OECD reluctantly added similar Services PE provisions not to the MC, but in the Commentary. So an *activities* type PE has in fact metastasized through the 1980 UN model into a significant type of PE which is both separate from but sometimes confused with the other Article 5 provisions which either create a discrete type of PE or recognize PE-free offices, agents and activities.

It took 80 years for a Services PE provision to emerge from the original 1899 Austria–Hungary/Prussia treaty 'bricks and mortar' *Betriebsstätte* concept of an assets PE. There from the beginning was also a second type of PE, the dependent agency PE which existed independently of a fixed POB. This second type of PE was amended by 1927 to include English concepts of agency and the PE-free independent agent.

Construction assembly sites emerged as a third type of PE based on a 1962 US – Japan treaty inclusion of such a site in response to a major US installation project in Japan and incorporated into the 1963 OECD draft. The 1977 OECD MC recognition of CAS PEs as not an Article 5(2) illustrative type of PE but as an Article 5(3) stand-alone PE, freed from the fixed POB requirements of Article 5(1) but tied to a 12-month timeline, set the stage for the UN MC's 1980 addition to the CAS article of a second type of pure services PE, also tied to the reduced UN MC 6-month timeline. Thus, this fourth type of 'Services' PE was born, freed of the fixed POB, authorized agent and geographic proximity requirements of the other three PEs.

7.2 THE SERVICES PE PROVISIONS

A. UN Model Provision

Under Article 5(3)(b) of the UN Model Tax Convention, the concept of 'permanent establishment' includes:

> '(b) The furnishing of services, including consultancy services, by an enterprise through employees or other personnel engaged by the enterprise for such purpose, but only if activities of that nature continue (for the same or a connected project) within a Contracting State for a period or periods aggregating more than 183 days in any 12-month period commencing or ending in the fiscal year concerned.'

Accordingly, under the UN Model Tax Convention, a 'permanent establishment' is deemed to exist where services are rendered by an enterprise in the source state through qualifying individuals (i.e. employees or other personnel) over a certain period of time which starts or ends in a given tax year.

B. Optional OECD Commentary Provisions

On 17 July 2008, the OECD updated its Commentary to include an optional Services PE provision which significantly expands the circumstances in which a Services PE may arise.[1] The addition of the optional Service PE provision in the OECD Model Commentary is a concession to the source country 'minority' view among the OECD Member States.[2] However, the OECD Model Commentary also clearly articulates the potential issues which the Services PE provision may raise, such as the risk of non-compliance, problems with tax collection, and profit attribution.[3] The optional OECD Services PE provision which the contracting states may consider including in their bilateral tax treaties reads as follows:

---

1. OECD Commentary, Article 5, para 42.11.
2. Pijl, 'The OECD Services Permanent Establishment Alternative,' 48 *European Taxation*, 9 (Sep 2008), pp. 472-476, at 472. According to Pijl, the reason underlying the inclusion of the service PE provision in the OECD Model Commentary rather than the Model itself can be attributed to the opposition of several countries to include the provision in their tax treaties. The inclusion of the Services PE rule in the OECD Model Commentary is a good starting point in treaty negotiations for countries which are in favor of such a provision.
3. OECD Model Commentary, Art. 5, paras. 42.12 and 42.13.

'Notwithstanding the provisions of paragraphs 1, 2 and 3, where an enterprise of a Contracting State performs services in the other Contracting State

a) through an individual who is present in that other State for a period or periods exceeding in the aggregate 183 days in any twelve month period, and more than 50 per cent of the gross revenues attributable to active business activities of the enterprise during this period or periods are derived from the services performed in that other State through that individual, or
b) for a period or periods exceeding in the aggregate 183 days in any twelve month period, and these services are performed for the same project or for connected projects through one or more individuals who are present and performing such services *in that other State* the activities carried on in that other State in performing these services shall be deemed to be carried on through a permanent establishment of the enterprise situated in that other State, *unless these services are limited to those mentioned in paragraph 4 which, if performed through a fixed place of business, would not make this fixed place of business a permanent establishment under the provisions of that paragraph. For the purposes of this paragraph, services performed by an individual on behalf of one enterprise shall not be considered to be performed by another enterprise through that individual unless that other enterprise supervises, directs or controls the manner in which these services are performed by the individual.*'[4]

These alternative OECD Commentary provisions address two different situations. Subparagraph (a) reflects the OECD's 2000 repeal of Article 14 (taxing the services of a self-employed individual who has a 'fixed base' in the source country for more than 183 days). Alternative (b) basically parallels the UN provision creating a Services PE if NRE employees or other persons engaged by it are present in the source country for more than 183 days during the year. But the OECD terms are more restrictive in three respects;

1) The OECD provision clearly requires the services be performed within the source country state; the UN provision is more ambiguous and some source country adherents have taken the position services need not be restricted to those performed in the source country
2) The OECD provision specifically excepts Article 5(4) PE-free type services

4. OECD Model Commentary, Art. 5, para. 42.23, emphasis added.

3) The OECD provision requires that services provided by non NRE employees, e.g., employees of a subcontractor or seconded employees, are not counted unless such employees are under the control and supervision of the NRE.

7.3 CRITICISM OF SERVICES PE PROVISIONS

While both models have historically had threshold rules for taxing the income attributable to the services of non-resident individuals through Article 14 (taxing self-employed entrepreneurs if attributable to a source country fixed base permanent establishment or if present there for more than 183 days)[5] and Article 15 (taxing persons employed by a source country company or PE if the person is present there for more than 183 days), the basic OECD concept of a 'permanent establishment' has always resisted source country taxation of corporate services rendered without a source country fixed place of business or dependent agent. The PE concept is after all meant to encourage international trade by providing bright line demarcations up to which businesses can internationally trade without incurring local tax.

The call for a Services PE provision, made by a minority of source country members of the international trading community, has been criticized[6] by developed countries.[7] Rather than accommodating minority attempts to override traditional PE concepts with source country 'nexus' taxation, the OECD could better have left the issue to individual countries to resolve by reservation or observation to OECD MC or commentary[8] provisions. Stating these minority positions as 'alternatives' in the Commentary has led to an erosion of the historical PE concept and blurring where clear guidance should be given.[9]

---

5. Article 14 was deleted from the OECD MC in 2000, being viewed as duplicative of Article 5 – a premise which some, including the authors, question.
6. *See e.g.*, Dunahoo, *Source Country Taxation of Foreign Corporations: Evolving Permanent Establishment Concepts*, 86 Taxes Magazine 37 (March 2008).
7. Notwithstanding, the US has adopted service PE provisions in some of its treaties. *See e.g.*, Service PE provisions in Australian, Indian, Norwegian and New Zealand treaties (as well as the Fifth Protocol to the Canadian US treaty).
8. Dunahoo and Sprague, '2008 OECD Model: Changes to the Commentary on Article 5 Regarding the Treatment of Services: More Choices, Less Clarity,' 63 Bulletin for International Taxation 5(2009), pp. 191-198, at 193-195. Dunahoo suggests rather than the minority express their different view by reservation to an MC provision or observation to a Commentary provision. The subjective approach of tax authorities may have been unwittingly encouraged by the OECD's 2006 Report on Attribution of PE profits. The Authorized OECD Approach (AOA) allows for alternative Article 7 profit sharing approaches which go beyond the strict Article 9 transfer pricing rules applicable to affiliates.
9. For a criticism of the 'optional' nature of the provision included in the OECD Model, Pijl considers that the reasons for the inclusion of an alternative Services PE provision in the

The resulting erosion of the PE concept is evident in not just some aberrational rulings and cases but more ominously in an emerging practice of tax authorities to assess source country PE taxes based on subjective concepts non-existent in either the OECD, the Commentary or case law. For example one US practitioner wrote in 2008 that she had encountered the following tax authority positions involving her clients:[10]

- A company selling goods or providing services directly to local customers automatically has a PE in that country
- An affiliate or other company that performs services for another automatically constitutes a PE of that company, and perhaps of other companies as well
- A cost-plus marketing support arrangement generally creates a PE
- A dependent agent PE may arise even where the dependent agent is not granted, and does not habitually exercise, an authority to conclude contracts
- A commissionaire or other limited-risk entity automatically constitutes a PE of the principal, either because it is deemed to bind the principal in an economic or commercial sense, although not a legal sense, or because its facilities are deemed to be always 'at the disposal' of the principal
- A PE automatically arises whenever there is a VAT liability (or vice versa)
- Positive taxable income must always be reported in respect of a PE where one is found, even if otherwise legitimate expenses must be disallowed to avoid a loss
- Profits may be attributed to a PE in a manner that prevents other transactional parties from earning even a routine return
- Profits may be attributed to a PE on the basis of a 'force of attraction' theory.

None of these propositions has a basis in current law, the OECD MC or the Commentary. To require clients to defend against these unwarranted assessments, some of which have actually been accepted by lower courts or tax rulings, underscores the need for bright line guidance.

OECD Commentary, rather than updating the text of the OECD Model, should be 'found in the strong opposition of some countries to include it in their tax treaties.' Pijl further argues that for those countries having this alternative provision only in the Commentary is beneficial in treaty negotiations, as in situations coming within the scope of the Services PE provision, the taxing rights under the OECD Model Treaty are still with the residence state. *See* Pijl at 472.

10. Dunahoo, 'Source Country Taxation of Foreign Corporations: Evolving Permanent Establishment Concepts' (2008) vol. 86, no. 3 Taxes: The Tax Magazine 37-56, at 42.

The reach of a Services PE provision is illustrated by some Indian decisions which are somewhat unique in taxing technical services under either articles 5, 7 or 12[11] and Indian variants of the UN model Services PE provision which can result in taxation of services rendered either to third parties or to group affiliates within very short time periods, including under the US–Indian treaty services rendered on one day to an affiliate.

In *Ruling No. 8 of 1999*[12] a US parent company seconded 5 of its employees to its Indian affiliate to look after the general management, finance, purchasing, services, marketing and car assembly manufactory activities of the Indian company. The seconded employees remained on the parent's payroll, but the parent was reimbursed their cost by the subsidiary. The AAR ruled that the services were not for technical services under Article 12, but did constitute a Services PE under Treaty article 5(2)(l) without the necessity for meeting the fixed place of business requirements of Article 5(1). The basis for this reasoning was the 'precedence' which Article 5(2) (illustrative examples of a POB PE) took as a *lex specialis* provision over Article 5(1) which is a *lex generalis* provision. This premise disregards the OECD view that Article 5(2) provides only examples, which the tax authorities must prove meet the various requirements of Article 5(1).

The Commentary of both models provides that this non exhaustive list of illustrative items will in fact be permanent establishments only if all the requirements of Article 5(1) are met. Commentary on Article 5(2), para 12 provides:

> 'This paragraph contains a list, by no means exhaustive, of examples, each of which can be regarded, prima facie, as constituting a permanent establishment. As these examples are to be seen against the background of the general definition given in paragraph 1, it is assumed that the Contracting States interpret the terms listed, "a place of management", "a branch", "an office", etc. in such a way that such places of business constitute permanent establishments only if they meet the requirements of paragraph 1.'

---

11. *See e.g., Worley Parson Services Pty Ltd, Australia vs DIT,* AAR No 748 of 2009) (involving an analysis of technical services provided to determine (1) which were taxed as royalties under Article 12, (2) which were not royalty taxable but were exempt from tax as no POB or dependent Agency PE existed under Article 5 and (3) which were taxable as a Services PE. The case is discussed in Mehta at 270.
12. Discussed in Mehta at 269.

7.4 PREVALENCE OF SERVICE PE PROVISIONS

Recent developments in other jurisdictions point to the increasing importance of the Services PE provision in tax treaty practice. For example, as part of the 2010 update, the Russian Model Tax Convention, which is used by Russia in tax treaty negotiations with its potential future treaty partners, was amended to include a Services PE provision following the 2008 optional OECD rule.[13] Since then an OECD-type Services PE provision was included in a number of recent Russian treaties.[14]

The concept of Services PE was historically contained only in the 1980 UN Model, the optional OECD provisions only being added in the 2008 Commentary. However, a comprehensive current study[15] reveals that the Services PE provisions become increasingly popular in bilateral tax treaties, even where both contracting states are OECD members.

Services PE provision in recent tax treaties:

	Treaties between two UN countries	*Treaties between a UN and OECD country*	*Treaties between two OECD countries*	**Total**
Entirely or partly based on the UN Model Services PE provision	57.74% (399 of 691)	34.87% (242 of 694)	14.92% (30 of 201)	42.3% (671 of 1,586)
Entirely or partly based on optional OECD Model services provision	0.00% (0 of 691)	0.58% (4 of 694)	2.48% (5 of 201)	0.57% (9 of 1,586)

13. Decree of the Russian government 'On Conclusion of International Treaties on Avoidance of Double Taxation and Prevention of Evasion From Taxes on Income and Property' 84, of 24 Feb 2010.
14. *See*, for example, the treaties with Malta (signed on 24 April 2013), protocol to the treaty with Luxembourg (signed on 21 November 2011) and protocol to the treaty with Cyprus (signed on 7 October 2010).
15. *Cf.* Wijnen, de Goede and Alessi, *The Treatment of Services in Tax Treaties*, 66 Bulletin for International Taxation 1 (Jan 2012), pp. 27-38, at 29.

The study covered 1,586 tax treaties entered into in the period from 1 April 1997 to 1 January 2011; 43% of the tax treaties concluded in this period included a Service PE provision following, entirely or partly, either the UN Model or the optional OECD Services PE provision. Only nine treaties contained a provision inspired by the 2008 optional OECD Services PE provision. Interestingly, more than 40% of the tax treaties concluded between two UN countries did not contain a Services PE clause, which may indicate that these countries adhere to the OECD policies in this respect of taxation of business profits.

It is worth noting that the Services PE provision is not the only approach which states may employ to tax non-residents' income from the provision of services. In non-treaty situations, many states chose to exercise their taxing rights over the services income derived by non-residents by way of withholding taxes.[16] Treaties often include provision on technical services fees which are subject to the same tax treatment as royalties.

7.5 INTERPRETATION OF THE SERVICES PE PROVISION

A. The Meaning of 'Services'

Neither the UN Model Commentary nor the OECD Commentary provides a definition of what constitutes services that come within the scope of the Services PE provision. The absence of a definition may lead to practical difficulties and potential disagreements between contracting states regarding the material scope of the provision. For example, what may be considered as a provision of a service by one contracting states may be deemed a transaction involving sale of goods or intangible property by another contracting state. This may, in turn, increase the risk of unrelieved double taxation where some states would strive to interpret the term 'services' broadly, while others would take a narrower approach to the interpretation of this term.

In India, for example, it may be difficult to make a clear distinction between (1) technical service fees which are subject to withholding tax and (2) fees for other service which may give rise to a Services PE. In *Ruling No. 8 of 1999*[17] the AAR ruled that the fees for the secondment of employees by a US parent company to its India subsidiary did not qualify as fees for

16. Where domestic law provides for taxation of technical fees paid to non-residents, tax treaties would normally override domestic laws and provide for source state taxation rights only where a PE is constituted in the source state. In addition, based on the non-discrimination provision, the non-resident would in these circumstances be entitled to a deduction for the costs incurred in the provision of these services.
17. Discussed in Mehta at 269.

technical services, and should be assessed as fees for services which may lead to a Services PE in India. In this particular case, the employees of the US parent company looked after the general management, finance, purchasing, services, marketing and car assembly manufactory activities of the Indian subsidiary.

In *Worley Parsons Services*,[18] the AAR summarized the factors relevant for characterization of a fee as a technical services fee (subject to withholding tax), as opposed to its treatment as 'services fees' for Services PE analysis. Technical services fees are, essentially, fees for transmission of special skills, know-how, technical knowledge etc. Such technical knowledge and know-how should be imparted to, and absorbed by, the recipient of technical services.

'Services' do not include stewardship activities performed by a parent's employees deputed on a transient or short term basis to a source country subsidiary. In *Morgan Stanley & Co. vs DIT*,[19] the Indian Supreme Court considered whether stewardship activities performed by the employees of a US company in India could give rise to a Services PE in India:

> 'Stewardship activities involve briefing of the MSAS [Indian subsidiary] staff to ensure that the output meets the requirements of the MSCo [the US parent company]. These activities include monitoring of the outsourcing operations at MSAS. The object is to protect the interest of the MSCo. These stewards are not involved in day to day management or in any specific services to be undertaken by MSAS. The stewardship activity is basically to protect the interest of the customer [MSCo] ... A customer is entitled to protect its interest both in terms of confidentiality and in terms of quality control. In such a case it cannot be said that MSCo has been rendering the services to MSAS.'[20]

B. Services to be Rendered 'in' the Source State

The OECD Model Commentary explicitly provides that only services physically performed 'in' the source state can give rise to a Services PE there. The OECD Model Commentary states that, despite disagreements on the rationale for the inclusion of a Services PE provision in tax treaties, all

18. *Worley Parson Services Pty Ltd, Australia vs DIT*, 23 April 2009, AAR No. 748 of 2009; IBFD Tax Treaty Case Law Database.
19. *Morgan Stanley & Co. vs Director of Income Tax*, Mumbai, 9 July 2007, Civil Appeal No. 2914 of 2007; IBFD Tax Treaty Case Law Database.
20. 844*Morgan Stanley*, para. 14.

OECD Member States agree that this provision should not apply in respect of services provided outside the territory of the source state.[21] Accordingly, services performed 'offshore' should not come within the purview of this provision. The OECD Model Commentary does not suggest that the services must be taxable on the basis of where they are utilized.[22]

This might not be entirely clear in the case of Services PE provisions following the UN Model. While the text of the UN Model refers to activities which continue 'within' the source state,[23] the UN Model Commentary does not provide any additional guidance on the matter. Govind points out the interpretational difficulties that the wording of the UN Model provision raises: '... as the term "within" is used in this article, it is a question of interpretation as to whether this requires a physical presence or whether a mere continuation of activities is sufficient.'[24]

These interpretational difficulties may explain why countries often claim that no physical presence is required for a Services PE to exist. The discussion at the UN Committee of Experts on International Cooperation in Tax Matters gives a good summary of the position of the tax authorities in some emerging economies, in particular India, on the matter:

> '... Ms. Kapur [the representative of India] indicated that she agreed that the service has to be furnished to an entity in the source State, but she disagreed with the fact that the performance of the service had to take place in the source State. Ms. Kapur considered that the physical presence of personnel or employees is not required by the wording of the article, which talks about where the service is furnished and not where it is performed. The requirement that "activities of that nature continue within a Contracting State" did not, in her view, imply "performance" in that State — it would meet this test if the service was furnished to the Contracting State. There was some discussion about these two interpretations, but no conclusion was reached.'[25]

In its Guidelines on Assessment Rules on the Eligibility for Income Tax Treaty Benefits, issued on 7 January 2010, the Ministry of Finance of Tai-

21. 845OECD Model Commentary, Art. 5, para. 42.18.
22. 846OECD Model Commentary, Art. 5, para. 42.31.
23. 847Art. 5(3)(b) of the UN Model. The relevant provision refers to 'activities ... within the Contracting State.'
24. 848Govind, The International Tax Treatment of Cross-Border Services, 66 Bulletin International Taxation. 1 (2012), section 4.
25. *See* UN Committee of Experts on International Cooperation in Tax Matters, Report on eighth session (15-19 October 2012), Economic and Social Council Official Records, 2012, Supplement No. 25, p. 15.

wan stated that, where the tax authorities believed that the services rendered overseas were associated with the services provided in Taiwan, days spent outside Taiwan would be taken into account is assessing whether or not a non-resident has a Services PE in Taiwan.[26]

In *Linklaters LLP vs ITO*,[27] the Indian Income Tax Appellate Tribunal (ITAT) held that income from the provision of legal service outside India was also attributable to the Service PE in India and taxable in India. The taxpayer was a UK based law firm which rendered legal services to an Indian company. The services were provided both 'onshore' in India and 'off-shore' from the firm's London office.

The aggregate days of presence in India for the providing the services in question exceeded 90 days in a 12-month period which was the time test under the India–UK tax treaty in order for a Services PE to be constituted.[28] The Services PE provision of that treaty was part of the PE illustrative examples (i.e., included in Article 5(2). Accordingly, the taxpayer argued that there must be a fixed place of business at the disposal of the taxpayer in India, in order for a Services PE to be created there.

The Tribunal, however, held that, unlike the other PE examples, the Services PE provision was 'autonomous' and was not subject to the 'fixed place PE' definition. Thus, a Services PE was constituted in India simply because the 90-day presence test was met. Interestingly, ITAT held that the income from the provision of services outside India should be taxable in India because that income was 'indirectly attributable' to the Services PE in India.[29] The Tribunal's interpretation of the 'force of attraction' principle by reference to the treaty term 'indirectly attributable' is highly debatable.

The majority view, however, seems to be that the services must be provided in the source state in order to give rise to a Services PE,[30] a view which is in line with the traditional role of the PE concept as a threshold for taxation of non-residents' business profits. Kirsch summarizes the significant international tax policy problems that arise as modern technological

26. *See* Ponniah and Susala, Developments, Asia-Pacific Tax Bulletin, March/April 2010, p. 200.
27. *Linklaters LLP vs ITO*, Income Tax Appellate Tribunal, 16 July 2010, ITA Nos. 4896/Mum/03 and 5085/Mum/03; IBFD Tax Treaty Case Law Database.
28. The relevant provision of the India–UK tax treaty reads: '2. The term "permanent establishment" shall include especially: ... (k) the furnishing of services including managerial services, other than those taxable under Article 13 (Royalties and fees for technical services), within a Contracting State by an enterprise through employees or other personnel, but only if: (i) activities of that nature continue within that State for a period or periods aggregating more than 90 days within any twelve-month period; ....'
29. In particular, the Tribunal referred to Art. 7(1) of the UK-India tax treaty: '... If the enterprise carries on business as aforesaid, the profits of the enterprise may be taxed in the other State but only so much of them as is directly or indirectly attributable to that permanent establishment.'
30. Govind, section 4.

developments facilitate the cross-border delivery of personal services (e.g. tele-surgery which extends the reach of robotic-assisted surgery by eliminating the need for physical proximity between the surgeon and the patient):[31]

> 'Given the ongoing progress in technology and communications, which continuously expands the range of personal services that can be performed remotely, as well as the significant time lag that can occur in modifying norms reflected in the OECD Model Treaty and OECD Commentary, it is important to continuously reexamine standards, such as a service provider's physical location, that might lose their continued viability in an ever-changing world.'[32]

C. The Time Test

Both under subparagraph (b) of the optional OECD Services PE provision and Article 5(3)(b) of the UN Model, for a Services PE to be constituted in the source state the services must be performed/furnished for more than 183 days in aggregate.[33] Under both models, the time test applies in respect of the same project or connected projects.

The OECD Model Commentary clarifies that in the context of paragraph (b) the period or periods apply in relation to the enterprise, and not the individuals that enterprise engages to provide the services. Accordingly, it is not necessary that the services be provided by the same individual or individuals.[34] The time test operates on the basis of 'solar days,' rather than 'man days.' Accordingly, a day for purposes of this provision will count as one day, regardless of how many individuals worked on the project on that day (i.e. regardless of the number of 'man days'), a practice that had been confirmed by case law.[35]

The time test contained in subparagraph (b) of the optional OECD provision is fundamentally different from that employed by subparagraph (a) of the same provision. For the purpose of subparagraph (a) the mere presence of the individual over the specified period of time is sufficient to create a

31. Kirsch, The Role of Physical Presence in the Taxation of Cross-Border Personal Services, 51 Boston College Law Review 993 (2010), p. 1079.
32. *Id.*, p. 1080.
33. Article 5(3)(b) of the UN Model initially referred to a six-month period, but was amended in 2011 to refer to a 183-day period. The change simplifies the application of the rule with respect to the portions of a month, something which could lead to controversies.
34. OECD Model Commentary, Art. 5, para. 42.39.
35. *See* OECD Model Commentary, Art. 5, para. 42.39. This conclusion was also confirmed by several judgments, see – for example – *Clifford Chance, United Kingdom vs Deputy Commissioner of Income Tax*, ITA No. 1328/Mum/2001, 27 September 2001; IBFD Case Law Database.

PE, while in the context of subparagraph (b) only the days when services are actually performed should be counted. This makes the analysis of the time test in the context of subparagraph (b) quite difficult. For example, should the weekends, holidays spent in the source state, or stand-by periods be included in the day count for purposes of constituting a PE under subparagraph (b) of the optional OECD PE provision? The OECD Model Commentary clarifies that, in the context of subparagraph (b) of the optional OECD Services PE provision, the time test 'would normally correspond to the working days' of the individuals performing the services in the source state.[36] This implies that weekends and holidays spent in the source state should not be generally included in the computation period. However,

> 'an enterprise that agrees to keep personnel available in case a client needs the services of such personnel and charges the client standby charges for making such personnel available is performing services through the relevant individuals even though they are idle during the working days when they remain available.'[37]

In other words, stand-by periods for which remuneration is received from the client should be included in the computation.

In respect of the time test, the UN Model Commentary states that some developing countries oppose the inclusion of a time test in the Services PE provision, or prefer a lower taxation threshold for services:

> 'A few developing countries oppose the six-month (or 183 days) thresholds in subparagraphs (a) and (b) of paragraph 3 altogether. They have two main reasons: first, they maintain that construction, assembly and similar activities could, as a result of modern technology, be of very short duration and still result in a substantial profit for the enterprise; second, and more fundamentally, they simply believe that the period during which foreign personnel remain in the source country is irrelevant to their right to tax the income .... Other developing countries oppose a time limit because it could be used by

36. OECD Model Commentary, Art. 5, para. 42.42. Pijl argues that it is an 'open issue' whether or not weekend days and interruptions should be included in the computation. The Draft Commentary on Service PE, before being amended, read 'individuals who were present and performing such services in that other state *or are present in that other state for the purpose of performing such services*,' where the part in italics – subsequently omitted – referred to week-end days and interruptions. The omission of this part could leave an open issue on whether or not week-end days and interruptions need to be considered in the counting. *See* Pijl, *supra* note 2, at 474.
37. *Id.*

> foreign enterprises to set up artificial arrangements to avoid taxation in their territory. However, the purpose of bilateral treaties is to promote international trade, investment, and development, and the reason for the time limit (indeed for the permanent establishment threshold more generally) is to encourage businesses to undertake preparatory or ancillary operations in another State that will facilitate a more permanent and substantial commitment later on, without becoming immediately subject to tax in that State.'[38]

The UN Model does not offer further guidance on the computation. As a consequence of the 2011 update of the UN Model, earlier reference to a 'six-month' period in the Services PE provision was replaced by the '183-day' time test. The UN Model Commentary states that this change seeks to better align this provision with the wording of Art. 14[39] on independent personal services which has referred to a 183 days' presence.[40] The time test in the UN Model is also aligned with the corresponding requirements of the OECD Model.

More importantly, the 183-day rule helps to avoid discussions with the tax authorities as to whether or not portions of a month during which services are performed in the source state should be considered as constituting a whole month. This has been an issue in some developing countries, and will probably continue to be perceived as an issue as most of the tax treaties currently in force continue to refer to 'months' rather than 'days' in their Services PE provisions.

For example, under Chinese administrative guidance,[41] the time period shall count from the month in which the first employee or other personnel arrives in China for the provision of services to the month in which the last

---

38. UN Model Commentary, Art. 5, para. 10
39. *Cf.* UN Model Commentary, Art. 5, para 9. Unlike the OECD Model, the UN Model contains an article on taxation of income from the provision of independent personal services, such as independent scientific, literary, artistic, educational or teaching activities as well as the independent activities of physicians, lawyers, engineers, architects, dentists and accountants. That provision operates with the term 'fixed base,' rather than 'permanent establishment.' An equivalent provision was also contained in the OECD Model, but it was deleted from that model in 2000, as the OECD Member States agreed that there were no intended differences between the concepts 'permanent establishment' and 'fixed base,' a view that is not shared by the UN Model. Accordingly, situations previously covered by the provision on taxation of independent personal services of the OECD Model (Art. 14) are now dealt with under the business profits article (Art. 7).
40. The time test in the context of Art. 14 is essentially a 'presence test' (similar to subpara. a) of the optional OECD Model Services PE provision), i.e. it cannot offer guidance on whether or not e.g. weekend, holidays or other period when the employees are idle should be included in the computation.
41. Guo Shui Han [2007] No. 403 (Notice 403), April 2007.

individual leaves China after the completion of the services. A single day of provision of services in a given calendar month can mean that the whole month is affected, regardless of the aggregate number of days for which the services are actually provided in that month. Where in the following 30-day period there are no employees or other personnel of the foreign enterprise providing services in China, one month is deducted. The rule is often referred to as the 'one day equals one month' rule, and – despite being abolished – it may in practice be followed by local tax administrators.[42]

There is a huge variation in the way actual tax treaties address the time test in the Services PE provision. For example, Services PE provisions in Indian treaties often differ from the UN Model in this respect. In many cases, the time test is substantially shorter than the 183-day rules contained in the UN Model, and often a 90-day threshold is used.[43] In addition, many Indian tax treaties contain shorter time limits in respect of services provided to related parties, and a Services PE in India may in such cases be created if the period over which the services are provided exceeds only 30 days.[44] Moreover, some Indian tax treaties would give India taxing rights over the services income virtually immediately if such income is derived by a non-resident related party, i.e. these treaties do not contain a time limit for the creation of a Services PE where the services are rendered between associated enterprises.[45] The following table summarizes the time thresholds contained in selected recent tax treaties.

42. *See* Eichelberger, Liu & DeSouza, China (People's Rep.) – Permanent Establishments, Topical Analyses IBFD (accessed 7 June 2013), section 2.1.2. The authors state that Notice 403 is 'no longer reflected in published regulations,' but was not replaced by any other administrative document. Therefore, it often continues to be followed in practice.

43. *See, e.g.*, India's treaties with Australia, Norway and Singapore.

44. See, *e.g.*, India's treaties with Singapore, Switzerland and the United Kingdom.

45. *See, for example,* India's treaties with Canada, Australia and the US. Under these treaties, a single day of the provision of services between related parties may create a Services PE in India.

Services PE time thresholds in selected tax treaties in force:[46]

	UN-UN Countries	*UN-OECD Countries*	*OECD-OECD Countries*
1 month	5	–	–
2 months	10	2	–
3 months	56	22	–
4 months	8	7	1
5 months	1	–	–
6 months	263	167	26
8 months	1	1	–
9 months	32	18	2
12 months	19	25	1
15 months	1	–	–
18 months	3	–	–

D. Individuals Providing the Services – Secondment and Independent Contractor Issues

The optional OECD Services PE provision[47] specifies that – in order for a Services PE to be triggered – the services must be performed in the source state 'through one or more individuals who are present and performing such services in that other State.' It is further clarified that the term 'individuals' essentially refers to the 'employees and other personnel' of the service provider.[48]

There is, however, an exception to this. The OECD Model Commentary clarifies that, in some circumstances, the term 'individuals' may refer to individuals other than 'employees or other personnel' of the service provider. Para 42.23 of the OECD Commentary states:

46. *Cf.* Wijnen, de Goede and Alessi at 29 et seq. The research covered 1,586 tax treaties and amending protocols concluded worldwide in the period from 1 April 1997 to 1 January 2011. Time thresholds are reported in months, even where these are expressed in days in the relevant treaty. Additionally, some tax treaties differentiate between services provided to associated enterprises and unrelated third parties which is not reflected in the table.
47. Para. 42.23 of the OECD Commentary on Article 5, subparagraph b).
48. See paragraph 42.32 of the OECD Model Commentary.

> 'For the purpose of this paragraph, services performed by an individual on behalf of one enterprise shall not be considered to be performed by another enterprise through that individual unless that other enterprise supervises, directs or controls the manner in which these services are performed by the individual.'

This provision is relevant in cases where all or part of the services are subcontracted, as well as where employees are seconded to an affiliate. The OECD Model Commentary optional provision provides for strict conditions under which the employees and other personnel of a subcontractor may be considered to be individuals through which the non-resident provides services in the source state – i.e. the non-resident must supervise, direct or control the actual manner of the provision of services.

The OECD Model Commentary language on subcontracting in the context of the Services PE provision seems to be inconsistent with the approach taken to construction and project PEs. In particular, Para 19 of the OECD Model Commentary on Article 5 does not require a general contractor's control over the employees or other personnel of the subcontractor.[49] De Goede notes in this respect:

> 'I observe tension between Para. 19 of the Commentaries where for the construction site PEs, time spent by any subcontractors is added to the time spent by the main contractor, and Para. 42.23 on deemed services PEs where the activities of individuals for subcontractors are only attributed to the (main) service provider, if the latter supervises, directs or controls these individuals in performing the services.'[50]

The UN Model Services PE rule, in contrast, does not contain any specific language on subcontracting arrangements. It simply refers to services rendered 'through employees and other personnel.' This has led some authors to believe

49. OECD Model Commentary, Art. 5, Para 19 provides: '… If an enterprise (general contractor) which has undertaken the performance of a comprehensive project subcontracts parts of such a project to other enterprises (subcontractors), the period spent by a subcontractor working on the building site must be considered as being time spent by the general contractor on the building project. …'

50. de Goede, 'Permanent Establishment: Relative Permanence,' In: VAT in an EU and International Perspective: Essays in honour of Kogels, IBFD Amsterdam, pp. 319-329, p. 325. See also the heavily criticised paragraph 19 of the 2012 OECD Discussion Draft permitting attribution of wholly contracted out activities concerning fixed POB and CAS PEs provided the general contractor has control over access to the site and overall responsibility for performance – discussed at length above in Chapter 2.1E5.

that the term 'other personnel'[51] also includes the personnel of the subcontractor. For example, Pijl notes that '... the UN Model ("through employees and other personnel engaged by the enterprise for such purpose") possibly also brings activities under its scope that are outsourced ....'[52] A certain degree of control over the employees of the subcontractor would normally be required.

This conclusion was confirmed, for example, by the *Income Tax Appellate Tribunal (ITAT) of Delhi in Lucent Technologies International vs DCIT*.[53] The case concerned the interpretation of the Services PE provision contained in Art. 5(2)(l)(i) of the India–US tax treaty.[54] The taxpayer was a US company which supplied software and hardware for telephone systems. The taxpayer entered into contracts for the supply of the software and hardware directly with its Indian customers. These customers, however, concluded separate contracts with the taxpayer's Indian subsidiary for the installation of the relevant hardware. The taxpayer's employees were also occasionally sent to India in order to conduct marketing activities, network surveys etc.

In its analysis of PE issues, ITAT observed that in addition to its own employees, the taxpayer also exercised control over the employees of its Indian subsidiary hired for the installation, commissioning, testing and bringing up to operation of the hardware and the software supplied by the taxpayer to its Indian customers. ITAT held that the employees of the taxpayer's Indian subsidiary (the sub-contractor) would come within the scope of the term 'other personnel' contained in Art. 5(2)(l)(i) of the India–US tax treaty. Accordingly, the conditions for the constitution of a Services PE in India were met, as services had been provided in India for longer than 90 days. The ITAT stated:

> 'The other personnel specified here would be persons over whom the enterprise would be having a control. ... These employees of the affiliates over whom the assessee has a control would fall within the term other personnel and consequently, it would have to be held that a PE did exist as per the inclusive term as provided in art. 5(2) (l) of the DTAA between USA and India.'

---

51. OECD Model Commentary, Art. 5, para. 10, a provision which is also included in the UN Model Commentary, states that: '[t]his personnel includes employees and other persons receiving instructions from the enterprise (e.g. dependent agents).'
52. Pijl, *supra note 2*, at 474.
53. *Lucent Technologies International vs DCIT*, Income Tax Appellate Tribunal (ITAT), Delhi, 19 December 2008, ITA Nos. 2224/Del/2001, 5204/Del/2003 and 716/Del/2006; IBFD Tax Treaty Case Law Database.
54. Art. 5(2)(l) of the India–US tax treaty provides: 'The term "permanent establishment" includes especially: ... l) the furnishing of services, other than included services as defined in Article 12 (Royalties and fees for included services), within a Contracting State by an enterprise through employees or other personnel, but only if: (i) activities of that nature continue within that State for a period or periods aggregating more than 90 days within any twelve-month period; ...'

Similarly, in the *German NATO* case,[55] the Supreme Finance Court suggested, in *obiter dictum*, that cleaning personnel formally employed by a Dutch subcontractor but working under the supervision of a German company could be deemed economic employees of that German Company.

In contrast, in a 2010 ruling[56] the Delhi ITAT held in the case of two US resident companies – eFunds Corporation and eFunds IT Solutions Inc., that the relationship of the taxpayers with their Indian subsidiary to whom the taxpayers had sub-contracted provision of software development and call center services, resulted in a PE of the taxpayers in India under the India–US tax treaty. The taxpayers provided various services to financial institutions, retailers, electronic funds transfer networks, government agencies and others under the following four broad business segments: (1) ATM management services; (2) electronic payments; (3) decision support and risk management and (4) professional services.

An Indian subsidiary, eFunds India, provided the following services to the taxpayers (1) call center services; (2) financial shared services and data entry and (3) software development services. ITAT held that a PE was constituted on account of activities of the subsidiary which effectively resulted in the taxpayers carrying on their business in India. It is not clear from the ruling whether a certain 'degree of control' was required for a PE to be constituted in India.

In fact the US parent had no office, employees or dependent agent in India and the facts resembled those of the *Morgan Stanley* case[57] – back office IT support activities which were integrated with the NRE's core business but preparatory and auxiliary to it. ITAT distinguished its holding on the grounds that the Indian subsidiary had joint customer liability (this however would not seem to make it a dependent agent), was inadequately compensated for its services (this would seem to be a transfer pricing not a PE issue) and that its activities were a part of the NRE's core business (this might establish an Indian 'business connection' but would not seem conclusive of a PE characterization.

The OECD Model Commentary provides the OECD view – with which India disagrees[58] – and correctly concludes that no Services PE exists in the absence of a certain 'degree of control' over the employees of the subcontractor:

---

55. *Bundesfinanzhof*, I R 30/07, 4 June 2008; IBFD Tax Treaty Case Law Database.
56. Delhi Income Tax Appellate Tribunal, *eFunds Corporation vs ADIT*, 30 September 2010, Nos. 3668 to 3676 and 3714 to 3722 (Delhi) of 2009; IBFD Tax Treaty Case Law Database. The ruling does not deal specifically with the Services PE provision; it is, nevertheless, identifies the circumstances in which a subcontracting provision may result in a PE of the non-resident
57. *See* the KPMG summary alert at http://www.us.kpmg.com/microsite/tnf-asiapacific/2010/India_Dec9_No4.pdf.
58. *See* Positions of Non-Member Countries; OECD Model Commentary, Art. 5, para. 40.

> '... where a company that has agreed by contract to provide services to third parties provides these services through the employees of a separate enterprise (e.g. an enterprise providing outsourced services), the services performed through these employees will not be taken into account for purposes of the application of subpara. b) to the company that entered into the contract to provide services to third parties. This rule applies regardless of whether the separate enterprise is associated to, or independent from, the company that entered into the contract.'[59]

The UN Model term 'employees or other personnel' may also raise interpretational difficulties in the context of employee secondments and Services PE exposure. Are individuals who continue to be legally employed by a foreign enterprise, but are seconded to the source state to work under the direction of a resident of that state still treated as 'employees or other personnel' of the foreign company? Or should such employees be deemed to be economically employed by the receiving company, thereby creating no PE exposure for the foreign enterprise?

There are various Indian decisions and rulings which have analyzed the Services PE exposure in the case of temporary assignment of employees to an Indian company. In the 2007 case of *Morgan Stanley & Co. vs DIT*,[60] the Indian Supreme Court dealt with a case where a US based entity (MSCo) subcontracted certain back office operation to its Indian group company (MSAS). MSCo sent certain personnel to undertake stewardship activities such as monitoring the operations of MSAS and maintaining quality control and confidentiality in operations. In addition, certain other personnel were seconded to MSAS for periods of several months to several years based on the requirements and specification of MSAS. These seconded employees worked in India under the direction of the Indian group company, while they continued to be legally employed by MSCo. The employees' salaries were paid by MSCo, and subsequently recharged to MSAS at cost. Among other issues, the Supreme Court had to decide whether or not the employees of MSCo created a Services PE of that entity in India.[61] The Supreme Court distinguished the stewardship activities from the provision of services in India, and held that the presence of the employees for stewardship activities did not create a Services

59. *See* OECD Model Commentary, Art. 5, para. 42.43.
60. *Morgan Stanley & Co. vs Director of Income Tax*, Mumbai, 9 July 2007, Civil Appeal No. 2914 of 2007; IBFD Tax Treaty Case Law Database
61. Art. 5(2)(l) of the India–US tax treaty provides: 'The term "permanent establishment" includes especially: ... l) the furnishing of services, other than included services as defined in Article 12 (Royalties and fees for included services), within a Contracting State by an enterprise through employees or other personnel, but only if: (i) activities of that nature continue within that State for a period or periods aggregating more than 90 days within any twelve-month period; ....'

PE for MSCo in India. As regards the creation of MSCo's Services PE in the case of seconded employees (or 'deputationists' as they are referred to in the decision), the Court states:

> 'As regards the question of deputation, we are of the view that an employee of MSCo when deputed to MSAS does not become an employee of MSAS. A deputationist has a lien on his employment with MSCo. As long as the lien remains with the MSCo the said company retains control over the deputationist's terms and employment.'[62]

It was clear from the facts that the employees seconded to India worked under the direction of MSAS, a company that could be considered their 'economic' employer in India. The Supreme Court, however, seems to rely on the legal employment relationship in reaching its decision. In its reasoning, the Court considers the following factors:

- The services were provided for a period of two years, and the time requirement for the existence of a Services PE under the US–India tax treaty was met; and
- MSCo was responsible for the work of the seconded employees, who continued to be on the payroll of MSCo (i.e. the employees 'retained lien' on MSCo).[63]

In *Centrica India Offshore Private Ltd. vs CIT*,[64] the Authority for Advance Rulings (AAR) New Delhi also dealt with secondment of employees to India re related Service PE exposure. A UK and a Canadian company had outsourced certain back-office function to a group entity resident in India. Under separate 'secondment agreements,' the foreign enterprises had agreed to second selected managerial personnel to the Indian entity.

The seconded employees worked under the direction of the Indian entity, and were fully integrated in the Indian business operations. The AAR found that the foreign enterprises had a Services PE in India as the foreign enterprises had rendered services in India through the seconded employees; this was in substance similar to the findings of the Supreme Court in *Morgan Stanley*.

However, in *Tekmark Global Solutions LLC vs Deputy Director of Income Tax*,[65] the Income Tax Appellate Tribunal, Mumbai (ITAT) held that the

62. *Morgan Stanley & Co vs Director of Income Tax*.
63. *Id*.
64. Authority for Advance Rulings, New Delhi, *Centrica India Offshore Private Ltd. vs CIT*, AAR No. 856 of 2010, 14 March 2012; IBFD Tax Treaty Case Law Database
65. *Tekmark Global Solutions LLC vs Deputy Director of Income Tax*, Income Tax Appellate Tribunal Mumbai, 23 February 2010, (2010) 38 SOT 7 (Mum); IBFD Tax Treaty Case Law Database.

secondment of employees did not constitute a provision of services in India, and did not create a Services PE for the foreign enterprise. ITAT in this case seemed to focus on the economic reality of the secondment, rather than the legal employment relationship between the seconded employees and their formal US employer.

Under a secondment agreement, Tekmark Global Solutions LLC (Tekmark) agreed to second to Lucent Technologies Hindustan P. Ltd. (Lucent India) personnel meeting specific qualifications set out by Lucent India. The seconded personnel worked under the direction and supervision of Lucent India, and Lucent India had the right to send this personnel back to the US where its quality standards were not met. The employees continued to be legally employed by Tekmark, and the salary of these employees was recharged to Lucent India at cost.

The ITAT held that the seconded employees did not create a Services PE for their formal employer in the United States because they worked under the direction, supervision and control of Lucent India and the services that they provided to Lucent India were not associated with Tekmark. The ITAT correctly found that no Services PE should exist despite the fact that the time requirement for the creation of a Services PE was met. The seconded employees were the economic employees of Lucent India, and their presence in India was not relevant for the assessment of the PE exposure for the US entity.

In reaching this conclusion, ITAT considered that no profits had accrued to Tekmark from the secondment of its employees to Lucent India, as Tekmark was only reimbursed for the salary of the seconded employees without any profit element. Whilst this decision is difficult to reconcile with *Morgan Stanley* and *Centrica* (see above), it seems to be in line with the OECD Model Commentary recommendations regarding economic employment and related PE exposures, and provides a sensible outcome.

In *DIT vs Stock Engineer & Contractors BV*[66] a Dutch company entered into a turnkey contract for constructing a petroleum refinery in India and established an Indian project office and a site office. Stock Engineer & Contractors entered into a subcontract with its Malaysian subsidiary to second the Malaysian' company's technical staff to Stock to work on the project in India. ITAT held that the Malaysian company did not have a CAS PE by reason of providing supervisory services to Stock exceeding the 6-month treaty period since the seconded staff worked under the direction and control of Stock.

---

66. 27 SOT 452 (2009 Mumbai) discussed in Mehta at 262 and reproduced in Mehta Appendix One

In *Tekniskil (Sendirian) Berhad vs CIT*[67] a Malaysian company entered into a contract to provide 100 skilled workers to an Indian customer to work under the customer's direction and control. The Malaysian company was required to pay the salaries, insurance premiums and all other worker expenses. The customer was charged these costs plus a profit margin. The AAR held the Malaysian company had no PE because it merely provided skilled workers to a customer in India.[68]

A different result was reached in *Siemens AG and 20 employees*.[69] Siemens AG's Norwegian subsidiary secured a contract to supply plant and machinery to a Norwegian customer. Siemens AG assisted by providing 20 employees to its Norwegian subsidiary. The Norwegian Supreme Court ruled that Siemens AG had a PE in Norway due to its active involvement in the project which went beyond the mere hiring out of personnel.

The OECD October 2012 Discussion Draft[70] offers some additional guidance on the term 'employees' through which a foreign enterprise carries on its activities in the source state. The Draft suggests that where seconded employees are economically employed by a source country company while continuing to be legally employed by the foreign enterprise, their presence in the source state should not lead to the creation of a PE for the foreign enterprise.[71]

Since the OECD Model Commentary deals extensively with economic employment in the context of the commentary on Article 15 (taxing non-resident employees of a source country company or PE if present in the source country for more than 183 days),[72] the UN Model Commentary includes the relevant parts of the OECD Model Commentary on economic employment which indicates that these provisions are relevant also for the interpretation of tax treaties following the UN Model.[73]

---

67. 88 Taxman 439 (1996) (AAR – New Delhi) discussed in Mehta at 276 and reproduced in Mehta Appendix One.
68. *See also* the comments of Deloitte Netherlands to the OECD 2011 Discussion Draft on the treatment of secondments. Analogous to the mere leasing of real property or equipment, the mere hiring out of labor should not create a PE of the lender.
69. (29 April 1997, Norweigian Sup. Ct.), *Siemens AG (SAG) and 20 Employees vs Ministry of Finance and Customs*, Case No. R.T. 1997, s.653, discussed in Mehta at 263. The borrower simply uses the employee in its own business.
70. OECD Model Tax Convention: Revised Proposals Concerning the Interpretation and Application of Article 5 (Permanent Establishment), 19 October 2012; see http://www.oecd.org/ctp/treaties/PermanentEstablishment.pdf.
71. *Id.*, p. 15.
72. *See,* in particular, OECD Model Commentary, Art. 15, paras. 8.11-8.15.
73. 'Often a UN Commentary quotes parts of the corresponding Commentary on the OECD Model and, where this happens, it is now clear that it does so approvingly, unless it makes its disagreement clear. This is something that was not so obvious under previous versions of the UN Model.' *See* Yaffar and Lennard, 'An Introduction to the Updated UN Model,' Bulletin for International Taxation, November 2012, pp. 590-597, at 592.

The following factors are relevant in assessing whether or not the formal relationship of seconded employees with the foreign enterprise should be disregarded for PE analysis:

- who has the authority to instruct the individual regarding the manner in which the work has to be performed;
- who controls and has responsibility for the place at which the work is performed;
- the remuneration of the individual is directly charged by the formal employer to the enterprise to which the services are provided;
- who puts the tools and materials necessary for the work at the individual's disposal;
- who determines the number and qualifications of the individuals performing the work;
- who has the right to select the individual who will perform the work and to terminate the contractual arrangements entered into with that individual for that purpose;
- who has the right to impose disciplinary sanctions related to the work of that individual;
- who determines the holidays and work schedule of that individual.[74]

The OECD Model Commentary also considers the relevance of the financial arrangements between the parties in the context of agreements on employee secondment, which is one of the many factors to be considered in assessing whether or not the foreign enterprise provides services in the source state.[75] Where the individual's remuneration is directly charged to the source-state company (for example at cost or by using the cost-plus method), this may indicate that the foreign enterprise is not providing services in the source state. In contrast, the absence of a (direct) relationship between the remuneration of the individual and the service fee charges[76] may indicate that services are being provided by the foreign enterprise. In summary, the OECD Model Commentary suggests that the presence of a nominal profit element in the fee charged by the foreign enterprise (e.g., cost plus 5%) may not itself indicate that the enterprise is providing services in the source state.[77]

---

74. OECD Model Commentary, Art. 15, para. 8.14.
75. OECD Model Commentary, Art. 15, para. 8.15.
76. This would also be the case where the remuneration of the individual is only one of the many factors which are considered in computing the service fee (e.g. hourly rates for the service provided by a business consultant). *See* OECD Model Commentary, Art. 15, para. 8.15.
77. It is worth noting that in *Morgan Stanley* and *Centrica*, the relationship between the remuneration of the individuals and the fee charged by the foreign enterprise was disregarded. A Services PE in India existed, despite the fact that the individuals' remuneration was recharged to

In an April 2013 *Circular*,[78] the Chinese State Administration of Taxation clarified the circumstances under which a foreign enterprise which has seconded employees to work in China will be deemed to provide services there. It addressed the opposite scenario to the OECD Commentary, i.e. when will an employee formally employed by the foreign enterprise continue to be deemed employed by that enterprise for the purpose of the PE analysis. In Article 1 the circular lists the factors which must be taken into consideration. These include, inter alia:

- Which enterprise bears the responsibility or risk for the results produced by the individuals;
- The nature of the payments made to the foreign enterprise (e.g. management fees or service fees);
- The payments made by the resident enterprise to the foreign enterprise exceed the total sum of the salaries, wages, social security contributions and other fees advances or paid by the foreign enterprise to the seconded personnel;
- The foreign enterprise does not pay to the seconded personnel all the fees and expenses paid by the resident enterprise; and
- The number, job qualification and rate of remuneration of the dispatched personnel as well as the location in China where they work are determined by the foreign enterprise.

In particular, the circular suggests that any profit element in the fee received by the foreign enterprise may indicate that the foreign enterprise is providing a service in China which could potentially lead to a Services PE there. As noted above, in line with the OECD approach,[79] a cost-plus arrangement under the secondment agreement should not imply that the foreign enterprise is providing services. Accordingly, the drafting of the circular is broader compared to the OECD Model language and may potentially affect a wide range of arrangements.

Regardless of the proposed OECD Model Commentary changes aimed at enhancing taxpayer certainty, the interpretation of the term ‘employees or other personnel’ will likely remain a contentious issue. It is unlikely that the countries’ conflicting positions on the interpretation of this term will be streamlined in the near future, although the OECD (and UN Model Com-

---

the Indian resident companies at cost, i.e. without any profit element. In contrast, in *Tekmark*, this aspect was taken into consideration.

78. Announcement of the State Administration of Taxation on Issues Concerning Enterprise Income Tax on Labor Services Provided in China by Personnel Dispatched by Non-resident Enterprises, 19 April 2013, No. 19.

79. This approach is also endorsed in the UN Model Commentary.

mentary) approach to the interpretation of the term and the conditions for an employee of the foreign enterprise to qualify as the economic employee of the receiving enterprise appear to reasonable and well-balanced.

E. Same Project or Connected Projects

The time test for a Services PE to be created must be satisfied in respect of the same project or connected projects. This condition is contained both in the optional OECD Services PE rule and the UN Model provision. Accordingly, where the foreign enterprise is rendering several 'connected' projects in the source state, the time spent on performing such projects should be aggregated.

The OECD Model Commentary provides some useful guidance on the interpretation of the term 'connected projects.' The term must be interpreted from the perspective of the foreign enterprise that provides the services, rather than the service recipient's viewpoint.[80] While the facts and circumstances of each case are determinative in assessing whether or not the projects are connected, the following factors are listed in the OECD Model Commentary as relevant:

> 'Whether the projects are covered by a single master contract;
>
> Where the projects are covered by different contracts, whether these different contracts were concluded with the same person or with related persons and whether the conclusion of the additional contracts would reasonably have been expected when concluding the first contract;
>
> Whether the nature of the work involved under the different projects is the same;
>
> Whether the same individuals are performing the services under the different projects.'[81]

Although the UN Services PE provision has a much longer history, the UN Model Commentary does not provide any guidance on the interpretation of the term 'connected.' It only states that the purpose of the provision is to prevent adding together 'unrelated' projects.[82] The UN Model Commentary, however, does not explain how to determine whether projects are connected.

---

80. OECD Model Commentary, Art. 5, para. 42.40.
81. OECD Model Commentary, Art. 5, para. 42.41
82. UN Model Commentary, Art. 5 para. 12

The OECD Model Commentary guidance discussed above may be useful, but is far from resolving the uncertainties around the interpretation of the term 'connected projects.' For example, a consultant may provide business advisory services to the same client under the same framework advisory agreement, but the advice may relate to entirely different projects using separate engagement codes for each project. Should these projects be aggregated just because one master contract is used? Or should a greater weight be placed on the fact that the nature of the projects is different? And how different must these projects be to justify non-aggregation? Unfortunately, there is only limited case law and administrative guidance with respect to the interpretation of the term 'connected projects.'

In *Worley Parsons Services*,[83] AAR New Delhi outlined the factors that need to be taken into consideration in aggregating projects. Strictly speaking, the ruling does not deal with the interpretation of the term 'connected projects,' as that term is not contained in the text of the treaty in questions.[84] Nevertheless, the AAR's elaboration on the term 'services' sheds some light on the factors which are relevant for project to be deemed 'connected.' As the AAR puts it:

> 'The point of controversy ... is whether the word "services" should be confined to a single contract where there is more than one with the same party and the number of days specified in sub-clause (i) of clause (c) should be counted Contract-wise.'[85]

Worley Parsons Services, a company incorporated and resident in Australia, was engaged in rendering professional services to the energy and natural resources sectors (e.g. engineering, procurement and project management services). Between 2001 and 2005, Worley Parsons Services concluded six separate contracts with an unrelated Indian client. These contracts related to two projects led by the Indian client. The issue was whether or not the time

83. *Worley Parson Services Pty Ltd, Australia vs DIT*, 23 April 2009, AAR No. 748 of 2009; IBFD Tax Treaty Case Law Database
84. Art. 5(3)(c) of the India–Australia tax treaty reads: '3. An enterprise shall be deemed to have a permanent establishment in one of the Contracting States and to carry on business through that permanent establishment if: ...(c) it furnishes services, including managerial services and those mentioned in subparagraphs (3)(h) to (k) of Article 12 but not those services in respect of which payments or credits that are royalties as defined in Article 12 are made, within one of the Contracting States through employees or other personnel, but only if those services are furnished within that State: (i) for a period or periods aggregating more than 90 days within any 12-month period ....'
85. *Worley Parson Services Pty Ltd, Australia vs DIT*, 23 April 2009, AAR No. 748 of 2009, para. 7.3; IBFD Tax Treaty Case Law Database

spent in provision of services under these contracts should be aggregated in assessing taxpayer's Services PE exposure in India.

The AAR concluded that the payment received by the taxpayer under one of the contracts at issue constituted a royalty, and was subject to withholding tax in India; that contract was left out from the PE analysis. The AAR further opined that the remaining five contracts should be aggregated. The following factors were decisive in reaching this conclusion:

- the contracts for the provision of services in India were with one party;
- the contracts related to the redevelopment of an area to increase the recovery of oil and gas,
- the activities were to be carried out in and around Mumbai (i.e. a well-defined geographical area); and
- broadly, the nature of the work under the various contracts was similar.[86]

In summary, the AAR found that, from geographical and commercial viewpoint, the services under the contracts at issue could not be dissociated from each other. Accordingly, the time spent on provision of services under these contracts had to be aggregated.

The requirement of geographical coherence for project to be 'connected' is explicitly rejected by the OECD Model Commentary (only commercial coherence is considered). The AAR's reference to geographical coherence in the Services PE context is debatable, as Services PEs do not operate with the notion of 'fixed place.'[87] However, that reference effectively narrows down the scope of aggregation of 'connected' projects, and it can be welcomed by taxpayers.

The other factors considered by the AAR are similar to those stated in the OECD Model Commentary, although the AAR did not seem to consider whether or not the services were rendered by the same individuals. However, the discussions at a session of the UN Committee of Experts on International Cooperation in Tax Matters reveal that this factor can play an important role:

> '... if an enterprise provides services to a consumer for two different projects through two different departments using different personnel, then the two projects are not related and therefore the provision on "same or connected projects" cannot be applicable.'[88]

---

86. *Id.*
87. Perhaps, the AAR was inspired by the Commentary on construction and fixed POB PEs.
88. See UN Committee of Experts on International Cooperation in Tax Matters, Report on eighth session (15-19 October 2012), Economic and Social Council Official Records, 2012, Sup-

Finally, the ruling in *Worley Parsons Services* also confirms that any aggregation of the periods must be assessed from the perspective of the service provider, rather than the client. Interestingly, the AAR in *Worley Parsons Services* was not alone in its reference to 'geographical' coherence for the purpose of aggregating projects. The Technical Explanation to the Fifth Protocol to the US–Canada tax treaty states:

> '... projects, in order to be considered connected, must also constitute a geographic whole. An example of projects that lack geographic coherence would be a case in which a consultant is hired to execute separate auditing projects at different branches of a bank located in different cities pursuant to a single contract. ...'

As discussed, while the requirement of geographical coherence is definitely relevant in the context of fixed place PEs, it goes counter to the very nature of the Services PE provision.[89]

In China, Notice 75 issued by the State Administration of Taxation[90] states that several projects undertaken by the same enterprise shall be considered as 'the same project or connected projects' if they are commercially related or connected. The Notice then refers to the factors included in the OECD Model Commentary.[91] The guidance of Notice 75 may not be always followed in practice, also because most the Chinese treaties in force contain a UN Model-type Services PE provision.

---

plement No. 25, p. 16. It is stated in the report that two members of the UN Subcommittee on the Taxation of Services disagreed with this view. Some members of the Committee of Experts also had differing views on this matter, as described on pp. 16-17 of the Report. In particular, according to some commentators, the term 'connected projects' shall – in certain circumstances – be considered also from the client's perspective.

89. Department of the Treasury Technical Explanation of the Protocol done at Chelsea on September 21, 2007 amending the US–Canada tax treaty, Art. 3.
90. *Guo Shui Fa* [2010] No. 75 (Notice 75), effective from 26 July 2010.
91. *See* OECD Model Commentary, Art. 5, para. 42.41

Chapter 8

Tax in the Cloud – The Permanent Establishment Concept and the Digital Economy[1]

8.1 BACKGROUND

To a large extent, new technologies facilitated the globalization of the world's economy and introduced new industries, such as e-commerce and cloud computing. Technological changes redefined companies' business models and promoted a sharp increase in the outsourcing of services. Such increase created a need for instant worldwide data transfer, visualization and analysis.

The digital economy is currently the subject of intense scrutiny by the OECD, the world's major tax authorities and governments as well as major media outlets. The primary issue is whether there are appropriate rules to equitably and efficiently understand and then tax the 'digital economy.' For example, the location and alignment of IT infrastructure assets is an uncertain area with regard to the ultimate taxation of such arrangements.

This has, in turn, fuelled discussions as to whether the current international tax system is adequate to address the new business models; in particular, whether or not the century-old Permanent Establishment concept will continue to be suitable as a threshold for taxation of business profits generated through 'virtual' business activities. Back in 1996, the US Treasury Report described the issue as follows:

> 'Electronic commerce ... may be conducted without regard to national boundaries and may dissolve the link between and income-producing activity and a specific location. From a certain perspective, electronic commerce doesn't seem to occur in any physical location but instead

1. For information on the direct taxation (withholding tax, nexus and Permanent Establishment aspects) as well as indirect taxation (VAT, sales, use, and consumption tax aspects) of various Cloud Computing business models in over 100 countries see the EY Cloud Computing Tax Guide, available at www.ey.com/cloudtaxguide.com.

> takes place in the nebulous world of "cyberspace." Persons engaged in electronic commerce could be located anywhere in the world and their customers will be ignorant of, or indifferent to, their location.'[2]

The author of 'Permanent Establishment: Erosion of a Tax Treaty Principle,' Skaar, asserts that traditional rules requiring physical presence are not entirely adequate for taxation of profits from the 'mobile international business':

> 'The attempt to deal with e-commerce by means of the conventional notion [of permanent establishment] seems to confirm this author's conclusions in previous writings, i.e. that the [more] mobile international business becomes, the less adequate are rules which require a physical presence of some sort at a specific geographical spot for a certain period of time.'[3]

The main challenges for taxation of business profits in the era of digital economy can be summarized as follows:

1) The place where an e-commerce enterprise has physical presence differs from the locations where it may derive substantial revenue;
2) In instances where a Permanent Establishment is found to exist, attribution of profits to such a Permanent Establishment may still be debatable; and
3) The classification of payments made in the context of e-commerce and cloud computing (and related tax consequences) may be uncertain.

These tax issues have been intensified by the absence of clear definitions of e-commerce (or e-business) and cloud computing. E-commerce is commonly understood as the use of computers (i.e., servers) by companies and customers to provide more efficient delivery of goods and services. The term e-commerce is used in a broad sense and encompasses numerous activities, including the following: (i) storage, monitoring and analysis of information, (ii) purchase and supply of goods, services and software, (iii) electronic funds transfer and (iv)financial and operational data management.[4]

---

2. United States Department of Treasury, Office of Tax Policy, Selected Tax Policy Implications of Global Electronic Commerce (22 November 1996), p. 25. Available at: http://www.treasury.gov/resource-center/tax-policy/Documents/internet.pdf.
3. Skaar, '*Erosion of the Concept of Permanent Establishment: Electronic Commerce*,' in Intertax, Volume 28, Issue 5.
4. Doernberg, Hinnekens, Hellerstein and Li, *Electronic Commerce and Multijurisdictional Taxation*, (2001: Kluwer Law International), p. 37.

In an e-commerce environment, no physical presence is required for carrying on business activities, as many products can be digitalized and delivered electronically. From the perspective of tax policy, the most important feature of e-commerce is 'the total irrelevance of geographical considerations.'[5] As Doernberg *et al.* highlight, '[s]ervers can easily be located almost anywhere and their location is generally unknown and unimportant in a business transaction.'[6] Because of its multi-presence, e-commerce transactions that occur in 'cyberspace' may be difficult to trace by tax authorities.

Services can also be delivered electronically. The present environment already encompasses remote tele-surgery and the future is sure to make physical and geographical boundaries even less relevant.

Even greater taxation challenges arise in the realm of cloud computing. Similar to e-commerce, the cloud computing business model is by nature borderless. It is an approach to sharing infrastructure costs which links large pools of systems to provide IT services, and represents a fundamentally new approach to delivering IT resources. Users of cloud computing services are typically not aware of the underlying technologies used and of the physical location of the servers on which the resources are stored; these resources (e.g. data storage capacities, IT applications, databases, etc.) can be purchased and used over the Internet. As a result, users of cloud computing services do not need to make investments in building up their IT infrastructure, and avoid regular maintenance costs.[7] The use of cloud computing services is economical, as users normally pay only for the resources they actually use. Cloud computing services can be divided into the following main categories:

1) *Software as a service ('SaaS')* – The provider of cloud computing services maintains an Enterprise Resource Planning (ERP) system on its server for use by its customers. Users pay to access the system and run reports, manage information, etc.;
2) *Platform as a service ('PaaS')* – The provider of cloud computing services maintains a website on its server. Users access the website to build and/or host applications/ services/games on the website; and
3) *Infrastructure as a service ('IaaS')* – The provider of cloud computing services owns server farms[8] and networking hardware (i.e., IT infrastructure). Users pay for server access and run websites. Customers

5. *Id.*, p. 7.
6. *Id.*
7. For more details on cloud computing related tax issues, please refer to the following EY publication: '*Working in the cloud. Tax considerations of cloud computing*' (EY: 2012) on which this chapter is partly based.
8. Server farm is another term for data sourcing: a large number of computer servers placed in a particular location.

have no physical control or formal ownership interest in/risk of loss for servers or hardware.

Cloud Computing adds 'scalability' to e-commerce by reducing hardware, software, database management, security and IT implementation costs. It has a myriad of applications: from sales and use tax or payroll management to full scale financial accounting systems, which digitalize the business operations of a company with enterprise wide, customer and/or supplier access.

'Cyberspace' does not mean outer space. It simply means 'any space.' It does have a physical locality. The concept of cyberspace can be illustrated by the following example: a large server farm community in New Jersey rents server infrastructure for database collection, management and analysis for many large enterprise tenants. The server farm has physical space (i.e., New Jersey), but its use – through cabling and satellite transmission – extends to any space in the world. Therefore, 'Cloud Computing' is really the scalability of Internet commerce in one physical outsourced location. The income and expenses associated with the provision and core business use of such hardware may be subject to taxation based on source or residence in the country where physically located. However, significant amounts of income can be realized elsewhere through Cloud Computing, which may or may not be subject to taxation based on residence or source.

Contrary to popular belief, it would seem that case law has adequately dealt with e-commerce within the existing OECD Permanent Establishment paradigm of a fixed place of business (i.e., server), which is controlled and managed by a Non-Resident Enterprise as a part of its core business.

8.2 OVERVIEW OF PREVIOUS OECD WORK ON E-COMMERCE

Electronic commerce and policy issues were discussion topics of several international meetings in the late 1990s. The OECD continued this trend by hosting two conferences. The first conference occurred in 1997 in Turku, Finland, followed by a Ministerial Conference in 1998, entitled 'A Borderless World – Realising the Potential of Electronic Commerce,' held in Ottawa.[9] This second conference was attended by participants from both the OECD member and non-member states and resulted in the formulation of the so-called Ottawa

9. *See* OECD: An International Conference Organized by the OECD and the Government of Finland in Cooperation with the European Commission, the Government of Japan and the Business and Industry Advisory Committee to the OECD: 'Dismantling the Barriers to Global Electronic Commerce,' on 19-21 November 1997. Available at: http://www.oecd.org/sti/2751237.pdf.

Taxation Framework Conditions, which broadly defines the principles that should apply to e-commerce.[10] The 1998 Ottawa Conference Report stated the following:

> 'While the OECD believes that the principles which underlie the international norms that it has developed in the area of tax treaties and transfer pricing (through the Model Tax Convention and the Transfer Pricing Guidelines) are capable of being applied to electronic commerce, there should be a clarification of how the Model Tax Convention applies with respect to some aspects of electronic commerce.'

In 1999, the OECD Committee of Fiscal Affairs established a Technical Advisory Group (TAG). Its main task is to examine whether or not the existing rules for taxation of business profits are suitable in the context of e-commerce.[11] In December 2000, the OECD Committee on Fiscal Affairs published a document, entitled 'Clarifications on the Application of the Permanent Establishment Definition in E-Commerce.'[12] The content of such document was derived from a consensus reached among the OECD Member States[13] on the application of the Permanent Establishment concept to e-commerce activities and, as part of the 2003 update, introduced certain additions to the OECD Model Commentary to reflect this consensus.[14]

In principle, the 2000 Report confirmed that the same taxation principles should apply both to conventional and electronic commerce. It was further noted that these conclusions were not shared by Spain and Portugal which took the position that physical presence was not a requirement for a Permanent Establishment to exist in the context of e-commerce.[15] These two OECD members considered that a Non-Resident Enterprise carrying on business in the source state through a website could have a Permanent Establishment in that state.[16]

---

10. See OECD: A Report by the Committee on Fiscal Affairs, as presented to Ministers at the OECD Ministerial Conference, 'A Borderless World: Realising the Potential of Electronic Commerce' on 8 October 1998. Available at: http://www.oecd.org/tax/consumption/1923256.pdf.
11. Apart from the Permanent Establishment concept, which will be the main focus of this chapter, the TAG also focused on the following areas relevant for e-commerce: company residence rules, attribution of profits to Permanent Establishments and the application of transfer pricing rules to e-commerce transactions.
12. OECD Committee of Fiscal Affairs, 22 December 2000, 'Clarifications on the Application of the Permanent Establishment Definition in E-Commerce.'
13. With the exception of Spain and Portugal, which entered observations to the new text of the OECD Model Commentary on Art. 5 dealing with e-commerce.
14. *See* OECD Model Commentary, paras. 42.1-42.10.
15. In 2008, Spain withdrew its observation to paras. 42.1-42.10 of the OECD Model Commentary.
16. OECD Committee of Fiscal Affairs, 22 December 2000, 'Clarifications on the Application of the Permanent Establishment Definition in E-Commerce,' p. 3.

The 2000 Report emphasised that the TAG would continue exploring the Permanent Establishment definition in the context of e-commerce, and would come up with recommendations as to whether or not the Permanent Establishment concept – as a threshold for source taxation – should be revised to better reflect the realities of the digital economy, or whether that concept should be abandoned altogether.[17]

An extensive report, entitled 'Are the Current Treaty Rules for Taxing Business Profits Appropriate for E-Commerce?' was published in 2005.[18] After a brief description of the prevailing e-commerce and e-business models, this Report concentrated on identifying and evaluating the alternatives to the Permanent Establishment concept as a threshold for source taxation. These alternatives were evaluated on the basis of a set of pre-determined criteria (roughly following the so-called Ottawa Taxation Framework Conditions):[19]

1) *Neutrality* – Neutral and equitable taxation between forms of e-commerce and between conventional and electronic forms of commerce shall be ensured. This, in practice, means that it would not be feasible to have two different sets of rules for conventional and electronic commerce;
2) *Efficiency* – Minimum compliance cost for taxpayers and administrative costs for tax authorities;
3) *Certainty and simplicity* – The rules should be clear and simple, so that the tax consequences of transactions can be anticipated and accounted;
4) *Effectiveness and fairness* – Taxation shall produce the right amount of tax at the right time. The potential for tax evasion and avoidance should be minimized by way of proportionate measures; and
5) *Flexibility* – the taxation system shall be designed to keep pace with technological and commercial developments.[20]

---

17. *Id.*, p. 2.
18. OECD: 'Are the Current Treaty Rules for Taxing Business Profits Appropriate for E-Commerce. Final Report?' (OECD: 2005). Available at: http://www.oecd.org/tax/treaties/35869032.pdf. This final report is based on a Public Discussion Draft of 26 November 2003 and reflects the comments received on that Discussion Draft.
19. OECD: A Report by the Committee on Fiscal Affairs, as presented to Ministers at the OECD Ministerial Conference, 'A Borderless World: Realising the Potential of Electronic Commerce' on 8 October 1998, p. 5.
20. In addition to the Ottawa Taxation Framework Conditions, the 2005 Report included the following assessment criteria: (1) consistency with the conceptual base for sharing the tax base between countries; (2) compatibility with international trade rules; and (3) the need to have universally agreed rules.

The 2005 Report evaluated various alternatives for taxing business profits from e-commerce activities. Certain alternatives would require fundamental changes to the existing rules, as outlined below:

- Source withholding tax on the gross payment made to the supplier in an e-commerce transaction;
- Withholding tax levied on payments made to the supplier, but only where the payor may deduct the payments in computing its taxable profits (the so-called base eroding payments);
- Introducing the concept of 'virtual Permanent Establishments' as a nexus for source taxation; and
- Replacing separate entity accounting and the arm's length principle by formulary apportionment.[21]

The 2005 Report also considered less 'revolutionary' approaches to the source taxation of e-commerce activities. These alternatives intended to modify certain aspects of the existing source rules, without making 'fundamental' changes. Below is a brief description of these methods:[22]

- Changes to the Permanent Establishment definition to exclude activities that do not involve human intervention. Under this alternative, in the absence of any personnel or dependent agents, no Permanent Establishment should arise as a result of maintenance in the source state of any type of automated equipment (e.g. servers). The exception would continue to apply even where the activities of operation and/or maintenance of the (automated) equipment had been subcontracted. The proponents of this alternative argued that only little – if any – profits would be attributable to such Permanent Establishments. On the other hand, its opponents of this alternative claim that this exception would create an unjustified distinction between businesses/functions carried out through automated equipment and those carried out through human intervention;
- Modification of the Permanent Establishment definition to provide that a server cannot, in itself, constitute a Permanent Establishment. This alternative is a more limited version of the previously discussed one, in the sense that the Permanent Establishment definition should

21. For more details on these alternatives, *see* OECD: 'Are the Current Treaty Rules for Taxing Business Profits Appropriate for E-Commerce. Final Report?' (OECD: 2005), pp. 51-71.
22. For a detailed discussion of these 'non-fundamental' alternatives, see OECD: 'Are the Current Treaty Rules for Taxing Business Profits Appropriate for E-Commerce. Final Report?' (OECD: 2005), pp. 30-51.

not cover cases where a fixed place of business is used to carry out automated function through a server. The proponents of this alternative argued that changes need to be made to the 2003 additions to the OECD Model Commentary, to emphasize the importance of the human factor for the existence of a Permanent Establishment (this view was not unanimously share by the TAG members). The proponents also maintained that the decrease of the compliance costs for business and the administrative costs for tax are the most relevant benefits of this option;

- Modification of the Permanent Establishment definition/interpretation to exclude functions attributable to software when applying the preparatory and auxiliary exception. This alternative suggests including new language to Art. 5(4) of the OECD Model to the effect that functions attributable to software are not subject to the 'auxiliary and preparatory' requirement. The main argument made to defend this option was that software is generally used as a tool to support business activities and, as such, it would be consistent with the treatment of other (non-electronic) business tools if the functions performed by software would be ignored;
- Elimination of the existing exceptions in Art. 5(4) or making these exceptions subject to the overall condition that they be preparatory or auxiliary. The TAG concluded that the elimination of all the exceptions contained in Art. 5(4) would be impractical. A less radical option of subjecting the exceptions to the overall condition that they be activities of 'preparatory or auxiliary' nature was also considered.[23] The TAG noted that this option would be in line with the OECD Model Commentary;
- Elimination of the exceptions for storage, display or delivery in Art. 5(4). The logic behind this suggestion was that these activities are considered as significant in the context of certain businesses, and can have significant profits attributed to them. The TAG, in particular, considered the consequences of removing 'delivery,' in line with the UN Model. This option could substantially affect e-commerce business with warehouses in the source state;
- Modification of the existing rules to add a force-of-attraction rule dealing with e-commerce. Under this alternative, profits from e-commerce activities carried out through a website would be attributed to an existing Permanent Establishment in the source state, provided that the products sold through that Permanent Establishment and the website

23. OECD Model Commentary, Art. 5(4), para. 21 which states that 'the common feature of these activities is that they are, in general, preparatory or auxiliary activities.'

are similar. Effectively, the functions performed through the website will be deemed to be performed through the Permanent Establishment existing in the source state; and

- Adopting supplementary nexus rules for purposes of taxing profits arising from the provision of services. This option essentially suggests introducing a Services Permanent Establishment provision to the existing treaties (similar to that already described in the U.N. Model). Such provision would permit the taxation of income from services, if the enterprise that provides such services is present in the other country for that reason during a certain period of time.

Having evaluated all these alternatives, the 2005 Report concluded:

> 'As regards the various alternatives for fundamental changes ..., the TAG concluded that it would not be appropriate to embark on such changes at this time. Indeed, at this stage, e-commerce and other business models resulting from new communication technologies would not, by themselves, justify a dramatic departure from the current rules. Contrary to early predictions, there does not seem to be actual evidence that the communications efficiencies of the internet have caused any significant decrease to the tax revenues of capital importing countries.'

8.3 ADDITIONAL GUIDANCE ON E-COMMERCE

A. OECD Guidance on e-Commerce

The OECD Model Commentary was updated in 2000 to include new sections on e-commerce.[24] In essence, these provisions of the Commentary clarify how the traditional Permanent Establishment notions and concepts apply to e-commerce activities; the OECD Model Commentary does not introduce new concept but rather clarifies the existing rules. As the relevant provisions from the OECD Model Commentary are included in the UN Model Commentary,[25] the same principles apply in respect of treaties based on the UN Model. The OECD Model Commentary contains the following statements regarding e-commerce:

---

24. *See:* http://www.oecd.org/tax/treaties/ecommercereportsandtechnicalpapers.htm for an overview of the OECD reports and technical papers on taxation of e-commerce and more specifically http://www.oecd.org/ctp/treaties/1923380.pdf on the OECD Model Commentary, Art. 5, paras. 42.1-42.10.
25. UN Model Commentary, Art. 5, para. 36.

- Confirmation that the normal 'bricks and mortar' Permanent Establishment rules should be applied, by analogy, in the context of e-commerce activities;
- A Permanent Establishment may be constituted where a Non-Resident Enterprise has at its disposal and operates a server in the source state which qualifies as a fixed place of business under the provisions of Art. 5(1); no human intervention would be required for such a Permanent Establishment to exist;
- Confirmation that a website cannot, in itself, create taxable presence in the source state as it does not qualify as a fixed place of business under Art. 5(1);
- A typical web hosting arrangement with an Internet services provider (ISP) should not lead to a Permanent Establishment, as the ISP should not normally qualify as a dependent agent; and
- It is possible to apply the exceptions to the Permanent Establishment definition in the context of e-commerce transactions.

As discussed in previous chapters, the starting point in the OECD Model Commentary is that the business of an enterprise is normally carried on through its employees and other personnel. The Commentary continues, however, by stating the following in Para. 10 (Art. 5):

> '... a permanent establishment may nevertheless exist if the business of the enterprise is carried on mainly through automatic equipment, the activities of the personnel being restricted to setting up, operating, controlling and maintaining such equipment.'

Specifically, in the context of e-commerce, the Commentary clarifies in Paras. 42.5 and 42.6 (Art. 5) that:

> 'Another issue is whether the business of an enterprise may be said to be wholly or partly carried on at a location where the enterprise has equipment such as a server at its disposal. The question of whether the business of an enterprise is wholly or partly carried on through such equipment needs to be examined on a case-by-case basis, having regard to whether it can be said that, because of such equipment, the enterprise has facilities at its disposal where business functions of the enterprise are performed.
>
> [w]here an enterprise operates computer equipment at a particular location, a permanent establishment may exist even though no personnel of that enterprise is required at that location for the operation of the

> equipment. The presence of personnel is not necessary to consider that an enterprise wholly or partly carries on its business at a location when no personnel are in fact required to carry on business activities at that location. This conclusion applies to electronic commerce to the same extent that it applies with respect to other activities in which equipment operates automatically, e.g. automatic pumping equipment used in the exploitation of natural resources.'

The OECD acknowledges, in its general commentary concerning automated equipment, that business can mainly be carried on through such equipment, the role of 'the personnel being restricted to setting up, operating, controlling and maintaining such equipment.' Specifically in the context of e-commerce (operation of servers), the OECD states that a server may be 'operated' without the presence of personnel at the location of the servers. This makes it clear that business can be carried on through a server even where the operation of the server is fully automated/remotely controlled, and there is effectively no personnel present in the source state. The business of the enterprise can be carried on through a server which is 'at the disposal' of the enterprise.

Even where a fixed place of business would be found to exist, it would still be possible to benefit from the exceptions to the Permanent Establishment definition for activities of 'preparatory and auxiliary character.' In the e-commerce context, the OECD Model Commentary lists the following examples of activities which may qualify as exception under Art. 5(4):

- Providing a communications link – much like a telephone line – between suppliers and customers;
- Advertising of goods or services;
- Relaying information through a mirror server for security and efficiency purposes;
- Gathering market data for the enterprise; and
- Supplying information.[26]

The OECD Model Commentary clarifies that the exceptions cannot be claimed where the activities constitute the core functions of the enterprise, i.e. an essential and significant part of the enterprise as a whole. According to the OECD Model Art. 5(5), an agent must be a person (i.e., an individual or a company). Thus, whether or not the Non-Resident Enterprise has a dependent agent Permanent Establishment in the source state would depend on the specific facts and circumstances and the 'normal' analysis under Articles 5(5) and 5(6).

26. OECD Model Commentary, Art. 5, Para. 42.7.

B. Case Law Guidance on e-Commerce

In the above context, it is worth mentioning that in countries which apply the 'substance-over-form' approach to the agency Permanent Establishment analysis, increased attention must be paid to the set-up of information systems, to avoid an effective binding of customers to Non-Resident Enterprise principals. For example, the lower court in the Norwegian *Dell*[27] case held that there was a dependent agent Permanent Establishment, inter alia, by reference to the integrated accounting systems of the Non-Resident Enterprise principal and its Norwegian 'commissionaire.' In particular, even though the commissionaire had no authority to legally bind the principal, the IT systems were set up to provide the Non-Resident Enterprise principal with full insight to the finances of its commissionaire, providing an indication of the dependence of the latter on the former.

In the *German Pipeline* case[28] in 1996, the Court held that the Dutch owner of an underground oil pipeline in Germany used to transport third party customers' petroleum products had a fixed place of business Permanent Establishment in Germany from the mere presence of this (fully automated) pipeline. Whilst this case did not involve the digital economy, it became a paradigm for determining whether the sole presence of stationary equipment constitutes a Permanent Establishment in Germany.

Notwithstanding the Permanent Establishment treatment on the *German Pipeline* case, the German Revenue Office issued a decree describing an inconsistent treatment two years later. The decree provided that a server installed overseas by a German resident company did not constitute a Permanent Establishment. The decree and the case appear contradict each other. However, the reason they diverge lies on the nature of the business. In the German pipeline case, the transport of oil was the company's core business whereas in the decree, the tasks performed by the server were auxiliary and preparatory.[29]

The *Piedras Negras* case,[30] contains parallels from radio transmission towers and advertising revenue to today's model of server run websites and advertising/service models. In *Piedras Negras*, the court held that broadcasting services are sourced where the services are performed, as opposed to where the benefit/revenue from such services is attained. The court sustained that radio broadcasting income from a Mexican corporation was sourced where the electromagnetic waves are transmitted from (i.e., the Mexican corporation's

27. T.Miyatake, 'Dell Products (NUF) v Tax East,' *International Taw Law Reports*, Part 5, 2011.
28. *Bundesfinanzhof*, No. II R 12/92 (30 Oct. 1996), discussed in Mehta, at 8.
29. Eicker, *OECD PE Guidance consistent with German case law and decree*, International Tax Review (2001).
30. 127 F.2d 260 (5th Cir. 1942).

radio station in Piedras Negras, Mexico). It reasoned that all income-producing contracts were effected in Mexico and all services described under the contracts were performed in Mexico.

A dissenting opinion stated that income should be treated as derived from U.S. sources because, among other reasons, much of the benefit from such income was derived in the U.S.: (i) the programs were primarily designed for U.S. listeners, (ii) ninety per cent of its listener response came from the U.S. and (iii) ninety-five per cent of its income came from advertisers in the U.S.; however, the decision was not reversed.

The dissenting opinion gave rise to other items of consideration in the source of income analysis. Specifically, *Piedras Negras* provided support for the use of stationary equipment as a place of business argument; however, *Tipton & Kalmbach, Inc.*,[31] for instance, discussed that the portion of income from ancillary activities (emphasis added) performed in a different jurisdiction should be sourced at that jurisdiction.

The use of stationary equipment as a place of business is an evolving area. Most of Australia's tax treaties, for instance, provide the following Permanent Establishment definition on stationary equipment:

> '"Permanent establishment" includes, by virtue of paragraph (b) of its definition in subsection 6(1) of the ITAA 1936:... a place where the person has, is using or installing substantial equipment or substantial machinery; ...'[32]

Such definition gave rise to several rulings, which generally evaluate the equipment's size, quantity (if multiple pieces of equipment are involved), value and importance (whether the equipment plays a core role in profit making activity. The most important criteria are substantial size and value. In ATO *ID 2006/337*, the Australian Tax Office (ATO) ruled that the computer system of a Non-Resident Enterprise engaged in securities trading was *not* a substantial equipment Permanent Establishment. The equipment consisted on ten pieces of hardware weighing 164 kilograms and worth $200,000, including servers and routers and software used for market access and trading algorithms.[33]

---

31. Pursuant to *Tipton & Kalmbach, Inc.*'s case, the portion of income derived from services performed in the U.S. – in connection with engineering services performed in Pakistan – should be treated as U.S. source. 32 AFTR 2d 73-5334 (10th Cir. 1973).
32. ATO Interpretative Decision (ID) 2006/337. All Australian tax decisions and rulings can be viewed online at http://law.ato.gov.au/atolaw/searches.htm.
33. *See also Games Co*, Administrative Appeals Tribunal (Australia) Case U162 dated 5 August 1987 (87 ATC 942) (discussed in Mehta at 28) which involved the taxability of a loan out company of a US professional golf player who earned substantial endorsement fees by competing for 24 and 28 days in Australian golf events; the Tribunal held that 'substantial equipment' could not include a set of golf clubs or anything else associated with the taxpayers' activities

In *TR 2002/5*, the ATO construed the domestic definition of a Permanent Establishment to include the word 'fixed.' Thus, the use or installation of substantial equipment or machinery in Australia should meet the OECD test of geographic permanence if carried on 'habitually' at a fixed place as stated by McHugh J. in *Thiel vs FCT*.[34] *TR 2002/5* states that, while the test of time permanence does not literally require 'permanence,' it is a question of fact and, in the absence of a treaty time requirement, will be assumed met by a period of six months.[35]

The use of hardware equipment as an e-commerce place of business Permanent Establishment was stretched well beyond its OECD confines in three Indian Income Tax Appellate Tribunal (ITAT) cases, discussed below, to emphasize the importance of avoiding the use of any source company equipment as a 'place' of business.

In *Amadeus Global*,[36] a Spanish based company developed a *fully automated* airline computer reservation system (CRS) with mainframe servers in Germany and accessed in India through the Internet by unrelated travel agents. Amadeus contracted with an Indian company to solicit Indian travel agents who subscribed to the CRS system through the Indian company. Amadeus had no office, employees or dependent agents in India. The Indian travel agents could access the CRS either through their own computers or through IBM computers with dumb terminals supplied free as an incentive by Amadeus to a minority of agents. These agents could not move the computers, which were only of use to send or receive information from the CRS system and could not process it. Agents not supplied with such a computer could access the CRS system through their own computers configured with a 'node' supplied by SITA, an unrelated French telecom company to whom Amadeus paid a service fee.

ITAT considered the OECD Commentary, paragraph 4 (the 'at the disposal' requirement) and found that it stated the law in India. However, ITAT went on to find that the dumbed down IBM computers handed out free as an incentive to some travel agents, together with linked leased telephone lines, constituted a 'fixed place of business' Permanent Establishment of Amadeus in India, over which it retained complete 'control' – despite the fact that Amadeus was not in the 'business' of providing computers or leased telephone lines, Amadeus

---

in Australia; cf. Article 17, taxation of artists and athletes. *And see*, *Golf in Dubai LLC*, In re [2008] 174 Taxmann 480 (AAR – New Delhi), also discussed in Mehta at 32 and reproduced in Mehta, Appendix One, which held that 2 Indian golf courses rented by a UAE company for a weeks' tournaments did not constitute a fixed place of business for failure of the permanence test.

34. (1990) 171 CLR 338 at 359; 90 ATC 4717 at 4728; 21 ATR 531 at 544.

35. *See e.g.* United States–Australia 5(2)(f & g) (9 months for CAS project; 6 months for oil and gas exploration).

36. *Amadeus Global Travel Distribution SA vs DDIT* (2011, 11 Taxmann.com 153 (Delhi), discussed in Mehta at 12 and Nitikman at 237 and reproduced in Mehta, Appendix One).

had no control over the travel agent's offices in which such computers were located, any Indian travel agent could access the CRS system through his/her own computer and Amadeus received no income from any person in India, had no personnel and no activities there.

The facts in the earlier *Galileo*[37] case were similar, but even more devoid of any Permanent Establishment connection to India. There, a US based CRS provider had a large US Master Computer System with 18 main-frame computers connected to airlines' servers, which continually exchanged flight and seat availability data on a real time basis. Six categories of unrelated players used or were involved with the CRS system: passengers, travel agents, an unrelated Indian solicitation agent, SITA, Galileo and the airlines. Galileo also provided computers to its unrelated Indian solicitation agent, but only for the first two years as the computers then became obsolete. The computers had no significant value and were provided to only 265 out of 800 Indian travel agents.

As in *Amadeus,* ITAT held that Galileo had an Indian fixed place of business Permanent Establishment due to the computers because the CRS system existed 'in part' in the dumbed down computers over which Galileo maintained complete control, as well as the SITA telecom connection. Not surprisingly, the Court also held that such use was not 'preparatory or auxiliary' to Galileo's business.

Interestingly, in a third decision, *Western Union*[38] the US based money transfer company, dealt with a variety of independent agents in India (e.g., at post offices, commercial banks, tour companies, etc.) with regard to the transmission of funds from the US to India via a Money Transfer Control Number (MTCN). ITAT held, in accordance with the OECD Commentary, that the mere use of software on the premises of its agents, could not be a place of business.

C. Implications for Cloud Computing

The OECD Model Commentary does not yet contain any guidance on source tax implications for providers and users of cloud computing services. Therefore, it might be useful to apply, by analogy, the existing guidance on e-commerce. The implications for providers of cloud computing services should be assessed on the basis of the same rules (above) as described for companies engaged in e-commerce activities. Accordingly, any source state taxation consequences for the providers of cloud computing services – just as for companies engaged in e-commerce activities – would depend on whether or not there are servers at

37. *Galileo International Inc. vs DCIT*, DDIT (2008, 19 SOT 257 (Delhi), also discussed in Mehta at 18 and reproduced in Mehta, Appendix One).
38. *Western Union Financial Services Inc vs ADIT* (2007, 104 ITD 34 (Delhi), discussed in Mehta at 25 and reproduced in Mehta, Appendix One.

their disposal of Non-Resident Entities in the source state which are operated by them.

The tax consequence for the users of cloud computing services may not be straightforward. If, however, the current guidance on e-commerce is applicable, the users of cloud computing services should not normally have a Permanent Establishment in the states where their data are stored. Data are not tangible assets and the fact that the data are stored on the server of the provider of cloud computing services in the source state cannot, in itself, create a taxable presence for the user of cloud computing services.

In many cases, the users of cloud computing services would have no knowledge of where their data are stored.[39] It would seem impractical if a Permanent Establishment would be created where the users of cloud computing services are not aware, or cannot influence the location of the servers on which the data are stored or processes.

8.4 THE WAY FORWARD

A. Overview of Base Erosion and Profit Shifting (BEPS)

On July 19, 2013, the OECD issued its much-anticipated Action Plan on Base Erosion and Profit Shifting (the Plan). The Plan reiterates the themes of the initial report on BEPS, addressing Base Erosion and Profit Shifting (the Report). In the OECD's view, gaps in the interaction of domestic tax rules of various countries, the application of bilateral tax treaties to multijurisdictional arrangements and the rise of the digital economy, with the resulting relocation of core business functions, have led to weaknesses in the international tax system. The Plan acknowledges that, in many circumstances, existing domestic law and treaties yield the correct result, but states that, without coordinated action in the areas that give rise to policy concerns, countries that wish to protect their tax base may resort to unilateral action that could result in a resurgence of double taxation, as well as global tax uncertainty. Thus, the Plan concludes, fundamental, consensus-based changes are needed to address double non-taxation and cases of no or low taxation where taxable income is artificially separated from the activities that generate it. The Plan contains 15 Actions, each of which is linked to specific outputs that are to be completed by September 2014 or De-

39. This might not be the situation in the case of certain types of 'private' cloud services where the recipient of these services could be aware of the location of the servers. Also, in certain circumstances, the recipients of the IaaS services may influence (or be aware of) location of the servers on which the data would be stored.

cember 2015. The first action item is to 'Address the challenges of the digital economy.'

The Plan recognizes the tremendous benefits of globalization for domestic economies, but expresses concern that the increasing globalization of the economy and of multinational corporations (MNCs), coupled with the growing digital economy, has made it easier for MNCs to locate many productive activities in geographic locations that are distant from the physical location of their customers. The Plan asserts that these developments have created opportunities for BEPS, which occurs through the interaction of different tax rules that leads to double non-taxation or less than single taxation and through 'arrangements that achieve no or low taxation by shifting profits away from the jurisdictions where the activities creating those profits take place.'[40] The Plan states that this has resulted in reduced revenue for governments and higher costs of enforcement, a shifting of the tax burden to other taxpayers and competitive disadvantages for businesses that do not engage in BEPS. It also has caused some interest groups to question the fairness of tax systems.

The Plan states that no or low taxation alone is not *per se* a cause of concern; the concern arises in situations involving artificial separation of income from activities. The Plan also states that the relocation of core business functions resulting in a different distribution of taxing rights that may lead to low taxation is not *per se* evidence of defects in the existing system; rather, an examination of how value is added and profits are made is necessary. The Plan states that, although certain of the Actions will restore both source and residence taxation where cross border income would otherwise be subject to zero or very low tax, the actions are not directly aimed at changing the current standards on allocation of taxing rights on cross border income.

B. Addressing the Challenges of the Digital Economy

The Plan recognizes that there a number of challenges that need to be addressed with respect to the digital economy, 'which offers a borderless world of products, and services that too often do not fall within the tax regime of any specific country, leaving loopholes that allow profits to go untaxed.'[41] The Plan lists the need to address the challenges of the digital economy as its first action item, although it is unclear if this is intended to convey that this action item has a higher priority or importance than the other action items listed. However, each action item is undoubtedly not mutually exclusive; the challenges identified

40. OECD (2013), Action Plan on Base Erosion and Profit Shifting, OECD Publishing. http://dx.doi.org/10.1787/9789264202719-en.
41. OECD press release, 19 July 2013, 'Closing tax gaps – OECD launces Action Plan on Base Erosion and Profit Shifting.'

in the other 14 action items and any subsequent recommendations may affect enterprises that are part of the digital economy as well.

The OECD goes on to summarize the current environment of the digital economy as one that 'is characterized by an unparalleled reliance on intangible assets, (by) the massive use of data (notably personal data), (by) the widespread adoption of multi-sided business models capturing value from externalities generated by free products, and (by) the difficulty of determining the jurisdiction in which value creation occurs.'[42]

Fundamental questions are raised about the character and sourcing of income and how enterprises add value to make their profits. The Plan notes that 'new ways of doing business may result in a relocation of core business functions and, consequently, a different distribution of taxing rights which may lead to low taxation (although this) is not per se an indicator of defects in the existing system. It is important to examine closely how enterprises of the digital economy add value and make their profits in order to determine whether and to what extent it may be necessary to adapt the current rules in order to take into account the specific features of that industry and to prevent BEPS.'[43]

As action one in the Plan, the OECD task force that will help address the tax challenges of the digital economy have been asked to develop detailed options to address these issues, 'taking a holistic approach and considering both direct and indirect taxation.'[44] The issues to be examined require a better understanding of the different business models and include but are not limited to:

- The ability of a company to have significant digital presence in the economy of another country without being liable to taxation due to the lack of nexus under current international rules,
- The attribution of value created from the generation of the marketable location-relevant data through the use of digital products and services,
- The characterization of income derived from new business models,
- The application of related source rules, and
- How to ensure the effective collection of VAT/GST with respect to the cross-border supply of digital goods and services.[45]

This has led to a Discussion Draft that was issued by the OECD on 24 March 2014 which contains a discussion of the key features and business models

42. OECD (2013), Action Plan on Base Erosion and Profit Shifting, OECD Publishing. http://dx.doi.org/10.1787/9789264202719-en, p. 10.
43. *Id.*, p. 10.
44. *Id.*, p. 14.
45. *Id.*, p. 14.

in a digital economy, the opportunities for BEPS that can arise in a digital economy and some potential options to address the tax challenges raised by the digital economy. The Discussion Draft first examines the evolution over time of information and communication technology (ICT), including emerging and possible future developments. Building on this discussion, the Discussion Draft provides examples of new business models and identifies the key features of the digital economy. It notes that advances in ICT have given rise to a number of new business models which, although not always completely distinct from traditional business, can often be conducted over greater scale and distance (remotely) and includes a description of examples of such new business models. Notably, it is worth mentioning that the 24 March 2014 draft report also references the Ottawa Tax Framework principles as critical to the success of their efforts; this is an important concept in this rapidly expanding area of the economy.

The Discussion Draft describes the continued increases to the potential of ICT and digital technologies as impacting nexus and the ability to have significant presence without being liable to tax. For example, the reduced need for extensive physical presence in order to carry on business allows for movement of business functions to a new location that may be removed both from the market jurisdiction and the jurisdictions where related functions are taking place. The Discussion Draft states that these considerations raise questions as to whether the current rules are appropriate.

With respect to data, the Discussion Draft focuses on the questions of how to attribute value created from the generation of data through digital products and services and how to determine the share of profit attributable to these value drivers as raising cross border tax challenges. Additionally, the Discussion Draft notes that the issue of how to characterize a person or entity's supply of data in a transaction for tax purposes (e.g., as a free supply of a good, as a barter transaction, or some other way) also raises tax challenges.

Income characterization in the context of new business models similarly creates challenges when products and services are provided to customers in new ways. According to the Discussion Draft, income characterization difficulties raise questions with regard to the rationale behind existing income categories and consistent treatment among similar types of transactions.

C. Summary of the Potential Options to Address the Broader Tax Challenges Raised by the Digital Economy

The Discussion Draft provides an overview of four potential options proposed to the Task Force to address the challenges of taxing the digital economy. The Discussion Draft specifically notes that while the Task Force has had initial discussions on several options, the options are still in the process of being developed.

The first potential option presented to the Task Force and listed in the Discussion Draft would modify the exemptions to Permanent Establishment status under paragraph 4 of Article 5 of the OECD Model Tax Convention (relating to preparatory and auxiliary activities). The Discussion Draft states that several variations of this option are possible. One approach would eliminate paragraph 4 of Article 5 entirely. Another variation would eliminate just the enumerated exceptions of paragraphs (a) – (d) of Article 5(4) or make them subject to the overall condition that the character of the activity conducted be preparatory or auxiliary in nature, rather than a core activity, thus making such exceptions unavailable to businesses if such activities constitute one of their core activities or functions.

The second option, a variation on alternative Permanent Establishment thresholds, would establish an alternative nexus based on significant digital presence to address situations in which businesses are conducted 'wholly digitally.' In such case, an enterprise engaged in certain 'fully de-materialized digital activities' would have a Permanent Establishment if it maintained a 'significant digital presence' in another country's economy. Potential elements of a test for when a fully de-materialized digital activity would be conducted and for when a fully de-materialized business would have a significant digital presence are provided in the Discussion Draft.

The third option is another variation on alternative Permanent Establishment thresholds and includes three broad alternatives: a 'virtual fixed place of business Permanent Establishment' (creation of a Permanent Establishment when the enterprise maintains a website on a server of another enterprise located in a jurisdiction and carries on business through that website), a 'virtual agency Permanent Establishment' (extension of dependent agent Permanent Establishment concept to contracts habitually concluded with persons located in the jurisdiction through technological means, rather than through a person), and an 'on-site business presence Permanent Establishment' (creation of Permanent Establishment through economic presence within a jurisdiction where the foreign enterprise provides on-site services or other business interface at a customer's location).

The fourth option provided in the Discussion Draft would impose a final withholding tax on certain payments for digital goods or services. The Discussion Draft notes that these types of options are intended to address the possibility of maintaining substantial economic activity in a market without being taxable in that market under current Permanent Establishment rules due to lack of physical presence.

Chapter 9

PE Issues Arising from Centralized Tax Models

9.1 INTRODUCTION

For 20 years or more multinationals have been moving away from country-based operating models, i.e. ones in which markets are essentially addressed with a full value chain in each country, towards regionally or globally 'centralized' operating models, in which strategic and control functions for a region or for the world are centralized and supported by country level units responsible for day to day operations. Whether we call this supply chain management, operating model effectiveness (OME) or value chain transformation, it is one of the reasons why electronic and other consumer products are today far cheaper, better and more readily and widely available than 20 years ago. This trend has led to the development of new cross border business models in which, typically, a regional or global company in which certain business functions are centralized (from here on in 'the principal') transacts with, or through, local entities that perform the domestic operations: the operations and functions that have not been centralized. As discussed in some further detail below, there are a number of variants in the transactional relationship between the principal and local country entities.

Because of the cross border nature of centralized operating models, there is the potential for the principal to be viewed by tax authorities as having a PE in the local operating countries. Indeed, in some cases, the design of centralized operating models intentionally includes the structuring of local operations as branches of the principal or of a regional sales company. But, in most cases, the intention is to minimize the risk that the principal will be deemed to have a PE in other countries. This risk is likely to increase though particularly as tax authorities seek to apply new and broader interpretations of Article 5 concepts in response to centralized tax models.

This chapter therefore provides:

1) A brief generic overview of centralized operating models;
2) An identification of key issues and discussion around several key pieces of jurisprudence related to the topic; and

3) A discussion of some design implications for centralized models

OME is a process that is driven by business efficiency and that business efficiency must take into account all the tax aspects associated with cross border trade. Within the framework of this book we only address some of the aspects of OME that affect the permanent establishment issues. There are however many other critical tax components to OME such as transfer pricing, trade taxes such as customs and duties, indirect taxes in the various forms of VAT and GST etc. These will not be addressed.

A. Centralized Operating Models

In general, centralized tax models have several key hallmarks:

1) functions and risks are centralized in a certain location and/or legal entity (the principal) from which they are more efficiently managed
2) the principal is directly responsible for controlling key risks, management functions and other value adding activities such as central procurement and finance in relation to its (regional or global) territory
3) the principal owns, cost shares or licenses in valuable intellectual property, technologies, business operating model management (such as logistics)
4) the principal contracts with (or in some cases operates through) local entities responsible for:
   - Research and development,
   - Manufacturing,
   - Country sales and marketing activities
   - Routine support services.

Variants do exist with some of the more common variations including direct sales models (including e-commerce), supply chain companies responsible for sourcing and manufacturing but not for marketing and sales, and companies only responsible for procurement and related sourcing processes. A high level overview of the various local entities with which a central principal company might contract, is depicted in the below diagram, with further descriptions following.

Although various types of local entities can raise PE issues, the vast majority of attention is centered on the relationship between the principal entity and the sales and manufacturing entities. Therefore, although a short description of type of local entities is provided below, the remainder of this chapter will focus on the issues and design implications related to manufacturing and sales.

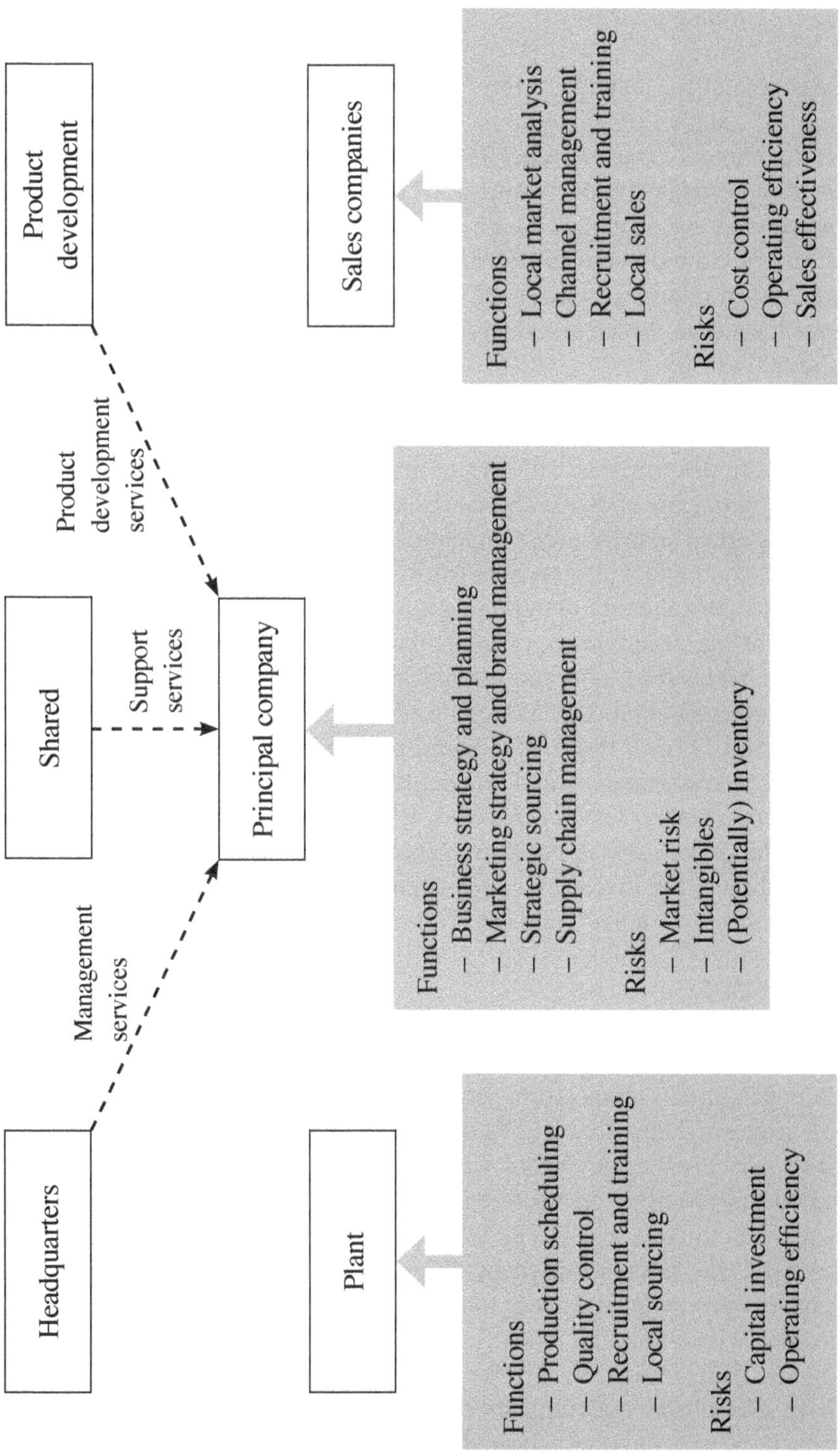
Headquarters
Shared
Product development
Management services
Support services
Product development services
Principal company
Plant
Sales companies
Functions
– Production scheduling
– Quality control
– Recruitment and training
– Local sourcing
Risks
– Capital investment
– Operating efficiency
Functions
– Business strategy and planning
– Marketing strategy and brand management
– Strategic sourcing
– Supply chain management
Risks
– Market risk
– Intangibles
– (Potentially) Inventory
Functions
– Local market analysis
– Channel management
– Recruitment and training
– Local sales
Risks
– Cost control
– Operating efficiency
– Sales effectiveness

1. Manufacturing

The spectrum for manufacturing entities includes: (i) a full-fledged manufacturer; (ii) contract manufacturers, (iii) consignment / toll manufacturers, and (iv) assemblers. The expected returns for companies characterized on this spectrum correlates with the functions performed, risks assumed, intangibles utilized, and the economic factors present in a specific industry. In general, the returns earned by an entity characterized as a pure contract manufacturer undertaking minimal risks should be subject to smaller variances and at a lower level than those earned by full-fledged manufacturers operating within a similar industry.

The transactional relationships associated with a centralized operating model can be characterized either as contract or consignment/toll manufacturing because the principal will own or license in the relevant IP and be responsible for managing non-operational risks.

A contract manufacturer typically undertakes the operational functions required to manufacture a product. However, a contract manufacturer typically does not undertake any entrepreneurial activities, which would result in risk bearing or the development of intangible assets. Contract manufacturers buy materials and components and sell finished goods to the principal.

A consignment/toll manufacturer is functionally equivalent to a contract manufacturer except that a consignment/toll manufacturer does not source or take title to raw materials and components; nor does it own work-in-process, or finished goods inventory. A consignment manufacturer therefore provides a manufacturing service to its principal rather than supplying goods. The principal owns the inventory which is physically located in the manufacturing location throughout the production process.

2. Sales

Similar to manufacturing entities, there is a spectrum of classifications for distribution entities. The spectrum generally includes: (i) a full-fledged distributor; (ii) a limited risk distributor (LRD); (iii) a commissionaire / undisclosed agent; and (iv) disclosed agent. Again, the expected returns for companies characterized on this spectrum correlate with the functions performed, risks assumed, intangibles utilized, and the economic factors present in a specific industry. In general, the returns earned by an entity characterized as an agent should be subject to smaller variances than those earned by a full-fledged distributor operating within a similar industry because an agent will undertake fewer functions and manage/bear fewer risks.

In centralized operating models, sales and marketing activities would normally be structured as a limited risk distributor or agent. However, in some cases the decision responsibility of local sales and marketing comes closer to a full-fledged distributor.

A commissionaire/undisclosed agent sells in its own name but for the account and risk of a principal. The commissionaire is a civil law concept and is not recognized as such in common law countries. The commissionaire is not required to disclose its principal. A commissionaire is responsible for typical sales functions such as: identifying potential customers; calling on active and potential customers; introducing new products; maintaining customer relations; and providing limited technical assistance. A commissionaire undertakes fewer operational functions than a marketer/ distributor and is typically not involved in any strategic marketing activities. A commissionaire negotiates with customers on the basis of general instructions received from its principal. The commissionaire concludes the (sales) contracts in its own name without disclosing its Principal, which in most civil law countries means that those contracts are (legally) not binding on the Principal. A commissionaire's remuneration should reflect the fact that the majority (although not the entirety) of the business risk lies with its principal.

A limited risk distributor is the legally the same as the full-fledged distributor except that certain risks and functions for instance inventory risks or marketing activities that are more efficiently operated on a group basis have been centralized with the principal. The circumstance that a limited risk distributor has less functions and risks than a full-fledged distributer should be reflected in its remuneration.

A disclosed agent generally operates as a sales representative that does not purchase products for resale, but receives a commission on the sale of products to customers contacted on behalf of the principal. An agent is responsible for typical functions such as: identifying potential customers; calling on active and potential customers; introducing new products; taking customer orders; maintaining customer relations; and providing limited technical assistance. The agent undertakes few operational functions and is typically not involved in any strategic or marketing activities. As compared to a disclosed agent, the operational concept of a sales representative acts in an even more stripped down functional capacity. A sales rep operates strictly in the context of representing the Principal in the local market and does not have the authority, legally nor de facto, to conclude contracts for its Principal. When a disclosed agent has, legally or exercises in fact its power to negotiated and conclude contracts in the name of another entity (e.g., the Principal), it creates a PE for that other entity.

3. Development

The relationship between the principal, responsible for controlling product and process development activities, and development centers which have the expertise and capacity to fulfil the development operations, is usually structured as a contract R&D service agreement. The contractual arrangement will specify the rights and obligations of the service provider and principal, usually providing for the principal (or another dedicated IP holding company) to prescribe the R&D activity it wants the service provider to render, to take on the costs and risks of the R&D and to be the legal registrant and economic beneficiary of any IP created under the development process.

4. *Shared Services*

The existence and nature of centralized shared services depends very much on the kind of business and on the organizational structure of the group, but in general may include routine or day to day processes in the areas of Marketing, HR, IT, Legal, Accounting and Finance.

5. *Service Companies*

In *addition* to the traditional shared service company, in today's economy many product companies provide services as part of the products sold – for example, a sale of equipment which includes installation and maintenance services, which are often performed either by the local entity, or by a virtual service team of the multinational.

6. *Procurement Companies*

Whereas principal companies house a range of centralized functions, procurement companies focus on a single set of related processes which add value and manage an important source of risk. These may include working with development colleagues to drive down sourcing costs and increase quality as well as identifying, qualifying and negotiating contracts with suppliers. The scope of activities range from raw materials and components to capital expenditure and indirect purchases, such as IT services.

B. Common Issues Associated with Centralized Models

There are a number of features of centralized models which may lead to challenges that the principal has a PE in another jurisdiction. These issues have been brought to light through highly publicized court cases and analyzed in great detail by various professional journals and publications. In particular, some of the more common issues arising in centralized models under Article 5 of the MTC include:

- Legal versus economic binding of the principal by the local entity;
- Whether the agent is of independent status;
- The 'full business cycle' concept;
- The performance of auxiliary activities by the local entity; and
- The performance of services

These five key issues will be discussed in further detail below.

1. Binding of the Principal by the Local Entity: Legal vs Economic Binding

A variation on the dependent agency issue as raised in Article 5(5) is whether or not a dependent agent is created through its activities which 'bind' the principal to 3rd parties, whether legally or economically. According to Article 5(5) of the OECD MTC, aside from a fixed place PE, a local entity can create a dependent agent PE of a foreign principal through habitually exercising the authority to conclude contracts on behalf of the foreign principal. This has been reinforced in the commentary, where it's stated that 'the phrase "authority to conclude contracts in the name of the enterprise" does not confine the application of the paragraph to an agent who enters into contracts literally in the name of the enterprise; the paragraph applies equally to an agent who concludes contracts which are binding on the enterprise even if those contracts are not actually in the name of the enterprise.'[1 2]

Normally one might assume that the authority to conclude contracts which are binding on the Principal must inherently have a legal context – in other words, that based on the legal contracts in place, the local entity has the (legal) authority to conclude contracts which are *legally* binding on the foreign principal. The question of, 'de facto' or economic binding of the principal was raised by the Norwegian tax authorities in the *Dell* case.[3] In the *Dell* case, Dell's products were resold in Europe through a network of related commissionaires, including through its related party in Norway. The critical issue in the *Dell* case was the interpretation of the phrase 'To enter into contracts on behalf of/' or 'in the name of' as stated in Article 5(5), and whether it was enough to create

1. OECD Model Tax Convention, Commentary to Article 5, paragraph 32.1, OECD 2010.
2. Consistent with this rationale, The US Model Treaty uses the term 'binding on the enterprise' rather than the OECD term 'in the name of the enterprise.' This difference is intended to be a clarification rather than a substantive difference. The OECD Commentaries indicate that this Article is intended to encompass persons who have 'sufficient authority to bind the enterprise's participation in the business activity in the State concerned.' The U.S. tax authorities interpret this provision broadly and would likely conclude that any contract executed on behalf of the principal was executed in the name of the principal. (US Model Treaty, Article 5, paragraph 5, United States Model Income Tax Convention of November 15, 2006).
3. *Dell Products*, HR-2011-02245-A.

a PE that the agreements entered into by a commissionaire in effect could bind a principal to 3rd party customers based on the totality of the circumstances – not just the legal implications of the inter-company agreement. Ultimately the Norwegian Supreme Court took a similar view to the French court in the *Zimmer* case (see below) in viewing the legal intention of the arrangement.

The US Tax Court in *Inverworld vs Commissioner* looked to the inter-company agreement in place between a foreign parent company and its US subsidiary. When reviewing the substance of the relationship between the foreign parent and the US subsidiary and reviewing specific language in the intercompany agreement, which allowed the US subsidiary to perform a number of binding acts on behalf of the foreign parent in connection with services provided by the foreign parent to its clients, the court concluded that there was in fact an agency relationship, whereby the US subsidiary had the authority to negotiate and conclude contracts in the name of the foreign parent.[4]

2. *Creation of Dependent Agents*

Being able to legally or economically bind a principal is not sufficient, in itself, to create an agency PE. Additionally, the agent must be either economically and / or legally dependent on the principal. This raises one of the more prominent PE issues occurring with centralized models: dependency. Under Article 5(5) and 5(6) of the MTC, if a related party acts on behalf of an enterprise and habitually exercises an authority to conclude contracts in the name of that enterprise, it creates a dependent agent PE in that jurisdiction unless the related party is of an independent status. Thus, the crux of the issue becomes 'what creates a dependent agent?'

A highly publicized court case that addressed this complex question of Article 5(5) and 5(6) was the *Zimmer* case (Societe Zimmer Ltd.).[5] In this landmark case, a UK principal engaged with its related party to act as a commissionaire for its products in the French market, whereas previously the same entity had acted in a buy-sell capacity. The French tax authorities concluded that the French commissionaire in fact acted as a dependent agent of the principal and it had the power to bind the principal in commercial transactions in the French market. The initial conclusion that a PE did in fact exist was based on the conclusion that the commissionaire was not an independent agent, but was acting under the instructions and control of the principal for all sales and marketing activities which can create dependency of the taxpayer according to the commentary on

4. *Inverworld vs Commissioner*, 1996 T.C. Memo 301 (June 27, 1996).
5. CE 31 mars 2010 no. 304715, 308525, 10e et 9e s.-s., *Sté Zimmer Limited*; and CAA Paris 2-2-2007 no. 05-2361.

Article 5.[6] Other factors taken into considerations were that under the agreement the principal assumed all the risks associated with the distribution activities and that the commissionaire's sole and exclusive activity consisted of distributing products of the one principal. Without the right to sell the principal's products, the commissionaire would have no other sustainable business. As pointed out in the commentary on Article 5, the number of principals an agent represents also can have a bearing on the independent status of that agent.[7]

The authorities asserted that the French company was able to bind its principal, in spite of the fact that the commissionaire was legally selling in its own name and not in the name of the principal when dealing with clients. The taxpayer won on appeal, where the French Supreme Court confirmed that the commissionaire was not binding the principal to 3rd party customers.

In addition to the highly publicized *Zimmer* case (Societe Zimmer Ltd.), a significant case coming from the US revolving around the dependent agent concept was *Taisei Fire & Marine Insurance Co*.[8] In this case, the IRS asserted that a US agent for four Japanese companies which operated as a reinsurance underwriter on their behalf constituted a dependent agent PE. In reviewing the facts, the court found that in order to be considered dependent, the agent needed to be both legally as well as economically dependent on the foreign principals. Regarding economic independence, the IRS argued that because the fee structure paid to the agent (a management fee to cover costs, plus a contingent commission based on the profitability of the reinsurance contracts that it underwrote) were paid by highly credit worthy entities, the agent bore no real entrepreneurial risk. The court rejected this argument on the grounds that the remuneration received during the years in question represented an economic return that was not representative of a 'subservient' company. Regarding the legal independence, the IRS argued that because the agent represented only 4 companies, it essentially had 'near exclusivity' in its business relationship, and therefore was legally dependent on the foreign principals. The court rejected this view of the IRS that the lack of exclusivity was a threshold for finding independence, but rather found that exclusivity should only be treated as a factor to be considered as part of the overall assessment whether the agent is independent.

3. Full Business Cycles

The question has been raised if Article 5(5) allows using a more holistic approach to determining whether or not a local entity creates a dependent agent

6. OECD Model Tax Convention, Commentary to Article 5, paragraph 38.3, OECD 2010.
7. *Id.*, paragraph 38.6.
8. *Taisei Fire & Marine Ins. Co., Ltd*, 104 TC 535 (1995); acq. AOD 1995-012.

of a foreign principal. Specifically the concept referred to as a 'full business cycle' considers the application of Article 5(5) more broadly than just the conclusion or negotiation of contracts. Under such full business cycle concept, Article 5(5) could also apply where the wider economic activities of the agent are subject to detailed instructions or control by a foreign principal; if the local entity is performing several tasks or operations as part of the inter-company relationship with the principal. Some factors for considering the application of the full business cycle in establishing a dependent agent include:

- Are the activities performed for the principal only?
- Is the local entity expected to follow the principal's guidelines exactly?
- Is the inter-company pricing implemented in such a way that the local entity assumes no real economic risk?
- Is the local entity performing multiple functions which, in their totality, result in the performance of both manufacturing of and promotion for the same products in the same market?[9]

The above factors were all taken into account in a 2012 Spanish court case involving the interpretation of Article 5 in the context of a centralized supply chain for the pharmaceutical company Roche Vitamins.[10] Under the fact pattern of Roche's business in Spain, the Spanish local entity was responsible for manufacturing and packaging products for sale to the foreign principal under a manufacturing agreement and for promoting those same products in the Spanish market, and leased a warehouse to the principal for the purpose of storing products prior to their distribution to customers in Spain. The Spanish Supreme Court noted that even though the Spanish local entity did not have the authority to conclude or negotiate contracts in the name of foreign principal, a dependent agency PE was nonetheless created. The court's reasoning could perhaps be understood by applying the 'full business cycle' concept to conclude that a dependent agent existed of the foreign principal in Spain, but this would likely be a misinterpretation. Rather the Court implies that the Spanish entity is in fact a nominee and attributes the manufacturing activities to the Principal as though the subsidiary did not exist (which also raises questions under Article 5(7)). The Court argues:

---

9. Particularly if these activities are neither geographically nor organizationally separated from one another and the totality of these (integrated) activities no longer constitute preparatory or auxiliary activities– see Commentary on Article 5, paragraph 27 and 27.1.
10. *Roche Vitamins Europe*, Spanish Supreme Court Judgment (Section 2) N 1626/2008 on January 12, 2012.

> 'Article 5.5 (the equivalent of Article 5.4 of the Spain–Switzerland Tax Treaty) authorizes contemplation of other activities different from that of an authority "to conclude agreements in the name of the enterprise", including those which the latter may have conducted through a fixed place of business, such as, precisely, the activity of manufacturing the merchandise that is then sold and distributed. ...
>
> This Chamber is mindful that production-to-order constitutes a normal practice in the market. Nor are we unaware that it is possible to establish a price for the manufacture as a function of the costs, plus a remunerative percentage for financing the production. And we can admit that the existence of companies with only one client is not outlandish. But the conjunction of the three factors supports the deduction that the case at issue here fulfils the defining characteristics of a dependent agent permanent establishment for purposes of the Spain–Switzerland Tax Treaty ...
>
> ... it cannot be argued that the said manufacturing activity was of an auxiliary, secondary or preparatory nature for its principal business.'

This reasoning of the Court seems an awkward interpretation of Article 5.5[11] that is at odds with OECD commentary and a denial of the CARCO example.[12] A contrary reasoning can be found by the High Court of Delhi.[13]

4. *Auxiliary Activities*

Article 5(4)(f)) provides that activities carried on at a fixed place of business of the foreign entity which are preparatory or auxiliary in nature, do not create a PE of the foreign entity. However, the correct application of this exception is not always easy to define.

---

11. OECD Commentary Article 5(5), para. 32, to which the Court refers, also states that an agent's mere dependency alone is insufficient and that every dependent agency PE must have authority to regularly bind its principal in its core business. *See* the discussion at Chapter 5.7 and fn 204 *supra*.
12. Fernández argues: 'The Court gives her a very "innovative" interpretation of the PE concept, under the consideration of the existence of what someone has called "industrial" PE (linked to the manufacturing activity on behalf of the foreign entity in the *Roche Vitamins* case), rather than the traditional concept of "commercial" PE. This "industrial" PE would appear when the combination of the different activities (not just commercial activities) performed by the Spanish entity in Spain create a sufficient link with the territory in order to create a PE.' (La Noción de Establecimiento Permanente en los Tribunales: Las Estructuras Operativas Mediante Filiales Comisionistas, Cronica Tributaria NUM. 145/2012 (39-57)).
13. http://www.ey.com/GL/en/Services/Tax/International-Tax/Alert--India-s-Delhi-High-Court-rules-that-outsourcing-of-services-by-US-company-to-Indian-affiliate-does-not-constitute-PE.

One example is the supervision by a local entity of contracts concluded by a principal entity and 3rd parties. In the *Philip Morris* case,[14] a German company that was a member of the Philip Morris Group received royalties from the Italian Tobacco Administration for the license to produce and supply cigarettes and tobacco products with the Philip Morris trademark. An Italian company also belonging to the Philip Morris group supervised the execution of the contract by the Italian Tobacco Administration and performed agency and promotional activities in relation to sales of Philip Morris products in 'duty-free' areas. The tax authorities claimed that the royalties derived by the German related party were subject to tax in Italy at the ordinary rates, due to the fact that they were attributable to a permanent establishment that the group maintained in Italy due to the fact that the tax authorities considered the supervision of the execution of the contract to be essential for the production of income for the German company, and not just auxiliary. Some of the points which were taken into account in adjudicating the *Philip Morris* case included:

- the supervision or control of the performance of a contract between a resident entity and a non-resident entity cannot be considered in principle to be an auxiliary activity within the meaning of Art. 5(4) of the OECD MTC;
- the participation of representatives or employees of a resident company in a phase of the conclusion of a contract between a foreign company and another resident entity may fall within the concept of authority to conclude contracts in the name of the foreign company;[15] and
- the entrusting by a non-resident company to a resident company of the management of some of its business operations makes the latter a permanent establishment of the former.

The *Philip Morris* case has been criticized by commentators. The principal function of the Italian subsidiary was the manufacture of cigarette filter tips for the PM group. After the *Philip Morris* decision and in response to the objection of the Tax Executives Institute, the OECD commentary was amended to provide that the mere participation of a subsidiary in contract negotiations would

---

14. Italian Supreme Court Decision No. 7682 of 25 May 2002 discussed infra at Chapter 5.15.
15. In the 2010 Commentary on Article 5 in paragraph 33, the Commentary states that just because a person has attended or even participated in negotiations with a client will not be sufficient, by itself, to conclude that the person has exercised an authority to conclude contracts in the name of the Principal. However, Italy has made an observation in paragraph 45.10 of the Commentary that its jurisprudence (e.g. the *Philip Morris* case) should not be ignored in interpreting paragraph 33.

not constitute the subsidiary a dependent agent,[16] an intended overruling of the rationale of the *Philip Morris* decision.

The U.S. Model and many U.S. tax treaties contain a similar provision for 'preparatory and auxiliary activities.' Generally, U.S. interpretations acknowledge a distinction between preparatory and auxiliary activities and core activities of an enterprise. In Rev. Rul., 72-418, a representative office of a German bank obtained credit reports on U.S. banks and information on banking and financial matters generally, assisted the bank's customers with information and letters of introduction, established and maintained contacts with U.S. banks and customers and provided information on German financial conditions, advertised for the bank in publications and by personal contacts, and on a few occasions communicated with the bank's U.S. obligors. These activities were deemed to be preparatory and auxiliary in nature, and the Internal Revenue Service concluded that the German bank did not have a PE in the United States.[17]

5. *Services*

As mentioned in the introduction, the performance of services in the context of a centralized model usually revolves around a few distinct concepts; either the services are provided directly by the foreign principal or the local entity sells products bundled with services or it provides support services which are part of the core activities of the business on behalf of its principal.

The OECD presents the view that profits from services performed in a foreign country should not be taxable by the foreign country if they are not attributable to a PE in that country (42.11 of commentary to Article 5). However there is a conflicting view that the country where services are performed should have the right to tax profits from the services, even when they are not attributable to a PE. The OECD therefore provided for an optional services PE provision in Para. 42.23 of the OECD Commentary to Article 5.[18]

In general, expatriate employees providing services in the US may create a PE to the extent the employee has the ability to bind the foreign enterprise in contract. Although most US treaties do not contain service PE provisions (and the concept is not defined in US domestic law), certain treaties, such as the US–Canada treaty do include a services PE provision, similar to the above mentioned OECD provision (Para. 42.23 of the OECD Commentary to Article

16. OECD Commentary, Paragraph 5, page 33; however if the NRO uses the office of a local affiliate, sales negotiation agents at that office may turn it into a POB sales outlet PE. Commentary, Paragraph 4, para 24.
17. Rev. Rul. 72-418, 1972-2 CB 661.
18. OECD Model Tax Convention, Commentary to Article 5, paragraph 42.23, OECD 2010.

5). The US–Canada treaty states that a PE exists if: 'Those services are performed in that other State by an individual who is present in that other State for a period or periods aggregating 183 days or more in any twelve-month period, and, during that period or periods, more than 50 percent of the gross active business revenues of the enterprise consists of income derived from the services performed in that other State by that individual.'[19]

The question arises whether services performed by a local entity on behalf of the foreign principal can give rise to a PE. Recent jurisprudence in India has shown that no PE risk arises where an Indian subsidiary provides such services[20] despite earlier counter indications.[21]

C. Design Implications of Article 5

This section will discuss some of the main design implications for centralized business models arising from the issues just discussed, covering first some of the more generic design implications, and then covering in more detail those arising in the context of manufacturing and sales activities within the value chain of a centralized model.

1. Generic Design Implications

In terms of generic design implications, some of the key considerations include:

- Management and control versus (economic) dependency
- Employee relationships to principal companies
- The 'full business cycle'
- Ownership of Inventory

Management and control versus (economic) dependency

As demonstrated by the case law above, one of the more complex issues encountered in designing a centralized operating model is the balance between risk management and control versus the creation of dependency. Fully efficient operating models may for business purposes require a degree of centralization of risk and functions that could create relationship of dependency at the local country level of the local entities. Highlighted throughout the jurisprudence is

19. 2007 Protocol with respect to Income Tax Treaty, September 26, 1980, U.S.–Canada, Tax treaties (CCH), Article 3, Para 9(a). The provision was added to overrule the Canadian *Dudney* case, discussed in Chapter 2, which held that a services PE could not exist in the absence of a fixed place of business, CAS or dependent agent PE.
20. http://www.ey.com/GL/en/Services/Tax/International-Tax/Alert--India-s-Delhi-High-Court-rules-that-outsourcing-of-services-by-US-company-to-Indian-affiliate-does-not-constitute-PE.
21. *See Rolls Royce Plc vs DDIT*, (2008) 113 TTJ (Del.) 446.

the risk that a PE will be deemed through the application of Article 5(5) if a local entity is perceived to be dependent, particularly economically, on a central principal company (although dependency alone cannot create an agency PE).

However, the challenge of balancing PEs and other tax-related concepts does not stop at dependency issues. Controlled Foreign Corporation ('CFC') rules, also present an inherent conflict with the evolving PE concept in case law. Earnings of foreign corporations generally are not taxed in the country of the parent until the foreign corporation repatriates its earnings through the distribution of dividends or not at all in full participation exemption countries. Various exceptions to this rule exist today often referred to as 'CFC regimes.' The US Subpart F is one such example.

When a CFC earns 'tainted' income the parent's jurisdiction generally taxes the corporation's parental shareholders currently on their pro rata share. This tainted income generally consist of passive income or related party sales or services. Income arising from core business transactions is typically not subject to anti-deferral rules. Examples of such business income would be:

- The sale of goods in which the entity has 'manufactured' the goods
- Active trading income
- Active services income

In order to stay within these categories and depending on the jurisdiction, the taxpayer has to meet rules like for instance the 50% third party trading test in Japan or the substantial contribution test[22] in the Unites States. There may be a tension between PE jurisprudence (e.g. Roche) which implies that the principal company must afford the local entity a certain level of entrepreneurial control in order not to be deemed a dependent agent PE, and the CFC requirements for a principal company.

Employee relationships to principal companies and their location of employment

Some of the larger challenges a multinational faces when it decides to implement a centralized model are:

- evaluating which key processes and functions need to be centralized;
- which roles currently are responsible for managing those key processes and performing those key functions; and
- where are those roles currently located and do they need to move?

22. Treas. Reg. §1.954-3(a)(4)(iv)

The results of balancing a range of commercial considerations, especially in a change management phase, including day to day operational requirements, and the location preferences of employees impacted by the centralization can include:

- a principal company employee is working temporarily in another office / location;
- a principal company employee works from a home office in another jurisdiction; or
- an employee of a local subsidiary of the multinational group is performing roles and responsibilities that are part of the core functionality of the principal company and are controlled by it.[23] This creates virtual principal structures, whereby principal functions are not co-located, at risk of creating a PE.

Only the second situation has been specifically addressed in the proposed revised commentary to Article 5.[24] The other two scenarios are not considered in the commentary despite their practical importance. Strict guidelines for how employees of the principal and employees of local entity's resident in other jurisdictions and performing principal functions should act under a centralized model are useful, but the risk of a PE challenge remains.[25]

---

23. *See*, for example, paragraph 10 of the Commentary on Article 5, whereby the OECD acknowledges that 'the business of an enterprise is carried on mainly by the entrepreneur or persons who are in a paid-employment relationship with the enterprise (personnel). This personnel includes employees and other persons receiving instructions from the enterprise (e.g. dependent agents)' In other words, if a local entity's employees have reporting lines directly into the Principal, this can be a situation whereby the local entity employees could be considered personnel of the Principal.
24. OECD Model Tax Convention: Revised Proposals Concerning the Interpretation and Application of Article 5 (Permanent Establishment). 19 October 2012 to 31 January 2013: 'Even though part of the business of an enterprise may be carried on at a location such as an individual's home office, that should not lead to the automatic conclusion that that location is at the disposal of that enterprise simply because that location is used by an individual (e.g. an employee) who works for the enterprise. Whether or not a home office constitutes a location at the disposal of the enterprise will depend on the facts and circumstances of each case. In many cases, the carrying on of business activities at the home of an individual (e.g. an employee) will be so intermittent or incidental that the home will not be considered to be a location at the disposal of the enterprise … Where, however, a home office is used on a regular and continuous basis for carrying on business activities for an enterprise and it is clear from the facts and circumstances that the enterprise has required the individual to use that location to carry on the enterprise's business (e.g. by not providing an office to an employee in circumstances where the nature of the employment clearly requires an office), the home office may be considered to be at the disposal of the enterprise.' See the discussion of 'home office' cases in Chapter 2.
25. *See* Chapter 7 on services and secondments.

Reallocation of business functions

Creating truly efficient operating models in some case requires a reallocation of functions and risks over different group entities sometimes even within the same jurisdiction. Such a reallocation of functions and risks must be well executed and properly documented for its non-tax business reasons. The OECD commentary on Article 5 provides anti-abuse language in case reallocation of functions was effected in order to avoid permanent establishment exposures, the Commentary states:

> 'An enterprise cannot fragment a cohesive operating business into several small operations in order to argue that each is merely engaged in a preparatory or auxiliary activity.'[26]

Reference can also be made to splitting up functions on a horizontal or vertical basis to avoid meeting the timeline requirement for a CAS PE.[27]

Ownership of inventory

There are several features of centralized business models, e.g. ownership of raw materials and work in progress of manufacturing inventory under a tolling agreement or finished inventory held by agents or in consignment, which require the principal to hold goods in a country. This creates an indirect tax presence in the countries in where the goods are held. There are countries (for instance South Africa[28]) in which an indirect tax presence has been argued by tax authorities to be sufficient to create a direct tax PE. This is inconsistent with the technical application of Article 5, as Article 5(4) generally provides that the maintenance of a stock of goods solely for the purpose of storage, delivery, display or processing does not create a PE.[29]

In particular in a number of Asian jurisdictions, direct tax nexus can be created through the ownership of inventory or, where local distributors hold the goods in consignment until an actual sale is made, as a result of a re-characterization of the local distributor as an agent under the argument that the local distributor de facto runs no risk with respect to the inventory and (in combination with other factors) as such should be treated as an agent of the foreign principal.

---

26. OECD Model Tax Convention, Commentary on Article 5, paragraph 27.1.
27. Chapter 3.
28. http://www.ey.com/GL/en/Services/Tax/International-Tax/Alert--South-African-permanent-establishments-face-further-scrutiny
29. Dunahoo's list of PE malapropisms– chapter 7.3

2. *Specific Design Implications: Manufacturing and Sales*

In the above section, the more generic tax implications were covered which can apply to most or all facets of designing a centralized operating model. However, as evidenced in the discussion on case law and the main issues arising in the context of Article 5 and the implementation of a centralized model, some of the more important design implications are centered on the manufacturing and sales pieces of the value chain. As such, these two areas of focus are addressed below.

3. *Manufacturing*

Aside from the generic issues discussed in the previous section, the specific relationship between the principal and manufacturing local entities can also give rise to a number of issues, including:

- Control of key decisions
- Ownership of assets

Control of key decisions relating to manufacturing

The trend towards manufacturing activities being undertaken under centrally defined and monitored standards increases the risk that a tax authority might argue that a deemed relationship of dependence exists between the manufacturing local entity and the principal, even though this relationship is insufficient to create a contractual agency PE concept (see discussion on *Roche*).

Leasing or ownership of plants and equipment

In addition to inventory ownership, ownership and / or leasing of equipment can cause potential PE issues depending on the facts and circumstances for a limited risk manufacturing entity. The commentary to Article 5 in paragraph 8 discusses the various scenarios where leasing or owning equipment could lead to a fixed place of business of the foreign (principal) company. In particular, paragraph 8 of the commentary notes that:

> 'If an enterprise of a State lets or leases facilities, I(ndustrial) C(ommercial) S(cientific) equipment, buildings or intangible property to an enterprise of the other State without maintaining for such letting or leasing activity a fixed place of business in the other State, the leased facility, ICS equipment, building or intangible property, as such, will

> not constitute a permanent establishment of the lessor provided the contract is limited to the mere leasing of the ICS equipment, etc.'

Paragraph 8 goes on to mention that:

> 'this remains the case even when, for example, the lessor supplies personnel after installation to operate the equipment provided that their responsibility is limited solely to the operation or maintenance of the ICS equipment under the direction, responsibility and control of the lessee.'

However, the commentary makes an important distinction that:

> 'if the personnel have wider responsibilities, for example, participation in the decisions regarding the work for which the equipment is used, or if they operate, service, inspect and maintain the equipment under the responsibility and control of the lessor, the activity of the lessor may go beyond the mere leasing of ICS equipment and may constitute an entrepreneurial activity. In such a case a permanent establishment could be deemed to exist if the criterion of permanency is met.'

As such, it is important to consider the context in which the equipment is being owned or leased, particularly when it comes to maintenance of that equipment by personnel in the jurisdiction of the manufacturing local entity.

4. Sales

Similar to manufacturing, the relationship between the principal and sales local entity can also give rise to a number of issues, including:

- Dependent agent creation; and
- Considerations around contract conclusion

Risk of creating a dependent agent PE

The principal's involvement in sales processes must be carefully designed and monitored in order to minimize the risk of creating dependent agent PE's. The risk that a dependent agent PE determination will be made on a de facto basis remains increases as functions and risks are centralized away from the local entities. Likewise the actual conduct and appearance of the personnel of the local entities can be determinative for the presence or not of a PE. Their job description in recruitment advertising, their role description on personal social sites and their conversations with clients, in short the manner in which they actually appear to be involved in the sales cycle is a very strong factor in whether a not a PE is created.

The risk is clearly greatest in relation to structures in which local country sales activities are structured as an agency or as support for direct sales by the principal. But a degree of risk remains when local country sales activities are structured as true distributors or commissionaires.

Conclusion of contracts

The other area which typically presents potential PE implications in a centralized supply chain model for the sales process is in regards to the conclusion of contracts with 3rd party customers. As demonstrated in the final resolutions of the *Zimmer* and *Dell* cases, it would appear that, where civil law commissionaires are used, as long as the inter-company agreements clearly demonstrate that the sales entity signs binding contracts only in its own name, then the legal interpretation should prevail. However, the implications – particularly around the commissionaire concept – are being re-examined in light of the international concerns around base erosion and profit shifting. Additionally, even if the sales entity is not binding the principal but merely securing orders, such a fact pattern can create potential permanent establishments in many Asian countries under certain treaties.

As such, this is another area to watch as the 'binding concept' for sales entities under centralized models may continue to evolve.

9.2 CONCLUSIONS

As noted in the introduction, centralized operating models are a development that has grown over the last 25 years but have accelerated in the last 10 years as a result of advancements in information technology. The PE issues they raise are complex and it is likely that fiscal challenges and experience will develop rapidly in the coming years as these models have the attention from national and supra-national organizations and authorities.

Perhaps the key lesson from experience to date is that there is not yet a settled and consistent approach to the notion of dependency across jurisdictions. What is apparent is that there is among tax inspectors and many lower courts an alarming disregard of the precise factors which define a POB or Agency PE and that in many instances these factors have been supplanted by local concepts of nexus and business connection in order to raise local tax revenues. The whole purpose of the PE concept is to override such local concepts and apply a uniform code of international taxation with regard to NRE business.

Chapter 10
Permanent Establishment and Partnerships

In common law countries, a general partner has broad authority to bind the partnership in matters affecting partnership business. The 2012 Revised OECD Discussion Draft clarifies the consequences of carrying on business in the source state through a NRE organized as a fiscally transparent partnership:

> 'In the case of an enterprise that takes the form of a fiscally transparent partnership, the enterprise is carried on by each partner 'and, as regards the partners' respective shares of the profits, is therefore an enterprise of each Contracting State of which a partner is a resident. If such a partnership has a permanent establishment in a Contracting State, each partner's share of the profits attributable to the permanent establishment will therefore constitute, for the purposes of Article 7, profits derived by an enterprise of the Contracting State of which that partner is a resident ...'[1]

Hence a resident in the host country or a nonresident general partner who regularly acts within the host country in a business capacity for the partnership will constitute a permanent establishment there for all foreign general partners. A general partnership may be within the dependent-agency concept if employed to conduct trading activity.[2]

Even if a true partnership is not created, joint venture business conducted through the office of a host country joint venturer might make that office 'available' to the foreign joint venturer – creating thereby a fixed-place-of-business permanent establishment for the foreign joint ventures. If a true general partnership exists, the host country partner may have a dependent-agency permanent establishment in each other country in which general partners are resident and transacting partnership business.[3]

---

1. 2012 Revised OECD Discussion Draft, Issue 9.
2. *See* generally Loengard, 'Tax Treaties, Partnerships and Partners: Exploration of a Relationship,' 29 Tax Lawyer 31, 54 (1975).
3. Similarly, under Section 875 of the 1986 United States Internal Revenue Code, if a partnership or trust is engaged in a 'United States trade or business,' each of its partners or beneficiaries is deemed so engaged. *See* Judgment of 28 September 1978, Lower Tax Court of Hesse, West

In *Johnston vs Commissioner*[4] a Canadian partner of a Canadian livestock dealership partnership, acting on its behalf, entered into an oral agreement with an Illinois partnership to ship Canadian cattle for resale by the Illinois partnership. The court held Johnston taxable on the sales under both Code[5] and treaty provisions. The two partnerships constituted a partnership. Hence, the Canadian partnership was deemed to have a permanent business or place of business by virtue of the Illinois partnership's 'permanent abode' in the United States.

The same result was reached by the *Canadian Tax Appeal Board in No. 630 vs Minister of National Revenue*[6] involving an American corporation engaged in with other corporations in a construction joint venture to build the Toronto subway. The Board held that the 'office premises of the partners collectively, were also the office premises of any one partner.'[7]

Doing business through a host country partner or partnership lowers the nexus or threshold for host country taxation appreciably. A permanent establishment can be found either under the 'continuity of activity' test applicable to a 'fixed place of business' or by reason of the regular exercise of contractual authority required by the dependent-agency concept. In fact, the two tests become blurred if a host country partner's regular business use of its own domestic office is attributed to the foreign partner by reason of the general authority in the former to bind the latter.

10.1 LIMITED PARTNERSHIPS

A. Common Law Countries

Under United States tax treaty doctrine, a limited partner can acquire a permanent establishment in any jurisdiction in which a general partner regularly

Germany, No. VIII 313-75, summarized at 1 International Tax Treaties Service, Art. 5, page 41 (Edwardes-Ker ed. 1986) (German–Austrian treaty, holding that an individual partner is attributed the fixed place of business of the partnership). However, such attribution may not apply in civil law countries to limited or financial partners. *See* Part B, *infra*.

4. 24 T.C. 920 (1955) (former 1942 United States–Canada treaty).
5. IRC § 219(a) (1939) (now IRC § 875).
6. [1959] 13 D.T.C. 300 (1942 former United States–Canada treaty).
7. *Id.* at 302. *See also* Judgment of 11 March 1970, HR, No. 16,290, Netherlands, BNB 1970-89, VN 1970-287, WFR 1970-798, summarized at 1 International Tax Treaties Service, Art. 5, page 55 (Edwardes-Ker ed. 1986) (Dutch-French treaty holding that a partner in construction job lasting three years had a permanent establishment).

conducts partnership business.[8] In *Donroy, Ltd. vs United States*[9] the court held that Canadian corporations that were limited partners in two California limited partnerships had permanent establishments in the United States by virtue of the general partner's power to contract on their behalf, despite their limited liability, in the day-to-day conduct of the business activities of the United States limited partnerships. It is believed a similar result obtains in the United Kingdom and perhaps other common law countries.

B. Civil Law Countries

In civil law countries, the tax treatment of partners and partnerships may differ from that dictated by the common law perspective. Several civil law jurisdictions do not automatically attribute entrepreneurial status to limited (*financial-commandite*) partners by reason of a general partner's trading activities within the country, the limited partner's status is compared to that of a creditor who provides financing.[10] Such attribution was discussed in a 1984 decision[11] in Germany and in 1983 in the Netherlands.[12] And although, as a general rule Japanese partnerships are deemed to constitute a permanent establishment in Japan for all non-resident partners (by sole reason of their interest in the partnership, all partners are deemed to conduct business through a fixed place of business in Japan), this joint business concept does not apply to a TK, given its unique (financial) character under Japanese commercial law and promulgated regulations. Additionally, Japanese tax law clarifies that a non-resident limited partner in an IBLP is not deemed to have a permanent establishment in Japan by sole reason of its IBLP interest, given its restrictive status as a passive investor (subject to certain criteria).

If the Limited Partner is considered to be a 'financier,' the remuneration may follow the treaty allocation rules for interest paid on a 'profit participating' loan. In the absence of a permanent establishment in the State in which the partnership is situated, the taxation rights of the source country may be severely limited.[13]

---

8. A fixed place of business would not be required if a general partner is conducting partnership business within the host country if he is regularly exercising his authority to bind the partnership contractually.
9. 196 F. Supp. 54 (N.D. Cal. 1961), aff'd, 301 F.2d 200 (9th Cir. 1962).
10. According to the Dutch Trade Code (Article 20), a financial partner is not permitted to be actively involved with the general management of the partnership. If the financial partner breaches this rule, he will become fully liable for all debts of the partnership.
11. BFH, 25 June 1984, GrS 4/82.
12. Dutch Supreme Court, 2 November 1983, Dutch Taxation Rulings No. 1983-330.
13. In not following the *Abfärbe* theory (see discussion in part B, *supra*), the German Courts (and also apparently, the Japanese) reject the apparent Anglo-Saxon rule attributing entrepreneurial status to financial or limited partners, although in Germany, this would apply in the rare cases

Thus, in a 1992 Dutch court case,[14] a resident of Belgium was a financial partner in a Dutch closed partnership. He was unable to carry on an enterprise in the Netherlands by reason of his financial partnership status. Because Article 7 (business profits) of the tax treaty between the Netherlands and Belgium was thus inapplicable, Articles 11 (interest) and 22 (other income) allocated taxation rights to Belgium. He was not considered taxable in the Netherlands on his profit share or interest on capital. This case is of particular importance since the Belgian financial partner was considered to be an entrepreneur for Dutch individual income tax purposes.[15] The Netherlands Supreme Court created an additional spin in a case involving a Swedish limited partner in a Dutch limited partnership that carried on a business in the Netherlands and was managed by a Dutch general partner in the Netherlands.[16] The Supreme Court concluded that the limited partner was subject to Dutch corporation tax by virtue of having a fixed place of business in the Netherlands because (a) the limited partnership interest was part of the limited partner's business assets and (b) the limited partner was directly entitled to profits of the Dutch limited partnership.[17]

In Germany, a foreign partner will have a permanent establishment only if the partnership is engaged in a trade or business through a permanent establishment attributable to the foreign partner in his role as an entrepreneur (*Mitunternehmerschaft*). If a foreign partner is acting as an entrepreneur, a permanent establishment of the partnership can be attributed to him either in the form of the partnership's fixed place of business, or by reason of a general partner's creation of a management PE.[18] In Germany, there are three types of financing by which a lender can participate in the borrower's profits (or profits and losses), while profit distributions/payments on the instrument to the lender may be deductible by the German borrower as interest.[19] If the capital partner

---

where a partner does not carry entrepreneurial risk or does not have rights typically granted to a partner.

14. Ruling Lower Court of Den Bosch, 8 July 1992, No. 4395-89.
15. Article 6 of the Dutch Individual Income Tax Act deems partners in partnerships to be entrepreneurs if they are entitled to hidden reserves upon liquidation of the partnership.
16. Supreme Court case of 10 March 1993, No 27 786. A similar ruling was given in Supreme Court case of 23 March 1994, No. 29 084 in relation to Belgium.
17. Furthermore, due to a specific provision in the Dutch corporate income tax act, a limited partner that is entitled to profit of an enterprise that has its place of effective management in the Netherlands is subject to tax in the Netherlands even if the foreign partner is not an entrepreneur.
18. A.H.M. Daniels, Issues in International Partnership Taxation 85-86 (Kluwer, 1991).
19. Hybrid financing is available through a (1) *Stille Gesellschaft* (sleeping partnership), (2) *partiarisches Darlehen* (participating loan) or (3) *Genussrechte* or *Genusscheine* (participating rights). Silent partnerships can be structured in such a way that a foreign partner creates a PE in Germany as he is deemed to have co-entrepreneurial status (so-called atypical silent partnership; this requires certain management rights regarding the business in which the silent

is thus not acting as an entrepreneur (or is prohibited from so acting) he should not have a permanent establishment.[20]

C. Partnerships and Trusts as Limited Partners (Tiering)

What is the result if a limited partner is itself an (upper-tier) limited partnership? Do the upper-tier limited partners have a United States permanent establishment because the lower-tier general partner has authority to manage the business of the lower-tier partnership? What if the lower-tier limited partner were a discretionary trust (and not a 'look-through' entity under United States 'grantor trust' rules)? Do the discretionary beneficiaries have a United States permanent establishment?

Section 875 of the United States 1986 Internal Revenue Code attributes the United States trade or business of a partnership or trust to its foreign partners or foreign beneficiaries, respectively. The application of this statutory rule was considered in Rev. Rul. 85-60.[21] The ruling involved these facts:

> 'A is a citizen and resident of a foreign country (FC). A is the sole beneficiary of TR, a testamentary trust established in FC for the benefit of A. A is not treated as the owner of any portion of the trust under any provision of [Subchapter J].
>
> Pursuant to the trust instrument, TR became a limited partner in PRS... PRS, a limited partnership formed in the United States ... is engaged in the real estate development business in State S and maintains a business office there. TR derives some of its income from the limited partnership interest in PRS. TR is required by the trust instrument to currently distribute all of its income to A, which TR does.'

The ruling applied *Donroy*[22] to attribute to the trust the dependent-agency United States permanent establishment created by the general partner who resided in the United States. The ruling then applied domestic law to attribute

partner participates, as well as up- and downside participation). See also BFH, Judgment of 21. July 1999 – I R 110/98, where a German resident held an atypical silent partnership interest re. a Swiss business and was found to have a Swiss PE, exempt from German tax under the German–Swiss treaty.

20. *See,* however, Judgment of 3 August 1973, BFH, West Germany, summarized at 2 International Tax Treaties Service, Art. 22, page 3 (Edwardes-Ker ed. 1990) (German–Swiss treaty, holding that a silent partner in a German partnership has a permanent establishment because an operating partner can bind the silent partner; it was held immaterial that the silent partner's share was taxed as a dividend).
21. 1985-1 C.B. 187, based on General Couns. Mem. 39361. See 27 Tax Notes 1034 (1985).
22. Cited in Part A above.

to the nonresident beneficiary the permanent establishment of the trust. A commentator criticizes the ruling as an abrogation of treaty law by United States statutory law.[23] But is it? The ruling holds that a foreign beneficiary was taxable as the holder of the income interest in a foreign trust which was itself a limited partner.[24] The trust clearly had a permanent establishment in the United States and would be taxable under United States domestic tax rules on its share of undistributed effectively connected income.[25] To the extent such income was distributed or was required to be distributed, the beneficiary becomes the taxpayer and the trust a conduit.[26] Accordingly, the ruling attributes not only the United States trade or business of the trust, but also its United States permanent establishment to the beneficiary. If instead the trust had been discretionary and had not made a current distribution, upon a later accumulation distribution of income previously taxed to the trust, the nonresident beneficiary would be subject to further United States tax if his United States tax rate exceeded the trust's rate (after gross-up and credit for the United States tax imposed on the trust). However, it is unlikely that any tax would be due because the trust's United States effective tax rate would equal or exceed that of the beneficiary.[27] Therefore, the only adverse tax impact which reattributed permanent establishment status could have on the trust beneficiary would be application of the limited force of attraction rule[28] which, in the absence of treaty protection, could attribute to the beneficiary permanent establishment income from United States sources which is neither investment income nor trade or business income.[29]

The multi-tier partnership case is even less compelling because each partnership will be looked through for United States tax purposes to the ultimate non-partnership partners.[30] To fail to attribute a permanent establishment to

23. *See* Nitikman at 261 and nn. 17-18.
24. If the trust were a grantor trust under Sections 671-77, 678 or 679, the grantor or the beneficiary would be the taxpayer pro tanto. A similar look-through applies to a life tenant with respect to income under §§ 652 and 662.
25. An 'investment' trust would be classified as a corporation under United States tax principles, and no permanent establishment would be imputed to the individual certificate holders. *See* Rev. Rul. 75-192: 1975-1 C.B. 384; *Howard vs United States*, 84-1 US. Tax Cas. (CCH) 9494 (Ct. CI. 1984) and *See* generally the authorities cited at 416 Tax Mgmt. (BNA) A-4 through A-6 and C&A-l.
26. IRC §§ 651-52 and 661-662.
27. *See* Section 1(e) of the United States Internal Revenue Code of 1986.
28. Section 864(b)(3) of the United States Internal Revenue Code of 1986.
29. *See* Bittker & Eustice, Federal Income Taxation of Corporations and Shareholders (5th ed. 1987, Warren, Gorham and Lamont) at pp. 17-19 and fn. 58 for a listing of the types of income attracted.
30. It is now settled that the sale of a United States trading partnership interest by a foreign person will be subject to United States business profits taxation under Rev. Rul. 91-32, 1991-1 C.B. 107, which taxes all or part of the gain by 'looking through' to the portion of the gain attributable to United States trade or business assets of the partnership.

such partners would mean that no United States tax would be due since for United States income tax purposes a partnership is not a taxpayer.

10.2 NATURAL RESOURCE PARTNERSHIPS

The mere ownership of natural resources or rights should not create a host country permanent establishment, while the exploitation of such rights through a joint venture generally will.[31] Although, for United States tax purposes the participants in a joint operating agreement can elect out of partnership status under Section 761 of the Internal Revenue Code, partnership status still exists for tax treaty purposes. A permanent establishment may arise either from the management authority of the United States operating partner or the availability of a United States fixed place of business.

In the United States, permanent establishment exposure can be avoided for natural resource exploitation by forming a host country subsidiary to engage in a 'cooperative' partnership. For example, a United States subsidiary taxable under subchapter T as a 'co-operative' entered into a partnership with another United States company to obtain phosphate rock. The subsidiary had a contract to supply its Canadian parent with phosphate. It distributed the profit to its parent as a 'patronage' distribution, and claimed a deduction for the distribution under United States rules. The Internal Revenue Service held that the subsidiary was not an 'alter ego' or agent of the parent and was therefore not a permanent establishment of its Canadian parent.[32] Hence, its patronage distribution of profit on arm's length sales of minerals to the parent was subject to only a 15% withholding tax (and was presumably exempt from tax in Canada).

Similar cooperative arrangements might be available for the purchase of oil products with resulting 'patronage' profit being subject only to withholding tax.[33]

---

31. *See* Ltr. Rul. 8316109 (holding that Dutch partners have a United States permanent establishment because a 'working interest' is a permanent establishment. In most American states a working interest itself conveys no interest in real property or minerals in place but is rather the right to extract and keep oil or gas at one's own cost (for a royalty on oil or gas extracted).
32. Ltr. Rul. 7918105.
33. *See* Ltr. Rul. 7918105, which states the rationale for such exemption in the following discussion:
'Rev. Rul. 66-53, 1966-1 *C.B.* 206 involved a U.S. cooperative engaged in purchasing oil products in the U.S. and their sale in the U.S. to its member patrons on a cooperative basis. Patronage dividends were distributed to the patrons, including nonresident aliens and foreign corporations or foreign cooperatives not doing business in the U.S. The Rev. Rul. held that withholding was required under section 1441 and 1442 of the Code as fixed and determinable annual income from sources within the U.S.

10.3 NON-TRADING PARTNERSHIPS

Although a partnership may have a host country partner, a permanent establishment may not result because the partnership is not considered to be trading under host country law. For example, in Greece, a permanent establishment will not exist unless the partnership is engaged in an active business in Greece.[34]

In the United States, an investment partnership (which is not a dealer) can effect unlimited transactions and trading for its own account in United States equities, securities and exchange-traded commodities without being viewed as 'engaged in a trade or business within the United States.' This statutory exception also extends to trading for one's own account through a United States resident agent with full discretionary powers, provided in the case of securities, that the foreign partnership (unless closely held by a few individuals) does not have a principal United States office through which such trading is conducted (if its principal business is such trading).[35]

In *Coastal Chemical Corporation vs U.S.*, 546 F. 2d 110, (5th Cir. 1977), the Court held that patronage dividends paid to a foreign patron were subject to withholding under section 1442 of the Code.

Since Coastal Chemical, *supra* and Rev. Rul. 66-53 considered patronage dividends paid to a foreign patron to be subject to withholding, the implication is that those patronage dividends were not effectively connected with a trade or business in the U.S. Section 894(b) of the Code provides, in effect, that for purposes of applying a treaty benefit with respect to income not effectively connected with the conduct of a trade or business within the U.S., a nonresident alien individual or a foreign corporation shall be deemed not to have a permanent establishment in the U.S. at any time during the taxable year. The special problem of the proper tax treatment of a patronage distribution to a foreign parent cooperative is the result of the special tax treatment given such a relationship under section 1381-1388 of the Code. If the subsidiary is merely the "alter ego" of the parent operating the phosphate mine, then a permanent establishment would result under the Convention. Rev. Rul. 77-1, 1977-1 C.B. 161 revoked the "cost company" concept in the mining area by treating "cost companies" as independent viable corporations similar to *Moline Properties Inc. vs Commissioner*, 319 U.S. 436 (1948). Section 1382 of the Code treats the cooperative and its member patrons as separate entities and specifically rejects any principal-agent relationship as a basis for domestic taxation of a cooperative. Therefore, the single fact that a cooperative mining arrangement exists is not sufficient to prove an agency relationship resulting in the finding of a permanent establishment in the U.S. under the Convention.'

34. 7 April 1988, Circular No. L 3519-451-Pol 132, Greece, summarized at 1 International Tax Treaties Service, Art. 5, page 47.5 (Edwardes-Ker ed. 1990).
35. IRC § 864(b)(2) and Treas. Reg. § 1.864-2(c)(2)(ii). There is also a 'trade or business' exception for trading in securities and commodities by dealers and brokers for the account of others, through independent United States agents, provided the partnership has no United States office through or by which such trading is effected. Treas. Reg. § 1.864-2(c)(i).

10.4 WHAT IS A PARTNERSHIP?

For tax treaty purposes, what is a partnership is usually defined under host country law. As a case in point, it is instructive to consider United States tax law. That law seems most concerned with three issues:

1) What constitutes a partnership;
2) How to distinguish partnerships from other economic relationships (employment, independent contractors, loans, leases and co-ownership), and
3) How to distinguish partnerships from corporations.

For United States tax purposes, a partnership includes every jointly owned profit-seeking venture which is not a corporation, trust, or estate.[36] Entities organized under state partnership statutes may not be partnerships for United States tax purposes.[37] Conversely co-proprietorship ventures may be classified as tax partnerships even though no legal partnership exists.[38] Three criteria are generally relevant to define a tax partnership:

1) The venture must be formed to seek profit.
2) The profit must be jointly shared.
3) The profit must be shared by two or more persons who have a proprietary interest in the venture.

Intent is clearly relevant, but a partnership agreement can be inferred from the circumstances. It need not be written.[39] A mere agreement to share expenses (research and development cost-sharing arrangements, for example) is not

---

36. IRC 7701(a)(2) and Reg. § 301.7701-2.
37. Rev. Rul. 76-435, 1976-2 C.B. 490.
38. *Rose & Chommie*, Federal Income Taxation 450 (3d ed. 1988).
39. McKee, Nelson & Whitmire, 3-9, citing *Commissioner vs Culbertson*, 377 U.S. 733, 742 (1949). Intent to act as a partnership is crucially relevant, as shown by a number of objective criteria (not all of which need be shown). As stated by the Tax Court in *Luna vs Commissioner*, 42 T.C. 1067,1077-1078 (1964) the relevant factors include: The agreement of the parties and their conduct in executing its terms; the contribution, if any, which each party has made to the venture; the parties' control over income and capital and right of each to make withdrawals; whether each party was a principal and co-proprietor, sharing a mutual proprietary interest in the net profits and having an obligation to share losses, or whether one party was the agent or employee of the other, receiving for his services contingent compensation in the form of a percentage of income; whether business was conducted in the joint names of the parties; whether the parties filed Federal partnership returns or otherwise represented to respondent or to persons with whom they dealt that they were joint venturers; whether separate books of account were maintained for the venture; and whether the parties exercised mutual control over and assumed mutual responsibilities for the enterprise.'

a partnership because the venture does not produce a single profit which is shared by the venturers.[40] Further, the venturers must have an ownership interest in the venture.[41] An arrangement in which one participant receives a fixed amount or a percentage of gross income, regardless of profitability, while the other retains the residual profit or loss, may be characterized as a loan, license, lease or sale, employment or independent contractor relationship.[42] A partner can contribute merely the use of his capital, retaining gain or loss from its sale. In such case however, a partnership may exist only as to the operational results and not as to gains from the invested capital.

Joint liability for venture losses is not a prerequisite for partnership treatment. One partner can agree to be liable for all losses.[43] Nor is a capital interest required of every partner. However, a partnership may not exist until a service partner acquires a vested interest in the partnership. Thus, a service provider who has neither an interest in partnership capital nor liability for losses may be an employee, an agent or an independent contractor.[44]

40. Treas. Reg. § 1.761-l(a). Another example is a medical 'partnership' to share office and staff expenses. Similarly, a 'general partner' who agrees to bear excess losses but does not share in venture profit is a guarantor, not a partner. The IRS ruling policy requires a general partner to have at least a one percent interest in each item of partnership income, gain, loss, deduction or credit. Rev. Proc. 74-17, 1974-1 C.B. 438.
41. *See, e.g., McDougal vs Commissioner*, 62 T.C. 720 (1974), acq., 1975-1 C.B. 2.
42. *See Allison vs Commissioner*, 35 T.C.M. (CCH) 1069 (1976). A 'partnership' without a general partner will likely taxable as a corporation under Treas. Reg. § 301.7701-3.
43. *McDougal vs Commissioner*, 62 T.C. 720 (1974), acq., 1975-1 C.B. 2.
44. *Dorman vs United States*, 296 F.2d 27 (9th Cir. 1961) (services 'partner' who contributed his notes payable only out of his share of partnership profits, after equity partner had recovered his capital, held an employee). A capital interest received by a services partner is taxable as compensation income. Prop. Reg. § 1.721-1(b)(1). *See also Diamond vs Commissioner*, 56 T.C. 530 (1971) aff'd, 492 F.2d 286 (7th Cir. 1974) (receipt of capital interest by a service partner represents service compensation income). *See also, McDougal vs Commissioner*, 62 T.C. 720 (1974), acq., 1975-1 C.B. 2 (A purchased a race horse which B agreed to train in exchange for an interest in the horse after A had recovered his investment plus a premium; held, no partnership created until B received his interest). And see three real estate cases to same general effect, cited in Bureau of National Affairs Tax Management Portfolio, No. 161-3rd at A-13 and n. 164. Note that if a nonresident services partner receives an interest in property in exchange for services, he is taxable in the United States only if the interest is received for United States-sited services. *See Ingram vs Bowers*, 57 F.2d 65 (2d Cir. 1932) (Caruso's contract to record master record disc in New York held United States services income even though compensated by an interest in worldwide royalties, where RCA retained disc ownership); *Karrer vs United States*, 152 F. Supp. 66 (Ct. CI. 1957) (Swiss scientist who contracted with Swiss employer to provide patent research for Swiss employer in return for a portion of United States patent royalties was held to receive foreign source income, not taxable in the United States even though scientist obtained the patent in his own name, assigning all rights to his employer).

This issue has arisen in investment partnerships established by fund managers. A case in point is *Estate of Smith vs Commissioner*[45] in which investors deposited cash with a fund management group to be invested by it in commodities. The management group and the investors agreed to split the net profit on a 40%-60% basis. The investors retained all interest in the venture capital and due to the investment nature of the venture, the management group had no real exposure to loss. The profit-splitting arrangement was held an independent contractor relationship, not a partnership.[46]

Lending transactions generally avoid partnership status if there is a fixed obligation to repay principal and interest, even if the obligation is non-recourse debt and interest is measured by a percentage interest in the borrower's income or gains.[47] Similarly, lease payments based on the lessee's gross income from the use of the property do not create a partnership between the lessee and his lessor.[48] Partnership status may be relevant in deferred payment sales, in which the purchaser attempts to deduct a deferred payment to a seller who continues in management.[49]

The mere ownership of property in the host country does not create a permanent establishment. Similarly, the mere co-ownership of property will generally not create a partnership where the parties retain their individual ownership interests and do not provide substantial services directly or through an agent.[50] Thus, net leasing and sharecropping arrangements by joint owners usually do not create a partnership.[51]

If a joint venture is taxable as a tax partnership under United States tax rules, but no legal partnership has been created, it is still necessary for the Internal Revenue Service to show that the nonresident venturer has either (1) available for his use, and regularly uses, a United States office (e.g., of the

45. 313 F.2d 724 (8th Cir. 1963). See also cases cited at 161-3rd Tax Mgmt. (BNA) A-13 and note 168.
46. Similarly, in Rev. Rul. 75-43, 1975-1 CB. 383, an agreement between a cattle owner and a cattle feeder to divide net profits was held not a partnership, where the cattle owner provided capital and the feeder provided feeding equipment and labor; the feeder lacked a proprietary interest in the venture.
47. *See Hartman vs Commissioner*, 17 T.C.M. (CCH) 1020 (1958). Thus 'equity kicker' loans can be used to avoid both partnership status and, if held to maturity, United States capital gains taxation under IRC § 897.
48. Treas. Reg. §§ 1.761-1 (a), 301.7701-3(a). But partnership status can exist if there is an agreement to share lessee expenses or loss. McKee, Nelson & Whitmire at 3-28.
49. *See McKee Nelson & Whitmore at 3-20 and Gant vs Commissioner*, 263 F.2d 558 (6th Cir. 1959).
50. Treas. Reg. § 1.761-l(a).
51. Rev. Rul. 75-374,1975-2 CB. 261 held that no partnership existed where apartment building co-owners paid a percentage of receipts to a management agent who provided tenant services, including heat, air conditioning, water, unattended parking, normal repairs, trash removal and maintenance of public areas.

United States venturer) or (2) that the United States venturer has the requisite contractual authority, regularly exercised, to bind the nonresident in the United States business of the venture. In other words, it cannot be presumed that simply because a tax partnership exists, the United States 'partner' has authority to bind the nonresident or that an office of the United States 'partner' has been made regularly available and was so used by the venture for the account of the nonresident.

In the United States, private rulings provide guidance on how to structure a manufacturing joint venture to develop and market a product internationally without creating a partnership or fixed-place-of-business permanent establishment. An illustration is Private Letter Ruling 7923075. In this ruling, a foreign manufacturing company (A) and United States manufacturing company (B) agreed jointly to design, develop, manufacture and sell 'product Z' as follows:

1) A & B would each design and develop a component portion of Z in their own facilities, retaining all patents, know-how, and other intangible property rights with respect to their respective component products (component Y with respect to A and component X with respect to B).
2) Each of A & B would have co-exclusive rights to manufacture product Z in its own facilities using the component product of the other, in accordance with a cost-sharing agreement with respect to product Z. That agreement provided that each would be assumed to have borne 50% of development costs.[52]
3) Product Z would be manufactured for United States sales by B in the United States; product Z being manufactured for foreign sales by A in its foreign plant.
4) Sales would be accomplished by jointly owned subsidiaries, C (incorporated abroad) for foreign sales and D (incorporated in the United States) for United States sales.[53]
5) A & B would each ship their respective component parts to the other, for contract manufacturing by the other into product Z, the supplier retaining title to the portion of Z accounted for by the component supplied.[54]

52. A cost-sharing agreement is not a partnership.
53. The related-party treaty exception applies to prevent subsidiaries from being permanent establishments of the parent. See, e.g., OECD Model 5(7).
54. *See* OECD Model 5(4)(c), contract-processing treaty exception.

6) A & B would then separately sell their portions of Z to the relevant sales subsidiary (C or D) which would resell product Z to third party customers.[55]
7) While the sales subsidiaries would exclusively market product Z, A & B would guarantee their performance for customer relations and after-sales support purposes.[56]
8) Spare parts would be sold directly by A & B to the sales companies for resale to customers.[57]
9) A & B agreed upon a formula division of the gross receipts from sales of product Z and the spare parts. The formula was unrelated to actual costs or cost experience of either Corporation A or Corporation B. It provided each party an independent opportunity for profit based on its cost efficiency, while insulating each party from the costs or inefficiencies of the other.[58]

The ruling holds that A has no permanent establishment in the United States because (1) A does no marketing in the United States, (2) A's component product Y is contract manufactured by another enterprise in the United States into product Z, and (3) A, as owner of a portion of product Z, sells its portion to D, the price paid to A, insulating A from B's costs. Because of the cost sharing agreement, A and B have co-exclusive ownership of the manufacturing intangibles. Accordingly, B charges A only for direct manufacturing costs plus a small profit (but without charging for manufacturing intangibles).

55. If a 'delivery agent' treaty applied, such sales would be exempt even if effected through a consignment sales arrangement; there is no delivery agent if title passes before delivery to the retail customer.
56. Performance guarantees do not constitute an agency relationship.
57. *See* note 157.
58. Tax partnership status was avoided because the co-ownership status was limited to the cost shared intangibles, while net profits were not shared as each party bore its own costs or inefficiencies.

Bibliography

DOUBLE-TAXATION CONVENTIONS

Conventions are cited throughout the book by the names of the contracting parties, e.g., United States–Netherlands. The term 'Article' is omitted from references other than references to model treaty commentaries.

London Draft – Model Bilateral Convention for the Prevention of the Double Taxation of Income and Property, London Draft, League of Nations Fiscal Committee No. C.88.M88.1946.II.A 59

Mexico Draft – Model Bilateral Convention for the Prevention of the Double Taxation of Income, Mexico Draft, League of Nations Fiscal Committee No. C.88.M.88.1946.II.A.58

OECD Draft – Draft Double Taxation Convention on Income and Capital, Report of the O.E.C.D. Fiscal Committee, OECD Document C(63)87 (1963)

OECD Draft Commentary – Commentaries on the Articles of the Draft Convention, Draft Double Taxation Convention on Income and Capital, Report of the O.E.C.D. Fiscal Committee, OECD Document C(63)87, pages 59-164 (1963)

OECD Model – Model Double Taxation Convention on Income and on Capital (1977) as currently updated in 2010

OECD Model Commentary – Commentaries on the Articles of the Model Convention, Model Double Taxation Convention on Income and on Capital (2010).

OECD Reports – 2010 Model Tax Convention on Income and Capital (full version, 2012 © OECD).

Reports of the OECD Committee on Fiscal Affairs (Volume II)

Report on taxation of income from container leasing (adopted by OECD Council 13 September 1983)

Report on taxation of software (adopted by OECD Council 23 July 1992)

Treaty characterization issues arising from E-commerce report (adopted by the Committee on Fiscal Affairs 7 November 2002)

OECD 2012 Discussion Draft – OECD Model Tax Convention: Revised Proposals Concerning the Interpretation and Application of Article 5 (Permanent Establishment), 19 October 2012 to 31 January 2013

OECD 2013 BEPS (February 13) Report advising on base erosion and profit shifting

UN Model – UN Dep't of Int'l Economics & Social Affairs, UN Model Double Taxation Convention Between Developed and Developing Countries, UN Doc. ST/ESA/102, UN Sales No. E. 80 XVI 3 (1980) as currently updated in 2011

US Model – United States Treasury Department's Model Income Tax Treaty of 1981, 1 *Tax Treaties* (CCH) 208 as updated in 1996 and 2006

BOOKS AND KEY ARTICLES

Avery Jones, J.F., and D.A.Ward, 'Agents as Permanent Establishments under the OECD Model Tax Convention', *British Tax Review 341, Eur. Taxn 5, Journals IBFD 16* (1993)

Avery Jones, J.F., 'The United Kingdom's Influence on the OECD Model Tax Convention', *British Tax Rev*. 6, pp. 653-683 (2011)

Baker, P., *Double Taxation Conventions*, 3d ed. (Sweet & Maxwell, London) (looseleaf)

Carroll, M., 'The Historical Development of Income Tax Treaties,' in *Income Tax Treaties* 51 (Bischel ed. 1978)

Carroll, M.B., 'International Tax Law, Benefits for American Investors and Enterprises Abroad,' 2 *Int'l Law*. 692 (1968)

Carroll, M.B., 'Evolution of U.S. Treaties to Avoid Double Taxation of Income Part II,' 3 *Int'l Law*. 129 (1968)

Dunahoo, C., 'Source Country Taxation of Foreign Corporations: Evolving Permanent Establishment Concepts', 86 *Taxes* 37 (March 2008)

Edwardes-Ker, M. (ed.), *International Tax Treaties Service* (1977, 1986)

Ehrenzweig, A., and F. Koch, *Income Tax Treaties* (1949)

IFA, *Is there a permanent establishment?*, *Cahiers de droit fiscal international* vol. 94a (Sdu Uitgevers, 2009), Online Books IBFD

McKee, William S., Robert L. Whitmire and William F. Nelson, *Federal Taxation of Partnerships and Partners* (1990)

Mehta, A., *Taxmann's Permanent Establishment in International Taxation*, (Taxmann Publishing Ltd, New Delhi, 2012)

Nitikman, J., 'The Meaning of "Permanent Establishment" in the 1981 U.S. Model Income Tax Treaty,' Part 1, 15 *Int'l Tax J*. 159; Part II, 257 (1989); 'The Painter and the PE,' *Canadian Tax Journal* (2009) vol. 57, no 2, 213-58 (a superb article on the meaning of 'at the disposal')

Pijl, H, 'Agency Permanent Establishments: "in the name of" and the Relationship between Article 5(5) and (6) – Part I', *I.B.F.D. Bulletin for International Taxation*, January 2013 pp 3-21 and 'Part II', *I.B.F.D. Bulletin for International Taxation*, February 2013 pp 63-99 (the best history and analysis of Agency PEs)

Reimer, E., N. Urban and S. Schmid, *Permanent Establishments – A Domestic Taxation, Bilateral Tax Treaty and OECD Perspective* (Kluwer Law International, Alphen aan den Rijn, 2011)

Rawal, R., *The Taxation of Permanent Establishments* (Spiramus Press Ltd, London)

Roberts, S., and W. Warren, *U.S. Income Taxation of Foreign Corporations and Nonresident Aliens* (1970)

Roberts, S.I., 'The Agency Element of Permanent Establishment: The OECD Commentaries from the Civil Law View (Part One)', *Intertax* 9, pp. 396-420 (1993) and '(Part Two)', *Intertax* 10, pp. 488-508 (1993)

Russo, Raffaele and Edoardo Pedrazzini, 'Permanent Establishments Under Italian Tax Law: An Overview' (2007) vol. 47, no. 8-9 *European Taxation* 389-97, at 395-96

Russo, R., and C. Romano, 'Italian Tax Consequences of Permanent Establishments', *IBFD Bulletin for International* 456, 457 (Aug-Sept 2010)

Skaar, A., *Permanent Establishment – Erosion of a Tax Treaty Principle* (Kluwer Law International, 1991) (the leading work in the area)

Tittle, Martin B., *Permanent Establishment in the United States, a View through Article V of the U.S.–Canada Tax Treaty* (Vandenplas Publishing, Lake Mary, Florida, 2007)

Tremblay, Richard G., 'Permanent Establishments in Canada,' *Proceedings, Canadian Tax Foundation* 41st Tax Conf., 38-1 *et seq.* (1989)

Vogel, K., *Klaus Vogel on Double Taxation Conventions; A Commentary to the OECD,- UN- and US Model Conventions for the Avoidance of Double Taxation on Income and Capital*, 3d ed. (Kluwer Law International, The Hague, 1997)

Table of Cases

Index